The Resurrection of Richard Nixon

Books by Jules Witcover

85 DAYS: THE LAST CAMPAIGN OF ROBERT KENNEDY

THE RESURRECTION OF RICHARD NIXON

JULES WITCOVER

The Resurrection
of Richard Nixon

G. P. PUTNAM'S SONS
New York

TO MY MOTHER

Acknowledgments

In November, 1962, *Time* expressed the accepted political wisdom of the day in appraising the defeat of Richard M. Nixon as the Republican Party's candidate for governor of California. "Barring a miracle," the newsmagazine said, "Nixon's public career has ended." Miracle or not, slightly more than six years later, the same Richard M. Nixon stood on the steps of the Capitol in Washington and took the oath of office as the thirty-seventh President of the United States. This book is an attempt to chronicle what happened to the man, to the country and to its politics in those six years that enabled him to fashion one of the great political comebacks in American history. In this effort, I am indebted for their recollections to many of Richard Nixon's friends and fellow Republicans, including members of his Cabinet and White House staff, and also to these colleagues who observed him over this period—Jack Germond, Carl Greenberg, Don Irwin, Walter Mears, Robert Novak, Don Oberdorfer, Tom Ottenad, Charles Quinn, Daniel Rapoport, Robert B. Semple, Jr., Bill Stout and Mike Wallace. My appreciation goes also to Robert Lescher, my agent, to Arthur C. Fields, my editor at Putnam, and above all to my wife, Marian, who not only typed the manuscript but also provided constructive editing along the way.

JULES WITCOVER

Washington, D.C.
April, 1970

Contents

Anybody in politics must have great competitive instinct. He must want to win. He must not like to lose, but above everything else, he must have the ability to come back, to keep fighting more and more strongly when it seems that the odds are the greatest. That's the world of sports. That's the world of politics. I guess you could say that's life itself.

In a televised campaign interview

—RICHARD M. NIXON, 1968

1

Down and Out

AT about ten o'clock on the morning of November 7, 1962, Richard Milhous Nixon sat glumly in front of a television set in Suite 724 of the Beverly Hilton Hotel in Los Angeles. He wore a dressing gown and held a watered-down drink in his hand, but there was nothing relaxed about him; typically, though he had been in the privacy of that suite all through election night, he still wore his necktie tight up against his buttoned collar. It was, most inappropriately, the Presidential Suite, a spacious seventh-floor apartment where Truman, Eisenhower and Kennedy all had stayed; now, the rich beige, white and gold tones of the room failed to lend either brightness or elegance to the grim scene. Around Nixon were his most trusted political advisers: H. R. "Bob" Haldeman, his campaign manager in the race for the California governorship, just now ending in disaster; Robert H. Finch, his closest political counselor and friend; Murray Chotiner, a key strategist and aggressive in-fighter; John D. Ehrlichman, an advance and logistics man; Congressman Patrick J. Hillings, another political aide; Ronald L. Ziegler, a young press assistant. Two old family friends, Ray Arbuthnot, a wealthy Pomona Valley rancher, and Jack Drown, husband of one of Mrs. Pat Nixon's old schoolteacher colleagues, also were there. In an adjoining room the candidate's wife sat alone, sobbing quietly. The two

13

Nixon daughters, Tricia and Julie, mercifully, were staying with friends.

The door opened and in walked Herbert G. Klein, the San Diego newspaper editor who periodically signed on as Nixon's chief press adviser and spokesman. Klein had just been in the Cadoro Room below, trying to placate the assembled election-night press corps, who had waited through the dawn for Nixon to appear and concede defeat in favor of the Democratic candidate, Governor Edmund G. "Pat" Brown. But Nixon kept holding off, hoping beyond all rational judgment that late returns from conservative Orange County and San Diego might turn the tide. The reporters, never very favorably disposed toward Nixon, were even more antagonistic than usual by now; on Klein's last visit to them, they had told him in effect to go back upstairs and get his candidate.

"They're all waiting," Klein said to Nixon in his customary low monotone. "You've got to go down."

The candidate stared at the emissary. "Screw them," he said, and sat there.

For about five minutes a gloomy discussion ensued. Though Nixon's dark mood was excruciatingly obvious, most of the aides advised that he ought to make the concession statement himself. It was traditional; it was the proper, the sporting thing to do; he could make it short and sweet and then it would be over with.

"Screw them," the former Vice President of the United States repeated several times to the entreaties.

Klein, a man with an unflappable manner and a perpetual squint that together give him a faintly Oriental inscrutability, persisted.

"I told them you'd make a statement," he said to Nixon, evenly.

"You make the statement," Nixon shot back. "You make it."

In the face of this acrimony and apparently unshakable resolve, the discussion among the aides then turned to what Klein should say, and it all was the predictable: congratulations to Brown and an observation from Nixon that he had done his best and the people had spoken. Klein made a few notes, dashed off some telegrams of thanks to party workers and then headed

14

downstairs, several of the other intimates at his side, leaving Nixon in his suite.

A car was waiting at a rear exit of the hotel. The plan was for the defeated candidate to slip quietly out while Klein was reading the concession statement. A group of campaign workers had collected in a room across the hall, and Nixon, having shed his dressing gown and put on his coat jacket, walked over to thank them on his way out. The mood among the candidate's fiercely loyal supporters was bitter and angry, fanned by derisive comments coming over the television set from impatient reporters in the press conference room below. As Klein and the others came into view on the screen and the press spokesman pulled out his notes, there were more protests from reporters about the candidate's failure to appear.

The defeated Nixon, haggard and unshaved, was being bombarded now with emotional excesses from both sides. Faithful workers, in tears, were spilling out their regrets to him and their ire at the press treatment; one of them came up to him, put his head on his leader's shoulder, and sobbed. At the same time, the voices of demanding reporters were coming into the room over the television set:

"Where's Nixon?"

Klein: "I have the text of two messages I'll read to you. The boss won't be down. . . . He plans to go home and be with his family . . ."

The reporters, after their long vigil, were not satisfied with secondhand concessions, and they told Klein, some of them deriding Nixon in the process, implying he was afraid to come down and face the music. In the room upstairs, the barbs coming over the TV set served only to escalate the bitterness. An aide turned to the candidate. "Don't let them bluff you," he beseeched. "Go down and tell them what you think." Nixon, suddenly bristling, turned and stormed down the corridor, about half a dozen supporters trailing him, onto a waiting elevator. "Oh, hell," he said to them or aloud to himself as they descended, "it was a pretty good fight. We fought hard. We fought clean . . ." On the ground floor, Nixon stepped out and started through the lobby. "Losing California after losing the Presidency," someone heard him say, halfheartedly. "Well, it's like being bitten by a mosquito after being bitten by a rattle-snake."

Upstairs, Finch, the tall and movie-star handsome lawyer who had been Vice President Nixon's right-hand man in Washington, had gone into another room as Klein left. He assumed that by now Nixon had made his way from the hotel. Some other aides had been telling Nixon on the way out of Suite 724 that "it looks like you're ducking," but the candidate had been so firm about not going to the press conference that Finch was certain that was the end of it. He was dumbfounded, therefore, as he watched Klein jousting with the reporters, suddenly to see Nixon striding grimly toward the microphone. He looked his worst. The small dark eyes, tight mouth, rubbery nose and self-conscious demeanor that had made Nixon the cartoonist's delight presented him at this moment in his least photogenic, most self-damaging aspect. He brusquely interrupted Klein, took the microphone and, face flushed, hands jammed into coat pockets, literally spit out the words heard round the political world:

"Good morning, gentlemen. Now that Mr. Klein has made his statement, and now that all the members of the press are so delighted that I have lost, I'd like to make a statement of my own . . ."

What followed was, in the judgment of any experienced political observer worth his salt, the funeral oration over the political remains of Richard M. Nixon, two-time loser for major elective office. It was the public act of hara-kiri of the century; the "real Nixon" as opposed to the "old Nixon" or the "new Nixon," finally unmasked by his own hand, revealing himself to be the whining, petty, patronizing political hack that most of the press always had thought he was. The voters of California had knocked him down, but no referee was needed to toll off the count over him; Richard Nixon, while flat on his back, was counting himself out.

The litany of the Nixon kamikaze of November 7, 1962, has become by now part of the folklore of American politics. Alternately berating and praising the reporters who covered his losing campaign, insisting he had no regrets, Nixon ranted on as thunderstruck newsmen first gaped, then scribbled frantically the words that once and for all were to seal the man's doom. It was not simply the vitriol that shocked, but the undisciplined, repetitious and contradictory thrashings-out by this most disciplined, organized and logical of all public speakers. To recapture the total impact of a man out of control on a mental seesaw, it is instructive to quote the performance at length:

"I appreciate the press coverage of this campaign. I think each of you covered it the way you saw it. You had to write it in the way according to your belief on how it would go. I don't believe publishers should tell reporters to write one way or another. I want them all to be free. I don't believe the FCC [Federal Communications Commission] or anybody else should silence [them].

"I have no complaints about the press coverage. I think each of you was writing it as you believed it. I congratulate Governor Brown, as Herb Klein has already indicated, for his victory. He has, I think, the greatest honor and the greatest responsibility of any governor in the United States. And if he has this honor and this responsibility, I think that he will now have certainly a position of tremendous interest for America and as well as for the people of California.

"I wish him well. I wish him well not only from the personal standpoint, because there were never on my part any personal considerations. I believe Governor Brown has a heart, even though he believes I do not. [Now it was starting—the bitterness he had held in so long. But it came out almost in spite of himself. He was too much the disciplined public man for it to happen all in an unbroken rush.] I believe he is a good American, even though he feels I am not. And therefore I wish him well because he is the governor of the first state. He won, and I want this state to be led with courage. I want it to be led decisively and I want it to be led, certainly, with the assurance that the man who lost the campaign never during the course of the campaign raised a personal consideration against his opponent —never allowed any words indicating that his opponent was motivated by lack of heart or lack of patriotism to pass his lips.

"I am proud of the fact that I defended my opponent's patriotism. You gentlemen didn't report it, but I am proud that I did that. [Now came the first traces of rancor toward those

17

men before him who had played God with his career. He glared at them, tough and on the offensive, his voice rising.] I am proud also that I defended the fact that he was a man of good motives, a man that I disagreed with very strongly, but a man of good motives. I want that—for once, gentlemen—I would appreciate if you would write what I say, in that respect. I think it's very important that you write it. *In the lead. In the lead.*

"Now, I don't mean by that, incidentally, all of you. [He saw a familiar face in front of him, and, his hostility arrested by it, he retreated.] There's one reporter here who has religiously, when he was covering me—and incidentally, this is no reflection on the others, because some of you, you know, weren't bothered. One reporter, Carl Greenberg—he's the only reporter on the [Los Angeles] *Times* that fits this thing, who wrote every word that I said. He wrote it fairly. He wrote it objectively. I don't mean that others didn't have a right to do it differently. But Carl, despite whatever feeling he had, felt that he had an obligation to report the facts as he saw them. [Greenberg, sitting directly in front, was mightily embarrassed about receiving such singular absolution, and later so informed his superiors. They told him to forget about it.]

"I say these things about the press because I understand that that was one of the things you were particularly interested in. There'll be no questions at this point on that score. I'll be glad to answer other questions."

But instead, Nixon went on. He commended the labors of his Republican volunteers. ("I think they did a magnificent job. I only wish they could have gotten out a few more votes in the key precincts, but because they didn't, Mr. Brown has won and I have lost the election," said the man who went under by 300,000 votes.) He commented on the previous day's Republican gubernatorial victories by Nelson A. Rockefeller in New York, William W. Scranton in Pennsylvania, James A. Rhodes in Ohio and George Romney in Michigan and predicted the Grand Old Party would be revitalized in 1964—without him as its leader. He saw President Kennedy as a tough foe as a result of the masterful way he had persuaded and pressured the Soviet Union to remove their missiles from Cuba in the crisis that had overshadowed the closing days of the 1962 campaign. But

18

maybe Kennedy really had not been tough enough against the Russians, and against the appeasers in his own ranks. ("What will happen in Cuba? Can we allow this cancer of Communism to stay there? Is there a deal with regard to NATO? Is there going to be with regard to NATO and the Warsaw Pact? Are we going to continue any kind of an agreement in Cuba, which means that Khrushchev got what we said we would never agree to before he made his threat with regard to his missiles and that is, in effect, ringing down an Iron Curtain around Cuba? Those are the things that Mr. Kennedy, of course, will have to face up to, and I just hope—and I'm confident that if he has his own way he will face up to them, if he can only get those who opposed atomic tests, who want him to admit Red China to the UN, all of the woollyheads around him—if he can just keep them away from him and stand strong and firm with that good Irish fight of his, America will be in good shape in foreign policy.")

Finally, it was time to look ahead. "One last thing: What are my plans? [He was being the helpful Nixon, the thorough Nixon, again—anticipating questions and answering them, thus retaining control of the conference.] Well, my plans are to go home. I'm going to get acquainted with my family again. And my plans, incidentally, are, from a political standpoint, of course, to take a holiday. It will be a long holiday. I don't say this with any sadness. I couldn't feel, frankly, more, well, frankly, proud of my staff for the campaign they helped me to put on. We campaigned against great odds. We fought a good fight. We didn't win. And I take responsibility for any mistakes. As far as they're concerned, they're magnificent people, and I hope whoever next runs in California will look at my staff and take some of these people—use them—because they are—they're great political properties, shall we say, putting it in the—in a very materialistic way.

"One last thing: People say, 'What about the past? [For he knew they would ask, and even in the heat of anger he was a man who sought always to touch every base.] What about losing in '60 and losing in '64 [sic]'? I remember somebody on my last television program said, 'Mr. Nixon, isn't it a comedown, having run for President, and almost made it, to run for governor?' The answer is I'm proud to have run for governor. Now, I

19

would have liked to have won. But not having won, the main thing was that I battled—battled for the things I believed in. I did not win. I have no hard feelings against anybody, against my opponent, and least of all the people of California. We got our message through as well as we could. The Cuban thing [Kennedy's preempting of public attention in the missile crisis] did not enable us to get it through in the two critical weeks that we wanted to, but nevertheless we got it through, and it is the people's choice. They have chosen Mr. Brown. They have chosen his leadership, and I can only hope that that leadership will now become more decisive, that it will move California ahead and, so that America can move ahead—economically, morally and spiritually—so that we can have character and self-reliance in this country. This is what we need to move forward.

"One last thing. [For the third time—but he had been watching the reaction to his ramblings, and he could see they were having a jolting effect, an embittering effect, on the reporters. Something drove him to defend himself.] At the outset I said a couple of things with regard to the press that I noticed some of you looked a little irritated about. And my philosophy with regard to the press has never really gotten through. And I want it to get through. This cannot be said for any other American political figure today, I guess. Never in my sixteen years of campaigning have I complained to a publisher, to an editor, about the coverage of a reporter. I believe a reporter has got a right to write it as he feels it. I believe if a reporter believes that one man ought to win rather than the other, whether it's on television or radio or the like, he ought to say so. I will say to the reporter sometimes that I think, 'Well, look, I wish you'd give my opponent the same going over that you give me.'

"And as I leave the press, all I can say is this: for sixteen years, ever since the Hiss case, you've had a lot of fun—a lot of fun—that you've had an opportunity to attack me and I think I've given as good as I've taken. [His voice was strident now, his face dark.] It was carried right up to the last day. I made a talk on television, a talk in which I made a flub—one of the few that I make, not because I'm so good on television but because I've been doing it a long time. I made a flub in which I said I was running for governor of the United States. The Los Angeles

Times dutifully reported that. Mr. Brown the last day made a flub—a flub, incidentally, to the great credit of television, that was reported—I don't say this bitterly—in which he said, 'I hope everybody wins. You vote the straight Democratic ticket, including Senator Kuchel.' I was glad to hear him say it, because I was for Kuchel [a Republican] all the way. The Los Angeles *Times* did not report it. I think that it's time that our great newspapers have at least the same objectivity, the same fullness of coverage, that television has. And I can only say thank God for television and radio for keeping the newspapers a little more honest.

"Now, some newspapers don't fall in the category to which I have spoken, but I can only say that the great metropolitan newspapers in this field, they have a right to take every position they want on the editorial page, but on the news page they also have a right to have reporters cover men who have strong feelings, whether they're for or against a candidate. But the responsibility also is to put a few Greenbergs on, on the candidate they happen to be against, whether they're against him on the editorial page or just philosophically deep down, a fellow who at least will report what the man says. That's all anybody can ask. [He went on and on, belaboring the point, as if he were in a debate and sensing that for all he had said, he still was behind because at the start he had resorted to rancor.] But apart from that I just want to say this: Among the great papers in this country that the people say that I should be concerned about— the Louisville *Courier*, the New York *Post,* the Milwaukee *Journal,* the Fresno and the Sacramento *Bee*—I couldn't be— disagree with that more. I want newspapers. If they're against a candidate I want them to say it. I believe they should say it. I don't mind reporters saying it. I would hope that in the future, as a result of this campaign, that perhaps they would try at least simply to see that what both candidates say is reported, that if they have questions to ask of one candidate, they ask the same questions of the other candidate.

[But it could not be left at that. Somehow in all the incredible ups and downs of this incredible monologue, the professional Nixon had been holding the personal Nixon on an elastic rein, letting him spring out for a moment, then snapping him

21

back when he had gone too far. But the personal Nixon—weary, bitter, disoriented—strained at the rein of years of discipline, and finally, at the end, snapped it.] "The last play. I leave you gentlemen now, and you will now write it. You will interpret it. That's your right. But as I leave you I want you to know—just think how much you're going to be missing. You won't have Nixon to kick around anymore, because, gentlemen, this is my last press conference, and it will be one in which I have welcomed the opportunity to test wits with you. I have always respected you. I have sometimes disagreed with you. But unlike some people, I've never canceled a subscription to a paper [an obvious reference to President John F. Kennedy's cancellation of the New York *Herald Tribune* in a fit of pique], and also I never will.

"I believe in reading what my opponents say, and I hope that what I have said today will at least make television, radio and the press, first, recognize the great responsibility they have to report all the news and, second, recognize that they have a right and a responsibility, if they're against a candidate, give him the shaft, but also recognize if they give him the shaft, put one lonely reporter on the campaign who will report what the candidate says now and then. Thank you, gentlemen, and good day." And with that, according to *Time* later, Nixon turned to an obviously chagrined Klein and said: "I know you don't agree. I gave it to them right in the behind. It had to be said, godammit. It had to be said."

It was over now, and the defeated candidate strode from the room as unceremoniously as he had come in; no smiles, no waves, no handshakes with the press. By this time, his car had been brought around to the front. Mrs. Nixon was waiting silently in the back seat, and her husband climbed in after having plowed through a last bunch of vexed admirers. Riding with the Nixons, in addition to the driver, was Chotiner, the old political mentor generally considered to be the architect of Nixon's slashing anti-Communist campaign style in the early, bitter California races for Congress against Jerry Voorhis and for the Senate against Helen Gahagan Douglas. The car set off for Nixon's ranch home with swimming pool in fashionable Trousdale Estates, north of Beverly Hills, and as far as the great

American public was concerned, that was the last that would be heard of Richard Nixon, seeker after high elective office.

Listening to Nixon's performance before the press on that morning was for the political community like stumbling unannounced into a man's monologue to his analyst. It revealed a capacity for deep bitterness in Nixon that through his long public career and long sparring match with the nation's press he nearly always had managed to control, or to cover up. It demonstrated likewise an ambivalence, as he strangely vacillated from vitriol to condescension and back, saying in one breath that "I have no complaints about the press coverage" and in the next that "for once, gentlemen, I would appreciate if you would write what I say . . ." Finally, it disclosed a humanness about the man, revealed privately moments earlier in his comments when Herb Klein had entered the suite to urge him to make a personal concession; a capacity to blow his top regardless—for once—of the political consequences. It was so startling because there always had been a punching-bag quality to the public Nixon; he came up smiling because it was the politic thing to do, like one of those dolls with a round weighted base that keeps bobbing back when a child pokes at it.

The private Nixon, of course, always had the capacity for being hurt, for bitterness. At times of great personal crisis he also had the guts to show it in private, even at the risk of damaging his own political self-interest, which in the public portrait of the man always was the paramount consideration. Ten years earlier, when the story of Nixon's private political fund broke in the midst of the 1952 Presidential campaign, nearly persuading Eisenhower to drop Nixon as his running mate, Nixon risked all by telling the indecisive Eisenhower straight out in the critical telephone conversation that led to the "Checkers speech": "General, there comes a time in matters like this when you've either got to shit or get off the pot." In 1962, in recounting the incident in his book, *Six Crises,* Nixon softened the phrase to "fish or cut bait." But others in the room that night at the Benson Hotel in Portland, Oregon, heard the angry Nixon use the more earthy expression to the man who in public he never ceased to treat as a deity.

Shooting from the hip in public, however, was something

Nixon did not often do. He was too aware of the damage that could come from blunt, impulsive talk in front of outsiders, and that was what made the 1962 "last press conference" all the more startling. Again ten years earlier, after the "Checkers speech," in a Los Angeles studio, Nixon became outraged to learn Eisenhower did not say at once he was keeping him. "For the first time in almost a week of tremendous tension, I really blew my stack," Nixon wrote in *Six Crises*. He returned to his hotel and dictated to Rose Mary Woods, his longtime, fiercely loyal personal secretary, a letter of resignation from the Republican ticket. Chotiner intercepted her in the corridor immediately afterward and tore it up. Nixon had not known that in a public speech that night, the general did in fact make it clear Nixon would stay on the ticket. Of his own short-fused reaction then, Nixon wrote in *Six Crises* something he obviously forgot a decade later in his celebrated attack on the press:

"The next day when I learned the whole story, and the accurate one, of Eisenhower's reaction, it was quite clear to me that I should have waited for all the facts before going off half-cocked. . . . The point of greatest danger for an individual confronted with a crisis is not during the period of preparation for the battle, nor fighting the battle itself, *but in the period immediately after the battle is over. Then, completely exhausted and drained emotionally, he must watch his decisions most carefully. There is an increased possibility of error because he may lack the necessary cushion of emotional and mental reserve which is essential for good judgment.*" (Italics added.)

And in his preface to the final chapter in the book, about his losing race for the Presidency in 1960, Nixon wrote:

"The most dangerous period in a crisis is not in the preparation or in the fighting of a battle, *but in its aftermath.* This is true even when the battle ends in victory. *When it ends in defeat, in a contest where an individual has carried on his shoulders the hopes of millions, he then faces his greatest test.*" (Italics added.)

On the morning after his California defeat, Nixon obviously had failed to remember that philosophy, though it seemed to have been sharply etched in his self-analysis. As a result of the lapse, he was burned and burned badly. The scars this time would be as deep and the scene so well remembered by others that he would not be able to forget the lesson again.

In any event, in November, 1962, there was no reason to quarrel with *Time* magazine's epitaph that "barring a miracle, Nixon's public career has ended." The California defeat could not have been more politically damaging or more personally humiliating. It was an article of political faith, until Nixon himself rewrote the dogma in 1968, that a successful candidate for the Presidency must have a big-state base, and in California he was through. Had he not run for governor, Nixon would have remained California's most prominent Republican and a live prospect for the 1964 Republican Presidential nomination. After all, in 1960 he had lost by the narrowest margin in American political history. Why did he take so foolhardy a step as seeking the California governorship?

The reason was simple: Nixon was not seeking a stepping-stone to a 1964 rematch against John F. Kennedy; he was seeking a sanctuary from it. Far from wanting to use the statehouse in Sacramento to launch another Presidential bid in 1964, as Brown successfully charged in the 1962 campaign, Nixon actually had hoped to use it as a four-year hiding place, from which he could avoid making another losing race against Kennedy. Inherent in his decision to run for governor was a Presidential timetable not of 1964, but of 1968, when he finally did make his second try. Thus, though he lost in California in 1962, the gubernatorial contest in the end served the political purposes intended at the start—to keep Nixon off the national ballot in 1964 and to make him the Republican Party's logical choice in 1968! The circumstances that produced both these results never of course were anticipated. But because Richard Nixon did not win in California in 1962 and did not run for President in 1964, he was able to emerge again in 1968, when his party found itself with a rare opportunity for victory, but facing a leadership vacuum.

It has been widely assumed that Nixon ran for governor in 1962 because he was unable to resist local and state pressures from important Republicans in California. Although it is true such pressures were great, the strongest persuasion came not from California but from Republican powers and friends in the

East, who agreed that if Nixon were to come back, he needed a major base that would give him a sanctuary in 1964 and then a stepping-stone in 1968.

Almost as soon as he got back to California in early 1961 and began to practice law as counsel to the Los Angeles firm of Adams, Duque and Hazeltine, local Republicans focused on the former Vice President as their strongest candidate for governor. The Republican Party in California was in great disrepair; the decision of Senator William F. Knowland in 1958 to leave his influential position in Washington as Senate minority leader, and seek the governorship as a Presidential stepping-stone of his own, had produced a disastrous domino effect. Reluctantly, Republican Governor Goodwin Knight agreed to step aside and run for the Senate. But he was upset by Democratic Congressman Clair Engle, while Knowland himself was going under at the hands of the same Pat Brown who later was Nixon's undoing. Also, both houses of the state legislature were in Democratic control.

If the low state of Republicanism in California was a local dilemma, however, it was a national opportunity for Nixon. By becoming governor, he could step in and take control of the state that by 1968 would be the nation's most populous. Just months before, when he ran for President, he had carried his home state by 35,000 votes, and according to statewide polls would be the Republican Party's strongest gubernatorial choice. Nixon himself was so impressed when he saw the polls that he derisively commented to one adviser that he would have to win by as wide a margin as the polls showed to pull in with him beleaguered GOP Senator Thomas H. Kuchel (who won reelection in spite of Nixon's 1962 defeat). Nixon was then, by any yardstick, a conventional politician, and the conventional wisdom dictated that he have a large home base from which to launch a second Presidential campaign. Realistically, though, he might still have had that base within his party as long as there was a Democrat in the statehouse in Sacramento, and the idea of *being* governor was not particularly compelling for a man so obviously oriented toward national and international issues.

For the first few months of 1961, Nixon busied himself with

26

his new law practice and with the writing of *Six Crises*. He took the latter project seriously, scribbling ideas on the yellow legal pads that had come to be a trademark and then dictating into a recording device for transcription by his secretary, Rose Woods. At the same time, as the titular leader of his party—that empty and meaningless distinction bestowed on losing Presidential candidates and as a former Vice President, Nixon remained a celebrity to be consulted and tapped for political capital. To follow his natural inclination to involve himself deeply in Republican affairs in California, but to pull back short of grasping the leadership reins, was a personal contradiction.

Not all California Republicans were pressuring Nixon to run. His good friend and former campaign manager, Bob Finch, urged him repeatedly in early 1961 to stay out. "It wasn't that I thought he couldn't win," Finch recalled later, when he became Nixon's Secretary of Health, Education and Welfare. "All the polls showed he could. But the problems of California were so great, tax problems and all the rest that later hurt Brown, that he stood to lose more than he could win. And I felt he had been going too hard for too long—for fourteen years in public life. Campaigning in California was tough, like another national campaign. The one against Kennedy the year before probably had been the hardest physically in history. Two young men going all out all year. I was afraid of the cumulative fatigue. Nixon wasn't run down, he seemed to be in fine shape. But who needed it?"

There were many others, though, who thought Nixon needed it if he hoped to make another serious try at the Presidency. They were the same members of "the Eastern Establishment"— that rather formless collection of Republican moderates best symbolized by the last Republican Presidential loser, Thomas E. Dewey of New York—who had masterminded Dwight D. Eisenhower's two party nominations and had helped Nixon nail down the Republican nomination in 1960. Several times in early and mid-1961, Nixon and Finch traveled back to New York and Washington to confer with Dewey, Herbert Brownell, Jr., William P. Rogers, Clifford Folger, the old Eisenhower and Nixon finance man, Leonard W. Hall, General Eisenhower's campaign manager, and even such non-Establishment figures as

Senator Everett M. Dirksen of Illinois and Representative Charles A. Halleck of Indiana, about what the former Vice President ought to do. From Washington, Nixon would drive to Gettysburg for a round of golf, dinner and the advice of General Eisenhower. The consensus heavily supported making the gubernatorial race, and the arguments were obvious: the need for a major political base, California as that ideal base, the need to speak from an influential forum that would attract national press coverage, the need for an immediate candidacy on which to focus fund-raising. Folger specifically stressed how difficult it was to raise money for Nixon's numerous political activities as a noncandidate. He would have heavy overhead expenses, secretaries and researchers to help him maintain his position as the national party spokesman, but no political income. Of the meetings, one participant said later, "It all came down to one simple thing: What do we do to keep Dick Nixon alive?"

On top of all these arguments for a quick candidacy was one other increasingly persuasive fact—the soaring national popularity of John F. Kennedy in the White House. Having lost to Kennedy by only 119,000 votes, or fewer than one per precinct, there always was the danger—and it came to be considered that—that Nixon might be called on to try again against the same man. His chances, of course, would have been much diminished by Kennedy's incumbency and Nixon's own departure from public office, but if other leading Republicans ran away from the Presidential nomination, Nixon might find himself trapped into running. Thus, the California governorship took on greatest appeal as a political sanctuary; Nixon could pledge at the outset of the gubernatorial campaign that he would serve a full four-year term, and then use that solemn pledge to turn away any entreaties in 1964 that he put his political neck on the block against President Kennedy.

This rationale seemed to serve the political objectives of both the local and the national Republicans weighing Nixon's future. For Californians interested in him primarily as a rallying point for party unity, and for Easterners interested in preserving him as a national political commodity beyond the pitfall of 1964, four years in Sacramento seemed the best solution.

"Eventually, practically everyone told him to run," Stephen Hess, the Nixon speechwriter, urban researcher and analyst, recalled later. "After he lost, some tried to rewrite history, but they were for it then. The main thing was, if he didn't run he would be the sacrificial goat for the party against Kennedy in 1964. From a political point of view, the commitment to serve as governor for four years made a lot of sense." Finch agreed. "I felt he really meant the four-year pledge. Kennedy looked awfully strong then, and the Republican Presidential nomination didn't appear to be worth much."

Not really burning with the desire to be governor of California, but pledging not to seek the Presidency in 1964, Nixon entered the 1962 race with forced enthusiasm. "He balanced the input of advice," Finch recalled later, "but once the decision was made, it was all systems go. Even when it began to turn against him, he never said, 'I wish I hadn't done this.' " But the built-in obstacles proved to be too much to overcome. Pat Brown, for all his reputation as a bumbler, knew when he had an issue. Though the hiding-place ploy had more validity in terms of the political realities, it required a bit more sophistication for voters to grasp; Brown settled for the stepping-stone argument to combat Nixon, which was simple, straightforward and easily understood. Stanley Mosk, the Democratic state attorney general, spelled it out clearly as soon as Nixon announced his candidacy on September 27, 1961, more than a year before the election. "Californians will hardly be flattered," Mosk said, "to have their governorship considered Nixon's consolation prize, a vehicle to satisfy his personal ambitions."

Before taking on Brown, Nixon had to get by a primary fight against the Republican state assembly leader, Joseph Shell, a doctrinaire conservative and a vanguard of the political sentiment that swept Ronald Reagan into the statehouse four years after Nixon's loss to Brown. Beating Shell was no problem, but it had to be done without further splitting the shaky Republican ranks and thus undermining Nixon's chances in the general election, in a state with a 3-to-2 Democratic registration edge. To carve such a moderate course, Nixon dissociated himself from the rising John Birch Society and got the influential California Republican Assembly to go along. It was a position

29

Nixon apparently took out of conviction as well as political reality. However, it shifted many ultraconservatives to Shell, and although Nixon won the June primary by a 2-to-1 margin, the contest left scars that endured through the general election. Eventually Nixon found himself behind Brown in the polls. (Nixon later sought to put major blame for his loss to Brown on the primary—and on his decision to reject John Birch Society support. At least one post-election analysis indicated, however, that he had won most of the Republican vote. His problem, as always, was with Democrats.)

While Nixon was disposing of Shell, Brown had been hammering away all spring with the stepping-stone argument, and in it he found an important ally: Nixon's own reputation as a national and international figure, and particularly as a foreign-policy expert. For all of Nixon's efforts to concentrate on state issues—he assembled impressive task forces to educate him and to produce position papers—the focus inevitably always came back to the man's interests beyond the state's borders. When anything happened in Vietnam, he was asked to comment, and press conference questions repeatedly turned to national and international issues. In March, 1962, when *Six Crises* was published and became a national best seller, it underlined his out-of-state orientation and again drew attention to his role as a national and global figure. "He still was the titular head of the party," Finch recalled. "He could remain mute on national issues, and look silly, or he could speak out. It was a very sticky wicket."

Nixon's national reputation was, of course, also a tremendous advantage to him in the California campaign. He had instant crowd recognition and a star quality (he often referred to himself as a "celebrity" in explaining this phenomenon to reporters; it was typical of his complete political concentration and ability to discuss himself as though he were his own campaign manager sizing up a prospective political property). These factors, and his determined campaigning, might have overcome the negatives if it had not been, ironically, for a cataclysmic development on the foreign policy front that reduced the Nixon-Brown campaign in its final days to secondary interest, in and out of California.

"How Many Street Views Watergate"

<u>Time</u>

28 may 1973

13-14

"The Decline and Fall"

Time

19 August 1974

pp. 53 – 55

On the night of October 22, President Kennedy went on nationwide television and disclosed the Cuban missile crisis— just as Nixon, running a measured campaign geared to "peak" as close to election day as possible, was pulling up to Brown in the public opinion polls. Watching Kennedy's speech with Steve Hess in his room at the Edgewater Inn in Oakland, Nixon felt at once that he was done in—again by events and by Kennedy. "He said then that it was all over," Hess recalled later. "He had been building the campaign, and this was the knife that cut into his ascending line. People stopped talking about local issues. We went to Disneyland the next day and he spent all morning making a unity speech, supporting Kennedy. He threw away his notes. It would have been superfluous and irrelevant to talk about anything but the Cuban crisis. He was a national leader; it was a strength, but it also was his weakness."

In the final week, Nixon labored valiantly to bring the spotlight back, even trying a defensive election-eve telecast patterned on the successful 1952 "Checkers speech"—the homey living room format, this time with family at the candidate's side. The Democrats had made a campaign issue of a loan made to his brother, Don, by the Hughes Tool Company (of the Howard Hughes empire), and Nixon indignantly denounced "malicious last-minute smears against me." It didn't work. It was a bad show, and he knew it. The Hughes loan did not hurt him nearly as much as the impact of the Cuban missile crisis, the stepping-stone issue and, in Nixon's view anyway, the split caused by the primary fight against Shell. The morning of the election, Hess, a youngish, scholarly-looking academic who moves easily in and out of political and government life, was in his hotel room packing for the trip back East when the phone rang. It was Nixon, calling to thank Hess for his help, because they probably wouldn't see each other again soon. "You still think you're going to lose?" Hess asked him. "Yes," Nixon answered. "You may be wrong," Hess said. "I'm not wrong," was Nixon's reply.

That night, it became pretty clear by midnight that Nixon's prediction had been correct. Hess typed out a concession statement for the candidate, gave it to Rose Woods and went to bed. He awoke in mid-morning, turned on his television set and was

31

surprised to see and hear Nixon in such a foul mood as he conducted his "last press conference." "Losing wasn't a shock to him," Hess said afterward. "He had expected it."

There is no reason to doubt, either, that Nixon at that bitter moment believed he finally was at the end of his own campaign trail. Unlike the six crises he had described in his book, written after his 1960 defeat, this seventh crisis seemed to have no redeeming political opportunity. Five of the first six—the Alger Hiss case in 1948, the Nixon fund and "Checkers speech" in 1952, President Eisenhower's heart attack in 1955, the Caracas riot in 1958, the "kitchen debate" with Soviet Premier Khrushchev in 1959—all were turned to Nixon's political advantage. And the sixth—his campaign for the Presidency in 1960—was such a narrow loss that it left him a live, viable political commodity, if he played his cards right. But the seventh—a resounding defeat for a lesser office at the hands of so unimpressive and parochial a politician as Pat Brown—plunged him to rock bottom.

Still, even in this debacle, Richard Nixon did have one sustaining strength: his commitment to the political life. That, in the final reckoning, and the unpredictable turns that political life can take, combined to bring about in 1968 what Nixon himself had every reason to think in 1962 was impossible. Even as he drove home in those first minutes of acrimonious defeat and public humiliation, he already was discussing his future, and whether he ought to leave California. By no means was the conversation the first plotting of a comeback, because Nixon had no illusions about his plight. "He felt he was through with politics," Chotiner recalled much later. "Not by choice, but by outcome. He didn't say so in so many words, but he felt his political career was over." Nevertheless, as an instinctive political animal, Nixon never permitted the thought to enter his mind that he would get out of politics—public life, party activity, discussion of issues—altogether. For sixteen years, as Congressman, Senator, Vice President and candidate for President and governor, he had been two things above all else: a fierce political partisan and a public man engrossed in public issues "Once you've hit the big leagues," he said long afterward, when private life on Wall Street had brought him wealth, but not fulfillment, "it's awfully hard to resign yourself to just puttering around."

Given that attitude, it was inevitable that Nixon would set out, or be driven by his own compulsions, to position himself to remain in the vortex of national political affairs. If he was not destined to be President of the United States, and it certainly looked that way, there was much that could be done in Republican circles to have an important impact on the party and the national life, short of that pinnacle. Thus, though the Presidency now may have seemed to Nixon beyond his grasp forever, his fixed determination to remain a voice and a force in the highest public councils set him on the course that, six years later, culminated in his resurrection from the political dead and his ascendancy to the White House.

Writing in a new preface to *Six Crises* in 1968 about the course of events that incredibly found him seeking the Presidency for a second time, Nixon professed to be unable to "analyze the workings of American democracy and the mystery of public opinion that took a man from 'finished' in 1963 to candidate for the Presidency in 1968. . . . There is no doubt, however," he said, "about what was *not* the reason for my candidacy today: It was not by dint of my own calculation or efforts. No man, not if he combined the wisdom of Lincoln with the connivance of Machiavelli, could have maneuvered or manipulated his way back into the arena."

In the strictest sense, this was true, considering the violent and divisive political developments that ultimately invited the return of Richard Nixon. He did not say, in that somber drive from the Beverly Hilton that morning in November, 1962, that he was not through yet, that he still would be President of the United States some day. But in the personal decisions he made in the ensuing months and years, and in the manner in which he conducted his affairs and himself, he was infinitely more than a leaf of fate, carried along by the winds of fortune and destiny and deposited finally on the front steps of 1600 Pennsylvania Avenue. Those winds, certainly, swept through a period of political upheaval so devastating and unpredictable that it cast tradition and precedence aside with utter irreverence, creating the improbable conditions Nixon required for a return to

33

power. But if it had not been for the way the man positioned himself politically immediately after his 1962 defeat and, just as critically, the way he addressed himself to himself—to what it was in him that not only made him lose but made others so pleased when he did lose—he would not be in the White House today.

For all Nixon's outward denials of maneuver and manipulation, there occurred from those darkest hours of public rejection through the next six long years one of the most effective exercises in self-analysis and self-rehabilitation in the history of American politics. It has been suggested, in fact, that Nixon actually underwent professional psychoanalysis in those years. The suggestion has been denied and no reliable testimony has been produced to support it, but the notion is almost irrelevant anyway. In the actions and statements of Richard Nixon from late 1962 through 1968, there is remarkable evidence of how the man's own introspection and ability to adjust his words and style reshaped his public image and eventually made him acceptable, if not wildly appealing, to a plurality of American voters. From the moment of his disastrous "last press conference," the man embarked on a determined effort never again to inflict damage on himself through lack of self-discipline. Instead, with the fierce single-mindedness that the American public really came to appreciate only much later, he set out to make a new beginning—personally, emotionally, geographically, politically. From the start, he hoped this new beginning would lead him somehow back to national prominence; not as President of the United States, perhaps, but as a force in American politics and public opinion.

It would not be easy. Richard Nixon was a two-time loser with an added handicap now—a reputation as a bad loser. But he was only forty-nine years old, and he was in good physical shape. And he was, above all, a political animal to the core. "Once you've been in the arena," he said in a private interview much later, when circumstances and his comeback ambitions were beginning to place him clearly on the road to the White House again, "you can't stay out." In November, 1962, though, what should have been understood about Nixon even in the ebb tide of his career was obscured by his apparent willingness to close out his political options publicly in one emotional venomous valedictory. The man had got his pent-up feelings off his chest, but not out of his system. The drive that had brought him this far still was very much alive; the next step was to select the most propitious way to channel it.

2

New York–and Dallas

THE day after Richard Nixon's "last press conference," Rose Woods, the indispensable secretarial guardian
of his time and interests throughout his career, placed a phone
call to the Los Angeles home of the one individual the defeated
candidate chose to accompany him on the start of a post-election vacation. Surprisingly, that individual was not Nixon's
campaign manager, nor one of his close political counselors,
nor even one of his longtime personal or family friends who
had been with him through the peaks and depths of success
and failure. Rather, he was a relatively minor appendage to
Nixon's California gubernatorial campaign entourage, an official of the Pacific Telephone and Telegraph Company assigned eight months earlier by his employer to be the official
communications representative.

The man, John S. Davies, is a large, mild-mannered, amiable
gentleman of unobtrusive political views who was the telephone
company's general sales manager when he met Richard Nixon
for the first time. His job during the campaign had been to
arrange the complex communications required for the candidate, his staff and the accompanying press as they moved swiftly
from one end of the state to the other—at hotels, at rallies, at
airports or at trainside in a day of whistle-stopping. In the
performance of these duties, Davies became absorbed into the

official family as such men usually do in a campaign, and in time he found himself a silent but trusted witness to innermost staff discussions and strategy sessions. He knew how to cut through communications red tape, and before long he was doing it for Nixon himself, placing rush calls for him, handing over the phone when the connection was made, then standing by to be of further service. He heard all and said nothing; in that trite phrase most often used in a demeaning context, he knew his place, and Nixon came to recognize that here was a man he not only could trust but could feel comfortable with.

Rose Woods told Davies that Nixon was going to the Bahamas in two days and wanted him to go along. It was a command performance of a sort, but also tangible evidence of the ties of friendship that had grown quickly between the two men of such essentially different backgrounds and interests. Davies accepted at once, and on the Friday morning after the election he met Nixon at the Los Angeles Airport, where they boarded a jet bound for Miami. Though the experience of the election still was fresh in their minds, on the long cross-country flight not a word was said between them, according to Davies, about any aspect of the late campaign or of Nixon's political future. "When he wants to talk and chat, that's fine," Davies said later in discussing their relationship. "When he doesn't want to, you give him that leeway. On the flight down, there were times he obviously was deep in thought, peering out the window, and then he would come back, and we'd chat again."

At the airport in Miami, Nixon and Davies were met by a third vacation companion, a short man of dark eyes and complexion and quietly friendly demeanor who like Davies was essentially nonpolitical and who had known Nixon mainly in a nonpolitical context. In fact he was a registered Democrat at the time. This man, Charles Gregory "Bebe" Rebozo, is a self-made millionaire who rose from a lowly station as a chauffeur for swank Miami hotels and an airline steward in the embryo days of passenger flights to an entrepreneur of laundromats and gas stations, and eventually to the heights of big-time real estate dealings. He had met Nixon in 1951, when the young Senator from California, suffering from a cold and weary from his hard race for election, went to Florida with a Senate colleague,

37

George Smathers. Smathers recommended Key Biscayne and asked Rebozo, a prominent member and developer of that community just south of Miami Beach, to take Nixon in hand. Rebozo, of Cuban parentage, was a bachelor who could give time to his friends and, like Nixon, a loner and an introvert. A warm personal friendship blossomed almost immediately, and they often swam and fished together.

Like Davies, Rebozo is a man who, because of his own lack of political ambition or desire for the limelight, is able to deal with Nixon on a personal basis divorced from politics. And, like Davies, Rebozo too is a man who knows his place; "I've seen him and Bebe sit in a room for three hours," Smathers told me once, "and neither ever say a word. Nixon's a little bit of a mystic. He gets all his information together, then he meditates and contemplates. And Bebe sits there." Nixon, Davies and Rebozo spent long days at Huntington Hartford's hotel, the Oceanfront, on Paradise Island in the Bahamas, without talking politics. "The three of us would go swimming in the surf," Davies recalled later, "swapping stories, talking about anything. Then he would get deep in thought and would walk down the beach. We'd wait for him, and sooner or later he would come back." At night there were small dinner parties hosted by Hartford and others, with politics and Nixon's own future seldom if ever the topic of discussion.

Nixon's choice of Davies and Rebozo as the two men with whom to vacation at a critical time in his career, out of the hundreds of important and sometimes brilliant leaders he knew in the fields of politics, law and business, is perplexing to outsiders. But Nixon political associates have come to recognize the role these men and others like them play in Nixon's life. They see them as emotional and conversational safety valves for him. "He can be comfortable with them," says Steve Hess, now a White House aide. "They don't want anything from him, and he doesn't have to be on guard with them. Men like Bebe have an old-shoe quality that helps Nixon relax." Others in this category, who have been selected by Nixon to accompany him at critical times before and after he reached the White House, include Hobart Lewis, the president and executive editor of *Reader's Digest;* Robert Abplanalp, a businessman who became a millionaire by developing the aerosol valve for dispensing sprays; and Paul Keyes, former producer of the Jack Paar and *Laugh-In* television shows, who is said to have a special talent for enabling the sometimes tense Nixon to see the humor in life.

In taking Davies and Rebozo with him to the Bahamas in 1962, Nixon was assuring himself political and personal privacy at a time he needed to think. At the end of the November vacation, at Thanksgiving, his wife, Pat, and daughters, Tricia and Julie, joined him for a few days, then they all returned to California to face the uncertain future. Almost at once, Nixon began to contact his closest political friends and advisers to help him chart his course. He was a two-time loser, but not forgotten. Only five days after his California defeat, that fact was demonstrated in a massive public protest against an American Broadcasting Company television special by Howard K. Smith called *The Political Obituary of Richard M. Nixon.* One of the individuals interviewed briefly on the show was Alger Hiss, the former State Department official convicted of perjury after the Congressional investigation into Communist espionage that had boosted Nixon into national prominence in 1948. Hiss said that "political motivation played a very real part" in Nixon's conduct of the case and that the then Congressman "was more interested . . . in molding appearances to a point of view that he began with, than in objectively developing the facts." Nearly 80,000 telegrams and letters poured in on the network. Smith conceded much later, after Nixon became President, that "it bothered ABC a great deal and it didn't leave me unshaken." Nixon issued a statement that said: "What does an attack by one convicted perjurer mean when weighed on the scales against the thousands of wires and letters from patriotic Americans?" Smith wrote to Nixon about the show but never got a reply (though in 1968, when Nixon was a candidate for President again, Smith—by now, like the Nixon of 1968, a "hawk" on the Vietnam War—received a cordial letter from him praising a more recent television commentary. And when Nixon first reached the White House, he phoned Smith to compliment him on a broadcast).

The defeated candidate was, after all, still a former Vice

39

President and Presidential candidate. A Midwestern university wanted him as its president, and so did a university in southern California. He received feelers to become chairman of the board at the Chrysler Corporation, then badly in need of an organizational transfusion. He was scouted as the possible next commissioner of baseball. Hess and Chotiner both suggested the chairmanship of the Republican National Committee as a natural outlet for his political experience and energies, and for his talents as a party unifier and spokesman. But Nixon apparently never seriously considered the idea. All of these, in fact, were unsatisfactory because they would have impeded his personal political activity. Bob Finch, who conferred with him often in those days, said later that "there never was any question of his withdrawal from the political arena, at least as party unifier. But he felt he would not run for political office again. He felt that since he had ruled himself out, since he was not a viable political product in terms of electability, he wanted to speak out for the party, travel and have ready access to the media."

As early as December, 1962, only a month after his California defeat, old Nixon hands were conferring again on his future, and in the first weeks of 1963 a meeting was held in a suite at the Waldorf-Astoria in New York, to take stock. In the group were Robert C. Hill, ambassador to Mexico in the Eisenhower administration and a longtime Nixon friend and supporter in New Hampshire; Hess; Keyes, then with the Jack Paar night television show; Bunny Lasker, head of the New York Stock Exchange; Tom Duggan, a Los Angeles newscaster, and a few others. Nixon presided and asked Hess to summarize all the alternatives open to him—including Hess' suggestion about the chairmanship of the Republican National Committee. No votes were taken; possibilities simply were discussed, with Nixon mostly listening. But out of the conversations, one door after another was closed as this job or that appeared to tie Nixon's hands in being what by nature as well as desire he had to be—a free political agent.

That requirement inevitably kept Nixon in the practice of law—but not in California. His political stock was too low there, and he would become embroiled in endless party wrangles that would only further diminish his voice as a national leader. Also, as another aide put it later, "There was no foreign policy angle in California. It had to be the East. He had to have his cake (money) and eat it too (his interest in foreign policy) ."

On the money point, Mrs. Nixon was particularly unhappy and was nagging him about their plight. The Nixons, in cold fact, were deep in financial debt, largely because they had bought the showcase Trousdale Estates home—6,500 square feet, four bedrooms, seven baths, three fireplaces, swimming pool and Harpo and Groucho Marx as neighbors. Also, as a former Vice President and Presidential candidate, he could not go anywhere or do anything at less than first class. He had been working as a lawyer for only two years, with much of that time out for politicking. He was not broke, but at the level he had to live, he was hard-pressed. And, finally, Pat Nixon felt humiliated by the gubernatorial defeat. She could not bear the thought of staying in California and being looked down on, after all she had been through. If her husband was an introvert, by comparison she was practically a recluse. He at least had his passion for politics. She told some friends that Dick had promised never to run for public office again, and none of them doubted it was the way she wanted it. "One reason he has been so thoughtful and kind to her," an old associate said much later, after Nixon had become a candidate again, "is because he knows she can't stand it."

The obvious destination for the Nixons—where the money, the prestige, the international focus and the action ("a fast track," as Nixon often put it later) all were—was New York. The political stepping-stones there were occupied by Republicans—Governor Nelson A. Rockefeller in Albany and Senators Jacob K. Javits and Kenneth B. Keating (later Nixon's ambassador to India) in Washington. But Nixon wasn't thinking in that vein anymore; he was in the same position Thomas E. Dewey had faced after a second loss for major office, and he knew how successful Dewey had been, and how influential he had remained, by turning to private law practice in New York. In fact, he discussed the move with Dewey and received encouragement. (Later, one close associate insists, Nixon became so frustrated at being shut out of the "political arena" in New York that he toyed at one point with starting all over at the

41

bottom of the ladder, by running for the House of Representatives. The idea seems incredible, and no doubt it was to him too if indeed he ever did consider it, because he never moved in that direction.) Nixon took a hands-off attitude toward Nelson Rockefeller's Republican Party in the state, even to the point of staying away from the big annual party dinner that no other Republican in good standing ever thought of missing.

In his new career in the law, however, it had to be New York. As matters turned out, though, the major law firms that often are havens for big-league politicians between elective offices were not beating Nixon's door down. "A lot of lawyers didn't want a tiger in their midst," one of his associates said later. They had their own vested interests and were not anxious to become bit players in Nixon's next unfolding drama. There also was, to some degree at least, resistance against Nixon himself in the Eastern bastion of Republican liberalism. One associate tells of the time, shortly after the Nixons finally did move to New York, when they met Irving Mitchell Felt, the Jewish philanthropist and head of the Madison Square Garden Corporation. Felt, the story goes, took an immediate liking to the Nixons and decided to have a small dinner party with five other couples, to introduce the newcomers around. "It took Felt two or three weeks to get the others," the associate says. "They just didn't want to go to dinner with Nixon."

These attitudes, and the fact that Nixon was looking for a special deal where he would get a fat salary and still be free to engage in politics, obliged Nixon's friends to do some hard scouting for him. "There just weren't too many places where he could get two hundred and fifty thousand dollars and all his time," said one member of his firm later. One of Nixon's oldest friends and benefactors, Elmer Bobst, head of the Lambert-Warner Pharmaceutical Company, finally cleared and greased the way with his law firm, a reputable but somewhat stodgy antique known as Mudge, Stern, Baldwin and Todd.

It was, in the words of another Nixon political associate, a "backwater" firm in which he clearly would be the top man. Whereas the new partner would have had to scramble had he joined a thriving powerhouse—and might not emerge on top—at Mudge he would have a relatively clear field, and could take credit for boosting the firm's fortunes. Another old friend, Donald M. Kendall of the Pepsi-Cola Company, helped by giving Nixon his lucrative legal account; it served as a kind of entrance fee into the firm.

Six months after his California defeat, it was all settled; Nixon on May 2, 1963, announced he would move to New York on June 1 and become a big-time lawyer in the toughest competition. He would be counsel to the firm until he was admitted to the New York bar, and then a full senior partner, with his name at the head. (On January 1, 1964, it became known as Nixon, Mudge, Rose, Guthrie and Alexander—the names of dead partners having been dropped and senior men added. The new lead name on the door brought more and more business, until the firm became one of the fastest-growing on Wall Street.) While awaiting admission to the bar, Nixon said in announcing his move East, "I shall engage in matters relating to the Washington and Paris offices of the firm." Washington and Paris—politics and foreign policy; Richard M. Nixon would be a private citizen, but a private citizen living in the communications center of the world who had positioned himself to be seen and heard on both the national and the international stages. Perhaps he didn't yet realize it, but already he was on his way back.

Actually, even before the move to New York, Nixon was taking steps to cement his reputation in the public mind as a foreign-policy expert. In April he was invited to address the prestigious annual meeting of the American Society of Newspaper Editors in Washington, and he seized the opportunity with zest. John C. Whitaker, a tall and good-humored Washington-based geologist who served as a volunteer advance man for Nixon's visits to the capital and remains among his most loyal and admiring aides, recalled later how Nixon came to Washington a day early, holed up in a room at the Madison Hotel and pored over research gathered for him. "From eleven o'clock that night until four in the morning he went over the material," Whitaker said, "scribbling away with the old fountain pen on the yellow legal pad. While he wrote, I typed. After a few hours' sleep, he got up again at seven and went until noon, working it over and over." It was Whitaker's impression at the time that

43

Nixon regarded the ASNE speech as a sort of valedictory on foreign policy, because he could not expect another invitation from the group if he remained out of elective office. Nixon told Steve Hess as much. "He was working on it in such a frantic way," Hess recalled later, "that I asked him why he was going at it like that. He had spoken to this group many times. He told me: 'It may be the last time I'm ever asked to give a speech to such a group. I have a number of things I want to say.' It was sort of his swan song, since ASNE asked only the leading politicians. It indicated he felt he was moving out of that category."

But beyond the "swan song" aspect, Nixon likely saw the forum as a means of reinforcing his position as the Republican Party's titular leader and its resident expert on world affairs. There were, of course, always high appointive jobs to be filled, including Secretary of State; although Nixon never publicly aspired to the post, by background and interest he would be one of the logical prospects in a future Republican administration headed by someone else.

The speech, as Nixon obviously hoped, was very well received by the editors—who always had been high on him—and it kept his name alive in political circles. It was Nixon's view that what a man said always received more attention and was likely to have more real influence if he spoke as one who might be a future Presidential candidate. Even if he himself did not see another candidacy as probable, his desire to remain a serious voice in national affairs was sufficient reason to help any such speculation along.

In the speech, Nixon severely castigated President Kennedy for what Nixon contended was, in the perspective of a year's time, an American defeat in the Cuban missile crisis of the previous October. Though the Russians had agreed to withdraw their long-range offensive missiles from Cuba, Nixon noted, the United States had agreed not to invade the island, and thus the Communist government of Fidel Castro remained secure. "No matter whether there are twelve thousand or seventeen thousand Soviet troops now in Cuba, Khrushchev's position, with American acquiescence, is firmer today than a year ago. . . . We must no longer postpone making a command decision to do whatever is necessary to force the removal of the Soviet beach-

head. The United States cannot tolerate the continued existence of a Soviet military and subversive base ninety miles from
our shore . . ."

The speech, in addition to underlining Nixon's determination to remain the cutting edge of Republican foreign policy
opposition to the Democratic administration, offered for those
with good memories a revealing insight into the workings of the
political mind of the man. Nixon's get-tough approach in April,
1963, was in sharp contrast to his moderate rejoinder in the
fourth and final Nixon-Kennedy television debate of 1960,
when the same basic matter of deposing Castro arose. Then,
Nixon severely criticized Kennedy for advocating active American support of anti-Castro Cubans in exile and in Cuba, charging that such action would violate American tradition and
treaty commitments. But Nixon in 1962 confessed in *Six Crises*
that he really agreed with Kennedy but had to take the opposite
position; that he had to protect plans going forward within the
Eisenhower administration—urged by himself—for just such a
Cuban invasion. He was like the geography teacher who, when
asked by a school superintendent whether he believed the world
was round or flat, said he could teach it either way. It all
depended, obviously, on where one sat, and now—in April,
1963—Nixon sat on the outside, where advocacy of a tougher
Cuban policy seemed good politics.

In every public man's career there usually are a few incidents
that stand out over the years as particularly revealing about
him. Nixon's fencing with Kennedy over Cuba is one of those
incidents and therefore warrants examination. A day before the
final Nixon-Kennedy debate in 1960, John Kennedy had made
a blatant appeal for support at an American Legion Convention
in Miami Beach, telling the cheering delegates that "we must
attempt to strengthen the non-Batista democratic anti-Castro
forces in exile, and in Cuba itself, who offer eventual hope of
overthrowing Castro." The Kennedy statement received wide
press coverage, and as expected, Nixon was asked in the debate
the next night to explain the difference in the two candidates'
approaches to Cuba. Nixon immediately attacked Kennedy.
"Our policies are very different," he said, though—he confessed
later—they really weren't. He called Kennedy's statement

45

"probably the most dangerously irresponsible recommendations" of the campaign and warned that if they were followed, "we would lose all of our friends in Latin America, we would probably be condemned in the United Nations, and . . . [it] would be an open invitation for Mr. Khrushchev to come in, to come into Latin America and to engage us in what would be a civil war and possibly even worse than that."

It was, obviously, a well-prepared response, and—in light of later developments—a prophetic one, anticipating the condemnation at the UN and elsewhere that did in fact descend on the Bay of Pigs invasion, conceived in the Eisenhower administration and carried out imperfectly and ineffectively by Kennedy. And it was a remarkably detailed and reasoned response, in light of Nixon's later admission that he wasn't himself persuaded by it.

Nixon, in *Six Crises,* explained why he had argued in 1960 against what he believed: *"There was only one thing I could do,"* Nixon wrote. "The covert operation had to be protected at all costs. I must not even suggest by implication that the United States was rendering aid to rebel forces in and out of Cuba. *In fact, I must go to the other extreme:* I must attack the Kennedy proposal to provide such aid as wrong and irresponsible because it would violate our treaty commitments." (Italics added.)

The 1960 Presidential debates have been criticized as not having really been debates at all, but it is quite clear from Nixon's confessional postmortem that he considered them to be debates in the fullest sense. A champion debater can be assigned either side of an argument, suppress his own personal views, marshal all the strongest arguing points for the side assigned to him and against the view he really embraces, and make the best of it. Not only is this precisely what Nixon did, but he volunteered that he had done it with American foreign policy and the Presidency in the balance.

That 1960 performance obviously stuck in Nixon's mind in the next years, for he considered it one of the decisive incidents in his defeat that year. In November, 1964, he again defended his debating position in an article in the *Reader's Digest,* which through his friend Hobart Lewis became a kind of house organ for him, helping him finance his trips abroad in return for articles that underlined his continuing foreign policy interest and involvement.

"Any number of factors could have made the difference in what was to be the closest Presidential election in history, where a shift of less than one-half a vote a precinct would have changed the result," Nixon concluded. "Most observers agree that our positions on the Cuban issue could well have been the decisive factor. But I have never had any regrets about this decision, or any doubt that it was *the only one I could make* under the circumstances." (Italics added.)

Why couldn't Nixon have protected the covert operation simply by emphasizing his own public campaign proposal—a strict diplomatic and economic quarantine of Cuba, which he had in fact mentioned? In the summer of 1966, in an interview in the study of his New York apartment, I asked Nixon about why he had to "go to the other extreme" and say something directly contrary to what he believed.

"*It was the only political position that was salvageable,*" he answered without a moment's hesitation. "I couldn't say what we were actually doing and what I was advocating in the government. But Kennedy was taking a highly popular position, and to simply say you were against it *would not have been enough politically.* I had to give the reasons it was wrong. It was one of the ironies of the campaign. But I had to do it. Many of my critics were against the decision to go into Cuba in the first place. They would have been happier if I could have stayed with the administration decision. All my intellectual critics would have been happier." (Italics added.)

In the same interview, Nixon also revealed that had he been elected President in 1960, he would have gone through with the very Cuban invasion he had debated against, and in fact would have asked Eisenhower to launch it even before Nixon succeeded him in the White House. "Time was of the essence," he told me. "I would have advocated to President Eisenhower that it be done before my inauguration, and if I had done so, I'm confident it would have happened that way. Eisenhower couldn't start that kind of undertaking and leave it to a new [Democratic] administration. But I was hard-line on Cuba and would have wanted to go ahead without delay."

47

Nixon contended that he would not have permitted the invasion to fail, that he would have committed whatever forces were required to throttle Castro, and that Khrushchev never would have had the chance or the encouragement to put missiles into Cuba later. "If the United States had dealt with Castro effectively at the Bay of Pigs," he said, "Khrushchev would not have miscalculated a year later in the missile crisis. Khrushchev, like all aggressors, all dictators, interpreted indecision as weakness. The way to avoid miscalculation is never give them a moment when they think you're weak."*

Appearing before the editors in Washington in April, 1963, Nixon no longer needed to play the champion debater taking the "wrong" side. His tough anti-Castro, anti-Communist speech plucked the patriotic strings of the predominantly Republican editors' hearts, and they applauded lustily. They applauded also his explanation for his 1962 "last press conference" outburst against the press: "I felt like returning for sixteen minutes some of the heat I had been taking for sixteen years." And they laughed when he said he agreed with his old archfoe, Harry Truman, that "if you can't take the heat, stay out of the kitchen." After his California defeat, Nixon said to more laughter, he had got out of the kitchen. Still, his performance before the editors was not completely convincing on that score. John H. Averill of the Los Angeles *Times* wrote of Nixon's appearance that "while he denied in response to one question that he has any plans to seek public office in the future, several of his listeners were heard to remark that he sounded for all the world like a man still seeking the Presidency."

This suspicion was reinforced in many minds when Nixon began to speak out more and more. In contrast with his old stump intensity, though, he now was much more relaxed, and it was not long before the "new Nixon" talk of 1960 had been upgraded to speculation about a "new, new Nixon." Feature writer Arthur Edson of the Associated Press was among the first

---

* In their book, *The Invisible Government,* David Wise and Thomas B. Ross have written that a Nixon aide told them Nixon actively was "hoping for" the Bay of Pigs invasion before the 1960 election because "it would have been a cinch to win the election if the Eisenhower administration destroyed Fidel Castro in the closing days of the presidential campaign."

to notice a change: "There's a new Richard M. Nixon politicking about the land," he wrote. "It's a Nixon most people never saw, a Nixon who is relaxed and quick with the wisecrack." He was, obviously, a man who had put his political ambitions behind him and was enjoying himself. Or was he? Nixon's idea of enjoyment was not the same as others' was. A few weeks after his Cuba speech to the editors, he returned to Washington. There he received a high-level foreign policy briefing at the State Department prior to a long summer vacation with his family in Europe and the Middle East, before settling down to his new law practice in New York. During the vacation Nixon found time to renew old acquaintances with Charles de Gaulle in Paris, Konrad Adenauer in Bonn, Pope John in Rome and lesser world lights—and to be photographed with most of them for consumption back home. It was the beginning of a series of overseas tours in the next five years that would effectively keep alive Nixon's reputation as a foreign policy expert in every quarter of the globe, and keep him acquainted with the problems and personalities with which any future candidate for the American Presidency would have to deal. His trips abroad at the same time illustrated how Nixon the political animal, not through any Machiavellian master plan to seize the White House but through a natural positioning dictated by his interests and his determination not to be cut out of the action, put himself on the road back.

That road, at the outset particularly, had many long stretches of routine and inconspicuous travel. Nixon's first months in New York as a lawyer, characteristically, were taken up with devotion to detail and self-education in a new arena. The man's capacity and even zest for hard work were turned to the task of establishing himself on Wall Street, and in this effort he had the cooperation of his new law partners and old political associates. They introduced him to the right clubs for lunch and golf, but that really was not his style. He preferred, if he was busy, to arrive early and stay late at work, reaching the office sometimes at seven thirty in the morning and working past six. His office on the twenty-fourth floor at 20 Broad Street was a museum of his past political life, and one could not enter it without the immediate feeling that it was a kind of sanctuary for a President-

49

in-exile. A two-pen set from President Eisenhower, his Cabinet and White House staff, inscribed "with high esteem and warm regards," was centered at the top of a large, antique wooden desk. Behind Nixon's swivel chair was another desk on which were perched the signed, framed portraits of ten world figures: Queen Elizabeth, Prince Philip, the Shah of Iran, Haile Selassie, President Ayub Khan of Pakistan, Antonio Segni of Italy, King Bhumibhol of Thailand, King Baudouin of Belgium, Nehru and President Radhakrishnan of India. Murals and sketches from Nixon's Asian travels abounded, and there were photographs on the wall with Ike and one from Lambaréné autographed "avec mes bonnes pensées" by Schweitzer. There were keys to assorted cities, Vice Presidential ashtrays and gavels and sundry other evidences that here a man of history could be found. (The only office quite like it was George Wallace's governor-in-exile layout in an office building in Montgomery, full of photographs of past glories, and American and Alabamian flags flanking his chair.)

When there were no pressing matters at the office, Nixon preferred to stay home rather than go in and get bogged down in routine and in office politics. His inclination, and as time went on his strength, was broadening the firm into areas of international law and trade, where his impressive contacts abroad were used to good advantage. Also, his knowledge of how Washington works attracted clients and, once they came in, enabled the firm to serve them better.

Nixon the Wall Street lawyer lunched perhaps twice a week at The Recess, the very exclusive club on the thirty-eighth and thirty-ninth floors of 60 Broad Street just down from his office in the heart of the business district. The membership roster abounds in famous names: Thomas E. Dewey; former Attorneys General Herbert Brownell and William P. Rogers (later Nixon's Secretary of State) ; former Secretary of Treasury Henry Fowler; Nixon's Secretary of Commerce, Maurice Stans; former disarmament negotiator Arthur H. Dean and many others known mainly in the legal profession. But unlike Nixon, most of them had made their mark on Wall Street before going into government service. "I don't think I ever thought of him as being a lawyer," said the manager of The Recess, Karl Brandon, after Nixon had reached the White House. "He was a lawyer, but to us he was the Vice President."

At The Recess, Nixon would be given the choice table at a corner where two picture windows meet, providing a sweeping view of the East River. With his law partners, clients or an occasional political visitor, he would eat sparingly, preferring clams, pompano or red snapper, and seldom drinking liquor. But the long, leisurely lunch and the comfortable pace of living it symbolized did not fit into his "fast track" concept of New York. Increasingly, he escaped to Washington or Europe or to political rescue work for the party around the country.

Nixon did not think too much of some of his senior associates at Nixon Mudge. The one he liked best was Randolph H. Guthrie, a corporation lawyer whose ideas on growth of the firm were close to Nixon's own. Another favorite was Leonard Garment, a onetime jazz clarinetist who ran the litigation department and later became a chief campaign brain truster on use of the media. Nixon found the two other major figures, Milton C. Rose and John H. Alexander, narrow and boring, and in time it often was Nixon and Guthrie against Rose and Alexander in internal struggles over policy. Nixon's interest in golf, nurtured while he was Eisenhower's Vice President, waned because when he went to Baltusrol in New Jersey or to Blind Brook in Westchester, he often ran into law partners and associates he didn't particularly care for. So he just stayed away. And any feelings of inadequacy, even of inferiority, about running on "the fast track" diminished as his bank account rose.

The Nixons weren't much, either, for socializing with the members of the law firm, or for that matter with any other New York social clique. They received invitations but turned most of them down. Instead, they gathered their own private favorites around them, particularly the nonpolitical types of whom the politicians and the celebrity-watchers never had heard and would not, because they shielded the privacy of the Nixons zealously—men like Bob Abplanalp, Elmer Bobst and Don Carnevale, a successful New York jeweler. Pat Nixon had not really wanted to part with the leisurely, sunshine life of California and the quiet familiar ways there, but she had been so hurt by the California political experience. In the words of one

New York associate, "it was like moving to another country for her to come to New York," and she usually took refuge in the tasteful thirteen-room Fifth Avenue apartment the Nixons bought for $135,000 and in the activities of her two daughters.

The apartment was refurnished in French provincial, with a preponderance of pastel yellows and golds. Over the next five years, about $50,000 was spent in remodeling; Mrs. Nixon converted a small maid's room into a large walk-in closet for the master bedroom, which contained twin beds and was only slightly larger than the adjacent rooms of Julie and Tricia, each with private bath. A fourth bedroom was converted into a television sitting room, and the servants' quarters were remodeled for storage of Nixon's papers and for a larger room off the modernized kitchen for Fina and Manolo Sanchez, the unobtrusive Cuban refugee couple who assisted in the quiet, at times almost sequestered life of the Nixons.

The former Vice President, having been caught up in the rush of political events and public life ever since the end of World War II, was able at last to do a great deal of reading. "Up to 1963," an associate said later, "his life had been a succession of urgencies that didn't allow for reflection. He acquired that from 1963 on. He could go back to the way it was at Duke Law School, when he was a drone, when he sat and read all the time." Whenever possible, he would put in three hours or more with a book before retiring for the night, and his preference ran heavily to current events. More and more, however, he said in a later interview, he was turning then to history. "It's escapist, but it also enriches your thought processes," he told me, and he listed as his favorites the eras of Woodrow Wilson, Theodore Roosevelt and Winston Churchill. Wilson and Teddy Roosevelt clearly were his latter-day American heroes and models. He admired the first Roosevelt, he said, "because of his great dynamic drive and ability to mobilize a young country and make it a responsible world power; his high idealism, his ability to lead." With Wilson, Nixon said, it was "his sheer intellectual brilliance. He led the nation through it. Roosevelt led by the force of his personality, his animal magnetism, the mystique of leadership. Wilson once wrote a speech at Princeton in which he talked of men of thought and men of action. Teddy Roosevelt was a man of action and Woodrow Wilson was a man of thought. Teddy Roosevelt was a man of action who could think and Woodrow Wilson was a man of thought who could act. You must judge the effectiveness of each world leader in terms of this combination."

Clearly Nixon, even in the relaxation of reading, always was focused on the political life. Few of the books on his shelves were novels ("I have no time for them," he said on another occasion). The comfortable, paneled den, overlooking the corner of Fifth Avenue and East 62d Street, was—like his Broad Street office—full of mementos of the activist public life and of political commitment. On his mantel was a collection of nineteen miniature elephants of marble and glass from all over the world, the symbol of his party and of his vehicle to national and world prominence.

Neighbors saw very little of the Nixons, but in New York there was nothing unusual about that. Those who did meet them on the elevator or in the lobby downstairs, including the building help, all found them to be congenial, going out of their way to make small talk and to put the employees at their ease. The effervescent Julie was the favorite of most of those who saw the Nixons at a distance, but her father was well liked for his lack of snobbishness and his interest in what his casual acquaintances were doing, reading—and thinking politically. In the manner of the old political reporter who takes soundings from taxi drivers and barbers, Nixon often would ask his doormen what they thought of this or that latest development, and the gesture if nothing else set this tenant apart from others of lesser fame who treated the hired help like hired help. Yet it was more than courtesy and cordiality; the man thrived on politics and the limelight it brought. Once, walking down the street, an Associated Press photographer came up to Nixon and asked permission to take some pictures. He snapped one showing Nixon standing at a corner with the people all around him looking straight ahead. The picture ran the next day over the caption: "The Forgotten Man." Nixon, furious, called the AP photo desk and complained. He pointed out that everyone on the corner was watching for a red light to change.

As the fall of 1963 wore on, and Nixon learned what it was

like to be a New York lawyer, others in the Republican Party were not professing their lack of interest in the 1964 Presidential nomination. One of them, Nelson Rockefeller, already was a declared candidate. He recently had been divorced and remarried to a mother of four, Mrs. Margaretta Fitler "Happy" Murphy, a development that severely jolted his Presidential prospects. But he was pressing on, and there was no doubt that the darling of GOP conservatism, Senator Barry Goldwater of Arizona, would actively oppose him. Other names also were involved in the usual pre-election-year speculation: George Romney, the Rambler Man who had shaken up Detroit with the compact car and who then got himself elected governor of Michigan; William W. Scranton, the aristocratic former Congressman and State Department official who to many Republicans projected a young, Kennedy-like image as governor of Pennsylvania; Henry Cabot Lodge, Nixon's 1960 running mate, who now was American ambassador in Saigon; long shots like Dr. Milton Eisenhower, brother of the retired President. To no one's surprise, but to the dismay of many, the contest was developing as a collision between Rockefeller and Goldwater, with neither of the two men appearing at this stage to have the support necessary to win. The prospect, particularly in the view of many of the men in the East who had engineered the Eisenhower nominations of 1952 and 1956 and the Nixon nomination of 1960, was for a bloody party-splitting stalemate, and no real alternative in sight.

That appraisal, of course, was woefully myopic, for while these prognosticators were peering into their cloudy crystal balls, the foot soldiers of Goldwater's conservative army were marching through the grass-roots ranks of the Republican Party, sweeping everything in sight under their banner. While the party's moderates and liberals concentrated on the old formula of kingmaking at the top, the Goldwater legions were methodically gaining control of the local party apparatus through caucuses or just plain power plays. Directing the strategy was New York public relations consultant F. Clifton White, a shrewd, soft-spoken technician given to floppy bow ties and intraparty conspiracies, with the ultraconservative Young Republicans as his personal brigade. Throughout the South and

Southwest, and in much of the Midwest, grass-roots Republicanism already was committed in heart and purpose to Goldwater, who had told them from the podium at the San Francisco convention in 1960, "Grow up, conservatives!" They had taken the cue with a vengeance, and after years of frustration and bitterness marked by repeated Republican nominations dictated or engineered from the "Eastern Establishment," they spread the gospel of Goldwater with a fervor that often approached, and sometimes reached, fanaticism.

Because most states select their delegates in ways other than the direct primary, the Goldwater movement was able to function as a sort of political underground. While the American press focused on the early primary contests as the battlegrounds on which the Republican nomination would be decided, the supporters of Barry Goldwater labored in the nonprimary states, at routine meetings, caucuses and later at county and district party conventions to win control. The primaries were ballyhooed as the ball game, but they were not; especially not in 1964. They did, nevertheless, provide a useful smoke screen for the conservative mobilization that was going on in the Republican Party, and they did keep the kingmakers harmlessly occupied.

In the Easterners' search for an alternative to the stalemate they thought they saw coming, Nixon was not a particularly favorite name, and not only because he had said repeatedly he was through with elective office. In the 1960 campaign, which Nixon had lost by only 119,000 votes, he had run as a loner, keeping his own counsel, insisting on making his own strategy, shunning the advice of some of his top campaign aides. Had he won, no one would have remembered it. But he had not won, and the second-guessing was inevitable, particularly because the margin of defeat was so narrow. If-only-he-had-listened-to-me became a familiar and consoling lament; the main lesson of the 1960 campaign for many of its veterans was that they didn't want to go through another one like it.

Still, Nixon was the previous Presidential nominee, he nearly had won, and he remained probably the best-known Republican after Eisenhower. In September, at an insurance agents' convention in Syracuse, he launched a series of policy speeches because, he said, the Republican position "was not getting through completely." The publicity didn't enhance his standing as a recluse. Neither did an interview by the Associated Press with Eisenhower at the former President's Gettysburg farm in the first week in October. Eisenhower said Nixon had told him he was removing himself completely from the 1964 race, but, Ike added, "I suppose that if suddenly there was a wave of support that threw him again into the race, there would be no question about his capacity to perform the job." And the next day Nixon made another foreign policy speech, criticizing a decision by Kennedy to sell wheat to the Soviet Union as "the major foreign policy mistake of this administration, even more serious than . . . the Bay of Pigs. What we're doing is subsidizing Khrushchev at a time he is in deep economic trouble." Rockefeller, at a press conference in Eugene, Oregon, where he was doing spadework for that state's distant Presidential primary, said he thought Nixon was a candidate for the nomination in 1964, no matter what Nixon said.

Rockefeller, and other Republicans, had heard by now that Nixon had not been exactly hiding out politically. He had been attending a number of dinners with business leaders and former close political associates, at which he was asking them to remain uncommitted for a while, until the Republican nomination picture became clearer. Columnists Rowland Evans and Robert Novak reported cases of state Republican leaders who had been publicly committed to Goldwater switching to uncommitted on the personal request of Nixon. To those who cared to believe—and their numbers grew daily—it sounded suspiciously like an effort to stop Goldwater or to create a stalemate between him and Rockefeller that would oblige the party to turn to Nixon.

Statements by Nixon to the contrary didn't stem the rumors. In an interview in *U.S. News and World Report* he was asked about it, and replied: "I'm not a part of and will not become a part of a stop-Goldwater or any such movement directed against any other candidate." Well, suppose there was a draft-Nixon movement? Would he accept? "I shall not be a candidate in '64—and that answers all questions of that type. Of course, there can be no draft unless a man stimulates it or encourages it. And, as far as I'm concerned, my statement that I shall not be a candidate means that there will be no draft."

Still the speculation grew. Nixon went off to Europe on business again, and on his return in late October told reporters, "There is a feeling that President Kennedy is trying hard and is sincere, but there is a quality of uncertainty. Too many voices are speaking out in Washington. I have never been abroad when American prestige was lower than it is now." Again, it sounded to some like Nixon the Candidate. Robert J. Donovan, the Washington bureau chief of the Los Angeles *Times,* wrote: "There is reason to think that former Vice President Richard M. Nixon wants to be considered a candidate for the 1964 Republican presidential nomination. Publicly Nixon says he is not a candidate. Yet it is significant that only within the last couple of weeks has former President Dwight Eisenhower, in his speeches, been including Nixon on his list of suitable Republican candidates for 1964."

Donovan also noted, however, that Nixon in Paris had said that "anyone who wants to run against John F. Kennedy would have a hole in his head if he didn't start now to build up a staff, especially a research staff," and Nixon was making no such move. Rose Woods and one other secretary were his staff, and as able as Miss Woods was no one had ever accused her of single-handedly nominating a President. Raymond Moley, the columnist and longtime Nixon friend and counselor, also referred to the Paris comment and wrote: "Much of the talk of Nixon as a candidate has been planted deliberately. In general, it has been done to injure or impair the chances of a Goldwater nomination. Such talk is projected not because some people love Nixon more, but because they love Goldwater less. . . . The fact that Nixon has recently expressed his views on national affairs is based upon a very human quality. A Republican with his experience, his past public service, and his status in the party has an obligation to make his views known. A man of his eminence simply cannot vanish from sight. And these expressions of his views can be of great value to his party and the country. But if every time he says something in public there will be raised the question of his possible candidacy, his influence will be completely destroyed." The man whose history was most like

57

Nixon's—Thomas E. Dewey—had managed to vanish from sight pretty quickly after his 1948 Presidential defeat, but that was his second Presidential loss, and Moley's argument had merit.

It was true, however, that General Eisenhower was keeping Nixon's name in the speculation. When Rockefeller was quoted in New Hampshire as saying that if a deadlock developed between him and Goldwater, Nixon "sure would be in the wings, I'll bet you that," Ike agreed. On November 10, on CBS' *Face the Nation* TV panel, Eisenhower said that if the party experienced a deadlock, Nixon would be "one of the likely persons to be . . . approached because he is after all a very knowledgeable and very courageous type of person."

Of his old boss' "endorsement," Nixon expressed appreciation but said he could conceive of no circumstances that could make him become a candidate in 1964. He would enter no primaries, and if anyone should try to enter his name he would move to have it withdrawn. As for Rockefeller's remark, Nixon said: "I am the one who is an expert on whether or not I am a candidate. . . . This is not a devious, conspiratorial plan on my part to be a candidate." And two days later: "My best role is to unite the party after the bloodletting . . . if I got into the fight now I could not serve in that role. . . . I'm not going to be a candidate. Anyone in the United States would want to be President, but there is a time and place for everything." And again, for Rockefeller: "I do not envision myself as others do, shaking out there in the wings, wringing my hands, waiting to be called by the party. Anyone who wants to run should get into the race right now. I'm not going to run and that rules me out as a candidate in 1964." And with that, Richard Nixon returned to his occupation, the practice of law.

On November 21, 1963, lawyer Nixon was in Dallas attending a meeting of Pepsi-Cola bottlers, unaware that an event so momentous was about to occur there that both the politics and the very spirit of the nation would be shattered in a few tragic seconds. He found the city seething with hostile talk about the arrival the next afternoon of President Kennedy. A month earlier in the same city, U.S. Ambassador to the United Nations Adlai E. Stevenson had been struck by a placard and spat upon in a right-wing demonstration after a United Nations Day speech. Nixon called a press conference in his Baker Hotel suite and urged the citizens of Dallas to give the President and his wife "a courteous reception." Those who would do otherwise, he said, "harm their own cause and help their opponents."

Concern for Kennedy's safety was only one of the matters on Nixon's mind in Dallas that day. He was in territory that was ripe for Republican inroads, Texas territory where Vice President Lyndon B. Johnson was particularly unpopular, and Nixon made the most of it. The fact that Kennedy and Johnson were in Texas together, he told the reporters, indicated that the President intended at that time to keep Johnson on the national ticket with him in 1964. "But we must remember that President Kennedy and his advisers are practical politicians. I believe that, if they think the race is a shoo-in, they will keep Lyndon. Otherwise, I think they will choose someone who can help the Democratic ticket. Lyndon was chosen in 1960 because he could help the ticket in the South. Now he is becoming a liability in the South, just as he is in the North." Racial demonstrations in the North—always a popular subject in the South—were at least partly the fault of the Kennedy administration, Nixon said. "Kennedy promised more than he could deliver. I don't think we should try to outpromise the Democrats." In Texas, that view hardly was likely to cost the Republicans votes.

The account of Nixon's press conference in the Dallas *Morning News* the next day was shunted to a back section, with only his remarks urging courtesy for the First Family making page one, in a general advance story on the Kennedys' arrival at Love Field that early afternoon. "Most downtown firms," the story said, "will give employees time off to see the motorcade. President Kennedy will ride in a blue convertible. If rain is falling, a plexi-glass bubble will protect him. The specially built car was flown here for use in the motorcade. Police said the motorcade will move slowly so that crowds can 'get a good view' of President Kennedy and his wife." The story also told of the vigilance of Dallas police; an anti-Kennedy group had scattered leaflets the day before, condemning the President for his positions on integration and foreign policy, and U.S. Attorney Barefoot Sanders reported he was investigating whether the activity violated any federal laws. Also, Police Chief Jesse Curry warned that anyone found tossing the leaflets would face prosecution for violating Dallas litterbug ordinances. Inside the paper, another short story noted there was a police guard at the Baker Hotel, but not for Nixon. It was for actress Joan Crawford, a director of the Pepsi-Cola Bottling Company, also attending the meeting. "There have been a lot of jewel thefts in New York hotels, and we didn't want to take a chance of having her jewelry stolen here," a Pepsi-Cola spokesman said.

Nixon that morning read the paper on his way to Love Field, and when he arrived for his 9:05 A.M. flight to New York, the crowds already were gathering to greet the President, who at that moment was addressing a breakfast group in Fort Worth, prior to departing on Air Force One for Dallas. The former Vice President boarded American Airlines Flight 82 and enjoyed an uneventful trip into what then was called Idlewild Airport. Much later, Nixon told me what happened next:

"I was in a taxicab when I got the news. It must have happened just as my plane was landing. My cab was stopped for a light in Queens, and a guy ran over and said, 'Have you got a radio? The President's been wounded.' I thought, 'Oh, my God, it must have been one of the nuts.' A half hour later I got to my apartment and the doorman told me he was dead. I called J. Edgar Hoover and asked him, 'What happened? Was it one of the nuts?' Hoover said, 'No, it was a Communist.'"

I asked Nixon how he felt personally when he heard the news, having known Kennedy and having come so close to being President instead of him.

"I didn't think of it in personal terms—'there but for the grace of God go I'—I never thought that," he said. "It was mostly in terms of he was so young, and so full of life. . . . I think of history in terms of tragedy. It's a tragic story, I thought, this is the supreme tragedy. When a man is old and dies, that's one thing. But a young man—the death of a man in his youth, so idealistic, so spirited. . . . I think that was one of the reasons Kennedy's death had a traumatic effect on the country greater than the death of Lincoln. It was not just the death of a man. The end of an era that had just begun. . . . We had been friends, as Senators are friends. I was as friendly with him as he was with any Senator on the Republican side. To some people he was President, to some a friend, to some a young man. To me he was all that, and on top of that, a man of history struck down in the tragic panorama of history. It probably had a greater effect on me than on some closer to him. Their feeling was personal. I thought of his age, his potential . . ."

I asked Nixon whether, after the assassination, he had experienced self-analysis, a kind of personal guilt and stocktaking to which many others had confessed in the immediate aftermath. "No," he said. "I'm somewhat of a fatalist. I've always felt you keep churning away."

According to an aide who was with him in his Fifth Avenue apartment the afternoon of the shooting, however, Nixon was personally very shaken by the event. Steve Hess, who was to participate in a meeting with Nixon that afternoon on a new book project, heard the news while having lunch with an editor from Doubleday, rushed to the Nixon apartment and was there when the former Vice President arrived.

"He was pretty shook up," Hess recalled later. "He told me how he had heard it, and I did feel there was a degree of 'there but for the grace of God go I' there. I felt it had been very hard for him to avoid that. He had the morning paper, which he made a great effort to show me, reporting he had held a press conference in Dallas and had made a statement that you can disagree with a person without being discourteous to him or interfering with him. He tried to make the point that he had tried to prevent it. He thought at the time a right-winger had done it [though J. Edgar Hoover had said it was a Communist]. It was his way of saying, 'Look, I didn't fuel this thing.' "

Rose Woods soon arrived at the apartment, and also Paul Keyes. Rose, at Nixon's request, phoned Tom Dewey and Roger Blough, the U.S. Steel board chairman, and canceled a golf date, and then a call was placed to General Eisenhower at his suite in the Waldorf Tower. The former President's military aide, Brigadier General Robert L. Schulz, took the call and reported that the general—at this cataclysmic moment for the nation—was taking a nap! He could not be disturbed, but he would be given the message when he awakened. Next, the call to Hoover, an old friend who logically would have the latest information, was made. The four of them—Nixon, Rose, Keyes

61

and Hess—sat in the study to the left of the entrance foyer. They talked about the crime and what kind of man might have perpetrated it. Tricia Nixon was in another part of the apartment, and her father went in to her for a while and then came back to the study again. He was, according to Hess, "pretty much in a daze." But there were practical things he had to attend to. All his appointments for the next week were canceled. A two-sentence press statement was drawn up and released: "The assassination of the President is a terrible tragedy for the nation. Mrs. Nixon and I have sent a personal message expressing our deepest sympathy to the members of the family in this hour of sorrow." Privately, Nixon wrote a personal letter to Mrs. Kennedy revealing what his public partisanship never quite obscured to the discerning: that he too was impressed by the Kennedy intellect and dazzled by the Kennedy wit, charm, poise and talent for leadership. And sometime later, after his nap, Eisenhower called back and Nixon discussed the assassination with him.

As the afternoon wore on, while the rest of the nation was glued to television sets, Nixon talked with his associates about the political ramifications. He said he felt Kennedy's death might cause a severe "bloodbath" in the Democratic Party between the new President, Johnson, and the brother of the old, Attorney General Robert Kennedy. The lack of rapport between these two Democrats was widely known, and Nixon speculated that the Democrats after a Johnson–Robert Kennedy fight might settle on Adlai Stevenson for a third time as their Presidential nominee in 1964. But by the next day, according to Hess, Nixon had come around to the belief that Johnson "would have it under control," that the country would unite behind him and that Johnson was a clever enough politician to take full advantage of his opportunity. The reading turned out to be exactly right.

Saturday morning was a dreary, rainy day that matched the mournful mood of the nation. As the country's and the world's great streamed in and out of the White House to pay private respects to the dead President lying in state in a closed coffin, Richard Nixon held political court in his New York apartment. Old political associates came by to discuss with him the impact of the assassination on the Republican picture, and what Nixon's own posture should be. A loose consensus seemed to emerge from the talks that the development had hurt Goldwater's chances, based heavily as they were on a Southern strategy. With a Southern President in the White House, the thinking was that Goldwater's strength would be undermined, and that he could not make it up in the North.

As for Nixon, the only sensible posture was a flexible one. The book project about which Hess had been talking to the Doubleday editor, an ambitious plan for the defeated Presidential candidate of 1960 to write a *Making of the President, 1964* of his own, would have to be shelved.* It would, quite obviously, tie Nixon up too firmly at a time when circumstances dictated that he stay available. The situation was just too volatile for Nixon to sign himself out of action by becoming a play-by-play reporter in the press box, when he might yet find himself in the ball game again.

That afternoon, the Nixons traveled to Washington, called at the White House and prepared with hundreds of others of the world's past and present great to attend the most solemn and sorrowful, yet also the most poignant and heroic, funeral the nation's capital ever had seen. On Sunday, clear and bright, the casket carrying the body of John F. Kennedy was taken by caisson up a Pennsylvania Avenue lined with tearful, silent Americans to the Rotunda of the Capitol. There, through the long afternoon and cold moonlit night, thousands more waited reverently in lines of astounding length for their time to walk by the coffin, touch it and feel the deadeningly heavy heartache of a personal loss. On Monday, the Nixons sat in St. Matthew's Cathedral next to Mrs. Nicole Alphand, wife of the French ambassador, and opposite President Johnson. On the way out to Arlington, their car was caught in the impossible traffic and they arrived late. "We were walking up when we heard Cardinal Cushing's voice booming out," Nixon told me later, "so we just stood where we were and listened."

---

* Hess was to have functioned as a kind of chief of staff, directing a number of "stringers" or reporters around the country and those traveling with the various campaigns, with Nixon at the head of the whole operation, feeding in his expert political analysis and his inside perspective.

When it was over, the Nixons walked back to their car. Quickly, they left Arlington and the man who by less than one vote per precinct had denied Richard Nixon the Presidency; who himself had been removed from it by the decision of one deranged man with a mail-order rifle. It was not the kind of thing Richard Nixon liked to dwell on. "Even now," he told me several years later, "women come up to me and say, 'I cried all night the night you lost the election, but now I'm glad you weren't elected President because you wouldn't be here now.' But I think it would not have happened to me. No two men are in the same place at the same time. I suppose the man would have sought out the President wherever he was, but the events would have been different and would have had a different impact on the man. I've never had any sense of fear or trepidation or superstition, none of that. When you see situations you walk into them, never worry about them. Once you make a decision, you just go."

At November's end in 1963, a new and totally unforeseen situation suddenly was confronting Richard Nixon. He had said he was not a candidate for the Presidency and would not be one. "There is," he had said less than two weeks earlier, "a time and place for everything." But those words were uttered in a context that was a whole political world away now. The man who on that same earlier occasion had admitted he still wanted the Presidency now had to ask himself anew whether fate had brought him again to a time and a place when he should reach for it.

3

The Camouflaged Candidacy

As the Presidential election year of 1964 approached, Richard Nixon was no more excited about the prospect of Senator Barry Goldwater as the party's nominee than was any other level-headed Republican. But Nixon, after two major defeats, was in no position to do battle with the Arizonan, clearly the sentimental and emotional favorite of most party regulars of conservative bent. Before the shock of John F. Kennedy's assassination, Goldwater's Southern strategy, for all its obvious weaknesses, could not be attacked persuasively by Nixon on tactical political grounds; Kennedy as a candidate almost certainly would have the populous Northeast locked up, along with all of the major, vote-rich cities outside the South. Any way one approached 1964, it loomed as a Democratic year; the Goldwater candidacy had the intraparty virtue, if nothing else, of giving awakening Dixie Republicans a vehicle through which to build the party in the South, and of giving long-suffering conservatives everywhere in the GOP something to beat their breasts about.

When Kennedy was killed, however, the whole picture seemed to have changed. The immediate impression was that the new President, Lyndon Johnson of Texas, as the first modern Southerner to occupy the White House, would himself have a lock on the Southern vote. At least Nixon so reasoned, according to one of his key political advisers of the time. It was not apparent then that Johnson instead, in his most brilliant and self-disciplined first months as President, would opt for holding John Kennedy's Northern, urban base by serving as his dead predecessor's regent in office, rather than moving out as his own man. The nation was to learn in due time that Lyndon Johnson was nothing if not his own man, but in these first months he subordinated his gigantic ego to the mood of the nation. With the words "Let us continue," he deftly harnessed that mood for domestic tranquillity and progress. And in so doing, he assured his own election the following November.

But the outcome of those first sorrowful months was not all that clear in January, 1964, as the American people sought to recover from a national tragedy that for most citizens had been a personal one as well. Lyndon Johnson in wisdom recognized this phenomenon and did not intrude upon it; only when time had worked its healing did "the real Lyndon Johnson stand up"—the domineering, overbearing egoist of his Senate days—and by that time he had been elected by the largest popular vote in history.

In the post-assassination uncertainty, however, it was natural for a political man like Richard Nixon to reassess his position. This was particularly so because the first Gallup Poll after Kennedy's death showed that Nixon, though not a candidate, had moved past Goldwater into first place as the man favored by most Republican voters to be the party's 1964 nominee. He received 29 percent to 27 percent for Goldwater, 16 percent for Ambassador Henry Cabot Lodge and only 13 percent for Rockefeller, the only declared candidate at the time. To put the latest developments into the perspective of his own future, Nixon one afternoon in January rented a suite at the Waldorf Tower and gathered a group of about fifteen old friends and supporters to counsel with him. Bob Finch was there, Bob Haldeman, Fred Seaton (Eisenhower's Secretary of Interior), John Whitaker, Steve Hess, Bunny Lasker, banker Walter Williams of Seattle and others. Significantly, the Eastern "king-makers"—Dewey, Brownell, Hall—were not present. The discussion ranged over the full spectrum of possibilities—of Goldwater, Rockefeller, the prospect of Scranton of Pennsylvania entering—and of Richard Nixon himself making a second run for the Republican Presidential nomination. Nixon mostly listened. Nelson Rockefeller's divorce and remarriage the previous May already had taken its toll of the New York governor's high hopes to be the 1964 Republican nominee. But the vast grass-roots apparatus that was to give Goldwater the nomination in a walk in July had not yet shown its hand, and thus the chances of a stalemate between the two men appeared to many of the Nixon advisers to be a distinct possibility. No one present said he thought Goldwater had the nomination sewed up. Yet, considering the passions of those who embraced and worked for Goldwater, it would not be wise for Nixon to move openly and aggressively into the picture. If he was to have a chance, it would have to be as an acceptable compromise in a deadlocked situation, as a man who had preached party unity and had not taken sides.

The talk turned, inevitably, to New Hampshire and the first of the nation's party primaries there in March. It shaped up as a bloodletting between Rockefeller and Goldwater. Rocky, in a first excursion into the state in October, had been met by a sample of what was to come from William P. Loeb, the ultra-conservative publisher of the Manchester *Union Leader*. Loeb wrote of the New York governor: "Apparently not being content with being a home-wrecker, Rockefeller now wants to be a party wrecker. . . . The United States has had enough multi-millionaire meddlers, be they Republican or Democratic."

As for Goldwater, though New Hampshire was a conservative state, all those present in the Waldorf suite knew the kind of candidate he would be: lemminglike. One of the most endearing traits of Barry Goldwater was his candor. There was a pioneer quality about the man, fearless to the point of folly; no Wild West gunslinger ever drew and fired with greater speed and abandon than Barry let words fly to nail a villainous liberal. Barry was good company, great theater, but horrendous politics. It was hard to believe that he could win in the open combat of the primaries. The appraisal was valid, as Goldwater's poor showing in New Hampshire soon established. But what was overlooked in the appraisal was one fact that Goldwater and his 'amateurs" recognized and exploited in full measure: primaries in themselves do not nominate candidates. Behind the façade of the traditional state races, the Goldwater legions would be working their will in the nonprimary states, picking up a handful of convention delegates in this state convention, collecting another in that county or district caucus, nickel-and-diming the Eastern liberal establishment to death.

The New Hampshire primary, though, could be significant in creating a logjam and starting a trend toward a compromise choice. The press, locked into precedent and tradition as much as the politicians were, also looked to the primaries as the make-or-break battleground for the major-party nominations. The spotlight the press would throw on New Hampshire—always strong for Nixon—could get something going for him, or at the very least keep his name in the running while the overt contenders destroyed each other. Former Ambassador to Mexico Bob Hill was the resident Nixon man in the state, and he would scout the situation.

One of the first problems to be considered was what to do about Wesley Powell. The former governor of New Hampshire, an unpredictable maverick who was one of the late Senator Joe McCarthy's strongest and last supporters, wanted to launch a write-in campaign for Nixon. Powell personally was not Nixon's cup of tea; in 1960, when Nixon won the New Hampshire Republican primary by a record vote, the then Vice President refused to ride in the same car with Powell in an official motorcade. But now, in 1964, Nixon could not afford to be all that independent; Hill would deal with Powell, and while Nixon did not openly sanction the write-in, he let it go forward. And that, in general, was the "decision" coming out of the Waldorf meeting; to do nothing overtly toward a declared candidacy, but to do nothing either that would prevent nature from taking its political course. It was far from clear, even in January, 1964, that the Republican nomination would be worth anything. Johnson's conduct in his first month in the White House was appraised and found to be impeccable. Nixon himself had great admiration for Johnson as a politician, and it increased as he saw the new President move deftly to stabilize and control the political climate in his own party and in the country.

Still, it was prudent always to be ready. There were a few steps Nixon could take in that regard, short of open pursuit of the nomination, and he took them. In mid-December, he already had touched base with General Eisenhower at Gettysburg and told a television interviewer that he and Eisenhower agreed they both would like to see Vietnam Ambassador Lodge "back here . . . discussing political matters." But Nixon had not communicated with Lodge in Saigon, he said. Just the mere floating of Lodge's name in advance of the impending primaries, though, could serve to keep the nomination picture more fluid.

On January 9, 1964, his fifty-first birthday, Nixon granted the Associated Press an interview in his Broad Street law office. He would not say outright that he would accept the 1964 Republican nomination, but he did say he would "make any sacrifice" to see that the GOP nominated "its strongest man." Reminded of the latest Gallup Poll showing him two points ahead of Goldwater, Nixon replied: "I believe that any man who has become a public figure belongs to the public, and as long as they want him to lead, to lead."

Nixon added, however, that "leadership doesn't always involve being a candidate." His role as the party's titular head was best served, he said, "by not getting into the scramble myself, but by talking about issues and attempting to give leadership in developing a program against the present administration and for a Republican alternative." Until it became clear who the party's strongest man was, he said, lapsing into his favorite sports jargon, he would remain "not on the sidelines, but in the thick of the battle—a blocking back, you might say, or to use a hockey term, the one who gives the assist. You know, you get just as much credit for the assist as you do for the goal." Nixon had handed out many an assist in his political career and would hand out many another; the credit he would get for them—in rebuilding the party and helping Congressional candidates across the nation—would play a major role in his eventual scoring drive.

But in early 1964, Nixon was not ready to make an overt move. Says Hess, who attended the Waldorf strategy meeting, "He was positioning himself in case lightning did strike. At the same time, he was deliberately keeping the door open as a way of giving more credence and play in the press to what he did say. If he was thought of as a possible active candidate, he would get much more play, and he knew that. He knew it always made the difference in whether you were on page one or the back pages."

In this effort, Nixon continued to get help from the opinion-makers. The prestigious Minnesota Poll in mid-January showed 74 percent of Republican voters approved of him, to only 53 percent for Goldwater and 52 percent for Rockefeller; the Harris Survey at the same time rated them Nixon, 43 percent; Goldwater, 23 percent; Rockefeller, 22 percent. Against Johnson, Nixon was first among all Republicans with 41 percent, to 34 percent for George Romney, 33 percent for Goldwater, 32 percent for Scranton and 29 percent for Rockefeller.

Nixon fueled the favorable trend with statements on radio and television of near-availability and finally outright availability. He taped a radio show with Arthur Godfrey and Jackie Gleason, and when Gleason asked him, "Are you going to run?" Nixon replied, "I never wear a hat, so it must always be in the ring." He declined to elaborate, whereupon Godfrey turned to Gleason and said, "I don't know how much clearer you want it, my friend." A few nights later, on Walter Cronkite's nationwide evening TV newscast, Nixon made it clearer. He didn't anticipate a draft, he said, but "if the opportunity should come again, I would accept it."

Always, of necessity, there was an accompanying disclaimer. "When I say that I don't want to be a candidate or a kingmaker, or attempt to be boss of the Republican Party, I mean exactly what I'm saying. I, however, do not mean that I reject public service. I feel that public service is the greatest opportunity that anybody can have. After all, I've been in it most of my adult life, and as far as I'm concerned, I have no regrets about having had the opportunity to serve. It was a great privilege. If the opportunity should come again, I would accept it. And I think I will know in the event that I feel that the people of this country, particularly in my own party, need me at that particular time. I don't anticipate that will happen now. I particularly don't anticipate it because I'm not in the arena. I don't intend to go out and stimulate a draft." But, Nixon added significantly, a candidate who entered none of the primaries could be nominated, because it appeared the primary results might be inconclusive.

Part of the positioning, too, was the now-familiar Nixon service to party. The traditional Lincoln Day period was at hand, and he plunged into the usual fund-raisers and other appearances, knowing they would yield a twofold benefit—the accumulation of IOU's from grateful grass-roots leaders and a forum for the declaration of policy views and positions. While Goldwater and Rockefeller worked the snow-and-slush beat of New Hampshire, Nixon addressed a party fund-raiser in New York (and told reporters inquiring about the New Hampshire write-in that it was the voters' decision and "I shall do nothing to influence that decision one way or another"). He gave a "strictly nonpolitical" foreign policy lecture at Pfeiffer College in Misenheimer, North Carolina (and attended a public reception in Salisbury by "the North Carolina Friends of Richard Nixon," who were so numerous the local National Guard armory had to be used). Next, it was a round of receptions, dinner and press conference in Philadelphia (and a widely quoted call for candor in Washington on Cuba and Vietnam); then a speech in the hotbed of Midwestern conservatism, Cincinnati, on civil rights and law and order; another in Miami Beach, another in Peoria, in Minneapolis, in Washington, D.C., in Kansas City. It was, for a man not "in the arena," a man not going out to stimulate anything, quite a schedule.

Nixon's hard-line foreign policy opinions were well known in and out of the Republican Party, and as a potential compromise candidate, he would be acceptable on that score to both the Goldwater and the Rockefeller wings. On the domestic front, however, Nixon had to tread more warily. A basic cleavage existed between the two active candidates, reflecting the fundamental split in philosophy between conservatives and liberals, particularly in the area of civil rights. Rising expectations among American blacks, the product of Lyndon Johnson's civil rights legislative victories and of his excessively optimistic rhetoric, already were creating apprehension among white blue-collar workers who saw Negro progress and their own modest

71

affluence as mutually exclusive. The term "white backlash" put a convenient handle on the whole complicated phenomenon, and Goldwater became its symbol, whether by design or by inadvertence. The emergence too of increasing black militancy, through demonstrations and boycotts, and the turning away from the goal of racial integration toward black power and separatism, fed the basic repressive quality of the Goldwater domestic posture. The Arizonan, as a kind of John the Baptist of the law-and-order gospel of 1968, hammered away at the problem of crime in the streets. He seldom mentioned blacks but he conveyed a message nonetheless to those who wanted to interpret it in racial terms. Goldwater's speeches came to be called "code" by his opponents—never overtly feeding the backlash but ever fueling it by implication.

Rockefeller, by contrast, eschewed the backlash in favor of the prevalent liberal view, which sought to direct attention and action to root causes of black poverty, illiteracy and crime. The battleground for the dispute was a pending federal civil rights bill, introduced after a long delay by the late President Kennedy and carried forward by Johnson, that would open the polling booths and most large public accommodations to blacks in the South and throughout the country. The legislation's potential for basic social change in the nation was tremendous; Goldwater opposed it, especially the public accommodations section, as an infringement on individual property rights (a "code" alibi, his critics said); Rockefeller supported it without qualification.

Nixon, in his Cincinnati speech on the Lincoln Day circuit, addressed the civil rights issue in a way that strongly suggested he was bent on making himself the reasonable alternative to Goldwater. After calling the pending bill opposed by Goldwater "a great step forward if it is administered effectively," Nixon said: "A law is only as good as the will of the people to keep it. The hate engendered by the demonstrations and boycotts has set Americans against Americans and has created an atmosphere of hate and distrust which, if it continues to grow, will make the new law a law in name only. It is time for responsible civil rights leaders to take over from the extremists . . ."

In what could be taken as a broadside at Rockefeller, Nixon

went on: "In this election year, Republicans will be urged by some to outpromise the Johnson administration on civil rights in the hope of political gain. I am completely opposed to this kind of political demagoguery. Making promises that can't be kept—raising hopes that can't be realized—are the cruelest hoaxes that can be perpetrated on a minority group that has suffered from such tactics for a hundred years."

To William S. White, Johnson's chief columnist-apologist, Nixon's Cincinnati speech was one of "great significance," opening the Republican challenge to the Texas-born President in the South, the border states, the mountain West and the suburbs everywhere by tying Johnson to civil rights extremists. But what the speech also did, quite obviously, was to remind the Goldwater legions that in Richard Nixon they had a man with whom they could live, if their first love died. That message was to be severely tested in the preconvention period by stop-Goldwater actions in which Nixon was involved, but it did survive, and it paid major dividends for Nixon in 1968.

Nixon's policy of potential but not declared candidacy did him no harm in the polls. In February, he widened his Gallup lead over Goldwater, 31 percent to 20 percent among Republicans, and he ran surprisingly ahead of both Goldwater and Rockefeller among independents (Nixon, 29 percent; Goldwater, 18; Rockefeller, 16). As part of the strategy of availability, Nixon also played the usual game with the Oregon primary, where the secretary of state declares what names shall go on the ballot, and where only an affidavit disavowing candidacy and rejecting the nomination can remove it. Since he already had said he would make "any sacrifice" for the party, Nixon said, he could not sign such an affidavit, so he would permit his name to remain on the ballot. But in Florida, where a delegate slate pledged to him filed for ballot position—and where Goldwater was considered a cinch to win—Nixon had his name removed.

There were times, though, when Nixon seemed overavailable. When Nixon appeared on NBC's *Today Show* four days before the New Hampshire primary, host Hugh Downs asked him if he would accept the Vice Presidential nomination. "I know you are going to expect me to say no because I have been Vice President for eight years and have run for President,"

73

Nixon said. "But I don't go along with the current talk among the present candidates for downgrading the Vice Presidency. I think it is time to upgrade it. And as far as I'm concerned I'm making it clear that I'm not a candidate for President and not a candidate for Vice President, but I will do whatever my party asks me to do, and I feel everybody else should too. The Vice Presidency, as Lyndon Johnson's position proves today, is as important as the Presidency." Later, Nixon was to back off this statement of Vice Presidential availability, but at this juncture it served the purpose of reinforcing his image as a man willing to make "any sacrifice" for his party—and to put heat on both Goldwater and Rockefeller to keep the door open to the second spot if called upon. Though both Goldwater and Rockefeller had drawbacks as Presidential candidates, each likely would add strength as the Vice Presidential nominee.

While the two active candidates and the one nonactive but available candidate busied themselves in and out of New Hampshire, four young Republican liberals from Boston—a thirty-four-year-old lawyer, David Goldberg, a forty-three-year-old businessman, Paul Grindle, and two twenty-three-year-old college girls, Sally Saltonstall and Caroline Williams—took matters into their own hands. In a singular example of initiative and imagination, they launched a classic write-in campaign for Ambassador Lodge that stole the Republican primary and made a farce of the expensive, "professional" thrashings-about of Goldwater and Rockefeller. Without an affirmative public word from Lodge in Saigon, the quartet from Boston fashioned a mail campaign that effectively filled a void left in the minds of New Hampshire's voters by Goldwater's verbal absurdities and Rockefeller's remarriage. Early in January, Goldwater casually had told reporters in Concord he'd make the social security system "voluntary," and after that, the shock waves through New Hampshire's older-than-average citizenry never leveled off. Rockefeller, in his bullheadedness or political naïveté, put his new, pregnant wife on display before old Yankee audiences and kept the tongues wagging nonstop until primary day. The voters clearly wanted somewhere else to go, and Goldberg, Grindle, Saltonstall and Williams gave them somewhere.

The results of the March 10 primary were considered at the

time to have hit Goldwater and Rockefeller hardest. Lodge won with 33,400 write-ins; Goldwater was far behind with 21,700, Rockefeller next with 19,500 and Nixon fourth with 15,700 write-ins. Nixon, after all, had not campaigned. But New Hampshire always had been Nixon country, and the former Vice President, in Kansas City two days before the balloting, had volunteered that the write-in for him would be "unprecedented" in size. The result, less than half what Lodge received, had to be disappointing. The primary was ripe for taking, but Lodge, not Nixon, took it. Still, the front-runners, Goldwater and Rockefeller, were damaged, and the possibility of a stalemate—and a turn to a compromise candidate—seemingly was enhanced by the New Hampshire vote.

At a press conference at the Military Park Hotel in Newark the next day, Nixon acknowledged Lodge's showing to be "spectacular" but said it would be a mistake to count Goldwater or Rockefeller out. As for himself, Nixon said the results "will have no effect on my political status." He expressed pleasure at his showing, and emphasized, for anyone who might think otherwise and hence denigrate the vote he got, that "it was done without help."

Once again Nixon said he would not become an active candidate, but once again there also was a teaser. His role as the party's titular leader was to "bring the case home against President Johnson." And in that regard, he added, "I feel there is no man in this country who can make a case against Mr. Johnson more effectively than I can."* Then, in what certainly could not have been considered an endorsement in the Goldwater camp, Nixon said he believed the Republican strategy against Johnson should aim at the Northern industrial states rather than at the South. Outside the hotel, young Goldwater pickets marched, indicating what they thought of Nixon's neutrality and noncandidacy.

* In an article in the *Saturday Evening Post* at that time, Nixon was quoted as saying of LBJ: "He's not only tricky, but he's good at it . . . Johnson is a master politician who works hard at it. . . . He has preempted the field when it comes to wheeling, dealing, fixing and picking the political situations that will satisfy everybody. If the Republican Party gets into that kind of a game with him, he'll kill us, because he's better at it." The observation was intended as criticism, but there seemed to be a note of professional admiration there, too.

It was a cloudy, uncertain time, and a propitious one for Nixon to embark on another of his business trips, this time across Asia to Saigon for a visit with Lodge, and on to Tokyo. The trip, Nixon explained, would give him "a holiday from politics" and a chance "to see how our foreign policy is working." Before departing, Nixon again underlined his official noncandidacy by asking two Springfield, Illinois, lawyers to desist from a write-in in his behalf in their state's primary because, they reported him as saying, "such a write-in effort might prove to be detrimental to party harmony in Illinois." Unmentioned was the fact that Illinois—like Florida—was shaping up as another cinch for Goldwater.

In the next three weeks, in behalf of client Pepsi-Cola, Nixon beat a well-publicized path to Lodge's doorstep. In Rome, he sipped a Pepsi at the airport and told reporters the June primary in California would knock out either Goldwater or Rockefeller; in Beirut, at the home of the Lebanese boss of a Pepsi bottling plant, he repeated that he would accept the nomination "if the party leaders ask me to run," but noted he planned to go to Latin America in May and to Europe in June, and "that proves I'm not campaigning, doesn't it?" As he spoke, and local TV cameras rolled, a waiter reached into view to turn a Pepsi bottle at his elbow so that the label showed. It was, quite clearly, a business trip.

In Beirut, however, Nixon found time to call on President Fouad Chehab, and in Rawalpindi, to have a long lunch with Pakistani President Mohammed Ayub Khan. In Bangkok, he addressed the Thai Council on World Affairs and International Law and then went on to Saigon for the meeting with Lodge. (Meanwhile, back in Oklahoma City, Oklahoma, Air Force Reserve Major General Barry M. Goldwater, dressed in fatigues, lifted himself out of the pilot's seat of a military jet and told newsmen that if he wasn't nominated by the Republicans, Nixon probably would be.)

Nixon and Lodge conferred for about two hours in the American Embassy in Saigon, and Nixon reported afterward that in addition to discussing U.S. policy in Vietnam, "we covered everything significant about this political year . . . a casual conversation about developments [that] had nothing to do with decisions—about what we're going to do in the political field." After Nixon had left, Lodge came out, submitted to newsmen's questions, shrugged and said: "There really isn't anything I can say. I'm sorry." There was no mention of Eisenhower's earlier call, which had been seconded by Nixon, for Lodge to return to the United States and campaign for the Republican nomination. Nixon spent the rest of his time in Vietnam dining with U.S. and South Vietnamese officials, visiting a hamlet recently recaptured from the Viet Cong and storing up political ammunition for use against the Johnson administration in the approaching campaign. Asked at one point whether he thought Vietnam would be an issue, he replied with a classic Nixonism: "I hope it doesn't; it will only become an issue if the policy has weaknesses worthy of criticism, if it is plagued with inconsistency, improvisation and uncertainty. That has been the case in the past."

In Hong Kong, Taipei (as Chiang Kai-shek's house guest), Tokyo (for visits with Prime Minister Hayato Ikeda and Foreign Minister Masayoshi Ohira), and Hiroshima (to open a new $1,000,000 Pepsi bottling plant), Nixon mixed business with politics, then headed home armed with the makings of a campaign—whether for himself or another worthy Republican. The United States, he said in New York, should deny the enemy a "privileged sanctuary" in North Vietnam. And in Washington, in yet another appearance before the American Society of Newspaper Editors, Nixon charged that American leadership in Asia had sunk to "its lowest point since Pearl Harbor" and insisted that "we cannot have a Yalu River concept in South Vietnam . . . the rules of the game must be changed." The "business trip" clearly had produced more than publicity for Pepsi-Cola; the Republican Party's most traveled spokesman, after a fresh look, was urging his most hawkish recommendations to date on Vietnam: escalate the war and the targets in North Vietnam and win a military victory.

In terms of Presidential politics, these views moved Nixon even closer to the prevailing sentiment of Barry Goldwater and his legions. Goldwater had said that if he himself were not nominated, Nixon probably would be; considering Goldwater's growing grass-roots organizational strength, it was becoming equally apparent—to Nixon certainly—that if Goldwater were not the nominee, he clearly would have a big say in selecting him. The same scenario seemed to be suggesting itself to others in the party. The AP polled 1,606 Republican county chairmen and other leaders on two questions: asked their personal preference for the nomination, Goldwater ran far ahead (Goldwater, 722; Nixon, 301; Lodge, 193; Scranton, 191; Rockefeller, 84); but when asked who they thought most likely would be nominated, Nixon won (Nixon, 526; Goldwater, 427; Lodge, 189; Scranton, 159; Rockefeller, 50).

Though Nixon continued to say he was not a candidate, his actions increasingly were being observed with interest—and skepticism. At a seemingly routine appearance in late April at Washington's annual Gridiron Dinner, the former Vice President inspired speculative stories with an apology of sorts for his 1962 "last press conference" outburst. "My friends in the press —if I have any," he said. "If I haven't any, maybe it was more my fault than theirs. I hope a man can lose his temper once in sixteen years and be forgiven for it." By intent or not, Nixon's Gridiron performance boosted his stock with many influential Washington correspondents and columnists who had not favored him. He also took the sharp edge off a long public and private feud with former President Harry S Truman by telling the audience how earlier that night he had passed a glass of bourbon to Truman at a private reception. "If this [Gridiron] party is supposed to be dedicated to love," Nixon quipped, "what better evidence is there than for Harry Truman to take a drink from Dick Nixon without asking someone else to taste it first?" As Nixon left the rostrum, Truman reached up and shook his hand; the crowd stood and applauded heartily.

Events, meanwhile, were moving rapidly in the Republican primary situation. Goldwater won Illinois comfortably if not overwhelmingly against Senator Margaret Chase Smith of Maine and weak Lodge and Nixon write-ins; Scranton carried his own state of Pennsylvania against no major organized opposition; a Lodge write-in gave him the Massachusetts primary virtually unopposed; Goldwater got three out of every four primary votes in Texas, with Lodge a surprising second on write-ins. In all of these except Texas, Nixon ran stronger than

Rockefeller. Then, after a breeze for Goldwater against only Harold Stassen in Indiana, came Nebraska.

Fred Seaton, a native Nebraskan who had helped sweep the state primary for Nixon in 1960 with nearly 75,000 write-in votes, refused to let the dream of a Nixon Presidency die. Accordingly, he set out early to convert the May 12 primary into a Nixon resurgence. As in New Hampshire, there was to be no formal, public Nixon approval or encouragement; such a statement would run the risk of embarrassment if the results were poor and would reduce the positive impact of spontaneity if they were good. Nixon, on a Midwest tour, happened into Omaha just five days before the primary for a "nonpolitical" speech to the National Conference of Christians and Jews. While ostensibly refusing to encourage the ongoing write-in plans in his behalf, he acknowledged at the inevitable press conference that he was ready to take on Lyndon Johnson if the convention delegates should decide he was "best qualified to lead the fight."

Conservative Nebraska, in spite of a history of write-in upsets, long had been considered locked up by the aggressive Goldwater forces. Rockefeller had conceded as much by staying out, and the expectation was a lopsided Goldwater vote. But Seaton, then publisher of a local paper, and a state senator, Marvin Strommer, launched a late direct-mail appeal pointing out that in the fall campaign against Johnson, foreign policy would be the main issue. There was only one Republican equal to the task—Richard Nixon.

When the votes were counted, Goldwater as expected ran first, but his margin was humiliating. The only candidate on the ballot, the Arizonan failed to win even half the total ballots cast (49.5 percent) ; write-ins for Nixon, Lodge and a few for Rockefeller had outpolled him. Of these, Nixon got the bulk, or 31.5 percent of the total vote. Goldwater's regional manager, Richard L. Herman of Omaha, put the best face on the outcome. "It is delegates and not the popular vote we were seeking," he said. Seaton saw it otherwise. "Nebraskans," he proclaimed, "have nominated the next Republican candidate for President with their write-in for Mr. Nixon." The vote in

Nebraska, he insisted, marked "the beginning of the Nixon surge" and the start of the Goldwater backslide.

Three days later, that bubble burst in Oregon. Nixon already had said he could not conscientiously ask that his name be taken off the free-for-all ballot there, and about two weeks before the vote he had sent a telegram to Donald F. Myrick, chairman of the Nixon committee in Portland, reiterating he would stay on. "I shall look forward to working with you in the final campaign," Nixon wired, "in whatever role our convention decides I can best serve the cause of Republican victory in November." It was diplomatically worded, but Myrick read into it what he wanted to. "We definitely have a candidate," he said.

The decision to stay on the Oregon ballot did not go down well with many Nixon political advisers, and it came amid professional readings of futility. Leonard Nadasdy, a former Young Republicans national chairman and Minneapolis public relations man, was sent to Oregon to take soundings with Nixon loyalists who had helped him carry the state against John Kennedy in 1960. Nadasdy returned with word that the old Nixon backers had split up to join Rockefeller or Goldwater, and he advised that Nixon forget any ambitious ideas about Oregon. But if strong showings could be put back-to-back in Nebraska and Oregon over a three-day period, restoring his reputation as a vote-getter while burying Goldwater and Rockefeller deeper and pulling Lodge back to earth, Nixon would be a creditable alternative. It would take money, though, and so Cliff Folger and others were asked to raise $50,000. Bob Finch in California pitched in, too, but they all found at this late stage that few contributors were interested. A disadvantage of a layback strategy is that the money men as well as the prospective candidate want to play it cautiously before really committing themselves. Even Elmer Bobst, Nixon's fatherly old friend who had helped him make his New York law connection in 1963, reportedly refused to contribute, arguing that Nixon had said he was through with Presidential politics, and ought to be.*

Still insisting he was not an active candidate, Nixon stayed out of Oregon through the primary period. Except for two days

* See Robert D. Novak, *The Agony of the G.O.P. 1964* (Macmillan, 1965).

in early April, Goldwater also shunned the state, apparently fearing another embarrassing loss to a strong Lodge write-in. He elected to concentrate on the more important June primary in California, with Rockefeller as the only ballot opposition and no write-ins permitted. But Oregon takes its primary seriously and likes to see its candidates. Rockefeller, campaigning on the slogan "He Cared Enough to Come," snapped back and won, receiving 93,000 votes to 78,000 for Lodge, 49,800 for Goldwater, and only 47,600 for Nixon, who failed to carry a single county in the state he had won in 1960. If Nebraska was, as Seaton said, "the beginning of the Nixon surge," Oregon was the end of it. If the former Vice President was to be the 1964 Republican nominee, the bid would have to come from the convention itself, and that possibility now hinged on the final primary in California between Rockefeller and Goldwater.

Nixon had predicted many times that California would knock out one or the other declared candidate; what he did not say, but what was a distinct prospect, was that this final primary could eliminate both—if Rockefeller won. Preference polls within the Republican Party continued to indicate emphatically that no matter what happened, the GOP in 1964 would not buy Nelson Rockefeller. Even a success in California, added to his one victory in Oregon, would not be enough to make him acceptable to a majority of delegates in the nonprimary states. But if Rockefeller did win in the final primary against Goldwater, the party might start looking in earnest for an alternative to the Arizonan. Thus, a Rockefeller victory in California was definitely in Nixon's interest.

Still, Nixon could not afford to back the New York governor there; any chance of emerging as the compromise candidate was rooted in Nixon's continued good relations with the Goldwater wing. In spite of great pressures from both Rockefeller and Goldwater for endorsement in California, Nixon would have to steer clear of his old home state, take neither side and await the outcome. To this end, Nixon went to unusual lengths of maneuver. When a group calling itself Californians for Nixon came out for Rockefeller, Nixon sent a telegram to Goldwater assuring him that "no one is authorized to speak for me or represent me in California by proxy or otherwise. I am not

81

supporting or opposing either of the two candidates running in the California primary." On the other side, when Nixon's mother, Hannah, accepted an invitation to be a guest at a Goldwater rally, she suddenly found herself flying to New York for a quick visit to her son.

Neutrality was the Nixon byword, but one of course always could look ahead. On the Saturday afternoon before the California vote, Nixon held another secret meeting in New York, on the fortieth floor of the Waldorf Tower. Seaton was there, Finch, Republican publicist Lou Guylay and other old political friends and advisers. The California primary was discussed, and what Nixon's strategy should be in the event of a Rockefeller victory there. On that very same afternoon, though, a matter of surpassing political importance was taking place elsewhere in New York—the birth of Nelson A. Rockefeller, Jr., the first child of the New York governor and his new wife, Happy. As had been his custom all spring, the father-to-be left the campaign trail and raced back East to be with his wife for the weekend. But this was the final weekend of the close California primary; the child's birth and Rockefeller's absence from the state flushed out anew all the public hostility toward his remarriage that had haunted his campaign efforts ever since New Hampshire. Had the birth of the child been a few days later, or had Rockefeller campaigned hard that final weekend, the outcome of the critical primary might have been different. As it was, Goldwater squeaked by with 51.6 percent of the Republican vote. Rockefeller was through, and because he was, so was Nixon; the strategy session at the Waldorf was for naught. The inevitability of Goldwater, though, did not become completely clear until the party's incredibly bumbling liberals—with Nixon in and out of their manueverings like a playing coach—had one more futile time at bat.

4

Last Lapse into Folly

THE arena for Nixon's last great folly before embarking on the road that was to lead to the White House was the 1964 National Governors' Conference in Cleveland. Here Nixon, after all the coyness and the disavowals of candidacy for 1964, finally was to reveal to influential fellow Republicans that he, at least, did not believe his political obituary notices. Here, over the advice and even the pleadings of associates, he was to make his last surrender to political wishful thinking, and come away bloodied in a futile and transparent bid to stop the nomination of Goldwater. It was from this failure that the coolness of the later successful Nixon was to spring—but not until the old, hungry Nixon had one last gasp. In the mythology of the Nixon comeback cherished and nurtured by his supporters, he never had the slightest interest in the 1964 nomination. But the events in Cleveland, and the recollections of key Republicans who participated in the critical private meetings, indicate otherwise.

It was now the eighth of June, only five weeks before the Republican National Convention in San Francisco, and it suddenly was dawning on the collected foes of Barry Goldwater that although he had won only one of the three contested primaries, there was no one between him and the Presidential nomination. The primaries had diverted their attention and energies from the nonprimary states where Barry's zealots, under the tutelage of Clif White, were inexorably building a convention majority. By the eve of the Cleveland conference, Goldwater already had committed to him publicly more than 500 of the 655 delegates needed for the nomination. The adage that you can't beat somebody with nobody rang in the moderates' ears, for now they had nobody.

Yet there was a small hope. All through the spring, while Governor Scranton professed lack of interest, his political associates in Pennsylvania had been working diligently, though often naïvely, to create the conditions that eventually would draw him into the race. Well-placed and well-heeled friends in Philadelphia and New York tried to drum up interest and money while the Harrisburg Hamlet sat in his statehouse office and pondered. Scranton seemed to be edging against his will toward a reluctant candidacy, and in fact had scheduled a meeting of Eastern Republicans in Harrisburg for the Thursday after the California primary, to assess the situation and his own position. But when Goldwater won, the conference was canceled. The next night, however, Scranton received a phone call from former President Eisenhower, his neighbor from over in Gettysburg, requesting a meeting. Scranton with proper deference said he would drive to Gettysburg the next morning, and the two men met there in Eisenhower's small office in town.

The strong prospect of Goldwater's nomination finally had hit Eisenhower too. He had hinted before the California primary, by issuing a statement describing his ideal candidate in terms of experience and outlook, that he did not relish this outcome. He had named no one, but the description was closest to Rockefeller and certainly could not be mistaken for Goldwater. But when Goldwater supporters began to cry foul, Eisenhower had backed off, declaring he had "never attempted to read anyone out of the party." Any inference that he had been aiming at Goldwater, he said, was "a complete misinterpretation." Now, in the wake of Goldwater's California victory, the old general's concern was mounting again, prodded by Scranton supporters. Whatever Eisenhower actually told Scranton at their meeting, it was clear that Scranton left for Cleveland thinking he had a go sign from the general to make an eleventh-hour bid to beat Goldwater.

Nixon, meanwhile, already had received reports of the situation from two unofficial political aides, Charlie McWhorter, an American Telephone and Telegraph official in New York, and Sherman Unger, who had left his Cincinnati law firm in the spring to help Nixon. Each had made informed nose counts of Republican delegate strength and reported that Goldwater now had a lock on the nomination. If Nixon was to have a role in 1964, it had become increasingly clear, it would be the very role he had stressed all spring, while warding off suggestions of his own interest in the nomination—as a party unifier. One place to start, obviously, was Cleveland. Nixon knew from past experience, however, what chaos these annual governors' conferences produced; television cameras and equally obtrusive reporters poking into every corner, fanning every rumor into a story, playing candidates and prospective candidates against each other. He knew too of the growing panic of the Eastern liberals and moderates and of Eisenhower's now well-publicized meeting with Scranton; he had a fair idea what Scranton would say when he got to Cleveland. The best thing for Nixon was to stay away.

Still, he was going to be in the Midwest that second week in June, speaking in Michigan before heading for London on law business. Four days before the conference officially opened, Nixon seemed to rule himself out of any stop-Goldwater effort. "Goldwater people by the millions across the country would sit on their hands if he was stopped by a blocking move or a conspiracy," Nixon said at a Long Island fund-raiser. "The Republican nomination would not be worth anything at all." As for his own chances, he dismissed the idea as "so remote that it isn't worth discussing."

In Detroit on Sunday, June 7, Nixon repeated he would have no part in a stop-Goldwater drive. "I think the party wants to search for a new man," he told his Michigan Republican hosts. "I think that search must go forward until it either finds that man, or decides it cannot find such a man. . . . I have consistently believed my best role is not to become involved in any such activities before the convention so as to be in a position to support the nominee and unite the party afterward." It was a clear disclaimer—except that Nixon also said again he would "willingly accept" any assignment the party gave him, and that "if the party should decide on me as its candidate, Mr. Johnson would know he'd been in a fight." Nixon seemed to be facing the fact that the 1964 nomination was beyond his grasp—and yet, maybe not entirely. If Goldwater *could* be stopped . . . but it would have to be done without Nixon—or without the *appearance* of Nixon having any role, if he was to be the inheritor of the Goldwater strength.

While Nixon thus was trying to play it both ways in Detroit, the political temperature already was soaring in Cleveland. At a Sunday morning breakfast meeting of the sixteen Republican governors, the independent-minded governor of Michigan, George Romney, decided to blow the lid off. Bothered by a host of Goldwater policy positions on civil rights, nuclear weapons, social security and other issues that in Romney's mind spelled disaster to the party, the governor had sought clarification from the Arizonan but had got none. Now he warned his fellow governors of the impending doom of a Goldwater candidacy; he demanded that they release a position statement that might somehow bring Goldwater to his senses on the issues, or, failing that, avert his nomination. The matter was discussed animatedly, but inconclusively.

With this anti-Goldwater head of steam already generated, Scranton arrived, primed to appear on the CBS television panel *Face the Nation* and, in light of his earlier talk with Eisenhower, apparently to announce his candidacy. He checked into the Sheraton-Cleveland Hotel, went to his ninth-floor suite—and found a message there to call Eisenhower. Scranton did so, to his regret. Eisenhower again was feeling the heat from Goldwater supporters, including his old Secretary of the Treasury, George Humphrey. He just wanted Scranton to know, Eisenhower said, he had no intention of entering into a "cabal" to stop Goldwater. Scranton, stunned, hung up the phone; with the ballyhooed television show approaching, he now would have to do some fast improvising.

As things turned out, he wasn't very good at it. He went down to the breakfast meeting of the Republican governors at which the earlier Romney tirade against Goldwater was being debated. He listened awhile and then headed for the TV studio. Shortly afterward, but before Scranton went on the sir, the breakfast meeting broke up in disarray. Romney, surrounded by reporters, told them that if matters continued as they were, it would mean "the suicidal destruction of the Republican Party as an effective instrument in meeting the nation's needs." Still contending he didn't know *what* Goldwater's positions really were, Romney said that if they were as contrary to the nation's and the Republican Party's needs as they seemed, he would "do everything within my power to keep him from becoming the party's Presidential candidate."

By now Scranton, however, was not similarly prepared. With Eisenhower's unexpected flip-flop still spinning in his head, the governor spent one of the most excruciating half hours on television ever suffered by a major political figure, awkwardly backing away from the challenge to Goldwater he had expected to crown with a TV announcement of candidacy. He was "available for the nomination" and he "would serve" if the convention called on him, Scranton said, but "I don't plan to go out and try to defeat Goldwater. I have no such intention. . . ."

The performance was a crushing blow not only for Scranton personally, but for the ebbing cause of his liberal and moderate Republican cohorts. Rockefeller, having himself carried the banner practically alone through the primaries, was openly disgusted. Asked by reporters whether he would support Scranton, Rockefeller replied: "Governor Scranton said that he was waiting to see where Senator Goldwater stood. And after listening to his press conference [the TV show], I think I've got to wait to see where he stands." Did Rockefeller think Scranton was showing "responsibility of leadership"? Rockefeller shot back: "Did you see him on television?"

It was, as Nixon might have known, chaos in Cleveland. But events and temptation were moving nevertheless to pull him in. Romney, having dropped his bomb, had set off a round of stop-Goldwater conferences among like-minded governors such as Rockefeller, Scranton and James A. Rhodes of Ohio—and had departed for Detroit, where he was to introduce Nixon at the prestigious Economics Club the next day. When Romney got

87

there, Rhodes phoned to ask when he would be back in Cleveland. The other moderate governors were ready, he said, to make the stop-Goldwater fight if Romney would be the point man. Romney said he would return the next night, after the Economics Club meeting.

That day, Monday, June 8, saw a remarkable demonstration of dexterity by Nixon. He had breakfast with Romney, during which the aroused Rambler Man briefed Nixon on all the latest maneuverings in Cleveland, including the pressure on Romney to make the race. If Nixon was not part of the emerging "cabal" —as Unger and other Nixon aides insisted later—he certainly was leaving himself wide open to the interpretation that he was. In his talk to the Economics Club, however, Nixon went to extreme lengths to try to make Goldwater sound more acceptable to party moderates. The Arizonan, Nixon said, "has moved to a position in which he accepts the major tenets of the Republican platform" and had "appropriately changed from a sectional to a national candidate."

All this looked very much like a Nixon effort to undercut any stop-Goldwater effort. Or was it a deft balancing act between the two forces? When asked by newsmen what he thought of Romney's tough anti-Goldwater remarks in Cleveland, Nixon said he thought that Romney's action would "in the long run help unite the party." Romney's comments, and Eisenhower's apparent urging of Scranton to become a candidate, Nixon said, had slowed Goldwater's drive for the nomination. If Nixon's delegate nose-counters of the time are to be believed, the former Vice President well knew at this junction that Goldwater had the nomination in hand. But in Detroit that day, Nixon was not talking like a man with that certain knowledge—or like a man who wanted to believe what he was hearing from those nose-counters.

Suspicion that Nixon was encouraging a "cabal," if not involved outright in one, was heightened by the fact Rhodes sent his plane to Muskegon, Michigan, where Nixon was speaking Monday night, to bring him to Cleveland. Rhodes met the plane and briefed Nixon on the latest efforts to persuade Romney to run. Romney, meanwhile, had raced back to Cleveland that night and, always a very early riser, presented himself at Nixon's suite the next morning before a breakfast of the Republican governors. There, Romney discussed his qualms with Nixon. Romney apparently felt trapped by his 1962 gubernatorial campaign pledge to complete a full four-year term in Lansing, and he explored the nature of that commitment with Nixon. Did the pressure from the other governors constitute a "draft" to which Romney ethically could yield? Nixon, according to Romney later, certainly thought so. Before any firm conclusions on a candidacy could be reached, however, the two men had to go downstairs to the breakfast, and there the discussion of the stop-Goldwater effort proceeded among small groups.

Presumably because he still was the party's "titular leader" and a guest at the breakfast, Nixon was invited to make a few comments. He told the governors, after a few opening niceties, that he had no prepared remarks but would be glad to take questions. Nixon stood there and the governors sat there, and nobody said anything. One of the participating governors later told Jerry Ter Horst, Washington bureau chief of the Detroit *News:* "It was so transparent. He was hoping that one of us, probably Romney or Scranton, would jump up and say, 'Okay, I'll run.' But more than that, it was pretty obvious that what he wanted most was a blocking back, somebody to run interference for himself until the right moment at the convention." Another governor told columnists Rowland Evans and Robert Novak: "After a moment or two, I realized what was happening. Nixon was waiting for us to ask him to run for President. It was unbelievable, just unbelievable." Nobody, of course, asked. Someone finally threw out a question about Republican chances against Lyndon Johnson, and Nixon warmed to his favorite subject, but that was the end of it.

During the breakfast, however, Scranton had been telling Romney how he and others could put together a quick campaign team for the Michigan governor. On the way out, Romney grabbed Nixon and ushered him into a convenient men's room for more moments of soul-searching. The two men agreed to meet again in Nixon's suite later in the morning. Perhaps all was not lost after all.

Romney went from there to a meeting with his fellow gover-

89

nors to discuss his own candidacy. Nixon meanwhile told waiting reporters he had detected a "lively interest" at the breakfast
for keeping the nomination open, for finding a "third-force
candidate." Romney and Scranton were the "likely possibilities" to challenge Goldwater, Nixon said, but Romney had
problems with Michigan backers "who want him to run for
governor." As for Goldwater, Nixon said, while it might be a
"short-term gain" to have him as the party nominee, "looking
to the future, it would be a tragedy for the Republican Party in
the event that Senator Goldwater's views, as previously stated,
were not challenged and repudiated." This was the same
Richard Nixon who in Detroit just the day before had suggested
that Goldwater already had adjusted to Republican realities on
most of his controversial views! Asked whether he himself
would accept a draft by the thirteen moderate governors (out of
the sixteen Republicans attending the conference), Nixon replied, "No comment." Did this mean he was not ruling himself
out as a possibility? Again, "No comment."

The impression now was spreading rapidly that Nixon had
come to Cleveland hoping the governors would get one of their
own to stage a holding action against Goldwater or ask Nixon
himself to run. Later, it was said Nixon already had urged some
of his supporters to draft a letter boosting him as the only sane
alternative to a disastrous Goldwater candidacy, and that the
letter was to go to all delegates and county chairmen at the right
moment. One longtime Republican tactician in New York
admitted later he had received phone calls from Cleveland from
both Romney and Nixon for appraisals of their chances. "Nixon
had Romney so convinced to go that Romney called me and
others after midnight that first night and said he was thinking of
taking a crack at it," the Romney-Nixon confidant told me. "I
told him, 'George, if you want to get your head bloodied, okay.'
And Dick was really pushing. He almost had Romney convinced. . . . But he was really gung-ho to be a candidate himself in 1964. I told him at one point, 'Dick, this is gone, and
you'll make a fool of yourself.' We had an argument over it."

A somewhat similar private conversation took place between
Nixon and Scranton. According to Scranton, Nixon launched a
long and rambling monologue, "highly political with very little

idealism in it," clearly suggesting that Goldwater did not have the nomination sewed up, and that "somebody else" ought to be supported. Nixon never specified who that somebody else ought to be, to Scranton's growing irritation. "It was such a beating about the bush," Scranton recalled later. "He never would come out and say it. It went on and on, and that was what disturbed me." Finally, Scranton said, in effect: "Dick, if you want to run for President, why don't you just go ahead and run?" That ended the conversation.

Shortly before Romney arrived at Nixon's suite for their second private meeting there of the day, Nixon informed reporters waiting in the crowded corridor that Romney would be coming along momentarily. Would they please make way for him to get through? The private talk would be about the nomination, he conceded. The newsmen had the distinct impression that Nixon did not want them to miss the Romney visit (as if they could) or its significance.

This bit of unsubtle scuttlebutt spread quickly, and there was an even bigger jam outside Nixon's suite when Romney arrived, characteristically bulling his way through as lights flashed and cameras ground away. The door was closed behind him; there then ensued a conversation that over the intervening years has been muddled in a crossfire of claims and denials. Romney insists to this day that at this meeting, Nixon came right out and urged him to run. "Nixon tried to persuade me to be a full-time candidate," Romney told me five years later, when he was settling in as President Nixon's Secretary of Housing and Urban Development. "I had said I would not be a candidate, but if I were drafted, I would do what any red-blooded American would do. When the other governors urged me to run, Nixon told me, 'That's a draft.' But I indicated I had a commitment [in Michigan]; that the most I could do would be to discuss the issues. Then Nixon urged me at least to indicate to the press outside that I was giving consideration to doing some campaigning on the issues. He never indicated to me he was available. In fact, he indicated the contrary. But he urged me to be a candidate, that unless someone did it, it would be all over."

The Nixon version is that he never urged Romney to run, that he didn't want to be in Cleveland in the first place, that any meetings he attended were set up by others, and that the only counsel he gave Romney was to proceed cautiously, not to be negative by singling out Goldwater as a target, and to be sure he had real support before venturing forth. "What Nixon was trying to do," Sherman Unger said later, "was to get through the convention with a party." Unger, who was in the room, remembers Nixon's telling Romney: "If you want to run to represent something affirmative, it won't hurt the party. But if you run just to stop Goldwater, it will split the party worse than it is." As soon as Romney left the room, Nixon turned to Unger and asked him to get him a reservation on the next plane east out of Cleveland.

Romney, encountering reporters as he left Nixon's suite, tried to waffle. He said Nixon and others had urged him to run and he was considering campaigning on the issues, a statement many of his listeners took to mean he was on the verge of candidacy. They were convinced of it when Nixon came out about forty-five minutes later and told the newsmen: "The Governor Romney effort is not a stop-Goldwater movement, but an attempt to write a good platform in keeping with the progressive traditions of the Republican Party." And with that, Nixon was off for Baltimore.

Another hour passed before Romney got word that stories were going out to newspapers across the country that he was in the race, or about to be. Frantically, he sent his press secretary, Richard Milliman, into the pressroom to squelch that impression. Romney was not running under any circumstancs, Milliman said; he merely was considering ways to "implement" his determination to get the best Republican candidate and platform. If Nixon was hoping to push Romney off the edge, it was clear now he had failed.

It may well have been, as the Nixon version insisted afterward, that the former Vice President had been dragged kicking and screaming to Cleveland, had been subjected to conspiratorial stop-Goldwater sessions not of his making, had tried only to keep any new candidacy by Romney or some other anti-Goldwater candidate within reasonable bounds, and had escaped at the first opportunity. But for a man bent only on party unity, his Cleveland observations on Goldwater and on his own availability were a strange way to project an image of neutrality. When Goldwater himself heard what Nixon had said in Cleveland, he made a bitter curbstone assessment that seemed well warranted by Nixon's own words. "He's sounding more like Harold Stassen every day," Goldwater observed, in an ironic reference to Stassen's 1950 efforts to dump Nixon as President Eisenhower's running mate. Later, Scranton told newsmen that Nixon at one point had urged Romney to run because the party "owed it" to the nationwide television audience "to provide some kind of contest at the convention; otherwise they'll be bored and turn it off." It was, in Scranton's view, "the most cynical argument I've ever heard a serious political figure offer."

According to one Nixon intimate, the former Vice President left Cleveland convinced in spite of everything that Romney *was* going to run. Romney's denials came while Nixon was flying east to Baltimore to catch his flight to London. As Nixon got off the plane, he was met by advance man John Whitaker, who told him: "It's on the radio that Romney's *not* going to run." Nixon seemed stunned. "What do you mean he's not going to run? He told me he was."

The whole Cleveland scene had been a fiasco, and Nixon had been in the thick of it. Because no anti-Goldwater candidate had been produced, the Arizona Senator emerged even stronger than before. Goldwater, commenting a second time on Nixon's observation that it would be "a tragedy" if Goldwater's views were not "repudiated," told Mary McGrory of the Washington *Star* acidly: "I guess he doesn't know my views very well. I got most of them from him." If Nixon was to maintain any role at all in 1964, Barry would have to be mollified.

That step, however, was not going to be easy, because with Romney declaring himself out, the pressure mounted on Scranton to enter the race—a development that also looked suspiciously to Goldwater supporters like an outgrowth of Cleveland and Nixon's quick visit. On June 11, the day after the governors' conference and Nixon's hasty departure, Scranton met with family, staff aides and Senator Hugh Scott of Pennsylvania, then called Eisenhower with his decision: he

93

would run. The final straw, after all the agonizing, apparently was an anti-civil rights vote by Goldwater in the Senate.

Scranton himself phoned Nixon in London with the news. "Watch out for the old man," Nixon told him. "You mean Ike?" Scranton asked incredulously. "Yes," Nixon said. And with that bit of very tardy advice, Nixon retreated into neutrality. The next day, when Scranton made his formal announcement, Nixon told reporters he would not endorse Scranton or anyone else before the convention. But Goldwater obviously was not convinced. "It's just like Nixon," he jibed, "to set this up and run off to London."*

It was pretty clear by now that Nixon no longer could have it both ways—he could not encourage a stop-Goldwater effort and at the same time remain sufficiently in the good graces of the Goldwaterites to be the beneficiary of a resultant stalemate. Returning to New York the day after Scranton's declaration, Nixon clearly signaled his fealty to Barry. If Scranton hoped to have a chance, Nixon said in another of his candid, surgical strikes, he would have to overcome the "weakness and indecisiveness" and the "very unfortunate impression" he had made on the television panel show during the Cleveland conference. Nor, in light of Scranton's phone conversations with Eisenhower, could Scranton "appear to be a puppet maneuvered by someone else." Of all of Nixon's talents, none surpassed his remarkable ability to give a man friendly advice in language and imagery that could make the man's foes wish they had said it first.

In the next few days, though, the moderate-liberal camp, led

* Four years later, after Nixon's election to the Presidency with his help, Goldwater told me: "Dick as far as I know had nothing to do with it [in Cleveland]. I don't believe he tried to get Romney or anybody else to run. Between his defeat for governor in 1962 and at least 1965, he never showed any interest in getting back into politics. Had he wanted to run in '64 I would have withdrawn for him. Hell, I didn't want it and didn't expect to get it until the last month, and then I felt I was trapped." Some of the governors, like Mark Hatfield, also gave Nixon the benefit of the doubt in discussing the episode later. "Here's a man who never had a great number of intimates among the governors," Hatfield said. "He wasn't extroverted like Rockefeller or Romney. He seldom confided his intimate thoughts, and as a result people were thrust into interpretation of what he was up to. He gave them less to go on, and people always are ready to believe the worst interpretation."

by Lodge's supporters, fell in behind Scranton for one last attempt to stop Goldwater. Nixon contented himself with resuming his fund-raising activities in Milwaukee and Chicago, insisting on his neutrality—and still seemingly clinging to the possibility that the convention might yet turn to him. In Milwaukee, asked about the prospect of a deadlock, he replied: "This is a two-man race. There can be no deadlock. It will be either one or the other. I exclude the possibility of any dark horse being nominated." But, he said in Chicago, if the convention failed to find a candidate "who can unite the party [and] if the party leaders turned to me, then I would undertake the responsibility of the nomination, and I would conduct an extensive campaign." Jimmy Durante used to sing a number that asked, "Did you ever have the feeling that you wanted to go, and then you had the feeling that you wanted to stay?" In these days, it seemed to be a perfect theme song for Nixon.

As June wore on, however, Scranton thrashed about ineffectively, and Goldwater's delegate count rose ever closer to the 655 needed for nomination. Nixon finally had to face the reality that there would indeed be no stalemate. Tying his own hopes to the prospect could only breed animosity among moderates and conservatives alike in the party. In the last days of June, he went to a favorite vacationing place at Montauk, Long Island, with Unger and Finch, and there made a basic reassessment of where he stood. If there was any point in his comeback when a first long-range decision was made that contributed directly to his 1968 election to the Presidency, it came at this informal meeting at Montauk.

Out of the talks with Finch and Unger, Nixon finally acknowledged what others had been telling him for months—that 1964 was not his year. More important, he concluded that the manner in which he conducted himself in what certainly would be a Republican disaster in the fall of 1964 could position him for a much more effective bid for the nomination in 1968. Nixon could foresee not only Goldwater's personal humiliation in the November election, but also the severe damage his name at the head of the national ticket would inflict on the Republican Party in Congress and even at lesser, local levels. The party would be in a shambles everywhere after the Goldwater candi-

95

dacy, and there would be a need for somebody who could rehabilitate it—someone who had not been at fault for the debacle, and who in fact had done all he could to avert or minimize it.

It was time, in other words, to stop playing games and to stop the wishful thinking. Goldwater was going to be the nominee, and the smart thing now was to make the best of it. Nixon ruled that the word be spread at once to his supporters to snuff out any potentially embarrassing effort to place his name in nomination. Also, since Nixon was sure that Goldwater would go down to inglorious defeat, the door had to be slammed on any possibility that Nixon might be saddled with the Vice Presidential nomination. He had in fact received a feeler from the Goldwater camp about being the No. 2 man. Nixon took the first available chance to back off, saying he could help the ticket more by not being on it. Finally, through Republican National Chairman William E. Miller (the same "Who is William E. Miller?" who finally ran with Goldwater), Nixon arranged to have his place on the convention speaking agenda switched to after the nomination, instead of before it. This way, the danger of any spontaneous activity in his behalf spurred by his speech would be removed, and as the retiring titular leader introducing the new one—the nominee—Nixon would be cast as the party wound-healer.

On July 14, as Nixon and his wife made a picturesque arrival in San Francisco by landing at Fisherman's Wharf in a helicopter, readers of the Los Angeles *Times* were able to read about the grand Nixon plan in a column by the director of the paper's editorial page, an old friend and former press aide, James Bassett. It said:

In certain quieter rooms of this extraordinarily quiet national convention, beyond the contrived celebrant noises, an informal group of erstwhile GOP leaders is earnestly working to make Richard Nixon the party's nominee for President. Not this year, however, but in 1968.

They are proceeding on the rather melancholy assumption that Arizona's Senator Barry Goldwater, who has the 1964 bid locked up, cannot beat Democratic President Lyndon B. Johnson, and that

"somebody else will have to pick up the pieces" four years
lence. . . . During the subsequent campaign, both Nixon and those
who are prominently identified with him will vigorously espouse the
Goldwater cause, just as the Arizonan himself labored mightily for
Nixon in 1960. But, they reason, unless a miracle passes, Goldwater
won't make it. "After November," they ask rhetorically, "who better
han Nixon can rebuild the Republican Party? In fact, who'll be
left?" . . . At 51, identified with the GOP center, Nixon would be
he likeliest man to weld together the dissident elements of right and
left. This he would accomplish by persuasion, by conferences, by
speech-making, by traveling and by writing, without seeking interim
public office as he did, regrettably, two years ago in California. Nixon
would, moreover, play a prominent role in the 1966 off-year congres-
ional campaign. . . . In the context of all this, Nixon's address to
he delegates on Thursday will be audited carefully by those who
profess to forecast the political future, both of parties and men. If,
ike Goldwater in 1960, he couples an appeal for post-convention
unity with a call to action by his own wing of the party, it's a fair
bet that Nixon hasn't for all time abandoned his presidential ambi-
ions. . . .

It was not necessary to wait for Nixon's convention speech to
confirm the accuracy of Bassett's column. At a press conference
hortly after his arrival, Nixon had charitable words for both
Goldwater and Scranton, and he emphasized that no matter
who won, "I for one Republican don't intend to sit it out, take
a walk." As for his criticisms of Goldwater at the governors'
conference in Cleveland, Nixon dismissed them out of hand,
aying the Republican platform being written in San Francisco
would be what Goldwater if nominated would run on. Asked if
Goldwater was qualified to lead the country in the realm of
foreign policy, Nixon called him "a reasonable man" who could
get for the United States "great respect from its enemies, some-
hing we don't have at the present time." (In prefacing this
esponse, Nixon again demonstrated his talent for doing the
opposition's work. The European press, Nixon said, had falsely
aricatured Goldwater as "some kind of a nut, a jerk, a wild
nan." He really wasn't, Nixon said—as Goldwater backers in
he room at the San Francisco Hilton blanched.)

97

As Nixon expected, Goldwater waltzed to the nomination. The job of healing the wounds inflicted during the convention, though, turned out to be much greater even than Nixon had contemplated. Before the vote, Scranton's staff in desperation sent off a vicious and personal attack on Goldwater over Scranton's name, charging that "Goldwaterism has come to stand for a whole crazy-quilt collection of absurd and dangerous positions that would be soundly repudiated by the American people in November." Goldwater assumed—correctly—that the usually mild-mannered and proper Scranton had not seen the letter, and he returned it. But the already breast-beating Goldwaterites who had come to coronate their leader did not take it so lightly. They were in a bloodthirsty mood, and Nixon's temperate let's-bury-the-hatchet-and-unite-behind-Barry speech after Goldwater's first-ballot nomination did nothing to cool them off.

Nixon recalled that in 1960 Goldwater as a losing candidate had told them, "Let's grow up, conservatives, let's go to work," and then went out and worked for the Nixon-Lodge ticket. "Before this convention," Nixon went on, "we were Goldwater Republicans, Rockefeller Republicans, Scranton Republicans, Lodge Republicans, but now that this convention has met and made its decision, we are Republicans, period, working for Barry Goldwater for President of the United States. There are some who may say they will sit it out or take a boat ride. I say 'Let's grow up, Republicans, and go to work,' and we shall win in November."

The Goldwaterites cheered Nixon's version of the 1960 Goldwater rallying cry. But unity really wasn't on their minds, and Goldwater knew it. When Nixon finally introduced him to the howling, frenzied crowd at the Cow Palace, the nominee basked for long minutes in the pandemonium of the true believers before him. Then, after shaking hands with wound-healer Nixon, he proceeded to undo all Nixon had said, by throwing raw meat to his hungry lions. Goldwater flatly told the party moderates who had tried so bumblingly to stop him that he could take them or leave them. "Anyone who joins us in all sincerity we welcome," he said. "Those who do not care for our cause we do not expect to enter our ranks in any case." The Goldwater legions cheered lustily at this casual dismissal.*

But they hadn't heard anything yet. In his rasping voice, delivered blandly as though the message were routine, Goldwater then uttered the phrases that were to dash at the very outset any hopes for party unity. "Extremism in the defense of liberty is no vice," he said. ". . . Moderation in the pursuit of justice is no virtue." As Goldwater spoke these words, underlined for emphasis in press copies of his text, the delegates in the Cow Palace erupted in a truly frightening display of fervor. Goldwater backers from Southern and Southwestern delegations sitting near the front let go with rebel yells, shaking their fists defiantly at reporters who gazed from the adjacent press section with awe and some disbelief at the uproar. The Goldwater delegates earlier had shown some of the same loathing when they booed and whistled during a speech by Nelson Rockefeller; this latest, invited so openly by their leader, was infinitely more venomous and visceral. Goldwater himself seemed somewhat surprised that his words had triggered such a reaction. For Nixon, the scene emphatically confirmed, if any confirmation was needed, that once the Goldwater spasm was over, this party would need above all else a unifier.

After the convention adjourned, and the party's moderates and liberals by the hundreds had indicated they would accept Goldwater's open invitation to stay home, Nixon set to work almost immediately to repair the damage. Among the prominent Republicans who expressed disapproval or at least reservations about the "extremism" remark was Eisenhower, who in a television interview a few days later said it "would seem to say that the end always justifies the means. The whole American

---

* One politician who "joined" Goldwater, in a sense, was Alabama's Governor George C. Wallace, who had cut a surprising and ominous swath through three Democratic Presidential primaries, winning 34 percent of the vote in Wisconsin, 30 percent in Indiana and 43 percent in Maryland. If he were to run as an independent in the fall, Goldwater might be shut out in the South and carry no states at all. But Wallace, wooed diligently by phone during the Republican convention by Representative James Martin, a Goldwater man, decided to leave the field to Barry in 1964—and to look ahead. About a week after Goldwater's nomination, Wallace announced he would not run as a third-party candidate in 1964.

99

system," Eisenhower added, "refutes that idea." Eisenhower wanted a "clarification" of the remark, and Nixon provided the vehicle by writing a prearranged letter to Goldwater that enabled the Arizonan, in the context of a reply, to soften the impact somewhat. The controversial phrase could be paraphrased, Goldwater wrote, "by saying that whole-hearted devotion to liberty is unassailable and that half-hearted devotion to justice is indefensible."

Early in August, Goldwater met with Eisenhower and Nixon at Gettysburg, again at Nixon's instigation, in a further effort to heal the breach underlined and aggravated by the convention. They discussed a Nixon idea for a party unity meeting to be held in Hershey, Pennsylvania, the next week, to which most major Republican officeholders and other leaders would be invited. Both Eisenhower and Nixon urged Goldwater to moderate his views in a way that would enable all Republican elements to support him. According to a transcript of that private meeting, Goldwater said he sought to "read no one out of this party" but to "make room for all, and to assure a climate within the party in which all of us will feel comfortable and at home." (Later, Goldwater told me: "The meeting didn't change any minds. We got the usual double-talk from Rockefeller and Romney. But Dick thought it was a good idea.")

Nixon acted as the meeting's moderator, introducing Goldwater and then summing up what was said in the ensuing discussion. His opening speech was as good an illustration as can be found of why he could remain a leading figure in the party for so long: "I think in order to win we must recognize that there are some states, for example, where a Goldwater position isn't the best position on a particular issue for a candidate or governor to take. And Barry Goldwater . . . will be the first man to say, 'Fine, take that position; campaign on those issues you believe in that are most helpful in your state and which fit the people of your state.'

"In diversity there are some problems if we create them or allow our enemies to create them for us," Nixon said, greatly minimizing the deep and basic split in the party. "But in diversity there is also strength, because . . . if we had complete unity and unanimity on views it would be forever a minority

100

party. In order to be a majority party, we must expand the base of our party, rather than to contract it. . . . I want all Republicans to win; I am just as strong for a liberal Republican in New York as I am for a conservative Republican in Texas, and I can go and just as enthusiastically campaign for both, because we need both liberals and conservatives to have a majority. And it is a majority we want in the House, in the Senate, among the governors, and for the Presidency."

In his summation, Nixon took the opportunity to remind all the other party leaders that he still was the best soldier in the ranks, ready to make any sacrifice for the cause. "With the great emphasis on TV, with the time that is involved," Nixon said, "it is very possible that Presidential and Vice Presidential candidates will not be able to get into all fifty states, or certainly not in the amount that you may want. It is there that you must make what we call the second line. As far as that second line is concerned, I want you to know that I am reserving five weeks, five weeks before November third, and I will spend full time and will be glad to go into states that the candidates will not be able to go into."

Through the fall, Nixon was true to his word. He brought his old logistics and advance man, Nick Ruwe, into New York to do his scheduling, and on September 30, at Garden City, Long Island, he launched a 33-day, 36-state personal speaking tour ostensibly in behalf of the Goldwater-Miller ticket. But Nixon of course knew they already were down the drain. What he really was engaged in, in the words of one of his strategists of the time, was "a salvage operation"—to save as many other Republican candidates as possible from going down with the ticket. Nixon made more than 150 stops in his 36-state swing, attempting to bail out Republican Congressional, Senatorial and gubernatorial candidates who through no fault of their own, and no change in their own political philosophy or policies, found themselves in jeopardy. At each stop, Nixon took three approaches—he lauded the independent virtues and strengths of the local candidate; he tried to paint Goldwater as a "reasonable" man in spite of Democratic contentions to the contrary; he gave Lyndon Johnson hell. "He was a one-man truth squad," one of his traveling aides said later. "He tried to

101

clarify what Goldwater was saying. But it was a Gordian knot and nobody had a sword."

None of Nixon's efforts, of course, made much difference as far as Goldwater's chances were concerned. It is difficult to make a clear-cut case, either, that Nixon did salvage much in the fallout that descended from the top of the ticket over lesser Republican candidates, sweeping them out of office at every level. In November, the Grand Old Party lost a net of two Senate seats, thirty-eight House seats and nearly five hundred in state legislatures. Middle-of-the-road Republican Congressmen as well as card-carrying conservatives were unceremoniously dumped in the avalanche of votes for Johnson—or, more accurately, although Johnson did not choose to recognize the distinction, against Goldwater.

Still, there were some Republicans who managed to squeak by, and they were grateful to Nixon for his help. More important in the long run was the fact Nixon had tried, and tried hard in the party's darkest hour. Those who went under as well as those who survived recognized that fact, and his conduct seemed all the more commendable when contrasted with the halfhearted or no-hearted response to the Goldwater dilemma by Rockefeller, Keating, Romney and others in the Eastern liberal camp.

Richard Nixon, for all his political experience, never had been a particularly subtle politician, and now that the Republican Party lay in ruin, he did not wait for others to note on their own the contrast between his behavior and that of others. Though Goldwater had lost, his conservative followers still held control of the party, and there was one sure-fire way to let them know whose side you were on: blast the hated Rockefeller. In a New York press conference two days after the election, he lit into Rockefeller as a "party divider" and a "spoilsport" whose own failure to work aggressively for Goldwater not only hurt the national ticket but lost Rockefeller his role as a national party leader. In practically the same breath with which he was urging Republicans to concentrate on "healing wounds, not opening new ones," Nixon accused Rockefeller of "dragging his feet" in the Goldwater campaign. "Anyone who sits on the sidelines in a struggle," he argued, was in no position to claim a national leadership role afterward. Nixon's performance, columnist Murray Kempton observed, sought to "bind up the wounds of the Republican Party with a tourniquet around the neck of Nelson Rockefeller." And Rockefeller, vacationing in Spain, commented that "this kind of peevish post-election utterance has unfortunately become typical of Mr. Nixon." But Nixon, with an eye to the Goldwaterites, knew what he was doing.

Nixon himself filed no formal claim for the party's leadership at the post-election press conference. His actions throughout the Goldwater campaign already had built his case as persuasively as could be done. All fall, Nixon had been administering to the sick party, trying to minimize the impact of the plague. Now, with political experts already saying eulogies over its prostrate form, the doctor remained in the house, insisting the spark of life was still there, and ready and eager to fan it. Richard Nixon believed, as he often said, in the American dream; among its favorite sagas was the one about the hopeless patient who miraculously recovered and married the doctor. Considering the dimensions of the Goldwater defeat in 1964, a Republican resurgence by 1968 seemed impossible. But Richard Nixon for one did not think so.

5

Rising from the Ashes

IN the shambles that was the Republican Party after the Goldwater debacle, Richard Nixon was an obvious candidate to lead the salvage work, having already started it during the fall campaign of 1964. In spite of the suspicions nurtured among both conservatives and liberals by his hot-and-cold flirtations with the 1964 nomination, and with the futile stop-Goldwater efforts prior to the San Francisco convention, he survived the November disaster better than most. Goldwater was utterly discredited by the landslide against him, but little better off were those liberals and moderates who had refused to give all-out help—Rockefeller, Romney, Lodge and the rest. Nixon himself had made sure Rockefeller would get tagged with a major share of the blame by immediately labeling him a "party divider" and "spoilsport." In the process, the former Vice President pointedly excused Romney and other Republicans who themselves had to seek reelection. But none who sold Goldwater short would be forgotten by his loyalists.

Nixon well knew that although the Goldwaterites had lost disastrously, they remained in control of the party machinery—particularly at the local levels. Even in the event they could be forced to yield the overt party leadership in the national committee, they would not fold their political tents across the land and slowly slip away. Unless forced out everywhere, they would remain a formidable power in party councils. Reality might rule out another Goldwater-type candidacy in 1968 (although an election-eve national telecast by movie actor Ronald Reagan already had the ultraconservatives buzzing about a new political star) . Even so, the men who had seized the party for Goldwater were bound to have a critical, or the critical, say in picking the 1968 nominee. And Nixon, for all his preconvention shenanigans, had performed tirelessly in Goldwater's and the party's behalf once the nomination fight was over. His post-election blast at Rockefeller shocked the liberals; it endeared him to the conservatives who still hung on.

To some Goldwater Republicans, Nixon seemed so logically the man to put the party back on its feet that they moved immediately after the election to give him the means. One governor who had been for Goldwater through the Cleveland fiasco took it upon himself to start calling his Republican colleagues around the country with the idea that Nixon ought to be installed forthwith as the Republican national chairman. Predictably, he got a cool reception from most of the governors who still remembered Nixon's machinations among them at Cleveland. Correctly, they saw in Nixon's talk about sacrifice for party and unity at all costs the makings of another candidacy of his own.

But running the national committee would have bogged Nixon down in administrative chores, and there was no indication anyway that he would have been interested. He always had been more valuable and more effective as a "celebrity" spokesman and fund-raiser, and if there was anything his career didn't need, it was the image of the professional political operator. His New York law practice, which gave him ample free time for politics and for world travels that reinforced his image as a foreign policy expert, remained a much better base.

Within that comfortable context, Nixon wasted no time in his transparent way planting the idea that the party now needed a man in a certain mold—and that Richard Nixon happened to fit that mold. In a page-one interview in the New York *Times* about a week after the election, Nixon said the GOP after the Goldwater nightmare needed "moderation" above all. "There is a strong conservative wing of the Republican Party. It deserves a major voice in party councils, and the liberal wing deserves a party voice, but neither can dominate or dictate—the center must lead."

If there is one word that Nixon has used most often in recent years to describe his own position in the political spectrum, it is "centrist." Republicans would be hearing that self-description increasingly from him as they sought to put 1964 behind them, and its memories of what the "extremism" label had wrought. In fact, after placing Romney at "slightly to the left of center, but primarily a centrist," Nixon was asked about himself. "I'm perhaps at dead center," he answered.

Ironically, up to this time, Nixon seldom had been thought of as a man either of the center or of moderation. His image was, above all else, one of fierce partisanship and combativeness. His lashing out at Nelson Rockefeller was a fresh example of that side of the man. Yet with his embrace of the unity-through-moderation theme, Nixon was obliged to soften his image. How well he was succeeding was not at first grasped by those who continued to see him only as the "old Nixon" and thus ridiculed the occasional political gossip that the man, having "made it" in New York, had mellowed. But that kind of talk—about a "new Nixon"—was heard with increasing frequency after the Goldwater defeat and into 1965 and 1966.

While other Republicans wrung their hands over the Goldwater disaster and were immobilized by it, Nixon was off again on another of his business trips to Japan—being interviewed en route, underlining his foreign policy credentials by his very presence, espousing the unity theme. At a Honolulu stopover he expressed confidence the GOP would come back with "new men, new leaders and new ideas that will put us on the offensive in 1966." At Tokyo Airport, he repeated the theme that the party needed new blood—but not brand new. "The leadership itself," he told reporters, "must be new in that it must have broad appeal to all elements of the party, but that does not in itself have to mean new people." Those perennial Nixon-watchers who saw a method in his moderation would get a particular kick out of that observation.

Before departing for Japan, Nixon had urged other Republicans to declare a moratorium on attacking and blaming Goldwater for what had happened in November; wisdom and prudence dictated a cooling-off period before moving to reorganize the party. Congressional GOP leaders were largely of the same view. But the nation's Republican governors, who through indecisiveness had failed to make even a respectable show of stopping Goldwater's nomination, were determined to make amends. As a first step, they wanted the young Arizona conservative Goldwater had installed as national chairman, Dean Burch, removed. At an early December meeting of the Republican Governors Association, a resolution was passed calling for a housecleaning that would bring "leadership which clearly represents a broad view of Republicanism and practices a policy of inclusion, rather than exclusion."

Nixon had said right after the election that the first of 1965 would be soon enough to address the issue of party leadership, but the pressure from the governors—and the implication that they intended to grab it themselves—persuaded him to move early. Back from Japan, he met with Goldwater and Eisenhower in New York a week after the governors' statement. Goldwater himself obviously had read the statement as a power grab by the governors, and he was not disposed to cave in to it. He had suggested blithely that if the governors had any thoughts about the direction of the party, they should submit them to the national committee. But the chairman of the governors' group, then Governor Robert E. Smylie of Idaho, said his colleagues would not accept a "secondary role" and he didn't believe anybody—meaning Goldwater—was "in a position to dictate policy to the party." Nixon, seeing the governors were not going to yield, enlisted Eisenhower to persuade Goldwater to make accommodations. The former President suggested a two-man leadership for the party, with someone like Ray C. Bliss, the unglamorous but highly respected Ohio state chairman known as a "nuts and bolts technician," handling organizational matters while somebody like the eloquent, conservative former Congressman from Minnesota, Walter H. Judd, acted as party spokesman.

The idea of a two-man leadership got nowhere, but others now were putting Bliss' name forward as a natural for the job. He had a solid reputation not only for diligence and effective-

107

ness but also for fairness. Nixon himself had tried to get Bliss to take the post on earlier occasions. Now, Nixon helped negotiate a face-saving arrangement whereby Bliss would be elected at a forthcoming national committee meeting in January and Burch would stay on officially until April, with Goldwater appearing to give his blessing to the switch. Goldwater didn't like the deal—because it obviously was the first clear erosion of his hold on the party machinery—but he reluctantly bought it.

Thus, as the new year started, a shift toward the "centrist" position where Nixon resided already had been accomplished by the removal of conservative Burch and his replacement by religiously nonideological Bliss. For Bliss as for Nixon, "moderation" was the byword in the party rebuilding job ahead. Bliss was officially elected at a national committee meeting in Chicago in late January. The meeting was dominated by the instinct for self-preservation that springs eternal from the political breast. Congressman Bob Wilson of California, chairman of the Republican Congressional Campaign Committee and a Nixon friend and ally, offered the best summation. "If I was in hell, with one leg gone, and one arm gone, and one eye gone," he told his brethren, "I'd still be thinking: How can I get out of here?"

The occasion also was marked by a final expression of appreciation from Goldwater to Nixon for his 1964 labors. Goldwater introduced Nixon to the assembled faithful at the Blackstone Hotel as the man "who worked harder than any one person for the ticket" in 1964 and, turning to him, exclaimed: "Dick, I will never forget it! I know that you did it in the interests of the Republican Party and not for any selfish reasons." Then Goldwater added: "But if there ever comes a time I can turn those into selfish reasons, I am going to do all I can to see that it comes about."

To this open invitation to be a candidate in 1968, Nixon merely smiled graciously. Instead of seizing the offer, he called on all Republicans to declare a moratorium on Presidential politicking in behalf of any candidate until after the 1966 Congressional elections. Before the party could even begin to think about a Presidential nominee for 1968, he told the national committee, it had to put the acrimony of 1964 behind it, develop an unprecedented unity in the ranks, and point to 1966 as an opportunity to recoup the major setbacks of November. Only with a restored base in a rehabilitated party, Nixon said, could any Republican candidate have a chance to win the White House in 1968. The speech, which received standing applause, effectively channeled the Republican comeback effort into an arena—the next Congressional elections—in which Nixon already was a proven performer. And dividends for the party in 1966 Congressional gains also would offer political dividends for Nixon.

A measure of how well Nixon had ridden out the 1964 storm was a January Gallup Poll that asked Republican county chairmen and rank-and-filers, "Who should lead the GOP?" He ran ahead among both groups, though Goldwater as the most recent standard-bearer was the traditional "titular leader." While Bliss set about reorganizing the national committee—he actually took over long before Burch's official departure—Nixon assumed the spokesman role, especially in the field of foreign affairs and the Vietnam War. In a New York speech in late January, he said flatly that the United States was "losing the war in Vietnam" and warned that unless strategy was changed "we will be thrown out in a matter of months—certainly within the year." He preached escalation of the war against the north by naval and air interdiction of Communist supply routes into South Vietnam and destruction of staging areas in North Vietnam and Laos. Such action did run the risk of triggering Chinese Communist intervention, Nixon conceded, but proposals to negotiate with the Viet Cong or to "neutralize" South Vietnam would be tantamount, he charged, to "surrendering on the installment plan."

Nixon's hawkish views, which had been hardening ever since his visit to Saigon and other Southeast Asian capitals the previous spring, were particularly timely. They were uttered just prior to Viet Cong terrorist attacks on American installations at Pleiku, Quinhon and Tuy Hoa on February 7, 1965, that provided the justification for the first major U.S. escalation of the war. President Johnson used the incidents to launch a new policy of air attacks against the north, first seemingly on a tit-for-tat retaliatory basis but actually as a continuing policy.

109

Back in August, 1964, Johnson had used another isolated incident, the reported North Vietnamese torpedo boat attack on American ships in the Gulf of Tonkin, to obtain a sweeping war authorization from the Senate. Retaliatory air raids were launched then too, with what some thought was excessive intensity, but Nixon was quick to support them. "The Chinese Communists or the North Vietnamese are being aggressive to test the United States during the election period," he had said. "It is now doubly important to overcompensate with firm action. . . . I don't think the 'war party' issue should be raised against President Johnson. If it's good politics to show strength, then I'm for it." (Then a choice Nixonism: "I think we should have been strong all along.")

The retaliatory attacks in February gave Senate doves the jitters. Democratic Senator Wayne L. Morse of Oregon called them "a black page in American history." But as far as Nixon was concerned the attacks didn't go far enough. At a party fundraiser in Philadelphia, he called on American planes and ships to bomb Communist supply lines and bases "day by day, and for that matter, night by night. . . . Failing to do more than we are doing will mean loss of the war . . . to imperial Communism."

In this and other Lincoln Day speeches in Chicago and Los Angeles, Nixon clearly established himself as the point man in the opposition party's criticism of the Johnson administration. And if "titular leader" Goldwater had any objection, he didn't demonstrate it. Instead of similarly touring the country in the Lincoln Day period, the 1964 Presidential nominee stayed in Arizona to speak to a small local group. He knew he was excess baggage nationally. "Nobody ever believes that 'titular head' stuff," Goldwater told me much later. "It doesn't mean a goddamn thing. The majority of the party would still go with me, but I wanted them to back him. I was not in a position to speak out for the party nationally. I just got to be persona non grata. It was mostly due to Bliss or imposed on him by those who thought I was the kiss of death. I was not invited by the national committee to speak to a fund-raiser after '64. But I was getting twenty-five to thirty invitations a day on my own, and still do."

110

In Goldwater's absence, Nixon demonstrated to party conservatives that they could have most of what they liked in Barry within the context of Nixon's "moderation." In Chicago, he fed Illinois county chairmen the kind of partisanship professional politicians like to hear. After describing himself as a "middle-of-the-roader," he lit into what he called "crackpot" liberal legislation and into the favorite whipping boy of conservative Republicans, Vice President Hubert H. Humphrey. During the 1964 campaign, Nixon had labeled Humphrey as "a dedicated radical," and he used similar language now. It was music to conservative ears.

While thus openly wooing the Goldwaterites, Nixon's general comportment gave moderates little to criticize. He spoke the conventional wisdom of most Republicans on the war—that the main thing wrong with Johnson's escalation was that there wasn't enough of it, or not the right kind of it. And, equally important to politicians of all shadings who always had to concern themselves with such parochial matters as fund-raising, Nixon, whose law practice was humming now, providing him money, prestige and freedom to travel, was as ever Mr. Available.

There seemed to be no end of opportunities for him to stress his past experience in foreign policy; when they did not fall into his lap, he improvised. In Finland with a group of American and Canadian industrialist clients in April, he finished his business early and on impulse—it was said—took off on a twenty-hour train ride to Moscow. At eleven o'clock at night, he sought out his old kitchen-debate buddy, former Premier Nikita Khrushchev, at the fallen leader's small Moscow apartment, but Khrushchev apparently wasn't home. Nixon did not leave Moscow, however, without a news-making debate with the deputy director of Moscow State University.

After Nixon's departure the official government newspaper, *Komsomolskaya Pravda,* described Nixon's quickie visit in language the Democratic National Committee, or even Nelson Rockefeller, probably could not have improved on. "Conceited by the fact that his person still means something," *Pravda* said, "the former Vice President and erstwhile candidate took to advertising himself even if it was scandalous, if only they wrote

111

and talked about him. On the street, Nixon for some reason accosted a policeman with stupid questions. He tried to start arguments with strangers and invited them to be his guests. In a word, as in a real clown's act, he tried to provide sensational material for the foreign newspapermen who followed on his heels." In spite of *Pravda's* "exposé," the Nixon visit received wide coverage back in the United States. The stories, of course, all harked back to Nixon's finest hour in 1959 when he took on the once fearsome Khrushchev in debate.

Life in New York, that "fast track" that had drawn him East in 1963, also provided Nixon with ample public exposure, and with a taste of sophisticated relaxing he seldom had had the time to enjoy. He and Mrs. Nixon went occasionally to the Broadway theaters—preferring the favorite if square musicals of the day, like *Hello, Dolly!*—and to the Metropolitan Opera. Nixon himself indulged in his lifelong interest in sports with more frequent visits to Yankee Stadium to see the Yankees or the football Giants and sometimes in winter to Madison Square Garden to watch the Rangers. He even was known to drop in once in a while at the renowned sports eatery, Toots Shor's, to talk sports; he golfed with the likes of old Cleveland Browns quarterback Otto Graham, then coaching at the Coast Guard Academy, and John Pont, who was to coach Indiana into the Rose Bowl several years later. Other favored golfing partners included Walter Thayer, president of the friendly New York *Herald Tribune,* and Bill Paley, chairman of the board at CBS. Julie, now sixteen, was going to the Chapin School, and Tricia, who was nineteen, was at Finch College, but both lived at home. Their parents often took them to dinner at the Edwardian Room in the Hotel Plaza just down the street from their Fifth Avenue apartment, or to the Metropolitan Club. When the Nixons went out alone, they would patronize the best-known expensive spots—"21," The Colony, Delmonico's, Le Pavillon, Lüchow's, the Stork Club. It was, quite obviously, the good life, and a relaxed Richard Nixon—a "new, new Richard Nixon," some who saw him suggested—really seemed to be emerging.

In addition to watching the lucrative Pepsi-Cola account and others at Nixon Mudge, the former Vice President busied himself attending meetings of various boards of directors to which he had been appointed—the Harsco Company, Investors Mutual Inc., the Investors Variable Payments Fund Inc., and his personal favorite, the Boys Clubs of America. (It is not known whether the latter connection was where he learned, as he said in later public criticism of the New Left student movement, that the [W.E.B.] Dubois Clubs had taken their name intentionally, in typical Communist treachery, to be confused with the Boys Clubs of America and thus wrap themselves in a cloak of respectability!)

It was, in sum, a time of watchful waiting, of consolidating Nixon's private and public resources, and of thinking. There was only limited opportunity in this off-year for overt political campaigning, with only two gubernatorial races—in New Jersey and Virginia—and the New York mayoralty election on the calendar. But the depths to which the Republican Party had been plunged by Goldwater required earlier and more extensive planning for the next year's Congressional elections. In May, after conversations with Congressman Bob Wilson, the GOP's House campaign captain, House Minority Leader Gerald Ford and others, Nixon was appointed honorary chairman of a new group called the Congressional Boosters Club, a Republican counterpart of Lyndon Johnson's "President's Club." A goal of $2,000,000 was set to find and support young attractive Republicans against vulnerable Democratic Congressmen and to help some of the Goldwater-debacle victims of 1964 to come back. Congressional districts that normally should have remained Republican were on the target list as well as seats of Democratic incumbents who barely won, even with Goldwater at the head of the Republican ticket. The overriding theory was that 1964, because of Goldwater, was an aberration; any Republican who survived then would need no special help in 1966, without the Arizona albatross around his neck. As the honorary chairman of this group, and inevitably as its ranking celebrity in grass-roots Republican circles in 1965 and 1966, Nixon had an ideal vehicle for maintaining and increasing his following among grateful toilers in the party vineyards.

Though it was only early 1965 some of those men around Nixon already could see the political possibilities of the situation. Several days in the spring they met with Nixon for lunch in Room No. 6 at The Recess on Broad Street, and for the first time as a group began to talk about a Nixon renascence. Seated at a large round table, with a picture-window view of lower Manhattan beyond, banker Maurice Stans, New York broker Peter Flanigan, Herb Brownell and a few others appraised the picture and decided the prudent thing would be to help Nixon remain visible. Garment, and later two other young lawyers in the firm, Thomas Evans and John P. Sears, began to give part of their time to political matters and the taking of political pulses. The Recess meetings continued, with other Nixon friends being brought in.

As summer advanced, their appraisal of Nixon's chances was confirmed in the public opinion polls. Gallup in late June asked selected voters to identify the man they thought would be the best candidate for the Republicans to run in 1968. The results gave Nixon a lead of nearly two to one over the No. 2 choice, Lodge (Nixon, 25 percent; Lodge, 14 percent; Goldwater, 13 percent; Romney, 11 percent; Dirksen and Scranton, 7 percent each; Rockefeller, 6 percent; Lindsay, 5 percent). Nixon was off again to the Far East, using each stop along the way to reassert his support of the war, shape a politically profitable Republican attitude toward it, and underline his position as the party's most experienced and most current expert on foreign affairs.

Finding a political focus on the war was made easier for Nixon by events. The spring of Nixon's content in New York had been one of secret crisis and turmoil for Johnson on Vietnam. The door to air assaults on the north that had been pushed open by the February attacks on American installations in the south by now was swung wide; escalation was under way inexorably, though without public awareness, in the air and on the ground; more attacks, more enemy infiltration in the south, more American troops. Democrats like J. William Fulbright, chairman of the Senate Foreign Relations Committee, began to grow more suspicious of a President who dissembled on what was being done militarily in Vietnam, and on how much more would be needed to be done. They pressed for more candor at home and for negotiations abroad, and in their demands Nixon saw the makings of political vulnerability at the polls.

Departing on his Far East trip from San Francisco in late August, Nixon told newsmen that such Democrats "encourage the Communist leaders to prolong their resistance" and that while saying they are for peace "they don't understand we are fighting in Vietnam to prevent World War III and to keep the Pacific from becoming a Red sea." In Tokyo, he included Johnson by inference, warning that "constant repetition by the United States of a desire to negotiate prolongs the war in Vietnam"; in Saigon, he called peace overtures "loose talk." And appearing on *Meet the Press* on his return in mid-September, Nixon repeated his call for more air and sea power to be thrown against North Vietnam and, while reiterating his support of Johnson, focused on the implication of growing Democratic "softness," this time specifically including the President.

"I don't know what President Johnson presently thinks with regard to negotiations," he said, "but certainly I think continued talk on his part, on the part of Secretary Rusk and others, suggesting that we only want peace, that we want to negotiate, has the effect of prolonging the war rather than bringing it to a close. I think President Johnson has got to make it clear to the world and to the people of South Vietnam that our objective is a free and independent South Vietnam *with no reward and no appeasement of aggressors.*" (Italics added.)

On the same program, Nixon was asked whether he still wanted to be President. "I am a very practical man," he said. "I believe that the Presidency seeks the man and that if a man is not destined at a particular time and place to lead the country, he will not be elected. I intend to do everything I can to strengthen our party, my party, so that when we get to 1968, whoever is selected—and it very probably is not going to be me—but whoever is selected, will be able to win, because I feel a certain responsibility, one for losing the election in 1960 and now a great responsibility for the weakness of this party, and I am devoting my efforts to building it up, without regard to what happens to me." Murray Chotiner, talking much later about Nixon's attitude at that time, wryly put it another, more succinct way: "He felt the party had been good to him and as a

115

national leader he had to help. If it was helping him politically at the same time, why, that was a calculated risk he'd have to take."

It was now the election season, limited as it was, and Nixon was ready to lend a hand to all Republicans who wanted him. One, John V. Lindsay, running for mayor right there in New York as the candidate of both the Republican and the Liberal parties, did not. There were only 600,000 registered Republicans in New York City, compared to more than 2,000,000 Democrats, and although Nixon now lived in Manhattan, he was no political folk hero there. Lindsay in fact had asked no outside Republicans to help him, and that decision was a convenient one for Nixon. As a registered Republican in New York, he told those who asked, he would vote for Lindsay but would withhold giving any "partisan" support because Lindsay was supposed to be running a nonpartisan race!

The other two major Republican candidates of 1965 did want him. One was A. Linwood Holton, a young Roanoke lawyer running an impossible race against the Byrd-machine candidate, Democrat Mills E. Godwin, Jr., in Virginia. Nixon, who had carried the state against John Kennedy in 1960, made a whirlwind swing with Holton that Virginia Republicans still have not forgotten. In a single day he visited every major population center in behalf of the unknown Holton, and when the candidate on election day captured 38 percent of the vote in losing to Godwin, ecstatic Virginia party leaders were quick to give Nixon much of the credit—and to tell fellow Republicans everywhere about it. Nixon's one day in Virginia that fall was one of his best political investments of the year. (Four years later, Holton became the first Republican governor of Virginia in the twentieth century, with Nixon, this time as President, paying another campaign visit.)

Nixon's other active intervention of 1965, however, was a serious misstep that, in the view of some of his political advisers, nearly derailed his 1968 Presidential train before it got out of the station. In New Jersey, a Republican state senator named Wayne Dumont was running for governor against the popular Democratic incumbent, Richard J. Hughes. Dumont was not going anywhere. The only issue that had created a stir concerned a Rutgers professor, Eugene D. Genovese, who in his antiwar fervor had said he would "welcome" a Viet Cong victory. Dumont argued that since Rutgers was a state university, the man should be fired. Hughes, though himself one of the staunchest supporters of President Johnson on Vietnam, took the traditional liberal position that academic freedom would be infringed upon by any such action against the professor. In the 1950's era of professional anti-Communism and Senator Joe McCarthy, the Dumont position might have turned the election around. Now, it didn't appear to be making a dent in the Hughes campaign, especially since the governor's own position on the war could not be challenged by Dumont.

A call for help went out to Nixon in New York. A good Republican was in need, and Nixon, as of old, lit out breathing partisan fire. Against the counsel of several members of his law firm and political advisers, Nixon joined Dumont in Morristown on October 24 and let Genovese and Hughes have it with both barrels.

"I do not raise the question of Professor Genovese's right to be for segregation or integration, for free love or celibacy, for Communism or anarchy, or anything else—in peacetime," Nixon said. "But the United States is at war. Genovese is employed by a state university, and he used the state college as a forum to, in effect, give aid and comfort to the enemy. World War II was a big war, and this is a little war. If anyone had welcomed a Nazi victory during World War II there would have been no question about what to do. . . . Leadership requires that the governor step in and put the security of the nation above security of the individual."

The reaction was almost immediate. The rumors of a "new Nixon" had been premature. The "old Nixon" of the California Congressional and Senatorial campaigns was suddenly found to be alive and spreading venom and innuendo in the state of New Jersey. Not only did local Democrats howl; newspapers including the New York *Times* took up the accusation. Nixon was shaken; his Republican friends with national ambitions for him were shaken; so were his law partners. "What happened was Dumont wasn't getting enough exposure on the issue, so he called on Nixon to get it going," said a Nixon intimate later. "The tactic worked all right, and we got clobbered with it."

At Nixon Mudge particularly, where shock waves from the liberal New York legal community were felt immediately, there was concern about what impact Nixon's "reversion to form" would have on the firm, as well as on the man the members now could see was moving back into the Presidential picture. A few advisers rationalized that the episode didn't hurt because it projected Nixon's name into the news. Nixon himself realized he had made a mistake. It was, said another aide much later, a spontaneous reaction— "You don't change all the colors of a horse at age fifty." Chastened by the experience, Nixon determined he would have to stick to his guns publicly, but he sought ways to temper the damage. Privately, he resolved never again to "revert" and open the door to the return of the "old Nixon."

The first step to recover ground was to put a face of good philosophy on what had been an act of bad politics. In a long letter to the New York *Times* in late October—about a week before Dumont went down to defeat in New Jersey—Nixon sought to defend his position as actually being a defense of academic freedom. "The question is, how do we preserve that freedom?" he wrote. "We do so by recognizing and protecting the right of individuals to freedom of speech. We do so by defending the system of government which guarantees freedom of speech to individuals. Unfortunately there are occasions— particularly in wartime—when the individual's rights and the nation's security come in conflict. . . ."

Nixon's argument also made it plain he did not look upon the Vietnam War at that time as any indigenous skirmish, but as the Cold War battleground on which the fate of the West would be determined. "The victory for the Viet Cong which Professor Genovese 'welcomes' would mean ultimately the destruction of freedom of speech *for all men for all time not only in Asia, but in the United States as well,*" he said. (Italics added.) (Not even General Giap or Ho Chi Minh himself, at his most braggadocian, ever had claimed that great a victory growing out of the Vietnam War.)

The Genovese case passed in most quarters with the defeat of

Dumont. But Nixon did not forget it, nor did the Eastern academic community, particularly in schools whose antiwar sentiment was fanned and extended as the stalemated conflict in Vietnam dragged on. The following spring, when the administration at the University of Rochester announced that Nixon would deliver the commencement address, a student uproar burst on the campus of the upstate New York school. There were demands that the invitation be withdrawn. It was not, and Nixon took advantage of the now spotlighted forum to expand and refine his views on academic freedom.

A distinction had to be drawn, he said, between freedom of speech as guaranteed in the First Amendment to the Constitution and academic freedom. The latter exists, he said, "not so much for the benefit of the academic community but for the benefit of the society which the academic community serves." Statements such as Professor Genovese's, Nixon told the Rochester graduates, cross "the line between liberty and license. . . . If we are to defend academic freedom from encroachment we must also defend it from its own excesses."

Nixon at Rochester appeared to be backing away from his earlier suggestion that Genovese's words were costing American lives. He disagreed, he said, with those who would sharply curtail campus dissent on grounds it gave "aid and comfort to the enemy." Those who would welcome enemy victory, however, just "do not know the enemy," he suggested.

Finally, in a prime example of his talent for turning political expedience into virtue, Nixon sought to picture himself as a citizen with such deep convictions on the subject that he had to speak out, regardless of the political risk to himself. "In the light of these convictions," he said, "I could not take what would have been the much more expedient course of refusing to comment on an issue of such importance to the freedom and security of the nation." When Nixon first spoke up about the Genovese case, of course, it was in the context of a partisan political rescue effort. Remaining silent might have been "the much more expedient course" personally, but that would not have helped Dumont much in New Jersey, and helping Dumont clearly was what motivated Nixon's first comments, not

119

some irrepressible obligation suddenly to defend academic freedom "from its own excesses."

Nixon by now had an amazing familiarity with Republican
personalities in the smallest towns and counties around the
country, and he cultivated them at every opportunity. When a
Western Republicans' Conference was held in Albuquerque in
November, he was there, telling the faithful how much
progress already had been made in healing old wounds. The
party, he proclaimed, would win at least thirty House seats in
1966—a massive comeback by any yardstick. Apparently satisfied
that his 1964 service in the Goldwater campaign, and Barry's
subsequent ringing endorsements, had secured his conservative
position, Nixon felt confident enough to underline his "centrist" posture even in a conservative section of the nation. He
criticized the John Birch Society as an extremist fringe, telling
the conference that "we have repudiated our radical right."
Thus, by inference, he painted the bulk of Republican conservatism as moderate and centrist itself. At the same time, he
defined the political enemy in terms the most ultraconservative
Republicans gladly embraced. The Democrats, he said, had a
much more serious problem dealing with their "radical left." In
other words, the responsible Republican Party had purged
itself, put its house in order, while the wild-eyes and revolutionaries who were bent on taking over the Democratic Party
remained at large.

Even to Deep South Republicans who had labored with
diligence and zeal in behalf of Barry Goldwater the year before,
the Nixon approach made sense. Though nowhere was Goldwater more revered or more effective than in the Deep South,
the folly of his candidacy was apparent there too. Typical of the
level-headed Dixie politicians who responded to the Nixon line
was Fred LaRue, a shrewd and unobtrusive party tactician who
was then the Republican national committeeman from Mississippi. He met Nixon for the first time at the Albuquerque
meeting and was marked down by the former Vice President as
a man who, in LaRue's own words later, "saw the pitfalls of
extreme ideology," and who therefore could be of use in the
Nixon plan.

That plan began to unfold in earnest almost immediately

with the approach of the Congressional election year of 1966. When Nixon intimates say, as they repeatedly do, that there was no long-range, cold-blooded Nixon "plan" to gain the Presidency, they cannot be refuted with documentary evidence, for there is no detailed battle strategy under lock and key somewhere. In a community of political sophisticates, it was not necessary to put in writing the possibilities and implications growing out of a Republican resurgence captained by Richard Nixon.

Maurice Stans, the aristocratic banker and prime Nixon fundraiser of 1968 who later became his Secretary of Commerce, recalls how he got the message. About five couples, including the Nixons and the Stans, attended the New York World's Fair one Sunday. "We made reservations at four or five of the principal exhibits," he said later, "and we planned to have dinner later at the fair. When we got there, the first exhibit we visited was the Johnson's Wax pavilion. We never got to any other. Dick was mobbed. He must have given a thousand autographs. There was a tremendous reaction to him. He had more charisma than anyone ever gave him credit for. That was my tip-off that he still had a political future—the awakening as far as I was concerned. From then on, I took every opportunity to help him."

Others who had experienced the "awakening" reacted similarly, and in Nixon they found a cooperative recipient of their assistance. He never told them in late 1965, his associates all insist, that he had his eye on the Presidency once again. He didn't have to. They realized the difficulties as well as he did, and the validity of his guiding philosophy of the time—that party revival in 1966 had to be the first priority; that until it was achieved, Presidential jockeying could only be destructive to the party and to the potential candidate who practiced it at the expense of party unity. If Richard Nixon was to come back, he would have to continue to demonstrate he was a party builder. What his friends could give him were the necessary building blocks, and this they set out to do.

6

Architect of Party Recovery

ONE night in the fall of 1965, Richard Nixon was in Belleville, Illinois, about twenty miles southeast across the Mississippi from St. Louis, at a cocktail party prior to a routine speaking engagement. Among the guests was a tall, husky twenty-eight-year-old editorial writer for the St. Louis *Globe-Democrat* named Patrick J. Buchanan, a serious student of conservative political philosophy. Young Buchanan, who as a Georgetown University student once had caddied for Nixon at Burning Tree Country Club, had an intensity about him that at first exposure was camouflaged by an easy and smiling manner. But this intensity was pushing Buchanan increasingly toward direct political involvement. At an opportune moment, he walked up to the former Vice President, introduced himself and said straight out that if Nixon was going to run in 1968, he wanted to get aboard early.

Nixon told Buchanan he could not say what he would do in 1968. But he needed somebody to help him in 1966, when he would be campaigning heavily in support of Congressional candidates. He asked Buchanan what he was doing. The young man described his duties as an editorial writer—heavy research and the sifting out of opposing points of view. These were just the services Nixon also required if he were to campaign in an informed and effective manner in 1966. He discussed Buchanan with his boss, publisher Richard Amberg, an old friend, and invited the young man to come to see him at his law firm in New York. In mid-January, 1966, Buchanan and Nixon talked for three hours at 20 Broad Street and Buchanan was hired—the first full-time recruit in an efficient political army that in the next three years would help Nixon march all the way to the White House. Nixon called Amberg in St. Louis and arranged for a one-year leave of absence for Buchanan. The young conservative intellectual never went back to his old job, and after Nixon's election in 1968 became a special assistant to the President.

The hiring of Buchanan was the first clearly visible evidence of a careful program that originally started not specifically to ready Nixon for another Presidential bid in 1968, but to help implement his immediate strategy of party recovery. Peter Flanigan, the New York broker who headed the 1960 Volunteers for Nixon-Lodge and was an officer at The Recess, Nixon's downtown lunch club, was the prime mover, along with Maurice Stans. They and a few other Republicans met and worked out a fund-raising program geared to assist the most promising GOP candidates for Congress. Nixon, who already had held discussions with another good friend, Congressman Bob Wilson of California, chairman of the Republican Congressional campaign committee, was to be the field general, selecting many of the target districts and going into them personally. Three separate fund-raising committees were formed: "Congress '66," "The Committee for the Election of Republican Candidates" and "The Committee for the Loyal Opposition."*

As Nixon's intimates describe the situation, the man in these days moved in the same atmosphere experienced by a baseball pitcher with a no-hitter going. Nobody, they say, ever mentioned to him the possibility that a Nixon-led success in the

---

* Fat-cat contributors, according to an Evans-Novak report, had a definitely conservative tinge: old Nixon friend Elmer Bobst ($5,000) ; Henry Salvatori of Los Angeles ($2,000) ; oilmen Gordon Reed ($2,000) and John G. Pew ($2,000) ; Jeremiah Millbank, Sr., a Draft-Goldwater founder ($5,000) ; DeWitt and Lila Wallace of *Reader's Digest* ($8,500) ; Milwaukee industrialist Walter Harnischfeger ($1,000) .

1966 Congressional elections could produce a Nixon Presidential candidacy in 1968, nor did he ever suggest it right out to them. But they all could read the scoreboard, and if they didn't realize when they first got together what was building politically for Nixon, the unspoken message soon began to come through. Buchanan said later, of his own decision to join Nixon, that he did not leave St. Louis with any commitment beyond that one year or any assurance that Nixon would run in 1968. But he was convinced Nixon was moving down that track and if everything fell into place, he would go.

The Flanigan-Stans group eventually raised $60,000 to finance Nixon's political activities in 1966, and to that was added $30,000 from Wilson's group. In these days of extremely expensive jet travel, it was not quite a treasure chest, but it did keep Nixon on the road, covering 30,000 miles and 86 Congressional districts in 35 states before November. Buchanan was his only full-time paid political assistant, but a network of about thirty "Nixon men" who had worked for him around the country over the years was ready to help again. Without the glamor and mythology associated with the "Kennedy men" who stood waiting for another call to political arms, the Nixon loyalists were just as strategically placed in their own party and, if not as numerous or colorful, just as efficient in advancing trips, arranging "spontaneous" welcomes and otherwise smoothing the way from one stop to the next. Nixon, in fact, brought his advance men to New York before the 1966 campaign to attend an informal school on advancing techniques. The list included many young men who later were to have staff positions in the Nixon administration—John Ehrlichman, John Whitaker, Nick Ruwe, Roy Goodearle, Ed Morgan, Dale Grubb, Dwight Chapin; Nixon's old political adviser, Charlie McWhorter, also pitched in, as he had done in every previous campaign effort since Nixon's days as Vice President.

If there was one commodity above all others that Nixon peddled from start to finish in 1966, it was confidence. In the past, his political crystal ball often had been fogged over by an excess of Republican zeal, but if Democrats ridiculed or despised him for it, Republicans liked to hear it, and needed to hear it more than ever now. Almost from the beginning of the year, Nixon exposed himself as a target by predicting a Republican comeback of record proportions in November. On the Lincoln Day circuit in early February, he told Republicans at a fund-raiser in Washington that he expected the party to recapture forty seats in the House of Representatives, four in the Senate, five or six governorships and six to seven hundred state legislative seats. All year he stuck to this prediction, though to many other politicians and pundits it seemed a pipe dream, just two years after Barry Goldwater had pulled the party over the abyss.

Actually, it took no crystal ball to foresee that the 1964 Goldwater candidacy had been an unnatural political phenomenon from which the Republican Party was bound to make some recovery two years later. For one thing, the party of a President traditionally suffers setbacks in Congress in off-year elections. For another, many of the Congressional losses in 1964 were in districts long considered safe for local Republican candidates. There could be no other rational explanation for these Congressional defeats than the presence of Goldwater at the head of the ticket. Also, Lyndon Johnson in 1964 still was operating under the sympathetic cover of the John Kennedy era, as its regent-protector against the trigger-happy Dr. Strangelove from Arizona. Now, after the first year of his own elected Presidency, "the real Lyndon Johnson" had begun to stand up; criticism of his conduct of the Vietnam War had begun to mount, especially within his own party, and he—not Goldwater—was becoming the whipping boy. Nixon proceeded in 1966 to focus on all these points—areas of likely Republican recovery, Johnson's increased vulnerability, and Vietnam dissension in the Democratic ranks—to help fashion the GOP's rehabilitation. Appearing on ABC's *Issues and Answers,* Nixon set the pattern for his year's activity. While Republicans would continue to support the President on the war, he said in the old familiar heavy-handed style, they would make a political issue of those Democrats "who have taken the soft line, the appeasement line." He did not identify the "appeasers" by name on the show, other than calling them those "well-intentioned but mistaken" Democrats who advocated such ideas

125

as a retreat to coastal enclaves in South Vietnam and indefinite suspension of air attacks against North Vietnam (policies later followed by Nixon himself as President) .

For part of his Lincoln Day speechmaking swing, Nixon's fund-raising friends chartered a nine-seat Lockheed Jetstar (the same plane in which James Bond was taken prisoner by villainess Pussy Galore in the movie *Goldfinger*) . En route from Seattle to the East Coast, Nixon laid out his strategy in modest terms to reporter David S. Broder, then of the New York *Times*. "I know that nobody gets anybody else elected," he said. "What I can do is get the candidate exposed to a bigger audience, get him on television and raise some money for his campaign."

Nixon seemed remarkably free of self-deception as he analyzed his own position as a unifier. "I can get the different factions to sit down together," he said. "I know the liberal fringe and the conservative fringe have no use for me, but they tolerate me, where they don't tolerate others." Nixon's word for the liberal and conservative wings—*fringe*—was a nice touch; it casually minimized the two wings and inferentially cast the Republican Party as a great middle ground—a party of "centrists," to use another of his favorite self-descriptive labels. And who was the greatest centrist of them all? Richard Nixon, of course.

As one way to remind Republicans, and voters generally, that he spoke for the party now that Goldwater had been rejected at the polls, Nixon in March began to write a monthly newspaper column, to be syndicated through the remaining nine months of 1966 by the North American Newspaper Alliance. Most of the research and much of the writing were done by Buchanan. The first column set the tone Nixon would follow throughout—hard, partisan campaigning in print: "Johnson inflation will be the major domestic issue of the 1966 congressional campaign. The President's deceptive guns-and-butter budget, which just a month ago was hailed as a political masterpiece, has turned out to be his first major political blunder. . . . As prices and taxes rise, administration spokesmen will try to blame labor for demanding higher wages, they will try to blame business for asking for higher prices, they will try to blame the war in

Vietnam. There is only one place to put the blame—the budget-brinkmanship of the Johnson Administration."

As readers digested such hard-hitting observations, Nixon was on the move through March and April—Montana, Arizona, California, Ohio, Louisiana, Texas, Mississippi, Alaska; his law business still needed and got attention, but it was the political season now and Nixon was in his element. He always seemed to Buchanan to be more concerned with what his political aide was doing than in the business of the law firm. Buchanan was trying to keep track of what Nixon called the political intelligence, and Nixon always was most interested in that. He told Buchanan once that if he had to practice law and nothing else he would be mentally dead in two years and physically dead in four.

There was, however, law work to do. Among the clients who had business with the firm that spring was a man named James J. Hill, who had won a $30,000 judgment from Time Incorporated in 1963 on a New York court's finding that his family's privacy had been invaded by a 1953 picture story in *Life* about the play *The Desperate Hours*. In the play, three escaped convicts take over a suburban home and hold its occupants in captivity. The playwright's files were found to include news reports of a similar invasion of the Hill family home in a Philadelphia suburb in 1952. The play itself describes incidents of violence and abuse to the family that the Hills testified never had happened in the actual episode. The Hills since had moved to Connecticut ostensibly to escape publicity, and had turned down offers to sell their story. During the play's Philadelphia tryout, a *Life* team visited the old Hill residence and took pictures of the play's cast in the house. The resulting article, Hill argued, defeated his efforts to avoid publicity and in fact had invaded his family's privacy.

When Time Incorporated moved in 1966 to appeal the $30,000 judgment before the U.S. Supreme Court, Nixon decided to handle the case. He had not actually presented a major case in court since joining Nixon Mudge, but that in itself was not unusual; senior partners were supposed to be responsible for major policy-making and for attracting new business. A prime reason he elected to take this one, according to one member of the firm, was the Genovese case. In the academic community, and in the law firm and the liberal New York legal fraternity as well, that case had left a cloud hanging over Nixon's views on individual freedom. *The Desperate Hours* case offered an ideal opportunity to dispel the cloud in a forum certain to receive national attention; the case came at the time the University of Rochester faculty and student body were demanding that Nixon be denied an honorary degree because of his position against Genovese. Additionally, the Hill case involved an effort to put legal limits on freedom of the press and to underline the press' responsibility toward the rights of the individual—an area of personal interest to Nixon made abundantly clear in his 1962 "last press conference."

Nixon's first appearance before the Court in late April was pronounced a triumph by nearly all observers. He informed his old California political foe, Chief Justice Earl Warren, that he had prepared for the case by reviewing sixty years of New York decisions in the area of invasion of privacy, and no one present had reason to doubt it. Throughout the two-hour hearing, Nixon conducted himself with confident reserve, eschewing his haranguing campaign style for courtroom decorum, yet displaying that same orderly marshaling of logic that increasingly marked his long, textless political speeches.

Life had erred, Nixon told the Court, in suggesting to its readers that it was presenting a reenactment of actual events that had occurred to the Hill family. If the *Life* appeal were upheld, he said, it would "give license—not to *Life,* but to every scandal sheet in the country—to lie about individuals for the purposes of trade." (Nixon usually was careful, in accusing the press of any wrongdoing, to exclude the present company. This I'm-not-talking-about-you-fellows-but-about-some-of-the-others approach always amused those reporters who had heard it more than once.) *Life* in turn defended the story as being within the protection of the First Amendment guarantee of freedom of the press. In spite of Nixon's solid performance, the case was held over for further argument in the fall. His law partners, however, were greatly impressed by Nixon's energy and thoroughness in preparing, briefing and arguing the case; the effort was worthwhile not only in terms of favorable publicity around the country, but also in shoring up his position at Nixon Mudge and in the New York legal community. Immediately on his return to New York the same night, Nixon took a dictaphone and unburdened himself of a long self-analysis of his presentation to the Court, noting where and how he could have improved upon it. Then he had the analysis transcribed and sent to his law associate and friend Len Garment for comment.

(In October, after another day and a half before the Supreme Court—in preparation for which he broke off campaigning for two weeks—Nixon lost the case. By a 5–4 vote, the Court held that the First Amendment gave the press immunity against such invasion-of-privacy suits. Associate Justice Abe Fortas, dissenting, urged Hill to seek a new trial, arguing that "if he can stand the emotional and financial burden, there is reason to hope that he will recover damages for the reckless and irresponsible assault upon himself and his family which this article represents." Nixon announced he would have the case retried, but eventually the Hill family and Time Incorporated reached an out-of-court settlement.)

For all his diligence in the Hill case, politics clearly was Nixon's main concern in 1966. He spent a great deal of his speechmaking time that spring in the South, cultivating the growing Republican Party there, still largely in the hands of the men who had worked for Goldwater in 1963 and 1964 and had won the only electoral college victories for him outside his native Arizona. Although Dixie Republicans had little leverage in Congress, and the specter of a 1968 Presidential bid by Alabama's George Wallace hung over the party's hopes of carrying even those five Deep South states again, the Southern bloc was crucial in GOP convention politics for 1968. The eleven Confederate states together, their delegations swelled by a bonus given to those states that went Republican in 1964, would constitute nearly half the total of delegates (667) needed for nomination. For all his emphasis on "centrist" politics, Nixon did not neglect the ultraconservative South in his gritty determination to remain a party leader. His middle-road approach was not lost on the more astute Dixie politicians. One of them, after listening to George Romney lecture a stilled and obviously resentful Atlanta Rotary Club on civil rights in 1967, was heard to say to another: "This fellow really means it. Dick Nixon comes down South and talks hard on civil rights, but you know he *has* to say what he does, for the Northern press."

Nixon provided a good example of the style that led to this observation on a trip to Jackson, Mississippi, in May, 1966. In town to speak at a party fund-raiser, he told reporters there was "no future in the race issue" for either party in the South anymore, and when asked about charges from liberal Northern Republicans that he was raising money for "segregationist candidates," Nixon replied: "I will go to any state in the country and campaign for a strong two-party system, whether or not I agree with the local Republicans on every issue." As for a segregationist plank in the Mississippi party platform, he said: "I am opposed to any so-called segregationist plank in a Republican platform. I would fight it in the national Republican platform and speak against it in any state I appear in." But then he went on to say what the Southern Republicans really wanted to hear—that he would limit his "fight" to words and let the state parties do what they chose. Recommendations that the Republican National Committee require state parties to repeal "without delay" any segregationist clauses in their state platforms, he said, were "unrealistic and unwise." The national party, he went on, should voice its own support for civil rights and then attempt to persuade state parties to go along. But, he said pointedly, "it cannot dictate to them." At the party dinner —attended by half a dozen blacks for the first time in local memory—Nixon was applauded when he urged both parties to stop campaigning on the subject of race and to turn to "issues of the future."

On the basis of the Jackson performance, Nixon legitimately could go North and say he had expressed his support for civil rights in the South as well as the North. But in so doing, he had made certain he remained in Southern eyes a man who understood the South's "special problem" and who would not jam Yankee solutions and Yankee impatience down Dixie throats.*

* As President in 1969 and 1970 Nixon further cemented that image with foot-dragging policies on school desegregation, nomination of Southern Judges Clement F. Haynsworth, Jr., and G. Harrold Carswell to the Supreme Court and a transparently specious charge that the U.S. Senate was anti-South for rejecting them.

Contrast his words in Jackson with his newspaper column released nationally almost immediately thereafter: "Southern Republicans must not climb aboard the sinking ship of racial injustice. Any Republican victory that would come courting racists, black or white, would be a defeat for our future in the South and our party in the nation. It would be a battle won in a lost cause. The Democratic Party in the South has ridden to power for a century on an annual tide of racist oratory. . . . Republicans should adhere to the principles of the party of Lincoln. They should leave it to the George Wallaces and the Lister Hills to squeeze the last ounces of political juice from the rotting fruit of racial injustice."

At that very time, George Wallace was indeed squeezing away, in an exercise that was to have a critical impact on Nixon's own future. Repulsed by the Alabama legislature in his bid to change the state constitutional prohibition against a second consecutive term for governor, Wallace ran his ailing wife, Lurleen. With all the backwoodsy trappings and racist overtones of his own earlier campaigns, he steamrollered her through the Democratic primary and over the political body of Republican James Martin, toward his own chair at the statehouse. While Mrs. Wallace would sit on the back of a flatbed truck, schoolgirlish in her blue blazer and white pleated skirt, a lifelike marionette with a how-many-times-have-I-heard-this look on her face, George would tell "the folks" that Lurleen's election was vital if "the movement" he had started in Alabama was to spread across the country. "I'm gonna be in a position," he would tell them, "to travel the length and breadth of this nation. I enjoy bein' on national TV and lookin' all them slick-haired boys in the face." And after George would finish describing the men who were running things from their high places in Washington, no right-thinking Alabamian could have any doubt that Wallace's "movement" represented the last best hope for America:

"Now you take a big sack and you put LBJ in there, and you put Hubert Horatio Alger Humphrey in there, and you put Bobby Kennedy the blood-giver in there, and you shake 'em all up. Then you put this Richard Milhous Nixon who with Eisenhower put bayonets in the back of the people of Little

Rock and in your backs, and you put in Earl Warren, who doesn't have enough legal brains in his head to try a chicken thief in my home county, and you shake 'em all up. And then you put in that socialist Nelson Rockefeller from the most liberal state in the country, and that left-winger George Romney who was out in the streets with the demonstrators, and that Clifford Case of New Jersey, and that Wild Bill Scranton of Pennsylvania, and that radical Jacob Javits of New York, and you shake 'em all up. Then you turn that sack over, and the first one that falls out, you pick him up by the nape of the neck and drop him right back in again, because there's not a dime's worth of difference in any of 'em, national Democrats or national Republicans."

The speech, in Alabama, was a guaranteed bell ringer, but it lacked the sophistication required for use in a nationwide campaign. At least that was the hope of the Nixon strategists. Voters across the country might be amused by George Wallace, but they expected much more in their Presidents than carnival humor. They expected substance, or at least the appearance of substance, and Richard Nixon could give them that. They wanted a man for all of the country, not just one section, and Richard Nixon knew how to project himself thus, while still demonstrating an appreciation of regional concerns.

Nixon at this time already was displaying his talents as the all-purpose, all-region campaigner in a steady stream of party-mending, treasury-replenishing trips to every corner of the land. But because he had been a two-time loser, his missions were getting very little national publicity, and it was possible for a political reporter to cover him and be the only member of the press along. I had not seen Nixon performing at close range for some time, so one week in late June I went along on a swing through the Midwest, Southwest and South that was a revelation. The stops along the way were typical of those Nixon was making all year under the cloak of his own supposed political extinction. There were no defensive entourages around him of the kind that later would seal him off as a candidate; only the very considerable defenses of the man himself, and one volunteer aide, usually former Congressman Pat Hillings, a jovial Irishman who had succeeded Nixon in his California house seat and now was Ford's West Coast representative. The very ordinariness of the trip provided an ideal opportunity to observe close-up the performing Nixon—not only as a political tactician but as the extremely well-compensated introvert he was. Looking over his shoulder for nearly a week, what I saw was the "new, new Nixon" about whom the political world already was whispering—mostly, at the time though, in jest and skepticism.

I joined Nixon in Detroit on a Sunday night at the Sheraton-Cadillac Hotel. On my way to see Pat Buchanan, who was accompanying his boss, I encountered Nixon as I got off the elevator. He was waiting for a down car, and as I approached he nodded noncommittally. But when it was clear I was going to make a full introduction of it, he smiled, shook hands and began at once to explain what he was doing there. "I just got in from the airport. I've just met with five or six of the boys—from what you would call the Establishment . . ." He seemed somehow obliged to account for his whereabouts. He was alert, defensive, but friendly; we discussed the travel schedule ahead, then parted, with Nixon promising that we would have a talk one night before the trip was over.

From that first brief beginning—cordial enough once I had intentionally capitalized on the chance encounter, yet sufficiently stilted to reveal a wariness on Nixon's part—a most curious relationship ensued. For the next five days, I accompanied Nixon several thousand miles by private plane and private car, often with only one other person in our presence. In all that time, until the last two hours when we finally talked at length, little passed between us beyond routine greetings at morning and evening and occasional small talk of a sentence or two on the run. I sat in at breakfast, lunch and dinner meetings at which he spoke, press conferences at every stop, and listened in on hurried conversations with local politicians on swift drives from airport to downtown hotel and back again. On flights in small private planes, I would sit just behind him as he filled the dead minutes and hours by retooling a speech on his ever-present yellow legal pad or by reading the sports pages of the local paper. Through it all, I would observe Nixon from time to time catching a glimpse of me, then looking quickly away, to our mutual embarrassment.

133

Sometimes, as he was standing shaking the hands of hundreds of well-wishers in a receiving line, I would post myself close enough to listen to what they had to say, and Nixon, having once noted my location, would not look that way again. Each night, after the last engagement, he would go directly to his room, usually at about ten or eleven o'clock, and I would retreat to the hotel bar for relaxed conversation with one of the volunteer aides traveling with him. He campaigned like an athlete in training; but one had the strong impression he lived a disciplined day not only to save his stamina but to preserve his privacy. At times it suddenly struck me that this man never seemed, even in a crowded room, to really be *with* anybody— and that he much preferred it that way.

In Detroit that first day, a morning press conference had been arranged at Cobo Hall by Nick Ruwe, the good-natured local broker who had been an advance man in 1960 and Nixon's personal aide in California in 1962. As photographers and television cameramen set up their equipment, reporters rehearsed gag questions like, "Mr. Nixon, are you going to run forever?" and other irreverent observations about the horse who had been around the track once too often. But the moment he entered the room the mood changed to one of mutual deference, slightly forced on both sides.

"How are you?" Nixon asked, smiling, breaking into an exaggerated grin, eyebrows way up in surprise at a familiar face, shaking hands with reporters in the first row who clearly hadn't expected the cordiality. "I'm sorry I held you up. I understand we had a camera crew late."

"Well," said one Detroit reporter, "we're all here now."

"It wasn't my fault," Nixon added, still smiling. (If Nixon had set down a book of rules, Rule One would have been: Don't offend the press.)

For the speech he was about to make before the 46th U.S. Junior Chamber of Commerce Convention, Nixon apologized and said: "You'll have to cover me live. I'm not equipped with staff for texts." Then he proceeded to tell the newsmen what he would be saying. (Rule Two: Make it easy for the press.) For one thing, he said, he would be commenting on difficulties Vice President Hubert H. Humphrey currently was having with his old liberal friends for standing by the Johnson administration for intervening in the Dominican Republic in 1965 and for stepping up the war in Vietnam. Some Democrats might criticize Humphrey, he said, but "history will be kinder" to him than his contemporaries because "the first responsibility of a Vice President is to carry out the policies of the President." (Rule Three: Be fair.) In a later interview, Nixon explained why this kind of praise for the opposition was a useful tactic. Talking about Republican women, he told me: "They're great workers, but they're idealists and emotionalists. They're the real haters. Any Machiavellian scheme, they go for. They die hard. They tell me, 'You didn't hit them hard enough. Why don't you give them hell like Truman?' I explain I not only have to appeal to partisan Republicans but also have to get Democrats to cross over. But the women don't understand that. Occasionally I say a good word for Johnson or Humphrey. *It's a device, of course, to show I'm fair-minded,* but the women don't see that. That's why the women liked Barry so. He didn't give a damn about Democrats. But to win, you have to."

Predictably, many of the press-conference questions went beyond the approaching Congressional elections. Nixon turned them all aside with a smile and a recitation of his determination not to discuss Presidential politics and individuals until after the party rehabilitation job was completed in November. (Rule Four: Be a unifying force.) "You can't make up the winter book on the Presidency until you get past the 1966 elections," said sports fan Nixon. And when the local reporters pressed him, he grinned gaily again and told them: "I must say you gentlemen are persistent and organized, but I've had them [the questions] all before, so there's no way you can get me off this position."

Nor would he discuss his own future as a Presidential prospect. (Rule Five: Be selfless.) Well, not directly, anyway. *Q:* Did he anticipate that his California defeat in 1962 would come back to haunt him? *A:* "Again we get back to 1968—in a very subtle way, I must admit. . . . A man has to live with his victories and defeats, and I'm no exception." *Q:* Would that "last press conference" be damaging? *A:* "Only history will tell." That remark didn't sound like it came from a man whose

135

political career was ready for history's judgment. But repeatedly Nixon emphasized he was doing his party's work, not his own. He had no political staff, he assured the reporters, and besides, "if I were concerned only about '68, why would I be making three fund-raising speeches in Michigan today?" Nobody offered an answer. But it wasn't because some of those listening didn't have a suspicion.

Out on the speakers' platform in the hall, Nixon followed Romney, who had delivered one of his patented inspirational sermons, full of generalities and appeals to individuals to do for others so that the government would not have to do unto them. The contrast was immediate and devastating. Employing a catechismal style, full of rhetorical questions and answers, repeating the questions, Nixon spoke for twenty-eight minutes without a note. (Rule Six: Be the voice of experience and self-confidence.) He moved easily from introductory humor to the planned praise of Humphrey, to a step-by-step review of American involvement in Vietnam and why it was necessary, to an attack on Democratic critics of the war, to excessive power in Washington, to giveaway government, to the need for decentralization, to the power of local action, to the strength of the Jaycees. "I know it's fashionable to sneer and look down on American service clubs with their lunches and all," he concluded, "but America needs more of them." Standing ovation, followed by recitation of the Jaycee creed as Nixon stood smiling but respectful.

It was an instant education for any Nixon-doubter. For all his obviousness, for all his forced gaiety, for all his apple-pie Americanism, he entertained these people, held their attention and, finally, roused them. He laughed at himself; he hit hard, but now his partisanship seemed tempered and fair; he dealt in facts, recited with supreme confidence and personal assurance; he was the man who had been there, whether the subject was foreign policy or coping with the Washington bureaucracy. Michigan was George Romney's home state, but had a two-man election been held at that precise moment in that hall, it would have been curtains for the governor.

Thanking the Jaycee president for an introduction that included references to his education, Nixon noted that one fact

had been omitted. "I was a dropout from the electoral college."
Laughter and applause. Then, pointing to a battery of photographers at work in front of him: "I want to be sure these people
get their pictures. . . . I've had trouble with pictures." Pause.
"I've had trouble with television too." A big grin, triggering
more laughter and applause. "A little girl came up to me on the
street in New York the other day with a copy of *Newsweek*
opened to a picture of me, and asked me to autograph it. I did,
and then she said, 'Mr. Nixon, that's a wonderful picture. . . .
It doesn't look at all like you.' " Another open grin, head back,
eyes wide, as the audience roared. Then a quick review of all his
travels. "I got stoned in Caracas. I'll tell you one thing, it's a lot
different from getting stoned at a Jaycee convention." Bedlam.

Then it was time to be serious. "Never has America been less
selfish than in Vietnam, let's get that one straight. . . . Why is
the United States in Vietnam? We are there because they
requested us to come in. . . . What are our goals in Vietnam?
Let us be sure we know what our goals are not . . . they are
not bases . . . our goal is to prevent the conquest of South
Vietnam. We believe this is a war that had to be fought to
prevent World War III. . . . What options do we have to
end the war? . . . What do we find? We find this is the first
war in which the party in power is not united, in which dissident Democrats—*and I say it in no partisan sense*—say we should
make whatever concessions are necessary to end the war, pay
whatever price is necessary to get out of it. Why must we reject
this thinking? I'll tell you why we have to reject it. We have to
reject it because peace at any price is always an installment
payment on a bigger war. If the United States makes the
mistake of peace at any price, it would forever destroy the
credibility of the United States. I recently asked Foreign Minister Thanat of Thailand what would happen if such a peace
were made, and he said to me, 'Mr. Nixon, no free Asian nation
will ever believe you again.' If we reward aggression it will lead
to a bigger war in three, four or five years. . . . It is a great
mistake to commit hundreds of thousands of American boys in
the bottomless pit of a ground war in Asia. We should not be
committed to fight their war, we should fight our war. . . ."

It went on like that—crisp, simplified, full of slogans that

137

were proven applause-winners. In addition to the seminar on Vietnam, the standard speech made five basic political points: a tide was sweeping nationally that in November would bring Republicans the greatest victories in twenty years; Republican unity and good candidates, coupled with the Democratic dissension, was the reason; only if the party was rebuilt in 1966 would its Presidential candidate have any chance in 1968; Johnson would be a drag rather than a help to Democratic candidates in 1966; the country had to vote Republican to preserve a strong two-party system.

Before the overwhelmingly white audience there would be no discussion of that major problem faced by the Republican Party—how to woo back black voters after the Goldwater desertion of even the relatively few who had voted Republican. A single line in the standard speech—"We say it is the responsibility of government to guarantee to everyone an equal place at the starting line"—disposed of the issue. Here in Detroit, Barry Goldwater was not mentioned; later, in Tulsa and Birmingham, Nixon lauded him and brought the crowd to its feet.

The standard speech concluded with an old party refrain—the eroding effect of big, centralized government on individual rights and local initiative. Nixon would warn of the day not too far off when a majority of Americans would have their rent subsidized, their medical bills paid, their income assured and their education determined by the federal government. Only the election of Republicans to Congress could prevent such a catastrophe.

Over the next several days, Nixon repeated the standard speech dozens of times, with only slight variations. That Nixon could make the same dull speech repeatedly, summoning up an appearance of enthusiasm and vigor each time, was a tribute to his dedication. And he *knew* it was a bore the second or third time around. "I don't see how you can listen to that speech of mine day after day," he once told a reporter traveling with him. "I'd go up the wall, myself." At large Republican fund-raisers it came in the context of an unabashed pep rally; at smaller, more exclusive affairs there was more emphasis on the personal humor, on the voice of national and global experience confiding in his special audience. Whatever the forum, it was clear that he was a hit.

"Some people say I oversimplify," he told me later when I asked him about his speaking style. "Well, that's the way I am. . . . I ask questions to wake up the guy in the audience. People come up to me and say, 'This is the first time I've understood Vietnam.' It's not that I say anything nobody else has said. I don't. It's the Socratic approach. I didn't invent it. But it drives the intellectuals nuts. They're supercilious. They say, 'If only he'd speak so *we* could understand.' What arrogance. . . . The worst sin is to be dull. That's the trouble with the intellectuals. They have no warmth when it comes to being interested in people. The reason I don't use a text is because I want to establish rapport with the little guy in the audience. That's the secret: not being too contrived, not practicing in front of a mirror beforehand, not writing every word out. It means my speech sometimes is looser than I want, but it's worth it. It's making a mistake once in a while. But that's worth it too."

Yet he seldom made a mistake. He had the speech down pat, and he moved from one theme to another smoothly and unerringly, sensing the reaction of his audience as he went along, making adjustments in emphasis to accommodate whatever the reaction was. Between events, on the plane, he would examine files containing local political intelligence prepared for him by Buchanan, or talk with a local Republican leader, then sketch out the speech on a yellow legal pad in terms of the demands of the local situation. The same basic speech got this treatment over and over again during the tour; he would move the key sections around like parts of a jigsaw puzzle from one stop to another, but when the speech came out, he delivered it—always without a note before him—without a jagged edge showing. (One reason he was able to do this, Nixon told me later, was that he never drank before going on. "I may have one beer after speaking, but never before," he said. "When I'm campaigning, I live like a Spartan. I've always been that way. I know what I can do. I've seen a lot of people who drink. They get up there and talk too long. I speak without notes, and I can't do that without intense concentration before and during the speech.")

He was, without doubt, at his best on the formal platform, where he could—despite his insistence that he speaks to "the little guy in the audience"—address the public in a mass; where he always was in control, where he could ask himself the questions and then answer them, where he could provide the sense of intimacy he sought through the use of the political catechism he long ago had mastered: "You ask me, 'Mr. Nixon, why do we have to reject appeasement?' And I tell you, we have to reject appeasement because peace at any price is always a down payment on a bigger war." Nobody, it seemed, ever asked him a question without preceding it with "Mr. Nixon." That appeared to be so whether it was the man in the street or Haile Selassie. You were just likely after a while to get the impression his was a household name, not only in this country but around the world. Which wasn't too far wrong. The ease with which Nixon moved from domestic to foreign policy issues and back again—peppering the monologue with the names of world leaders who had said to him concerning this or that, "But, Mr. Nixon, what about . . ."—was impressive as both propaganda and technique. On the stump, he had become much more formidable than in 1960 and, if you had to put it negatively, as those who remembered the "old Nixon" still did, less offensive.

And while he was best at a distance and with a big crowd, he was effective too up close, though at times embarrassingly transparent and cloying. After his speech in Cobo Hall, a woman obviously in her thirties came up and handed him a paperback copy of *Six Crises* to autograph. As he signed it "Dick Nixon," she told him: "My first election I voted for you." He looked up at her, pulled his head back in disbelief and asked, "Were you old enough?" Thrilled to the core, the lady confessed that she was. And at an oldtimers' Jaycee reception afterward, he walked through the crowd, "remembering" greeters who reminded him of what they had done for him in the 1952 campaign, or 1956 or 1960. When one came up wearing a large I'M FOR NIXON button from an old campaign, Nixon gave him the wide-eyed, incredulous look and asked, "Well, *where* did you get *that?*"—as if it were a one-of-a-kind relic from the Hayes-Tilden race.

Standing on a chair in the crowded private room filled with past leaders of the Jaycees, Nixon was relaxed and charming.

"Except for the women in the room, I'm probably the only one here who never made President." Pause. "The Vice Presidency's a pretty good office." Another pause. "I'm not knocking anything." Laughter, grin, applause, wider grin.

Then Nixon told about the Arkansas preacher who needed money for his church: "Well, the preacher looked out over the congregation and he said, 'Brothers, this church gotta walk.' And the response came back from the amen corner, 'Amen, preacher, this church gotta walk.' And then the preacher said, 'Brothers, this church gotta run.' And again the response came back, 'This church gotta run.' And then the preacher said, 'Brothers, this church gotta fly.' And it came back, 'This church gotta fly.' Then the preacher said, 'Brothers, it takes money to fly.' And the response came back, 'Let's walk, brothers.' " Shouting over the laughter, Nixon added the political punchline: "This year, we gotta fly!"

At other stops, this kind of cornball approach clearly was out of order. Leaving Cobo Hall, Nixon went to the exclusive, crotchety Detroit Club, where he lunched in private with thirty-three big Republican contributors. They greeted him like an old friend, and he knew his way around the club like a member, shaking hands with crusty octogenarians, inquiring about their families and businesses and throwing in a quick boost for the Grand Old Party.

From Detroit, he motored to Flint, arriving shortly before four o'clock. Nixon was to confer with Donald W. Riegle, Jr., one of the new young-breed Republican candidates for Congress who won that November, and then was to hold a press conference. When the car pulled up to a Howard Johnson Motel, Nixon asked Hillings to get out his electric razor. Hillings couldn't find it, so Nixon went inside the motel and his aide drove over to a nearby shopping center to buy one. He was unsuccessful, but to everyone's relief Nixon's razor was found after all. On a Nixon tour, the razor was vital equipment. He shaved two or three times a day and applied a shave-stick whenever possible before going on television, rather than pancake makeup, which gave his face a clammy look and accentuated his already prominent jowls. At every stop, neatness definitely counted.

Inside the motel, Nixon met with some more Republican contributors, predicted Riegle's victory to reporters and gave the young candidate a pep talk. "Beat 'em, now. Get going," Nixon told him, slapping Riegle on the back, playing the old coach unabashedly, then climbing into the car for the next stop, Bay City to the north. There, 400 guests who paid $100 each were waiting at the dingy Wenonah Hotel to have dinner with him. They lined the entrance as Nixon came in, and they applauded and reached out to shake his hand. He went up to his room, changed clothes and came out for another press conference. The local newsmen, including TV cameramen, had been waiting for some time, and he apologized. "I would have come right in, but I had to get shaved," he told them. The third shave of the day. Then he gave them the capsule of his speech and invited questions. Was there going to be a contest in 1968 between him and Governor Romney? "The obsession of the moment about the two names you mentioned is somewhat naïve," he told his questioner. Then, quickly, lest he offend and violate Rule One: *"Not on your part.* But the 1966 election will furnish the stable [of candidates]."

Local Republican candidates had crowded into the small room, ogling Nixon like tourists, so he cut the press conference short and waved them in, greeting them profusely, posing with each in turn for pictures. "Make these guys look good," he urged the photographers. "Don't worry about me." The locals loved it. Later, Hillings told me: "They keep coming over to me and saying, 'We're with him. We're ready to go. But is he running?' I tell them, 'What do *you* think?'"

After the standard speech at dinner, as Nixon was making his way from the hotel to catch a private flight, a local party official, agitated, came up. He explained how he had taken great pains to get a few Bay City black couples to attend, and how they had been shunted to the rear of the hall. Could they ride out to the airport with Nixon? Maybe that would smooth things over. There was a quick conference, then Nixon left. The functionary herded the blacks into another car and raced out to the airport with them. There, on the runway next to the plane, Nixon greeted them, chatted amiably for a few minutes and left. Thus was the open-door policy of the Republican Party in Bay City, Michigan, confirmed.

In Tulsa the next afternoon, Nixon went to the home of Republican Mayor James M. Hewgley, Jr., for a private cocktail party to which only major local contributors were invited. About twenty Cadillacs were parked on the front lawn when he arrived. John Thomas, a local oilman who footed the bill, stood on a chair on the broad patio and told the assembled: "This is real low pressure. We don't want anybody to give more than five thousand dollars—that's the limit. As you go in here you'll see some blank checkbooks. Just think now of what you want to give and then write it right out, while you still have a chance. You may not get the chance again." There were laughs all around, and none heartier than Nixon's. But sure enough, inside in the living room, perched casually on the back of a gold upholstered chair, was an open checkbook, and others similarly placed on the back of a long sofa!

Nixon spoke next, candidly referring to the guests as "the elite . . . part of a small group in the major cities around the country who keep the party going when things are at their toughest." As he spoke, Mrs. John Thomas whispered to me, obviously an outsider: "Everybody here is in oil. Tulsa is an oil town." The women particularly looked as though their husbands were "in oil"—many in their forties and older, but all tanned and well preserved; more and bigger diamond rings than I had seen in one place in years. Republican Governor Henry Bellmon was there—later to be a Nixon-for-President chairman—and the man running in 1966 to succeed him, Dewey Bartlett, a rank long shot who Nixon predicted would win, and did.

After a few more drinks and some hasty check-writing, the guests began to back their Cadillacs off the mayor's lawn and head for the ultramodern Tulsa Assembly Center. There 850 festive Republicans, paying $25 a plate for a nondescript dinner, roared a welcome to Nixon. Tulsa County party chairman Bert McElroy assured him that "Tulsa has been, is and will be again a Nixon city," to which the noncandidate merely smiled and waved. Then a long list of state and local officials paraded up to speak, and to bask in the political spotlight drawn by their guest. As they droned on, Nixon sat stiffly, looking a bit tired now, but being the attentive party soldier. Finally, Congressman Page Belcher rose to introduce him. After saying he was not going to recite Nixon's record, he proceeded to recall the Alger Hiss case, the Helen Gahagan Douglas race and the 1960 loss of the Presidency. Nixon smiled wanly at that reference, and struggled to do the same when Belcher next reminded the audience that Nixon didn't stop fighting after "his humiliating defeat in California" in 1962. Then Belcher went back to the 1952 "Checkers speech." "Here was a young man with his back to the wall. He literally set the Republican campaign on fire. This is the kind of man we should have at the helm . . ." Nixon's spirits lifted appreciably. "America faces a storm and I only regret we don't have this man at the helm. A few Republicans who didn't vote kept him from where he is needed now." The 850 faithful rose and gave Nixon a tremendous hand. He was, as the county chairman had noted, in friendly country, but even so, the reaction was startling. One would have thought he had just received the party's Presidential nomination—cheers and stamping and minute after minute of applause.

Here in conservative Oklahoma, the forgotten man could be mentioned. "Whether it was Barry Goldwater or Bud Wilkinson [who ran unsuccessfully for the U.S. Senate], Oklahoma Republicans in 1964 got out and fought when others didn't," Nixon reminded them. "I was proud to have been on the side of these men." After the disaster of 1964, he said, some Republicans "in New York and Washington" wanted to get out of the party, and some even defected to the Democrats (no names supplied). But the loyalists stuck, and now they would bring the party back. After the speech, a long line formed along the head table, and Nixon patiently stood and shook hands with everyone. "You must run," some of them told him, and he just smiled.

The next morning, the small Nixon party flew from Tulsa to Birmingham in a six-seat Lear Jet loaned to Nixon by Bill Lear, the World War II aviation electronics pioneer who built the planes. Nixon went over his speech notes and advance dope sheets on Birmingham, then read the sports pages of the Tulsa newspapers. At the Birmingham airport, he was met by the

Alabama Republican chairman, Alfred Goldthwaite; on the drive to town, Nixon pumped him about Republican prospects and difficulties in the state, and about the Democratic situation. Republican Congressman Martin, running for governor against Lurleen Wallace, wasn't given a prayer.

Nixon: "How do Wallace and Sparkman get along?"

Goldthwaite: "Wallace can't stand the sight of the man."

Nixon: "What kind of governor has Wallace been?"

Goldthwaite: "There's been some reports of chicanery, but nobody has gone out after him."

Nixon: "Alabama is a proud state. How in hell can the people vote for a woman who is going to be just a stand-in?"

Goldthwaite: "I was down in the Black Belt the other day, strong Wallace territory, and I asked a fellow in a store what he was going to do. 'I got to think about it,' he said. 'Well, you know it's not gonna be Jim Martin against George,' I told him, 'it's gonna be Jim against Lurleen.' 'Yeah,' he said. 'That's what I got to think about.'

Nixon: "How's Martin going to handle Lurleen?"

Goldthwaite: "So far, he's been saying Wallace will help LBJ if she's elected."

Nixon: "No, that's no good."

The car pulled up to the Parliament House, under a sign that said: WELCOME RICHARD NIXON, GLAD TO HAVE YOU BACK IN BIRMINGHAM. At a press conference inside, Nixon blandly told reporters there was a chance to elect Martin governor, and to pick up legislative seats because the tide was running against the national Democratic administration. He thumped hard for the development of the Southern Republican Party and said it "has been the subject of a great deal of maligning" on civil rights. Republicans in the North, he said, had come to know Southern Republicans as responsible men, and they did not have to agree on "the so-called civil rights issue" to work together, any more than Northern and Southern Democrats had to. Northern and Southern Republicans alike knew the party was being built "on the issues of the future rather than the issues of the past." The leaders of the New South in both parties faced problems crying out to be solved that had no relation to civil rights, "and they should have top priority." In a two-party

145

system, there must be room in both parties for liberals and conservatives. "The Democrats always got in bed with each other so they could always keep their noses in the trough," said the veteran phrasemaker. "Why not Republicans?"

As for the prospect of a third party in 1968 led by Wallace, Nixon was contemptuous. "Any American interested in implementing his ideas has to work through the existing parties. You can't do anything with a splinter. You have to be part of a board."

In coming into Alabama, Nixon since Goldwater's defeat had visited all eleven states of the old Confederacy. The reception in Birmingham, even more than in Tulsa, was overwhelming and left little doubt that Nixon already had a good lock on Dixie Republicans for 1968. There was interest in Reagan, but Reagan still had not won in California and the party pros did not know him the way they knew Nixon. Maybe Reagan would win and become a national prospect, but if not, Nixon looked fine to them, and what he said gave them no offense.

In Birmingham's Municipal Auditorium that night, 1,200 of the faithful showed up at $50 a plate for the largest fund-raising dinner in the short history of Alabama Republicanism. Nixon strode down the center aisle under a sweeping spotlight amid wild cheers, and Senate candidate John Grenier, a leading Goldwater organizer in Dixie in 1964, raised the pitch with his introduction. In 1960, he recalled, "Birmingham gave its heart and sixty percent of its votes" to Nixon, and if fate chose him in 1968 "to lead this country from the swampland of socialism to the bright sunshine of liberty . . . the electoral vote of Alabama will be cast for Dick Nixon."

The words set off rebel yells and stomping that was reminiscent of the Cow Palace in 1964. Here, clearly, was a place to pull out all the stops, and Nixon did not hesitate: "You'll notice as I came down the aisle I shook the hands on the right. It's hard for me to turn left. . . . Any Republican who believes LBJ is a conservative would believe Richard Burton married Elizabeth Taylor for her money. . . . The loyal opposition is needed. You show me a business without competition and I'll show you a second-rate product. . . . These Democrats who want peace at any price; let's call them the appeasement

146

Democrats for lack of a better term. . . . The bombing of North Vietnam is a case of too little and too late. If it had been done months ago, thousands of American boys wouldn't be dead today. . . . If you have conservative friends who are looking where to go, tell them to come to the Republican Party, because the Republican Party is the party of conservatives. The Democrat Party on the national level hasn't been conservative for thirty years and never will be, so get out of it and join the Republican Party."

The speech was an unqualified triumph. The audience surged around Nixon afterward, and he needed a police escort to get out of the hall. At another private reception later at the suburban home of a big Republican contributor, Nixon was elated. He had one drink, talked Republican resurgence for about an hour with his hosts, then returned to the hotel, tired but buoyant.

One of the knowledgeable Southern politicians who conferred with Nixon in Birmingham was Fred LaRue, the Mississippi national committeeman who had met Nixon in Albuquerque a year earlier. LaRue gave Nixon an optimistic report on his chances in the South; if Reagan did win in California, he would be the prime threat in Dixie, but not an insurmountable one. "Nixon's dilemma was that he had to win the nomination basically with the same forces Goldwater had in 1964," LaRue said later, "but without associating with them, or being associated." The candor of this remark from a man who himself was a Goldwater worker in 1964 underlined the coolness of the Nixon operation. Nixon agreed with LaRue about Reagan's being a threat in the South, but his victory in California was needed by Nixon as part of the party comeback image that would justify Nixon's own comeback.

Nixon left Birmingham about half an hour behind schedule the next morning because his one-man press corps misunderstood the departure time. As I raced to the airport in a taxi, he sat patiently in the jet, rejecting advice from others in the party to leave without me. When I finally climbed aboard, full of apologies, he smiled and waved me off, then changed the subject to save me further embarrassment. I was grateful and genuinely impressed by his courtesy and act of generosity (even when I

147

learned later he had told those aboard who wanted to leave me behind: "He's the only reporter we've got").

The final stop on the tour was Roanoke, Virginia, for a speech at the state Republican convention choosing Senatorial and lesser candidates for the fall campaign. A large crowd greeted him at the airport, led by Linwood Holton, the local lawyer for whom Nixon had labored so extensively in the 1965 gubernatorial campaign. At a press conference at the Roanoke Inn, the questions predictably focused again on Southern Republicanism. In Tulsa and Birmingham he had fielded similar ones, and by now he had honed his position finely, so that he could deliver it smoothly at the first query, tempering it somewhat because this was Virginia now, not Alabama, but remaining basically consistent. And at a candlelight dinner that night, he again was greeted with unbounded enthusiasm by a black-tie, more sophisticated crowd than in Tulsa or Birmingham. He responded with a more sophisticated version of the standard speech, giving the audience none of the raw meat he had thrown to the rebel-yellers in Alabama. Afterward, he conferred with Virginia leaders on the fall ticket, then drove to the airport for a flight to Washington.

Bill Lear's jet had returned to Tulsa, and waiting on the runway at the Roanoke field, looking like *The Spirit of St. Louis,* was a tired old Beechcraft, the only plane that could be chartered that night. John Whitaker, the Washington-area advance man who later became the President's appointments secretary, and Hillings were in the cabin. Nixon sat in the rear and I took a seat up front. After a rumbling, groaning takeoff, Hillings came forward and motioned me back. Nixon was relaxed and cordial now. He apologized profusely for not having had an occasion to talk with me earlier. Whitaker had arranged for a bottle of Scotch and some ice, and we all had a drink. The conditions were not ideal for conversation, because the old plane droned incessantly, but Nixon talked over the noise, openly, in a strong voice with no trace of weariness. He declined to discuss his political future, dwelling instead on the kind of man he saw himself to be right then, and how he had been affected by the turbulent events in his past.

The self-appraisal was remarkable. It clashed sharply with the stereotype of the man as a purely political tactician, an operator, a supersensitive product of the television age, a hater of the press. It was as though the Nixon that Nixon saw and the Nixon that the general public saw were two different men. It was either pure revelation or one of the great put-ons of the year:

"I wish I had more time to read and write. I'm known as an activist and an organizer, but some people have said I'm sort of an egghead in the Republican Party. I don't write as well as Stevenson, but I work at it. If I had my druthers, I'd like to write two or three books a year, go to one of the fine schools—Oxford, for instance—just teach, read and write. I'd like to do that better than what I'm doing now. I don't mean writing is easy for me, but writing phrases that move people, that to me is something. What memorable phrases have ever come from the Republican and Democratic national committees, or from speechwriters? My best efforts—my acceptance speech in 1960, my Moscow speech, my unity speech at the 1964 convention—all were dredged out by writing my head off. . . .

"The appeal of teaching or writing is in being able to take time to contemplate. Think of the great young leaders of the Jeffersonian era. They weren't out shaking hands, keeping airline schedules, meeting boards of directors. They had time to contemplate. Our greatest problem as a country is that we take our most competent people and keep them so busy doing things that others have to do their thinking for them. If we could find a way to take away the ceremonial trappings of the President it would be a great thing. That's why the Vice President must be constantly upgraded. The President should have the luxury of several days just to think—no Congressmen to see, no Senators to see. The danger today is that the American executive submits things to his highest advisers and then decides on the basis of what they tell him.

"In order to make a decision, an individual should sit on his rear end and dig into the books. Very few executives do it. They listen to this side and that, but they don't go to the sources. In this respect I'm like Stevenson. He was criticized as governor of Illinois because he always wanted to do his own work and research. Stevenson was a century late. He would have been more at home in the nineteenth century. He was an intellectual and he needed time to contemplate. [Linking himself to Stevenson certainly was an original thought—and one that doubtless would have appalled the bookish, erudite Illinoisan. Nixon in his Congressional, Communist-hunting days had been accused by liberals of practicing guilt by association; this time it was eggheadism by association.]

"Even many college presidents are primarily doers. They never do any thinking, they're so busy handling administrative chores. Men of superior ability are selected for top executive jobs and not used as they should be, in doing research and investigation, the hard thinking, the balancing of forces, in reaching a decision. In my own Supreme Court case, I read every case in the field to prepare for it. Some of my lawyer colleagues were surprised I took so much time. But I was complimented on being well prepared. That's why I seldom fall on my face in a press conference when an unusual question comes up. It's when a man doesn't do his own thinking that he gets into trouble."

As a self-described egghead and a man who yearned to write and lead the contemplative life, however, Nixon repeatedly expressed a low opinion of those who did—particularly those who also found time to put their oar into politics. Asked about Arthur Schlesinger, Jr.'s book on President Kennedy, in which Nixon came off badly, he said: "Frederick the First said that the surest way to destroy a state was to have it governed by professors. I don't know Schlesinger. He writes in an interesting fashion, but he's hardly objective. I don't fault him, because objective history is dull. Churchill wasn't objective. He put all his prejudices into his history of World War II, but that was what made it so interesting. When anyone sits down to write, he's going to be influenced by whether he's for or against his subject. . . .

"Many intellectuals have a double standard. If you happen to support their point of view you can be a drunk, a stupe, fall on your face in a press conference [the number of times he referred to the press conference as a standard of performance was noteworthy], and they will still back you. But if you take the unfashionable point of view, it doesn't matter to them how liberal it is; they're against you. In Rochester, when I spoke on academic freedom, I got letters from college people who thought it was a good speech, but none of the liberal press did. Some honest intellectuals admit it: they have a great difficulty in applying a single standard in evaluating public officials. If you're not one of them, anything you do will rile the living hell out of them. If you are, you can do no wrong."

Nixon professed to be unconcerned about the reaction to him by "the intellectuals and the liberal press." All he wanted to be, he insisted, was his natural self, and let the public take him or leave him. This in itself was a revelation, in light of the stereotype that existed about his obsession with image. He went on:

"I'm not one of those guys who reads his press clippings. I believe in never being affected by reports about me. I may read some selected clippings a week or so later, when somebody sends them to me, but never the next morning. I never look at myself on TV, either. I don't want to develop those phony, self-conscious, contrived things. One thing I have to be is always be myself. At a press conference, I try to reply to questions responsively, and you can't do that if you have to worry about keeping your chin up or down. It may be a weakness, I admit, but that's the way I am."

(In being himself, Nixon nevertheless very often seemed ill at ease—contrived—during the trip just ending. Before the television cameras particularly, he had the manner of the fighter who is willing to get in there and mix it, but who always is on guard for a rabbit punch from an unexpected source. He would permit himself to steal quick but ever so discernible peeks at the cameras as he talked, and he would punctuate his remarks with a tentative smile that would generate more self-consciousness than personal warmth. Though Nixon is far from photogenic and is the first to admit it, he does have a radiant smile that is capable, when he lets go, of illuminating his countenance. But in those days, except in response to partisan cheers, he seldom let go.)

In that now-famous "last press conference" in California, Nixon said, he was being himself and it had worked out for the best after all: "California served a purpose. The press had a guilt complex about their inaccuracy. Since then, they've been

151

generally accurate, and far more respectful. The press are good guys, but they haven't basically changed. They're oriented against my views. But I like the battle. I like to take them on in a give-and-take. I used to be too serious about it. Now I treat it as a game. I'm probably more relaxed, and not so much is riding on it. . . . I have a lot of friends in the press. They tell me, 'I like to cover you. You're news.' I do give the correspondents a lot of news. And I like the press guys, because I'm basically like them, because of my own inquisitiveness. . . . The press is very helpful with their questions. I'm better on TV in a panel format; I'm a Q-and-A guy, not a set-speech guy. Their questions are always tough, but they're more responsible, more objective, since California. After '62, the press could have said, 'Let's give it to the S.O.B.' But they didn't do it."

(Nixon's remark that he and the reporters who cover him are cut from the same bolt certainly would have amused most of them. Most, perhaps excluding several White House "regulars," remain unreconstructed cynics about Nixon and regard him as the personification of the all-technique politician of the TV age. But his observation that they hadn't "given it to the S.O.B." was borne out by this trip. At every stop, the inevitable press conference had been marked by mutual deference. Nixon was an egg-walker before the press, and in turn he always received more than the customary courtesy, even from the Dead End Kids of every city's press corps, the news photographers. It was an attitude that was to be continued—and capitalized on by Nixon—as he moved toward open candidacy for the White House.)

Nixon's family was not able to be quite so philosophical about his press treatment, he said. "Families never take it very well when their man is criticized. The difference is that the man can fight it. You can get back at a press conference. But the family is always on the sidelines and they get damned irritated. A wife and children are extremely sensitive—overly sensitive. Most public men are heroes or villains, but their families can't accept that. The family tends to view every little bit of fly-specking prejudice as a bitter attack. I don't look at it that way. I have my friends in the press who knock my head off every once in a while. I realize it's difficult to write objectively. But

152

there still are good reporters in Washington and New York and a few places around the country. Bert Andrews, the old *Herald Tribune* Washington bureau chief, once told me that the trouble with the greatest young reporters is that they want to write with their hearts, not with their heads. I said, 'Shouldn't reporters have hearts?' Bert said, 'Yes, they wouldn't be in this low-paying business unless they felt strongly about things. But they must write with their heads, not their hearts.' Columnists are different. They must write with their hearts. Often pure objective reporting is dull. That's why the columnist puts the shaft in men in public office. It's more interesting, let's face it. Evans and Novak are more interesting than Roscoe Drummond, and why? Because it's gossip, it's more yeasty, but it's not better journalism."

The ancient Beechcraft was descending into Washington National Airport now, over and past the White House Nixon hoped to occupy as President in 1969. When we landed, he glanced at the illuminated Washington Monument out the left window, put down the single Scotch and soda he had been nursing throughout the interview, shook hands and was off into the night. This time there were no crowds waiting, and he seemed relieved about it. In the last eleven days, stretching back to before I had joined him in Detroit, he had spoken in seven states from coast to coast, bringing his total for the year to thirty. In the process, he had constructed the beginnings of what the pundits were saying he lacked—a base from which to launch a national campaign. It appeared true, as Richard Nixon had said repeatedly, that he was not seeking commitments for 1968. But political activists know about such things, and nothing direct had to be said. The seeds were being planted, and were taking hold.

7

Help from an Unexpected Source

SHORTLY after Labor Day, Richard Nixon launched his planned five-week blitz on behalf of House and Senate candidates. Since 1964, by his own estimate, he already had helped raise between four and five million dollars for the off-year election effort, and now he was committing his time, his prestige and his own political future to its successful outcome. In the last two years he had traveled around the nation and the world shaping the issues on which he believed the Republican Party could come back; now he set out to use them to best effect. Before he was through, he not only would rally his party to a remarkable comeback but—thanks to the improbable assistance of Lyndon B. Johnson—would be projected suddenly and incontrovertibly into the Presidential picture once again.

During the summer of 1966, Nixon had been keeping his lines out on both the domestic and the foreign fronts. On the night of August 23, he had met privately at the Shoreham Hotel in Washington with about twenty leaders of the major conservative political groups in the country. Republican Congressman John M. Ashbrook of Ohio and former Congressman Donald C. Bruce of Indiana, representing the American Conservative Union, were there, and so were Charles McManus of the Americans for Conservative Action, Lynn Mote of Barry Goldwater's Free Society Association, Tom Charles Houston of the Young

Americans for Freedom, and William Rusher, publisher of the *National Review*. According to one participant, Nixon made no direct mention of a possible 1968 candidacy but "lines of communication were opened that should be helpful later on." Another reported that Nixon had predicted the election of twenty-five to thirty conservatives to the House in 1966 and said that by 1968 "responsible conservatism" on governmental fiscal and economic policy would be "politically respectable" again. It clearly was the kind of talk to convince the collected conservatives that they didn't have to look beyond Richard Nixon for a man who saw things their way.

And on the foreign policy front, Nixon during the summer had made yet another round-the-world tour, bolstering his diplomatic credentials and collecting useful campaign material. Passing through Saigon in August, he had said he was there to gather information on the political and military situation, but he pointedly denied any intent to use what he learned as ammunition against the Democrats in the fall. Nobody, of course, believed him. At nearly every stop on his trip, Nixon reiterated support of President Johnson on the Vietnam War—and in the same breath pointed out that members of Johnson's own party were undermining the effort. On leaving Saigon, he had called for not just "a marginal number [of troops] in order to accomplish our objectives, but more than enough, because the more power we have concentrated, the sooner this war can be brought to a conclusion." Clearly, Nixon was looking for daylight between the administration and a responsible Republican position on Vietnam, a way to support the President in what he did, but to make clear he wasn't doing enough.

During Nixon's trips to Saigon, the Johnson administration had been gradually raising the manpower level, and Nixon apparently was convinced from the military briefings that the trend had to continue. He seemed to be uncertain how to handle this trend politically. On September 11, appearing on *Face the Nation*, Nixon warned that "there is grave danger . . . that the administration will go overboard in increasing American forces in Vietnam. We might be able to win the war, but by doing so we would have on our hands a dependency for a generation to come. That's the wrong way to handle it." But the next day, speaking at an Overseas Press Club luncheon in New York, he predicted that after the election Johnson would "find it necessary to announce a substantial increase in our forces in Vietnam" and that he "owes it to the American people to come clean and tell them exactly what the plans are. The people should be told now, and not after the elections." Nixon appeared to be courting the hawk vote by urging troop increases while planting suspicions among the doves by suggesting Johnson was deceiving them. Asked whether he was accusing the President of deliberately misleading the public on a prospective additional troop buildup, Nixon replied lamely: "I wouldn't charge the President with misleading, because he may not have thought this thing through."

This penchant of Nixon's to try to milk every possible political advantage from a situation, and yet to back off when his implications were laid out before him, made him very transparent at times. He seemed to realize that some observers were aware of this tactic, and to be embarrassed by that fact. One of those who saw his Overseas Press Club performance and the politics in it, columnist Murray Kempton of the New York *Post,* captured this quality in a column the next day:

His [Nixon's] smile across the room at the intruder is almost and unexpectedly beseeching. The first thought is that he is faintly crying mercy; but he must long ago have ceased to expect mercy anywhere; a man who has so doggedly followed his star without ever asking quarter from history is certainly above asking mercy from journalists. But then you understand; he is speaking on Vietnam, he has counted the heads at the Republican convention and he knows already what the rest of us will be surprised to learn in the spring of 1968; the Goldwater people believe that he is the man to stand up to Mao Tse-tung although, from what I know of his native courtesy, I would not ask Richard Nixon to stand up to the general secretary of the Communist Party of Albania.

Out on the hustings, beyond the Eastern seaboard and its relatively liberal, sophisticated press, Nixon was less deferential in his references to Johnson, whom he saw as the Democrats' political soft spot. In a late September swing through Alaska and the Midwest, Southwest and South, he hammered away at

156

one hawkish theme: " 'All the Way with LBJ' means higher taxes, tighter money, a five-year ground war in Asia with American casualties greater than in Korea. . . . Now that we've come part of the way with LBJ, we want no part of the rest of the way." And to bring the Democratic-controlled Congress under his assault, Nixon tied it to Johnson's sliding stature in the public eye. He repeatedly called Congress "a toothless old lapdog of Lyndon Johnson" and a "stacked deck . . . the country hasn't won a hand since he started to deal." While calling for more diplomatic efforts to end the war, Nixon ridiculed an administration offer of a bombing halt against North Vietnam in exchange for a corresponding deescalation on the ground as a "pathetic exercise in instant diplomacy [that] creates the impression of American weakness and confusion."

Up to this time Nixon was flailing away without an effective focus. Then, suddenly, Johnson made a move that gave Nixon his target. The President announced a meeting in Manila with the ranking South Vietnamese and other allied officials, to be held just three weeks before the November elections. Nixon, anticipating some such Democratic strategy, hit even harder. He had been saying all year that the President would try by some device at the last minute to boost himself and his party in the polls, and said as much in his syndicated column: "From diplomats in Tokyo to members of the President's own party in Washington, the question is being posed: Is this a quest for peace or a quest for votes?"

Considering the growing inclination to distrust Lyndon Johnson that was spreading through the country, Nixon's remarks were politically well aimed. And when Johnson himself heard them, he reacted in a manner ideally suited to Nixon's purpose—with a blatant partisanship that gave Nixon still more ammunition. Johnson actually was being no more partisan than Nixon when, in a speech in Wilmington a few days before going to Manila, the President warned that votes for Republican Congressional candidates could cause the nation to "falter and fall back and fail" in Vietnam. But Nixon, full of righteous indignation, countercharged that Johnson had jeopardized bipartisan support for his Manila trip with a "vicious, unwarranted assault upon a Republican Party that has given Presi-

157

dent Johnson the support for the war that his own party has denied him. . . . The Republican Party has not failed America. The only failure has been President Johnson's. He is the first President in history who has failed to unite his own party in time of war." (Nixon also warned that Johnson's voice at Manila already had been weakened by "speculation in the press that his trip is more a quest for votes than a quest for peace." He did not point out that it was a sometime columnist named Richard M. Nixon who had aired that speculation in those very words in his syndicated column two weeks earlier.)

The Manila meeting was, as Nixon had charged, a carefully staged and publicized extravaganza obviously aimed at the opinion polls and voters in the crucial days before the off-year elections. Nixon grew increasingly apprehensive; in 1956, he knew, the outbreak of the Hungarian revolution and the British-French attack on Suez had focused national attention on President Eisenhower, had rallied public support around him, and had wiped out what little chance Democrat Adlai Stevenson had of beating him. And closer to his own career, Nixon could recall only too clearly the impact of major foreign policy activity on his 1962 race for governor of California. By his own judgment, the Cuban missile crisis had blunted his uphill drive in his home state and stopped him cold. Would the same thing happen again, with Johnson returning from Manila full of optimistic claims about the war, washing away all Nixon had done to bring the Republican Party back? Nixon had pinned his reputation and hopes on "the biggest Republican victory in twenty years." If Johnson managed to scuttle that prediction, Nixon would be a prophet without honor in a foundering party.

Yet there was little he could do while Johnson was in Manila. During the conference of war allies, Senator Robert Kennedy was severely criticized for saying in a question-and-answer period at the University of California that he didn't believe the people of South Vietnam really wanted the cocky, swashbuckling General Nguyen Cao Ky as their leader. Nixon immediately joined the chorus, charging that such "highly irresponsible" statements only "weaken the hand of the President" at Manila. Having taken this tack, it was very difficult for Nixon

158

himself to say anything about the Manila talks while they were going on.

The dilemma concerned him increasingly. Anyone could project what might happen in the last days of the campaign: Johnson returning and campaigning all over the country, pulling political chestnuts out of the fire with glowing accounts of Manila and visions of that elusive "light at the end of the tunnel" in Vietnam. In Australia, White House press aide Bill Moyers already had talked to reporters about an exhausting Johnson campaign schedule into key Congressional districts across the nation where the eleventh-hour Presidential presence might turn the tide. Even as Johnson talked with Ky and leaders of six other allied countries in Manila, Democratic politicians in more than a dozen states were initiating the special steps that had to be taken for a Presidential visit.

Thus, as a man already haunted by the intercession of damaging developments beyond his control in the past, Richard Nixon was sweating out the end of the campaign. Johnson compounded his fears by making much-publicized side trips to visit American troops in South Vietnam and South Korea—trips virtually certain to have a favorable impact on public opinion polls at home. Nixon could not simply stand by and let it happen. On the night of October 27 in Boise, Idaho, Nixon returned to his room at the Boise Hotel after a speech at the local college gymnasium. According to the *Wall Street Journal* a few days later, "Mr. Nixon's worry over possible political effects of the post-Manila Johnson campaigning became so gnawing that, unable to sleep, he summoned aides to his room at 4:30 A.M. to begin plotting a counterattack against the claims of accomplishment the President is expected to make. In the pre-dawn hours in Boise, Mr. Nixon reached the decision to make the Vietnam issue a major theme in his final week on the stump."

Nixon also felt growing concern about another development —the noisy surge of white-backlash candidates in the Democratic ranks in the South. There were at least four of them running for governor—George Mahoney in Maryland, Lester Maddox in Georgia, Lurleen Wallace in Alabama and Jim Johnson in Arkansas—and Nixon recognized them as threats to the growth of the Republican Party in Dixie. In his next syndicated column, a week before the elections, he pulled back on his earlier prediction for big gains in the South as well as the North—for "the coming of age of the GOP in the South." The picture now appeared to have changed, he wrote. "While my optimism about national Republican prospects has sharply increased, my predictions in the South must be revised—downward. The reason is that the Democratic Party—in a desperate throw of the dice—has gambled upon racism, demagogy and the backlash to win for it what the caliber of its candidates cannot. The gamble will pay off in some backwaters of the South. But the Democratic Party has made a fatal mistake. It has risked the next generation, just to win this next election."

As matters turned out, Nixon was overstating the threat to Republicanism in the South. On election day, of the four backlash Democrats, only one—Mrs. Wallace—won a majority. A second, Maddox, lost a plurality of the popular vote to Republican candidate Howard "Bo" Callaway in a three-way race, but in the absence of a majority for anyone as required by state law Georgia's Democratic-controlled legislature installed Maddox

At any rate, a Republican comeback nationally would have to be made largely in the North, where the Vietnam issue was critical. Vietnam had been a major emphasis of Nixon's campaigning all along, but in the last week he intensified it ever more. Two days before the Boise session, Nixon had said at a $100-a-plate fund-raiser in Grand Rapids, Michigan, that Johnson was "trying to cushion the fall" of massive Democratic setbacks on election day by dreaming up the Manila conference When the conference was concluded and Johnson and Ky had issued their communiqué in all the trappings of a major state paper, the apprehensive Nixon moved quickly to shoot it full of holes. His critical response was destined to set off a reaction by Lyndon Johnson that perhaps more than any other public utterance since 1962 was to propel Richard Nixon back into prominence as a Presidential prospect.

From Johnson City, Tennessee, where he was speaking in behalf of Senator Dirksen's son-in-law, Senate candidate Howard Baker, Nixon released an "appraisal of Manila," painstakingly prepared himself the night before, in which he warned of significant pitfalls. (The concern he was to voice in 1968 about loose tongues jeopardizing peace talks obviously had not yet seized him.) The Johnson-Ky communiqué had announced an offer of mutual withdrawal of American and other allied troops from South Vietnam in six months "as the military and subversive forces of North Vietnam are withdrawn, infiltration ceases and the level of violence thus subsides." In the meantime, it said, the necessity for continued military action and support "must depend for its size and duration on the intensity and duration of the Communist aggression."

Nixon blasted the withdrawal offer in words that were to have an embarrassing ring less than three years later, when the burden of achieving peace in Vietnam fell to Nixon himself and he put all his chips on "Vietnamization" of the war. But politically in 1966, the words were on target. The Johnson offer, he said, "states clearly that if North Vietnam withdraws its forces back across its border, and the violence thus subsides, we shall withdraw all American forces out of Vietnam, most of them ten thousand miles back to the United States. The effect of this mutual withdrawal would be to leave the fate of South Vietnam to the Viet Cong and the South Vietnamese Army. . . . [It] simply turns back the clock two years and says, 'Let the South Vietnamese fight it out with the Viet Cong.' The South Vietnamese Army could not prevail for any length of time over the Communist guerrillas without American advisers, air support and logistical backing. Communist victory would most certainly be the result of 'mutual withdrawal' if the North Vietnamese continued their own logistical support of the Communist guerrillas. . . ."

Tying allied military action to the scope of enemy action, Nixon said, again in words that would take on new perspective in 1969, "implies that a diminishing of the Communist military effort will bring a corresponding reduction in the allied effort. If this implication is accurate, then we have offered to surrender a decisive military advantage at the Manila Conference. We have offered to leave it to Communist generals to determine the timing and intensity of the war. . . . I know of no successful military effort that ever keyed its own intensity simply to

161

match that of the aggressor—thus deliberately surrendering to the aggressor the initiative for major offensives. . . ."

The Nixon thrust, aimed squarely at Johnson's credibility and diplomatic judgment, was a politically deft one at the time, though it attacked policies that Nixon himself later adopted and pursued as President in 1969 and 1970.

But in 1966, Nixon's prime objective was to turn the forthcoming Congressional elections into a referendum on LBJ. And in his wildest dreams, he could not have guessed how LBJ would help him do just that. Not only was Johnson going to make a villain of himself on the eve of the Congressional elections; he was going to make a hero of Richard Nixon—and thereby greatly enhance Nixon's political stock in his party and in the nation.

Abruptly, on Johnson's return from Manila on the day Nixon's critique appeared, the President's press office announced he would be undergoing some minor surgery and had decided to go to Texas to rest up for it. There would be no eleventh-hour campaign swing. Then, the next day, Johnson held a press conference in the East Room of the White House. It began mildly enough—until a reporter asked him: "Does the cancellation of your big campaign trip mean that you do not intend to do anything to help Democratic candidates for election, such as one little speech in Texas, or maybe a TV pep talk before election?"

Johnson's eyes narrowed. "First, we don't have any plans, so when you don't have plans, you don't cancel plans," he said curtly. Reporters in the audience who had been briefed by the President's aides on the very plans he was denying existed could not believe their ears. "We get invited to come to most of the states," Johnson went on, disdainfully. "In the last six weeks we have been invited to forty-seven of the states by the candidates for governor, the Senate or the Congress. We have been invited on nonpolitical invitations to the other three states, I might say. But we have not accepted those invitations. We do contact the local people who extend them. We do investigate in some instances going there, and we do express the hope that we can go. But until it is firm, until we know we can, we do not say 'We accept,' and schedule it." And then, with even more vitriol he added: "The people of this country ought to know that all these canceled plans primarily involve the imagination of people who phrase sentences and write columns and have to report what they hope or what they imagine. We have no plans for any political speeches between now and the election. We know of no requirement that we go to them. I just don't think they are necessary. I have had a very active year, and I would hope I could spend a relatively quiet weekend and go and vote on Tuesday morning. I hope every American will go and vote on Tuesday morning. If they do, I have not the slightest doubt but what their good judgment will prevail and the best interests of our country will be served."

Johnson's bitter and caustic noncancellation of his nonplans to campaign produced one immediate conclusion in the minds of political writers present: that his best political advisers had counseled him not to spend his Presidential prestige on a lost cause. The nonplans certainly had been well advanced by now. During the President's Asian trip, several White House aides had been sent back to Washington to coordinate the preelection travel. Secret Service men had gone to at least eleven states to check speaking sites and travel routes. In Boston, plans had been made to meet the President at the airport and take him by motorcade to a huge outdoor rally; in Chicago, there was to have been a massive noonday parade; in Memphis, extra phones for the Presidential press had been installed at the airport; in Portland, Democratic volunteers were rounding up guests, bands, placards and the other necessities for a big political show; in Billings, Montana, the Great Northern Hotel was holding 125 reservations for a White House entourage. As noncampaigns go, this one was shaping up as a corker—at least in the imaginations of "people who phrase sentences and write columns and have to report what they hope or what they imagine."

The President, obviously seething now, was not through with politics in his press conference, nor was he going to succeed in keeping himself out of the picture in the key last days of the campaign, even by going to Texas and shutting out the world. A reporter asked him to comment on Nixon's critique of the Manila communiqué, that "it appeared that you had proposed, or the seven powers had proposed, getting out in a way that would leave South Vietnam to the mercy of the Viet Cong."

That did it. Johnson bristled, yet tried to contain himself. Sarcasm dripping from every phrase, he unloaded on Nixon: "I do not want to get into a debate on a foreign policy meeting in Manila with a chronic campaigner like Mr. Nixon. It is his problem to find fault with his country and with his government during a period of October every two years. If you will look back over his record, you will find that to be true. He never did really recognize and realize what was going on when he had an official position in the government. You remember what President Eisenhower said, that if you would give him a week or so he would figure out what he was doing.

"Since then he has made a temporary stand in California, and you saw what action the people took out there. Then he crossed the country to New York. Then he went back to San Francisco hoping that he would be in the wings and available if Goldwater stumbled. But Goldwater didn't stumble. Now he is out talking about a conference that obviously he is not well prepared on or informed about."

Johnson went on to defend the Manila communiqué at length. "Why would we want to stay there if there was no aggression, if there was no infiltration and the violence ceased?" Johnson asked with more sarcasm. "We wouldn't want to stay there as tourists. We wouldn't want to keep four hundred thousand men there just to march up and down the runways at Cam Rahn Bay. But we felt if we state it again and each of us subscribe to it . . . that it would probably clarify our position. We think we did that, until some of the politicians got mixed up in it and started to not clarify it but confuse it. It shouldn't be confused. Every participant in that conference, acting on good faith, with the best of motives, wanted to say to North Vietnam and every other nation in the world that we intend to stay there only so long as our presence is necessary to protect the territorial integrity of South Vietnam, to see that the violence there ceases, and the infiltration and aggression ceases.

"They know that, and we ought not to try to confuse it here and we ought not try to get it mixed up in a political campaign here. Attempts to do that will cause people to lose votes instead of gaining them. We ought not have men killed because we try to fuzz up something. When the aggression, infiltration and violence ceases, not a nation there wants to keep occupying troops in South Vietnam. Mr. Nixon doesn't serve his country well by trying to leave that kind of impression in the hope that he can pick up a precinct or two, or a ward or two."

It was, in the memory of veteran reporters, the most brutal verbal bludgeoning ever administered from the White House by Johnson, or any other President for that matter, to a leader of the opposition party. Intentionally or not, the President's words immediately swung the national spotlight on Nixon at a time he was climaxing one of the greatest personal efforts in behalf of other candidates ever launched by a political leader not himself running for public office. Not only that, but the President's attack bestowed at once upon Nixon the image of *the* leader of the opposition.

At the time of the President's press conference, Nixon was at LaGuardia Airport in New York talking to television reporter and commentator Mike Wallace of CBS. Nixon boarded an old Constellation for a flight to Waterville, Maine, and en route Pat Buchanan, who had learned about Johnson's tirade just before boarding, excitedly told his boss about it. When he heard what Johnson had said, Nixon could hardly believe his good fortune. He immediately resolved to play the wronged party, and to play it cool, and as the old plane lumbered toward Waterville, Nixon prepared the answer he would make when he arrived. Wallace, meanwhile, also had heard about the Johnson outburst and had chartered a Lear jet to be on hand when Nixon's plane reached Waterville. Wallace met Nixon—bland, mild, statesmanlike—as he came down the ramp.

The President's criticism of him, Nixon said, was a "shocking display of temper," but he was not going to be drawn into a battle of personalities with Johnson or silenced by such outbursts. "Despite the Presidential temper," he said calmly, "I will continue to speak out" on Vietnam. He again demanded that the President say whether he intended to call up more American ground troops for Vietnam and how he intended to pay for increased costs of the war, by new taxes or by nonmilitary budget cuts, as the Republicans urged. Nixon said he was

165

"somewhat surprised" at the vehemence of Johnson's remarks, but added righteously: "Let the record show that all over the world I have defended the administration's announced goal of no surrender to aggression. I have defended it in the capitals of the world and here at home against members of the President's own party."

It was a masterpiece of self-congratulation. In two short sentences, he had managed to establish himself as loyal to the man who had just stabbed him; a world statesman who had used his global eminence to support this same man's policy; a selfless American who was more loyal to the President than members of his own party, who had deserted him. Two other surefire elements were included, too—praise for his opponent (a device to show he was fair-minded?) and putting patriotism before personality. "I respect the President," Nixon said with sincerity, "as a man who works vigorously, probably the hardest-working President of this century." But, he added, "the lives of men, the future of freedom here and abroad, are more important than what happens politically to me or to President Johnson." Both sides, he said, should discuss the issues "like gentlemen." (After this press conference performance marked by sweet reasonableness and a refusal to descend to the gutter, the New York *Times* reported, Nixon stepped back from the microphones and in an aside asked, "Was I too hard on him?")

The reaction to the exchange was immediate and one-sided. The ogre Johnson, with all the power of the Presidency behind him, had been the crude cowboy again, and Nixon's decision to turn the other cheek underlined that impression. From Gettysburg, there came a quick defense of Nixon from his old boss, General Eisenhower. Concerning Johnson's recollection of the famous 1960 Eisenhower remark that if he had a week, he might be able to think of some major policy decision Nixon had made, the former President said Nixon "was one of the best informed, most capable and most industrious Vice Presidents in the history of the United States, and in that position contributed greatly to the sound functioning of our government. He was constantly informed of the major problems of the United States during my administration. Any suggestion to the contrary, or any inference that I, at any time, held Dick Nixon in anything less than the highest regard and esteem is erroneous." (Nixon told me once that the 1960 remark "always bothered Eisenhower. He called that afternoon—I was out playing golf—and he said, 'Dick, I've been trying to get this damn thing explained. Frankly, I was kind of taken aback because the question was on decisions, and decisions are made by the President. You were always informed, but I made the decisions. I wanted to make it clear I didn't mean it that way.' ")

Johnson clearly was thrown on the defensive. Press Secretary George Christian, speaking from the ranch in Texas, stretched reporters' credulity even further than they were accustomed to having it pulled by his boss. "For those of you who were there," he said to newsmen who had seen and heard the President unload on Nixon, "I don't think the President showed any temper or personal attack toward Nixon. I think the President is in as good a humor as he ever has been in his life. I know for a fact he rather likes Mr. Nixon personally." (This sort of hyperbole came to be almost institutional in the Johnson White House. One of Christian's predecessors was asked at a briefing once what Johnson's relationship was to his old Senate protégé, Bobby Baker, then in deep legal troubles. "To be perfectly candid," the press aide replied confidentially, "he hardly knew the fellow.")

To take advantage of the unexpected windfall, Nixon's allies on the Republican Congressional Committee immediately turned over to him a thirty-minute television slot made available by NBC for Sunday afternoon. The time originally was to be filled with a controversial film documentary. Prior to Johnson's attack on Nixon, it had been decided to give Nixon fifteen minutes of the free time, cutting the film down; afterward, the movie was thrown out altogether so that Nixon could make a full defense against the President's assault.

On Saturday, November 5, Nixon issued a statement on his plans to reply on TV the next afternoon. "By attacking me rather than responding to the points which I raised," Nixon said, "he has struck at the very roots of the right of dissent. Is every public figure who rationally questions the means to achieve our goals in Vietnam to become the victim of a presidential attack to silence his dissent?" Nixon taped the response on Saturday night, again repeating his concern about the Manila communiqué and his determination to be a gentleman no matter what Johnson said about him. On Sunday afternoon, Nixon had an additional thirty-minute forum on ABC's *Issues and Answers* show. Chiding Johnson for his intemperate attack, Nixon claimed the high road and at the same time accused the President of "cheap political demagoguery." The President, he said indignantly, "tends to have an attitude that unless you go all the way with LBJ you don't go any of the way. He isn't going to get away with that with me." Reactions to both shows, Republican surveys indicated later, were sweepingly positive and instrumental in the heavy gains the party made on November 8.

Nixon was sure now that Johnson had committed a major political blunder on the eve of the off-year elections, and he wanted to capitalize on it right until the last possible hour. He proposed to National Chairman Ray Bliss that a film of Johnson's tirade against him, and his own answer, be shown on nationwide television Monday night in place of a planned—and predictably dreary—campaign roundup featuring Senator Dirksen and other GOP old faces. But Bliss refused to put up the money, reportedly on grounds that the national committee had to remain neutral among all prospective 1968 Presidential candidates. The refusal incensed Nixon; it was the final straw in an adamant attitude by Bliss and his national committee against giving Nixon any kind of campaign aid in 1966, and it is said to have been the real reason Nixon insisted, after his election to the Presidency in 1968, on dumping Bliss. "The national committee didn't help us one damn bit in 1966," one of Nixon's close campaign aides of the time told me later. "They were going to provide us with a plane but didn't. We were the only ones out there. We felt the national committee should have answered Johnson's charge with the strongest voice the party had in that situation—Nixon himself." Nixon partisans considered launching a telephone blitz against the national chairman, having friends of the former Vice President call him from all over the country demanding that Nixon be put on TV. But they felt it would only get Bliss' back up more. John Whitaker the Washington advance man of normally moderate mien,

wanted to send Bliss a telegram that said: "Screw you. Strong
letter follows." Others talked him out of it.

As matters developed, however, the election-eve replay wasn't
needed. Nixon, determined not to miss any last-minute opportunity, flew from New York to Anderson, Indiana, for a statewide television show and rally for all Indiana Republican
Congressional candidates. "Everybody call ten people," he told
2,500 cheering faithful. "Tell them a Republican Congress will
bring progress with peace and prosperity without inflation.
Now go out and win! Make Tuesday National Price Protest
Day. Kick the spenders out and send the savers in!"

On election night, the Nixon campaign team gathered in a
suite in the Drake Hotel on Park Avenue and 58th Street.
Nixon was elated by the results as they came in from across the
country. It was a sweeping Republican triumph of the dimensions that he—and only he of the leading political figures—had
publicly predicted. Nixon had said the GOP would pick up 40
House seats, 3 in the Senate, 6 governorships and 700 state
legislative seats. The actual gains were 47 House seats, 3 in the
Senate, 8 governorships and 540 state legislative seats. Even his
late doubts about the South had not been warranted, as already
noted. In Dixie, the party gained eight new House seats, one in
the Senate, and two governorships—Winthrop Rockefeller (Nelson's brother), in Arkansas, and a fellow with the unlikely
name of Spiro T. Agnew in Maryland, running as a moderate
on the racial issue against George "A Man's Home Is His
Castle" Mahoney.

With John Davies, his telephone representative friend from
California, placing the calls, Nixon, Buchanan and John Sears
phoned each winning Republican candidate as the news of his
victory flashed on television. Nixon spoke to Rockefeller,
Romney, Reagan, Percy, Senator-elect Edward Brooke in
Massachusetts and most of the other big winners. He was so
buoyant at one point, seeing Walter Cronkite on the screen, he
had Davies place a call to him. Cronkite still was on camera
when the call came in, but he got off to take Nixon's call and to
congratulate him for his clairvoyance. The former Vice President gave Cronkite a short briefing on the significance of the
results, but it wasn't necessary. The GOP had made a phenome-

nal recovery in two short years, and Nixon was the man who not only had predicted it would happen, but had a major role in making it happen. (Warren Weaver, Jr., the New York *Times'* knowledgeable political reporter and elections statistician, calculated that of 66 House candidates for whom Nixon had campaigned, 44 won, for a percentage of .667. The winning average of 319 Republicans who didn't have his help was only .448. Of all 86 candidates running for various offices Nixon had helped, 59 won, or a percentage of .686. Democrats for whom the Kennedy brothers had campaigned fared worse—.397 for those Ted Kennedy helped and only .391 for those for whom Robert Kennedy spoke.)

Nick Ruwe, the Detroit broker and advance man, was down in the lobby of the Drake buying a pack of cigarettes when Nixon and Davies stepped off the elevator, heading for home now that most of the results were in. "This is too great a night to go home," Nixon proclaimed. The three went out into the rainy night to hail a cab. Nixon still was on Cloud Nine. "We won! We won!" he shouted to Davies, slapping him on the shoulder. "Let's go to El Morocco and have some spaghetti!" And off they went. The three happy Republicans had a few drinks and spaghetti, interrupting their mild revelry occasionally for Nixon to accept the congratulations of customers at other tables. (The choice of fare at this famous nightspot intrigued me when I first heard about it. "Why spaghetti at El Morocco, of all places?" I asked my informant. "We were hungry," he said.)

Later, when Nixon finally got back to his apartment at about 2:30 A.M., he phoned Sears, who had remained at the Drake to check late returns. Sears read them to him, and Nixon asked for some of the better ones over and over again, as if he wanted to be sure they were real, to be sure they soaked into his mental political computer for future reference. "We've beaten hell out of them," Nixon told Sears, "and we're going to kill them in '68."

8

Ambush of the Front-Runner

On the Sunday before the great Republican comeback victory of 1966, the resident swami of the Washington political press corps, Bill Lawrence of ABC, looked into his crystal ball (the same one that was telling him Lyndon Johnson would not seek reelection) and clearly saw a GOP candidacy in it. On the *Issues and Answers* television interview show that Richard Nixon was using mainly to defend himself against President Johnson's press conference excesses, Lawrence asked: "Mr. Nixon, now that you have toured thirty-five states, seventy districts, renewed all your political due bills, when are you going to start running for President yourself?" And Nixon, to the surprise of some of his most intimate supporters, replied: "After this election, I am going to take a holiday from politics for at least six months, with no political speeches scheduled whatever."

The declaration of this self-imposed moratorium on political comment and activity—carefully preplanned by Nixon—stirred a mild debate in the ranks of Nixon strategists. Governor George Romney had won a smashing reelection victory in Michigan; the fear was that he would be off and running, giving the party the "new face" for which it constantly was searching, and restoring the role of the liberal-moderate wing of the GOP in selection of the Presidential nominee. Nixon himself had no

171

such trepidation. He knew what he was doing. In fact, he hoped Romney would put himself out on public exhibition—and on the firing line—at the earliest opportunity. Nixon, the man with the loser image, needed to knock somebody over, and he saw Romney as the ideal straw man. The governor had the looks and the winning record to be a candidate but, Nixon suspected, not the political savvy. Romney's indecisive performances and obfuscating self-explanations at the National Governors' Conference in Cleveland in 1964 and at Los Angeles in 1966—where he got himself impossibly snarled during a long, rambling discussion of Vietnam—had convinced Nixon that the Michigan governor could not make it. Succeeding in state politics and playing around the fringes of national politics was one thing; surviving in the national "arena," as Nixon liked to put it, under the pressures of complex domestic and foreign policy issues and a skeptical, merciless press corps, was quite another.

Ironically, Nixon looked to the press, who in his view had helped bring him down in 1960 and 1962, to be his ally in setting up Romney as the Nixon foil. For all his forgive-and-forget attitude toward the press after his 1962 outburst in California, Nixon continued to regard those newsmen who covered national politics as a very dangerous element in the whole political equation. He had seen for himself how a hostile press could harpoon a candidate. There was room for debate about its motivation, whether it was personal dislike for a candidate or his politics, or simply professional aggressiveness. But whatever the motivation, the ability of the press to inflict damage on a candidate, and even at times to force him to change the focus of his own campaign, was indisputable. Nixon himself had learned to cope with this threat quite well in the question-and-answer sessions that stimulated his debater's mind. To Nixon, the press conference was a legitimate field of combat, and he tended in conversations about the press and public figures to equate general excellence with a man's deft performance in that format. Even his own great confidence in dealing with what he fraternally referred to as "the Q-and-A" did not prevent him, however, from purposely end-running the press as his own Presidential stakes began to climb.

But Romney, Nixon reasoned correctly, had not yet learned the lessons about the press that Nixon's experience had taught him, and even if he had, he could not go into hiding. A moratorium on politics by a former Vice President, Presidential candidate and conspicuous globe-trotter would make little difference, since his face and his views already were widely known in the country; Romney, however, needed exposure in large doses on the national scene if he hoped to graduate to the status of a national candidate. That exposure, Nixon was confident, would be Romney's downfall. Yet as long as Romney was actively involved, the man Nixon regarded as more of a threat to his nomination, in 1968 as in 1960, could not make his move—Nelson Rockefeller. Meanwhile, Nixon himself could sit back, let Romney's destruction happen, and emerge all the stronger by virtue of the contrast between the way he and Romney conducted themselves in the pre-election-year shakedown.

The validity of Nixon's judgment about his own position, as a firmly established national figure bolstered by recent events, was incontrovertible. Two days after the off-year elections, the Nixons left New York for a Florida vacation. Mrs. Nixon and Rose Woods went out to Kennedy Airport ahead of the former Vice President while he attended to some last-minute business details. Although he now was observing his no-politics moratorium, he permitted me to accompany him on the drive to the airport so that I could finish a magazine article about him I had begun long before. It was a gloomy, overcast day, but the weather could not put a damper on his spirits. He was positively buoyant as he talked about the events of the previous week, highlighted not only by the election results but also by President Johnson's attack, which had unquestionably elevated him as *the* spokesman for the opposition party.

"I publicly predicted forty [new Republican House seats], but I thought it could go as low as thirty-two," he confided happily, now that the increase of forty-seven seats had been posted. "There was a big swing vote in the last days. Johnson's attack made it swing our way. The undecided vote was very high and interest was low in the campaign until the last week. I always have a thing about campaigning—you must keep going

173

to the last [a "thing" he learned to do without in 1968], and here the people weren't listening until the last. He played into our hands by hitting at us on the one issue he should have left alone—Vietnam." Of that attack, Nixon said with a trace of sympathy, perhaps born of his own past lapses, "Politically astute people can make mistakes too. Johnson was tired and irritable, and he just snapped a little. He had it made, but he attacked me on the wrong basis. He can attack my position, that's all right. But he attacked my credentials on Asia, and most people would agree I have a little more background, because of my travels, in that part of the world than he does. Here's the thing. He didn't have the experience of going abroad as a President. Any President who goes abroad gets a tremendous reception. To go see the troops and the high morale, as he did in Vietnam and Korea, you come back thinking, 'We're right and everybody else is wrong.' Well, to come back and find people asking questions burned the hell out of him. It was a mistake. And it takes only a very small mistake to swing a close election in the last few days."

Attacking him on Vietnam was a particularly poor move, Nixon said, "because it fired up Republicans who knew that I had defended the policy—the goal—all over the country and the world." He was astounded, he said, when he heard about it. "I couldn't believe it. It was too good to be true. I disagree with Johnson, but I have great respect for his political skill. But you never build up a major spokesman on the other side. In my view, controversy builds up, not tears down. That's a standard rule. There's an old saying: 'Never strike a king unless you kill him.' In politics, you don't hit your opponent unless you knock him out."

Johnson compounded his mistake, Nixon insisted, by getting too personally involved, and as a result weakened himself for 1968 as well as his party. "This is the difference between Johnson and Eisenhower," he said. "Republicans lost nineteen House seats in 1954 and forty-seven in 1958, but Eisenhower didn't lose, because he was always apart. He maintained the dignity of the President. With Johnson, it was 'my Congress,' so his prestige suffered. He identified himself too closely with Congress. Johnson is always right in there." As Nixon made this point, he leaned forward, pumped his fist like a piston and gritted his teeth. Then he sat back, relaxed. "Well," he went on, "he was well advised not to make that last campaign trip, even if his physical condition permitted it. He would have lost in every major state he appeared in. People abroad would have said, 'He's been rejected.' I know he couldn't have saved those guys [Democratic candidates] in California, Illinois, Michigan, Massachusetts. He could have gotten some more votes but he would have lost."

As Nixon unwound about the campaign, his views poured out without any prodding. He ran on for long periods, anticipating questions and answering them, obviously enjoying the exercise. With the Republican Party on the mend now and himself credited with being the chief doctor in the case, he looked back with satisfaction.

"It was a risky business," he said, "going into all those close districts. I could easily have picked incumbents to campaign for. But I felt anyone who could win in 1964 would win in 1966, and they did. We lost no seats we had in the North. It was the close ones that needed help. I also went into about ten I didn't think we could win. You've got to encourage them all, or nobody will take on the tough races."

Nixon admitted he had stuck his neck out in predicting a Republican victory of dimensions few others had imagined. If he had been wrong, he acknowledged, he would have been discredited as a pundit. But he said he had to strike an optimistic note, for pragmatic political reasons. "I don't mean you lie about predictions," he said, with a disarming candor. "You don't do that. I never predicted we'd win much in the Senate, for example. But you must always predict on the optimistic side. I took what I thought would happen, then gave the most optimistic view. You have to encourage the troops. In finances especially. These guys don't kick in unless they think we'll win."

Nixon, of course, was not the only big Republican winner. Those who actually were elected to office—Romney, Reagan, Rockefeller, Percy—all moved up in the 1968 Presidential speculation. Insofar as his own campaigning contributed to the Republican victory, he had helped build up competition for the

175

nomination. Wasn't he working against his own best interests? He would not acknowledge he had firm aspirations. "But let's assume I had decided to be a candidate in 1968. The interest of any candidate should be getting elected, not nominated. If I had conducted my campaigning this year as a delegate-seeking thing instead of working to get candidates elected, I could probably have locked it up by now. But the nomination, not the election. Now we have an immensely strengthened party. We now have a twenty-five percent better chance to win than we did in 1960. Then we had only fourteen governors and both houses in only six states. Now we have twenty-five governors and about eighteen state legislatures. Boy, that's a base! It doesn't assure your victory, but in a close contest it could be the difference. In 1960, Kennedy had the stronger party base. If I had been campaigning this year in the interest of being nominated, you could say I damaged those chances, but in the interest of being elected, if I were nominated, I helped them. I had no choice. I endorsed Romney and Rockefeller though in each case I helped a potential rival. This isn't altruism; it's the only thing that makes sense. I try to pound this into the heads of Republicans. We have to win. Republicans are jumping all over now, because we won. We'll be more divisive now, there will be struggles for power, but Republicans will become more exciting and that will be better for the party and the next candidate."

When the chauffeured car arrived at Kennedy Airport and we walked through the terminal, Nixon was greeted as if he had just been elected President. Men and women rushed up to shake his hand and to congratulate him. "You did a great job," one gray-haired man said. Nixon beamed. Inside the VIP lounge, another man with a small flash camera asked Nixon to pose and snapped a picture. As he went across the room to where Pat Nixon and Rose Woods were waiting, drinking coffee, another familiar figure, dressed in a tan sport jacket, slacks and a brown bow tie—astronaut John Glenn, yesterday's hero—slipped out of the lounge without a head turning his way. All eyes were on Nixon, and anyone who witnessed the phenomenon could not doubt its political significance.

Although the 1966 election-night results clearly had pointed not only to a party rehabilitation but a personal comeback for Nixon, those who shared that victory night with him insist he made no mention then of the prospects for 1968. "He's a man who does a great deal of keeping his own counsel," John Davies said later. "But those of us around him, seeing the possibilities, began to hope." Maurice Stans, who also was there, remembers "sometime in the course of the evening saying to him, 'Let's go for '68.' He laughed it off in a somewhat embarrassed way, and nothing more was said of it. But his mood was very gay, very spirited." John Whitaker had little doubt, either, after the 1966 victory. "He never told me, but I was sure he wanted to go and was going to go after that," he said later. "It was the right thing for him emotionally—he had to have another crack at it. The party unity thing didn't give him a full plate." Buchanan, who had told Nixon a year earlier that his own eye was on 1968, took his own reading; his leave of absence from the paper was almost up, but nobody said he should go back to St. Louis. The fact was, nobody—not even Richard Nixon—had to say anything. The Republican Party was back in business, and so was Nixon as a live Presidential candidate.

The Nixons spent the Thanksgiving holidays in Florida with old friend Bebe Rebozo, and as soon as they returned, in early December, Peter Flanigan and Stans were on Nixon's doorstep ready to go. "We told him," Stans recalled later, "we wanted to organize a Nixon-for-President Committee for '68. As far as I know, we were the first. He said it was something he wanted to give a lot of thought. He had declared a moratorium, but we went ahead." Flanigan and Stans met with Fred Seaton, Bob Hill, Walter Williams, John Lodge and Linwood Holton to form the nucleus, a steering committee that would take steps only by unanimous agreement. "We wanted to go even without his permission," Stans said. "We had several conversations with him, and he finally said he would neither approve nor disapprove. That was good enough for us."

Others came on their own to urge him to run. One was former Congressman Robert Ellsworth of Kansas, who was first elected to the House on Nixon's coattails in 1960 and never forgot it. In October, 1966, when Nixon wound up his Supreme Court case and rushed onto a commercial plane to resume campaigning, Ellsworth happened to be aboard. They talked and Nixon invited him to drop by in New York after the elections. Ellsworth did, with a straight-out piece of advice: "Romney doesn't have it. Let him have his run for six months. I think they've made a big mistake putting all their chips on him. I hope you'll go for it. Johnson, with all his troubles, will be easy to beat." Nixon was "inscrutable," Ellsworth said later. But he was listening. Soon there were other meetings, bringing in other Nixon stalwarts like Bob Finch and Bob Haldeman from California; John Sears, Len Garment and Tom Evans from the law firm; publicist Bill Safire, Fred LaRue, Hobart Lewis and Don Kendall. Ellsworth became a key operations man in all that was done. "They were not big decision meetings," one participant recalled later. "But you could look around the room and see who was in on the plot. It built camaraderie. It was exciting to think you were in on a plot to elect the next President."

Also on the scene now, as a new member of Nixon Mudge, was a stern-looking, stern-minded fifty-four-year-old municipal bond lawyer named John Newton Mitchell. He and Nixon had been colleagues in bond cases and had traveled to Washington together to appear before federal regulatory agencies. They had decided in 1966 to merge Mitchell's smaller firm, Caldwell, Trimble and Mitchell, with the Nixon firm, and on the first day of 1967 Mitchell's name had been tacked to the end of Nixon Mudge, Rose, Guthrie and Alexander. Mitchell had no professional political experience as such, but his legal work had given him a wide exposure to local officials around the country. At first his associations with Nixon were professional and social, including an occasional round of golf. But as time went on, Nixon turned increasingly to Mitchell—who was tough and competent—on matters of political organization. It was not until the late spring of 1968, however, that the bald, pipe-smoking former Navy commander emerged as the central figure in the Nixon Presidential campaign, second only to the candidate himself.

The first step was for John Lodge to dispatch a letter to leading Republicans expressing his own "strong personal feeling that it is time Dick Nixon received recognition for his dedicated efforts for the Republican Party, in this and other years." Lodge included a glowing full-page article by publisher Richard Amberg in his St. Louis *Globe-Democrat,* reviewing the Nixon record from 1964 through 1966 and concluding: "Whether by design or not, the Nixon performance over the last two years, capped by the final week's collision with a unanimous decision over LBJ, has annihilated the argument that Nixon is a loser, a candidate who cannot win. . . . There is no question that Richard Nixon is the Big Winner in 1966." It was, of course, a bit premature to suggest that Nixon had proved he wasn't a loser anymore. But his 1966 record was something Republicans could not dismiss out of hand.

Still, the focus was elsewhere—on George Romney, whose image might have been vulnerable for other reasons, but not for losing. He had just won his third straight term as governor of Michigan, by a bigger margin than ever, and also had demonstrated impressive coattail power. He pulled in with him the underdog Republican Senatorial candidate Robert P. Griffin and also twelve congressional and a host of state legislative candidates. Romney, who never had any difficulty believing in himself and honestly couldn't understand why others did, was proud of this 1966 record and confident it would dispel the doubts.

Although John Lodge and Dick Amberg were sure that Nixon was the big winner in 1966, the Harris Survey taken right after the November elections indicated otherwise. Of five prospective Republican candidates for 1968—Nixon, Romney, Rockefeller, Percy and Reagan—only Romney led President Johnson in a direct test. The poll gave the Michigan governor a clear 54 percent to 46 percent lead over the President; Nixon, Rockefeller and Percy all trailed Johnson by 46 percent to 54 percent, and Reagan was far behind, 33 percent to 67 percent. Prior to the elections, Johnson had led the pack in the polls, holding a two-point edge over Romney, the closest contender. To Romney boosters, the message was clear: the husky, square-jawed, photogenic former Rambler Man with the full head of silvering Presidential hair was the "new face" the party needed.

Almost at once there was pressure on Romney to get out into the open. He had to build a national following, and to do that

179

he had to demonstrate a grasp of national issues. Some of his most astute aides in Lansing, knowing the governor's limitations, saw only disaster ahead in a premature, breakneck rush into the national spotlight. Their counsel was weighed against more persuasive voices at the State Capitol and elsewhere. At a meeting of the Republican governors in Colorado Springs in early December, the liberal-moderate bloc already had begun to apply the heat, and Romney was not temperamentally conditioned to withstand suggestions that he had the stuff to be President of the United States. Indeed, the idea had crossed his mind as early as 1962, when he won his first term as governor.

The spotlight at the 1966 Colorado Springs meeting, in which Romney delightedly basked along with the new Republican glamor boy, Governor-elect Ronald Reagan of California, nudged him toward an early start, and the persuasions of Nelson Rockefeller and Bill Scranton did the rest. Rockefeller and his family pledged financial support that according to one knowledgeable source reached $300,000 before Romney was through, and with that kind of backing waved in his face, Romney acquiesced. He gave his staff the green light to arrange an "exploratory" trip of a low-key nature to areas where he could expect a receptive mood, and he confidently looked forward to it as the beginning of an uphill journey to the White House. As things turned out, it was merely the beginning of the end. But in the chronicle of Richard Nixon's political comeback, the Romney pilgrimage to nowhere was to be of great significance. In addition to providing a diversion behind which Nixon's own planning could go forward with minimal unwanted publicity, the Romney effort unwittingly would supply the means for Nixon to demonstrate dramatically that he no longer was a loser.

Obviously fearful of getting too far ahead of the field too early, Romney insisted at Colorado Springs that he needed at least six months and maybe longer to decide whether he actually would be a candidate in 1968, and to educate himself further about national issues, particularly the Vietnam War. Accordingly, he steadfastly refused to say what he would do about the war if he were President until he had a chance to examine the situation in greater depth, possibly including a visit to South Vietnam. The self-imposed moratorium was a gamble; the longer he remained silent, the greater would be the pressure on him to produce a solution. Unfortunately for Romney, he did not have the imperturbability to stick to his plan when the persistent national press corps began to probe on Vietnam. Far from keeping his own counsel, he was stampeded into responses that revealed with destructive clarity his own uncertainty and in the end proved to be his undoing. Later, Richard Nixon demonstrated how the same basic device of keeping one's mouth shut on Vietnam solutions could pay off, if resolutely employed.

A week after the Republican governors met in Colorado Springs, the National Governors' Conference held what was billed as a "working session" in White Sulphur Springs, West Virginia. But as usual politics was destined to dominate, in ways that would have important implications for 1968. Romney collared a number of his liberal-moderate colleagues, indicated he was going to try his luck at national exposure and asked them to remain uncommitted to anyone else until he had a chance to see what his prospects were. He promised that if he found at any point he could not make it, he would withdraw so that another liberal or moderate could make a run. It was a promise soon forgotten by most, but one that Romney eventually would keep, to the astonishment of everyone.

Although there already was great interest in the Republican jockeying for position for 1968, a totally unexpected development among the Democratic governors shunted the GOP maneuverings to the background and provided the first solid indication of Lyndon Johnson's political vulnerability. On the first night of the long weekend at the grand old Greenbriar Hotel in the West Virginia hills, eighteen Democratic governors got together to discuss some politics; after they were through—several hours later—Lyndon Johnson's ears probably didn't stop ringing for a week. Indiana's fiery old warrior, Roger Branigin, kicked things off with a diatribe against the President; he had failed to inform the governors on planning for his Great Society legislative program, thus leaving them holding the bag on its local implementation and on the adverse political fallout. When the President's old friend (Governor

John Connally of Texas) agreed, an avalanche of bitter criticism was set loose. One after another, the governors sitting around a long table blamed Johnson for Congressional, state and local setbacks in their states in the November off-year elections. They were so irritated that they made no effort to hide from the waiting press what had been spilled out in the private meeting. Soon the nation knew that Johnson had serious internal problems in his own party, and the fact was duly noted by all the Republican hopefuls. If Romney had reservations about challenging an incumbent President, this outburst by the Democratic governors was a persuasive argument to dismiss them.

The first public word of Romney's exploratory trip—which started as a modest swing to Alaska, Idaho and Utah, the base of his Mormon religion—came in late January at a meeting of the Republican National Committee in New Orleans. It was the first such meeting ever held in the Deep South, and Ray Bliss and others made much of the symbolic meaning—the presence finally of a two-party system in Dixie. As is the custom at such meetings, even two years before the next Presidential election, all the major prospective candidates had their agents or at least their supporters on hand; sniffing the political air, trading denials of their own activity and speculation about what others were up to, taking soundings. The most obvious of these unofficial activities was in behalf of Romney. Michigan's national committeeman, John Martin, longtime Romney lieutenant Richard Van Dusen (later his Cabinet undersecretary) and publicist Travis Cross held forth in a hospitality suite. They spread the latest favorable polls and told selected national political writers about the little trip the governor would make, for which there just might be room for a reporter or two.

While the Romney men operated openly at the New Orleans meeting, the agents of Richard Nixon were moving less obviously, but more productively. There was one overt move, and although it was widely publicized it was less significant than other private maneuvers it tended to screen. A letter "surfaced" from Seaton to 900 national committee members, state and local Republican leaders, extolling Nixon's virtues and inviting the recipients to get aboard his Presidential special early. "It is my belief," Seaton wrote in what clearly was part of the preliminary strategy, "that Dick Nixon is the single Republican with the stature, the requisite abilities and the qualities of leadership essential to unite us and maintain our current momentum—to the end that we shall enjoy many more victories at all levels in 1968, including the office of President of the United States."

It was, of course, little more than a temperature-tester. Nelson Rockefeller, in an Albany press conference, indicated he didn't think much of the idea. "I don't think he would get much of a response," he said. "I can't imagine that they are making responses to a former Cabinet member." (Seaton later reported, to nobody's surprise, that the response was "very favorable," and without further ado he predicted Nixon's nomination and election.) Rockefeller, asked whether he thought Nixon should be permitted a second chance at the nomination, was charitable. "I think that anybody is entitled to any chance he wants," he said. "Whether he gets the chance will be determined by the party. Mr. Nixon is an able and dedicated Republican who has devoted his life to public service." This last word of commendation suggested to veteran Rockefeller-watchers that he couldn't bring himself to believe Nixon was in it again; he could afford to throw him a bone. As for himself, having just been reelected after pledging he would not seek the Presidency again, Rockefeller was unequivocal: "I am not, will not and under no circumstances will be a candidate again."

As the Seaton letter grabbed momentary headlines, the Nixon operation was moving ahead secretly in other tasks, the most important of which was to cement the South. Fred LaRue, who had told Nixon in Birmingham in June, 1966, that Reagan would be his greatest Dixie threat, joined forces with at least two other 1964 Goldwater men—Senator John Tower and State Chairman Peter O'Donnell of Texas—to head Reagan off and stash the South away early for Nixon. LaRue among others had told Nixon that in order to "anchor the South, you have to nail down the flanks," and the flanks were Tower on one end and Senator Strom Thurmond of South Carolina on the other. Tower, more the realist of the two, saw before Thurmond where the strength was and where it was moving, and he became the point man of a favorite-son strategy that was to keep Reagan at bay most of the next year and thus keep the South

183

soft for Nixon. Tower himself confirmed at the meeting that he intended to be his state's favorite-son nominee, and that he expected similar favorite sons in Florida, South Carolina, Arkansas and some non-Dixie states like California and Colorado. All these were considered strong for Nixon or at least possible. When put together with hard-core Nixon states like Virginia, Georgia, Alabama, Tennessee, Mississippi and Louisiana, they made an impressive base for a Presidential nomination bid.*

There was, however, a real danger of image. Nixon, running on a Southern base after the Goldwater debacle, would weaken himself in the North, where he had to add strength to shut off the challenge of Romney or some other, later, liberal-moderate threat such as Rockefeller. The favorite-son approach therefore suited Nixon's needs perfectly; it tied up his Southern strength without the requirement that he be clearly tied to the South in the preconvention period. "After 1964," LaRue told me later, "Republicans in the South operated sophisticatedly. They didn't insist on making Nixon a Southern candidate. We were very slow in seeking open commitments; in fact we soft-pedaled them and encouraged the favorite sons."

While thus giving early attention to this veiled Southern base, the strategy also called for a national organization. To this end, the Nixon insiders looked for a man with an activist reputation inside and outside the party, and one whose mode of operation was in keeping with the bedrock of the Nixon push—party unity. One such man had emerged from the 1966 campaign, so obviously that Romney already was after him. He was Dr. Gaylord Parkinson, who as Republican state chairman in California had been instrumental in Reagan's election. Parkin-

---

* While Nixon looked to the South as a key region in his nomination, he knew he could not depend too greatly on it in the general election to follow. George Wallace, now installed as regent for his wife, "Governor Lurleen," already was laying plans for a Dixie-based third-party Presidential bid. In a secret meeting at the Woodley Country Club in Montgomery on the night of Lurleen's inauguration, his backers from Alabama, Louisiana, Missouri and Texas talked tactics, timing and money. Hosts were Asa Carter, a Wallace speechwriter, and the former Dallas County segregationist Sheriff Jim Clark. Among those present were Kent Courtney, the New Orleans right-wing publisher and head of the Conservative Society of America, and Floyd G. Kitchen, chairman of the newly formed Missouri Conservative Party.

son, an obstetrician turned political huckster, put what he liked to call "pizzazz" into Republican politics, but more important than that, a dictum that he called "the Eleventh Commandment." It quickly was renamed "Parkinson's Law," and it ordered, with Biblical simplicity: "Thou shall not speak ill of any other Republican." The phrase was the quintessence of party unity—and especially helpful for any candidate who might be vulnerable to personal attack. Such a candidate in 1966 had been Reagan the politically inexperienced movie actor, but under Parkinson's Law Reagan's Republican primary opponent, former Mayor George Christopher of San Francisco, was unable to capitalize on this personal vulnerability and was snowed under. Nixon himself, having adopted a similar posture of intraparty love (except when calling Rockefeller a "spoilsport"), could use an apostle like "Parky" to preach his unity gospel in the crucial year ahead.

Parkinson, on the way to the New Orleans meeting, had stopped off in Michigan to talk with Romney, who asked him to head his own unofficial campaign. Parkinson said only that he would consider it. When he arrived in New Orleans, however, he met with Tower, O'Donnell, LaRue and Tom Evans, and they urged him to speak to Nixon. A dinner meeting was arranged at the Quo Vadis in New York, and Parkinson flew there, along with Robert Walker, a San Diego public relations man active in the Republican political organization in California. O'Donnell and LaRue followed on a later flight and met with Nixon the next day. Nixon had been persuasive, and it was all set: there would be no announcement for the time being, but Parkinson would be coming aboard as head of the first above-the-table Nixon-for-President Committee. (The Romney forces, irked at having Parkinson snapped from their grasp and concerned about Nixon's staff-building, leaked the word to reporters in the hope of smoking out the fact that his self-imposed moratorium on politics was a deceit.)

As the Nixon campaign thus was going forward underground, Romney's was rapidly becoming an extravaganza, though it still was more than a year before the first Presidential primaries. As word spread of Romney's "exploratory" tour, more and more political reporters clamored to get aboard. It was, as many of

185

them put it, "the only show in town" that far in advance of the election year. Besides, there was a growing interest in finding out whether Romney could "cut it." The governor's past difficulties in stating his positions, on Vietnam particularly, had caused the press to react like hunting dogs who had caught the scent. Here was a man who wanted to be President, but couldn't make himself understood; was he simply unpolished, or was he a lightweight? The reporters set themselves the task of getting the answer for the public, and they pursued it with unusual zest. In the process, though few realized it, they would be playing a role Nixon had cast for them in his own strategy to use Romney.

Afterward, when Romney's encounters with the press had left him badly bruised, the governor blamed it all on what he called "the Teddy White Syndrome." Theodore H. White had made preelection maneuverings so interesting to readers with his *The Making of the President* books, Romney said, that reporters now felt obliged to latch onto anybody who faintly resembled a Presidential prospect, at the very first stirring. This was partly true, but a greater catalyst was Romney himself—his verbal meanderings and the gnawing question: Could he cut it?

The trip, a six-day tour to Alaska, the mountain states, New Mexico and Arizona, provided no final answer, but suspicions grew—as Nixon expected—that it would be "No." On the surface, Romney did well enough; hard-working, earnest, friendly, he drew more than 16,000 persons to formal speeches and raised an estimated $200,000 for local party tills. He was not so stuffy when you got to know him, and he had a sense of humor, though that too, like his views on Vietnam, sometimes got him into hot water. In Anchorage he raced a dogsled and rode a horse, and in Idaho he reminisced appealingly about his country boyhood there. As his campaign bus drove through his old hometown of Rexburg, Romney took the microphone and nostalgically pointed out places he'd been and things he'd done. "See that drugstore on the corner?" he suddenly asked. "I'll tell you, the biggest thrill was to come down to the Rexall drugstore on Sunday and buy a banana split, and while you were there you probably swiped fifty cents' worth of candy and other stuff." (Voices from the rear: "You just blew the Mormon vote.") Speaking at Ricks Junior College in the same town, Romney regaled the students with tales of the young George. Recalling how he was entrusted by a neighbor to drive home a harvesting machine and, after a series of lesser mishaps, finally crashed it into a fence, the governor blurted out: "As you can see, I was really a stupid kid." The Ricks students roared at this and other confessions. Romney, enjoying himself thoroughly, grinned at the reporters accompanying him and added: "The national press here won't think these mistakes are unusual for me."

The Romney humor was not as helpful to him as it might have been because he seemed to have a particular fondness for bathroom stories—clean bathroom stories, of course, but often more effective at getting audiences to squirm than to laugh or applaud. One mild one was about the time his friend Art Linkletter asked a little girl on television "what it's hardest to do without," and she replied, "Toilets." His idea of a big Halloween back in Idaho, he told the Ricks students, was tipping over "those little buildings out back." One morning on his charter plane, Romney switched on the intercom and apologized for being so sleepy. He had got up during the night to go to the bathroom, he explained, and couldn't get back to sleep "because the toilet wouldn't stop flushing."

Romney's wife, Lenore, although in general a tremendous campaign asset to him, had somewhat the same weakness for bathroom stories and for telling them. She loved to fire up her audiences with inspirational anecdotes taken from her own life, and she often would tell how being George Romney's wife wasn't always so rosy. "One day when our children were small," she was fond of recalling, "something went wrong with the bathroom plumbing, so I called a man in. He adjusted a few pipes and gave me a bill for twenty dollars. 'Twenty dollars?' I said. 'For two minutes' work?' And he said to me, 'Lady, you ought to see where I have to put my hands.' Well, I led him right up to the nursery and over to the diaper pail. I opened it and said, 'See where I have to put *my* hands?' " (When the Romneys appeared together, the outcome always was unpredictable and sometimes uproarious. After a very noncommittal introduction by conservative Governor Don Samuelson in Idaho, as Mrs. Samuelson and Mrs. Romney sat uneasily next to their husbands, Romney struggled for something complimentary to say. Finally he blurted: "He and I share a common asset—our wives.")

While the study of the Romney scatological collection was amusing, it was not especially persuasive that here was the next President (although the occupant of the White House at the time had a pretty fair collection of his own). With a contingent of more than thirty reporters along for nearly a week, the pursuit of the substantive Romney was inevitable. The governor had vowed not to enunciate his position on Vietnam until he had been able to take a thorough "fresh look" at the situation, but he could not have known how difficult it would be to sustain that self-pledge. Of more than a dozen speeches and talks during the tour, Vietnam was the major topic in none. But there were, alas, the press conferences. Romney held five, and Vietnam dominated the questioning; with each question Romney was drawn a little closer to the abyss of his own indecision. The press conferences were intended primarily for the local reporters at each stop, but the traveling newsmen could not be excluded, and they monopolized the questioning time, pursuing at the next press conference what they couldn't get answered at the one before. The Romney staff had signed on an itinerant inquisition and couldn't turn it off. "We wanted this to be off-Broadway," Romney lieutenant Walter deVries said at one point. "You take your soundings, and if your staff makes some mistakes or your candidate makes some mistakes you correct them. Well, it's off-Broadway, but they've flown the critics in with us."

Asked about Vietnam almost immediately at his first press conference in Anchorage, Romney said the Johnson administration was "locked in" on the war, with many of its options used, whereas he and the Republican Party had an opportunity to take a fresh look at it. But at Salt Lake City, Romney charged that Johnson was ambivalent about the war, talking peace one day and escalating the fighting the next. When a reporter recalled that in Anchorage Romney had said Johnson was "locked in," Romney issued a clarifying statement saying that the President "is locked into his own mistakes and a rigid defense of his position," but that "the Republican Party is not locked in; it has not exhausted its options. It is free to take a fresh approach." (Romney was forever "clarifying" what he had said. Jack Germond of the Gannett Newspapers, the Groucho Marx of the national political writers, insisted he had a special key installed on his typewriter for the governor's trips that printed at a single stroke: "Romney later explained . . .")

At Pocatello, Idaho—a name that in Republican circles quickly took its place alongside the Cow Palace as synonymous with political disaster—the reportorial circuit riders, unable to get clear answers from Romney aboard the plane, really zeroed in. They tried to establish what options Romney thought he had that the President didn't. For nearly forty minutes, Romney deftly if testily parried the questions, and as long as he stuck to a defense of his moratorium he did not get burned too badly. But then he chose to charge the Johnson administration with "political expedience . . . getting this country in trouble at home and abroad, including Vietnam." That set the inquisition off again. Would he provide an example?" "No, I will not." "Why not?" "Well, because I choose not to." "You're just going to make a charge like that and not substantiate it?" "At this point," Romney replied, his Maginot Line of a jaw jutting out stubbornly, angrily.

From there it was all downhill for Romney. He flatly declined to answer any more press conference questions on Vietnam. But the harm was done. He had been made not only to look uninformed and uncertain, but inept and undisciplined. The badgering of the press was said at the time to have caused Romney to lose control. It was partly that, but it also was the man's abiding dislike for the political style of Lyndon Johnson. Romney considered him a conniving operator of the worst sort, and he was enraged at what he saw as outright misrepresentation by Johnson of what was happening in Vietnam. "This whole war is shot through with politics," the governor told me on his plane one day. "This whole administration is excessively political. The President is a political animal through and through. He's never known anything else." That element of personal pique about Johnson was present later in the year when Romney complained he had been "brainwashed" by the Johnson administration during a 1965 visit to Vietman—a complaint that inflicted the mortal blow to his own Presidential chances.

Although Romney persevered with incredible doggedness the rest of the year, the wounds opened on his shakedown swing through the West never healed. His experience was a classic documentation of the power of the press, and of the use of that power in the guise of informing the electorate. The traveling reporters set out to learn whether George Romney could cut it, and they found out that he could not—at least in the rough-and-tumble of public discussion of issues. For some politicians—notably Richard Nixon—the ability of a public man to take care of himself with the press was indeed a legitimate measure of the man's ability to lead. For those who accepted that yardstick it probably was fair to say that George Romney was not equipped to be President, and it was better for him and the nation to find out early. From the very start of the tour, it became apparent that Romney was an easy mark—easily rattled, combative and hence easily goaded, perfectly willing to play the press' game, even when they greatly outnumbered him and—yes—outthought him on the implications of some of his Vietnam statements. Seeing this vulnerability, the press bore in.

In dealing with Richard Nixon, on the other hand, there seldom was the same relentless pursuit by the press in 1967 or 1968. He had had more than his share of an aggressive press in earlier years, of course, but he was right when he said that reporters had changed in their attitude toward him after the 1962 California press conference. Maybe they didn't have, as he suggested, "a guilt complex" about their accuracy and fairness toward him. But the constant public recollections of that affair certainly encouraged them to think they should. The climate of mutual deference that marked Nixon press conferences during his comeback effort attested to the intimidation of the past. In 1967 and more significantly throughout the campaign year of 1968, when Nixon also invoked a self-moratorium on discussion of Vietnam, the press with very few exceptions let him get away with it. For one thing, he was not the easy mark Romney was; he was deft in turning a touchy or damaging question aside. But one might have thought that would have been all the more reason for relentless interrogation. Nixon reached the White

House without ever saying what he would do about the one major foreign policy issue facing the nation—Vietnam; part of the reason he managed to do so was that he successfully bluffed the press out of applying toward him the same fierce and unremitting pressure for straight answers that undid Romney. If there was press irresponsibility in 1967 and 1968, it existed just as much in giving Nixon a free ride on Vietnam as it did in hounding Romney to political death on the same issue.

In a comeback full of ironies, one of the greatest surely was this: that the press that Nixon in 1962 had charged with giving him "the shaft" was now playing a prominent role in the undoing of the man who was the first major barrier to Nixon's success. That undoing of George Romney was not yet complete, but from Pocatello onward, it was only a matter of time. Richard Nixon realized this fact and he waited—still well out of the line of fire.

9

The Cool Pre-Candidacy

WHILE George Romney was licking the wounds incurred on his Western swing—he told Republicans at a big fund-raiser in Washington that the formula for political success was "blood, sweat and avoiding press conferences"—the Nixon strategy of remaining above the battle proceeded on schedule. The former Vice President departed in early March for another of his well-publicized European tours, accompanied by Bob Ellsworth. (It was a two-man entourage, which was the way Nixon wanted it. "Do we need somebody along to carry the bags?" he asked Ellsworth. The young former Congressman from Kansas said they didn't—and toted them himself.) While Nixon was abroad—not coincidentally—Dr. Parkinson announced to the surprise of nobody that he was indeed taking charge of a Nixon-for-President Committee and would be opening a national headquarters in Washington. His job, "Parky" said with a straight face, was to "convince Dick that he's got enough delegates so that he ought to run." Nixon (the man who had asked Parkinson to take on the job in January) had told him, "Parky" reported, that "I'm not going to give you the red light, I'm not going to give you the green light."

The noncandidate himself, leaving a meeting with German Foreign Minister Willy Brandt in Bonn, acknowledged he had been "informed" of Parkinson's move. "Dr. Parkinson did talk to me about his interest in starting a committee," Nixon said, "and I did indicate to him that I had made no decision with regard to my own political activities, and would not make one in the foreseeable future. But I said that if he desired, he could participate in such activities provided those activities were not directed against any other individual and were positive in their nature." Parkinson breaking his own Eleventh Commandment? Would Lester Maddox start drinking and smoking?

This development did not mean, however, that Nixon did not have some doubts about a 1968 candidacy. According to one intimate, they were in his mind often now. He was, as his opponents kept noting, a two-time loser, and a bad loser the last time out. The impact of his Presidential and gubernatorial defeats and of his bitter outburst after the latter really was unknown. Often in talking with his closest friends, he had discussed what strategy to adopt to cope with these problems from the past. It was suggested at one point that he write a magazine article on the responsibility of the press in political campaigns, a vehicle that would enable him to make reference to his "last press conference" and to put it in a more favorable perspective. But instead he took the tack of laughing it off, and that tactic proved effective. As for the "loser image," Nixon at one point seriously considered writing a book about losers who had come back, or at least had continued constructive political life—Henry Clay, William Jennings Bryan, Robert Taft, others. But the idea was abandoned, apparently because it would only remind people that he was a two-time loser. One Nixon insider, old pro Murray Chotiner, counseled that the "loser image" could be a political plus if handled deftly to paint Nixon as an underdog. "Whenever you heard something about him politically," Chotiner told me later, "everyone would say it was out of the question. So it became an asset, because it made his bid the political comeback of the century, and Americans like underdogs and comebacks. I told him: 'Never try to hide something when you can't hide it. The political comeback of the century— talk about that as an asset.' "

But underdog thinking did not dominate the Nixon strategy. Romney's circumlocutions on Vietnam and other issues increasingly were monopolizing that image; Nixon accentuated the positive at every turn, and these periodic trips abroad were part of that approach—an almost constant reminder that Nixon was the man who had been there, who had met and talked with the *other* famous world figures.

Not everybody was cooperative in this strategy. Prior to Nixon's departure for Europe on this latest trip, the Polish government had denied him a visa, and when he arrived in Moscow after seeing Pope Paul in Rome, Nixon was conspicuously snubbed. Specific requests for interviews with Kremlin leaders were not simply ignored, as often happened; they were flatly rejected.

Nixon was given permission, however, to tour south central Russia—Tashkent, Samarkand and Alma-Ata—and there he engaged in his customary practice of debating with whichever Russian was in sight. In Alma-Ata, a crippled World War II veteran who said he had participated in the linkup with American troops at the Elbe accosted Nixon and demanded, "Get American troops out of Vietnam." And during a factory tour, 200 workers crowded around him, some demanding an American withdrawal from Vietnam. "We too want peace," he said, "but it takes two to make peace." "Yes," a worker shot back, "the two are North Vietnam and South Vietnam." It was hardly a sequel to the kitchen debate with Nikita Khrushchev that had yielded high political dividends in 1959. Before leaving the country, Nixon paid a return visit to Sokolniki Park in Moscow, the site of that debate, but of course Khrushchev no longer was available to take him on. Nixon left Moscow with the reason he went no clearer than when he arrived.

Nixon finished off the trip with visits to Czechoslovakia and Rumania; in the first, after his Moscow snub, he was given a second-echelon treatment by the wary Czechs, but the Rumanians, moving increasingly to an independent posture on foreign policy, gave him a full-dress welcome. He had interviews with Nickolae Ceaucescu, general secretary of the party, and Foreign Minister Corneliu Manescu; the talks, along with the nature of his reception, planted the seed of his later campaign contention that the time had come to "build bridges to Eastern Europe." In the 1968 campaign and later in his inaugural address, Nixon stressed the theme that the two great blocs were moving "from an era of confrontation to an era of negotiation," and Rumania's decision in 1967 to cultivate a prospective candidate for the American Presidency contributed to that idea. The visit undoubtedly figured also in Nixon's decision to visit Rumania in the summer of 1969.*

After his European trip, Nixon moved on to the Far East, this time accompanied by a new addition to his political staff, Raymond K. Price, a thirty-seven-year-old former editorial writer for the New York *Herald Tribune*. Price, signed on as a researcher and speechwriter, provided an ideological counterweight to the conservative Buchanan. It was on this trip that Nixon firmed up his thoughts on the need for a system of Asian regionalism to guarantee the peace after the Vietnam War. A few months later, after Nixon had completed his fourth foreign trip of the year, Price helped him put together a provocative article on "Asia After Vietnam" in the prestigious *Foreign Affairs*. Perhaps more than anything else he had done or said, this article impressed serious students of foreign policy.†

There was, of course, more of Nixon's patented brand of foreign-dateline politicking along the way. In Saigon he again used that spotlighted forum to paint himself as a hawk on the war and to underline President Johnson's inability to unite his own party behind him. It was a "monstrous delusion" to suggest, he said, that any more than 15 or 20 percent of the American public wanted negotiation on the war.

Such statements reaffirmed the public impression of Nixon as a hawk, and if the country generally was moving increasingly away from that sentiment, there was little evidence that Republicans as a party were doing the same. The Gallup organization polled registered Republicans while Nixon was abroad and found a clear majority now favored him over George Romney. The Michigan governor, beset with problems of making his own Vietnam position clear, had lost a 51–42 edge he held over

* It is interesting to note that Nixon's career is dotted with occasions on which he has returned to a scene or a circumstance of triumph or defeat. Hence, the attempt to call on Khrushchev in Moscow in 1965, the return to Sokolniki Park in 1967, the Rumanian visit in 1969. Others are pointed out later in this chronicle.

† See page 217.

Nixon right after the 1966 elections, and now trailed 41–53, and was sinking.

But Romney was holding on—and it was important to the Nixon strategy that he was. Although it was becoming more and more evident that Romney was no match for Nixon, the governor was going to be the instrument of the Nixon reemergence. Like the expert fisherman in political waters he was, Nixon was giving Romney plenty of line, and patiently sitting back while his quarry thrashed himself into exhaustion and defeat. It was a slow and often boring playing-out process, but it was well worth watching for the insight it offered into the strategy and the remarkable self-discipline of the determined Richard Nixon of 1967. Pressure now was mounting on Romney to abandon completely his moratorium on Vietnam, which already had been thoroughly eroded by the press' inquisition and Romney's own fuzziness. While some aides urged him to shove Vietnam discussion to the back burner and talk about other problems, it was clear that something drastic had to be done on that subject to stem the slide. Obviously, he could not continue to accuse President Johnson of "political expedience" in his conduct of the war, and then clam up when asked for examples. The result was a major Vietnam speech in Hartford, Connecticut, in early April, 1967—covered by the national press as if it were an inaugural address—that put Romney on a tightrope. On one hand, he warned against "Americanization" of the pacification program in Vietnam and inflating American peace objectives, yet brushed aside the doves' clamor for a bombing halt and said flatly: "Our military effort must succeed. We must use military force as necessary to reduce or cut off the flow of men and supplies from North Vietnam, to knock out enemy main force units and to provide a military field for the South."

The Hartford speech was a well-prepared and well-delivered effort that showed Romney to be a man of balance on Vietnam. But for the very reason the speech was neither black nor white, it did not really get him out of the woods on the charge of fuzziness. After vacillating so long, Romney had been expected by many to come down on one side or the other. When he failed to do so, it was easy to dismiss him as a force. Johnson himself was quick to take that reading. Deftly, even before Romney had left the hall, the White House rushed out with a statement of the President's "appreciation" to Romney for his "strong endorsement of the fundamentals of the Administration's position on Vietnam." With that one shrewd comment, Johnson blurred the criticism in the speech and helped create the impression that after all the soul-searching, Romney really didn't have much new to say. The President's remarks infuriated Romney; he later said Johnson had given him a "bear hug" that squeezed the impact out of his speech. He was right. (Nixon, in the Far East, had the text of Romney's Hartford speech cabled to him, but made no comment. After what Johnson had said, anything from Nixon would have been overkill.)

A Gallup Poll of Republican county chairmen, released a week after the Hartford speech, showed the dimensions of Romney's troubles. Nixon now led him by nearly four to one; in the East, which was supposed to be Romney's stronghold, Nixon was ahead, 260–177; in the South, it was Nixon, 663, Romney, 53. In spite of his dismal standing in Dixie, Romney resolved to go there and show he was no ogre; or, at the least, to establish for the record that he said the same things about civil rights North and South. In Williamsburg, he spoke to a state Republican organization that already was solidly in the Nixon camp, and he said nothing to budge it; in Atlanta, as was his style, Romney lectured the Atlanta Rotary Club on racial equality, George Wallace and the folly of third parties, and got a cool reception for his troubles. Even when he spoke to a friendlier audience at the predominantly black Morehouse College, he was booed for his views on Vietnam. The Southern venture of the handsome Yankee was a case of little ventured, little gained, but he plunged doggedly forward.

While Romney was getting nowhere in the South, another major figure with a potential for political impact on Nixon even greater than Romney's was just returning from a much more noteworthy excursion into the North. George Wallace, having installed his wife, Lurleen, in the governor's chair, had grown restless with his consort's job and finally had moved to convert his "Stand Up for Alabama" movement into a "Stand Up for America" crusade. Although Wallace since his own election as governor in 1962 had been largely a Deep South

197

segregationist phenomenon, he had been quick to see the possibilities for applying his peculiar political charms and rhetoric to the white backlash in the North. After testing the waters in three Democratic Presidential primaries in 1964, he had found the temperature inviting. It was just a matter of timing, and the right time, in his view, was at hand. Wallace's candidacy in the North, ultimately, would have as profound an impact on Nixon's drive for the Presidency in 1968 as his predictable appeal in the South, and its development accordingly was integral to the Nixon comeback story.

All through early 1967, as Mrs. Wallace carried out the ceremonial duties of her office, George had sat in a smaller office across the corridor in the state capital, running the government and fidgeting. In late afternoons, after Lurleen had gone home, George would cross over and occupy his old chair, like any other second-in-command when the boss was away. For hours he would regale visitors with his personal glories of the past and his imagined future, chain-smoking cigars and knocking ashes in and around the gubernatorial wastebasket. He had it all doped out: eleven American Presidents had been elected without a popular majority, and three of them—John Quincy Adams, Rutherford B. Hayes and Benjamin Harrison—had won without even a popular plurality. The same could happen with him, and he liked to dwell particularly, and with whimsical irony, on one of the eleven named Abraham Lincoln. "Lincoln was a plurality winner, and I'll be a plurality winner," he would explain to a visitor. "In a four-man race he didn't get a majority of the people's votes, but he had enough to get a majority of electoral votes. Well, if I run, this will be at least a three-man race, and the same thing can happen." It was "if" then, but only for public consumption. That George Wallace could be elected President was pure fantasy, but he *could* deny enough electoral votes to either of the major-party candidates to throw the race into the House of Representatives, and the man was raring to go.

There was nothing that gave George Wallace more pleasure than the sound of his own voice retelling how in 1964 they had loved him in the North. "All I have on my side," he was fond of saying, "is the people." And "the people," Wallace made clear, were the taxi drivers, the waitresses, the beauty parlor operators, the steelworkers—"the workin' folks" who were fed up with "bureaucrats in Washington, pointy-headed intellectuals, psuedo- [sometimes pronounced *swayed-o*] intellectual morons tellin' 'em how to live their lives." The statistics (pronounced *stastistics*) of his 1964 primary triumphs tripped easily from his tongue, and the fact was, they were ominously impressive. So while Lurleen was playing lady governor, and George was standing behind her, the Wallace "movement" prepared to go national. A tour of four large Yankee states—New York, Pennsylvania, Ohio and Indiana—was organized, a beat-up relic of a prop plane was chartered, and one of the most ramshackle entourages to hit the road in the history of American Presidential politics headed out from Montgomery.

The first stop was Syracuse, where Wallace spoke to an overflow crowd at a huge field house that big-time football had built. It was a curiously ambivalent audience, picketing him, booing and jeering him, walking out on him, but also applauding him. He hardly had warmed up when a group of blacks came charging up an aisle wearing white sheets and pulling one of their number with a rope around his neck. "Hey, George, we got one!" one of the demonstrators yelled. They all began to chant, over and over again: "Oong-gowah, Black Power!" Wallace watched with a slight smile for a minute, then sat down. Most of the crowd applauded the demonstration, and when Wallace was introduced for a second time, he was thunderously booed. "There's a hot time in the old town tonight," he said, weakly, nervously.

He plunged into a long and often rambling speech, defending Lurleen's candidacy in 1966, insisting he was no racist, attacking the press ("The *Time,* and the *Life* and the *Newsweek*—they all out there in front, they here to dis*tort* what I say"), ridiculing college professors and excoriating "that left-winger in New Jersey who says he *longs* for—that's what he said, he *longs* for—a Viet Cong victory." At almost every sentence there was an interruption of boos and catcalls, and they became so intense that the usually impervious Wallace got edgy, stopped, lost his trend of thought. "Man, this is tough," he said at one point. But he wouldn't quit; he picked himself up and

199

pressed ahead, his little bulldog face pushed out, his fists jammed in the pockets of his navy blue suit, the sneer of defiance-amusement on his little bow lips.

Finally the hecklers got bored and left. Wallace turned cute and flip now, waved at them and thanked them for coming by. The crowd laughed at his outrageous aplomb. Before he was through, Wallace had many in the audience applauding his digs at Lyndon Johnson and his hawkish challenges about Vietnam. But until the heavy police guard had whisked him through pickets outside and into his car, an atmosphere of imminent violence hung heavily over the scene.

Later, back at his motel, when reporters asked how he felt about the picketing and heckling, Wallace professed to be "highly elated" over what he—but apparently nobody else—saw as a royal welcome. "When you can come to Syracuse and get that kind of reception from college students it makes you feel good," he said. "You know I'm not supposed to have any support on college campuses." And then he was off: "If you get that kind of reception from college students up here near the Canadian border, what kind of reception would I get from steelworkers? . . . You ever talk to any of 'em about me? They all for me. . . ."

The rest of the trip was more of the same, though not as raucous as at Syracuse. In Pittsburgh the next night, civil rights protesters marched in orderly fashion around and around the Penn-Sheraton Hotel as Wallace addressed the "Amen Corner," a bunch of Western Pennsylvania fat cats who beamed and purred at the Northern version of his Dixie pitch. Federal open housing legislation, he said, was "an attack on property rights in this country"—just what they wanted to hear. So was his insistence that there was no backlash on grounds of race in the country, just "a backlash against the theoreticians in Washington" who try to undermine local autonomy. After putting on the same basic show in Cleveland and Terre Haute, Wallace headed back to Montgomery, convinced that in North as well as South, he could strum chords of discontent that ran through the American mood. One thing was certain: George Wallace had no trouble translating his Dixie-oriented sales spiel to national politics. He was not a racist; he was not trying to impose school segregation on anybody who didn't want it; civil rights wasn't what worried him; it was the breakdown of law and order. The 1964 Goldwater "code" was operative again, and if George Wallace did not remotely resemble a man who could be elected President, he did emphatically demonstrate his potential for muddying the political waters for the major-party Presidential candidates in 1968.

Through all this temperature-testing by Wallace and by Romney, Nixon resolutely kept his head down, storing up more datelines and foreign leaders for effective name-dropping in the critical year ahead. In Lahore, Pakistan, screaming demonstrators took off their shoes and pounded the hood of Nixon's car, but the veteran of Caracas plunged on. Back in New York, he reported there was "a monstrous myth abroad, created and believed by Hanoi, that the United States is so divided that they can win in Washington and the United States the victory they cannot win on the battlefield." It was America's unofficial ambassador to the world reporting to his only constituency, the people, and his words were transmitted by an American press that began to recognize, what with Romney's floundering and no one else in sight, that this might well be the next Republican Presidential candidate speaking.

Nixon's six-month moratorium on politics now was approaching its end, but he still had a quick trip to South America scheduled, so he put off any major political speechmaking until his return. His old friend Bebe Rebozo accompanied him on an uneventful swing through Peru, Chile, Argentina, Brazil and Mexico, Nixon seeing the President in each country and also finding time for the people-to-people confrontations that always were such good copy back home. In Rio de Janiero, Nixon walked through a slum called Praia do Pinto, shaking hands, jostling dirty kids, chatting with miserable shopkeepers. At one point, the New York *Times* reported, he stopped to talk with a toothless pregnant woman who had three ragamuffins clinging to her. "What do you need most to improve your life?" the solicitous American visitor asked. "Money," the woman said. "What does your husband do for a living?" Nixon inquired. The woman began to laugh—she had no husband. "Thank you very much," Nixon said, and walked off. Did the woman know to whom she had been speaking? "I think he's connected with the movies," she said.

Back home, however, there was no such confusion. As Nixon returned, still another Gallup Poll was out, as if to confirm the wisdom of his six-month policy of "nonpolitical" globe-trotting. His nine-point lead over Romney in April had jumped to fifteen, and among independents, where he had trailed Romney by eight percentage points, he was five ahead.

The plan now called for the first real public exposure of Richard Nixon the likely candidate for President. It would not be too much, because Romney had not yet talked himself thoroughly out of contention and there was no sense in getting in his way. Also, overexposure was more of a threat than underexposure to a man who had been around as long as Nixon had been. Three forums were selected for late May. All were billed as "nonpolitical," in Chicago, Toronto and Philadelphia, just before Nixon was to make still another trip abroad, to fourteen countries in Africa and the Middle East. As usual, there were press conferences in advance of each speech. In these and in his formal remarks, it became clear at once that his six months of globe-trotting had been no mistake. Nixon was treated like, and sounded like, an unofficial Secretary of State. Each speech was tailored to show off his foreign policy credentials; each was a recital of doors opened to him abroad by illustrious world figures, many of them old friends from his days as a global troubleshooter for Eisenhower.

In Chicago, reporting on Latin America, Nixon held the attention of about 2,000 farm-feed manufacturers with a brilliantly presented if somewhat oversimplified hour-long analysis of the continent's woes, a subject not ordinarily of interest to this particular audience. But the man's sense of organization and his self-assurance were nothing short of awesome as he performed without a single note, reeling off statistics on production, population growth, educational levels and gross national products. In Toronto, in what surprisingly for this world traveler was his first speech in Canada, about a thousand businessman members of the prestigious and stuffy Empire Club, after toasts to Queen and President, sat intently in their tuxedoes and listened to Nixon take them on a sweeping hour trip around the world, again extemporaneously. Nixon's views on each area were livened by perspectives of visits only days or weeks ago ("As the President of Chile told me just last week, 'Mr. Nixon . . .' ").

In Philadelphia, Nixon spoke briefly at a luncheon of the World Affairs Council and then fielded timely questions about the Middle East, which now was showing every sign of exploding under the pressure of Arab closing of the Gulf of Aqaba, Israel's sole access to the Red Sea. Nixon's central argument was that if the United States and the Soviet Union saw avoidance of a big-power confrontation in the Middle East as mutually desirable, there would be no war there, because the immediately involved countries could not fight one without outside help. "One of the reasons I do not believe there will be war in the Mideast," he said, "is that those parties who seem to want war lack the power to wage it. And those parties who have the power to wage war in the Mideast do not want it. . . ."

Leaving for Africa almost immediately after his Philadelphia speech, Nixon was flying with Pat Buchanan from Paris to Rabat aboard a Moroccan Airlines plane when the Arabs jolted the world by sending their tanks racing across the Suez desert toward Israel. All was in turmoil as Nixon's plane landed and he learned for the first time what had happened. At a brief press conference he told reporters: "I do not believe that either side has the capability, without massive assistance from a foreign power, of winning a quick victory." Then he and Buchanan were whisked off to the American Embassy, where they waited during the decisive phase of the lightning six-day war that ended in the Arabs' humiliating defeat.

One of the lesser casualties was Nixon's crystal ball—the war did happen, and it was over quickly. His prognostications offered a particularly revealing insight into the workings of Nixon's mind. He was, and remains today, a man of logic with a lawyer's reliance and dependence on it. One of Nixon's great strengths as a speaker was his logic, honed through the years in debate and exchanges with the press. Speeches of an hour or longer flowed with a logical progression that gave his narratives a sense of unity. Listening to him, one could all but see the speech outlined on one of his lined yellow legal pads—one, two, three, four—as the points rolled off his lips. In answering press conference questions, Nixon often would go back, repeat the question, set up a number of possible answers, present them all, reject all but one and say why, then give the one he embraced and say why. In addition to being a debater's clever technique to buy time (Nixon readily admitted as much), the approach projected thoroughness, conviction and self-confidence. It also had the virtue of anticipating follow-up questions and defusing them before they could be asked. ("You're going to say to that, 'Well, just a minute there now, Mr. Nixon, if what you say is so, then how about . . . ?' And I say. . . .")

But Nixon's logical mind could get him in trouble too, as it did in his predictions on the Arab-Israeli war. If one believed that the Arabs and Israelis were dependent on big-power military support to fight a successful war, and that it was not in the interest of the United States and the Soviet Union to have a local war that could lead to a big-power confrontation, then it was logical to expect that the big powers would withhold the necessary support and the war would not happen. And since it was logical to expect that it would take big-power action to give either side enough of a military advantage to start a war, it was logical to assume that if a war nevertheless did start, neither side on its own would be able to win quickly, and thus it would drag on. It was logical, but it was wrong.*

The strengths or weaknesses of Richard Nixon's logic, of course, were not having any appreciable impact on the Presidential picture. His strategy was going according to plan, and

---

* Sometime after Nixon's twin errors of judgment on this war, I referred to them in an article about his reputation as a prognosticator. The reference generated a friendly letter from Pat Buchanan that said: ". . . I think it would be fair to say that Mr. Nixon was right about the Syrians and Egyptians lacking the power to wage war, that he was right that the Israelis had the power to wage war, that he was right . . . that the Israelis did not want a war. The error came, I think, in the underlying assumption that the Israelis could or would tolerate the new status quo imposed by Mr. Nasser. Mr. Nixon held the assumption that there was still a chance that it could be worked out peacefully—but about that time the Israelis had obviously concluded otherwise. So much for the record; the prediction was wrong. . . . For my own part I don't know the origin of Mr. Nixon's prediction that it would be a 'long war' once started, and, indeed, this would seem inconsistent with his statement about the belligerent parties 'lacking the power' to wage war."

although by June it still was more than a year from convention time, the smell of defeat was beginning to pervade the party's liberal-moderate ranks. Romney was running like a dry creek, and there was the usual confusion, lethargy and even backbiting in his wing of the party. One of the freshman governors then identified with the liberal-moderate wing—Spiro T. Agnew—was launching a one-man campaign to draft Nelson Rockefeller, and Rockefeller, who almost alone among the leading liberal governors was thumping for Romney, allowed to an interviewer that as a "last resort" he might be willing to be New York State's favorite-son candidate at the 1968 convention, to hold the 92-member delegation for Romney or some other moderate. The remark seemed to undercut Senator Jacob K. Javits, who was nursing Vice Presidential ambitions and whom Rockefeller earlier had advanced as the state's favorite son. At the same time, even the suggestion of Rockefeller's going to the convention as a favorite son shook the Romney camp and spurred speculation that Romney was indeed, as Nixon himself believed, a stalking horse for Rockefeller. Rockefeller attempted in a second interview to minimize the impact of the first, emphasizing that he had said "might" and insisting he would "do everything within my power to avoid" having to be a favorite son to hold the delegation. Javits and Rockefeller talked by phone and reported that the governor was just as solidly behind Romney as ever.

Whether the seeming disunity in New York Republicanism was a factor or not, ranking members of the Nixon-for-President Committee in Washington began expressing interest in this heretofore off-limits Rockefeller bailiwick. Ellsworth contacted the national political reporter of the New York *Times,* Warren Weaver, Jr., and nonchalantly raised the possibility of New York City Mayor John V. Lindsay as Nixon's running mate. The astonished Weaver checked the Constitution and confirmed that a Nixon-Lindsay ticket would forfeit New York's forty-three electoral votes, since electors can't vote for two men from their own state. Nixon could have cleared that barrier by moving his residence, perhaps to Florida, where he owned property. But Ellsworth made no such suggestion to Weaver. Also, a Long Island lawyer named Vincent L. Leibell, Jr., who had bucked Rockefeller in 1964 and gone to San Francisco as a

Goldwater delegate, announced he would run as a Nixon delegate in 1968. Nixon later disavowed Leibell's support; to the Romney camp, though, it all looked suspicious.

Beyond the personal and financial support of Nelson Rockefeller, George Romney no longer had much going for him. His fellow governors, who had been brushed aside in 1964 and were determined to have a major say in selecting the 1968 nominee, were immobilized by their own indecisiveness and lack of leadership. The Romney camp decided it was time to twist some arms. Two occasions in late June would offer the opportunity—a meeting of all the Western states' governors at West Yellowstone, Montana, and immediately afterward a gathering of all twenty-five Republican governors at Jackson Hole, Wyoming. Romney agents headed for West Yellowstone, but even before they arrived, their hopes were being dashed by some of the very governors they had hoped to corral. Two of the GOP's most outspoken liberals, Governors Tom McCall of Oregon and David F. Cargo of New Mexico, who had got wind of the Romney plan to seek commitments, ran the other way; neither they nor their colleagues were anxious to commit themselves to a man who was looking less like a winner every day, they said. McCall observed flatly that Romney's campaign was "lying dead in the water now."

This kind of talk deflated the Romney blitz even before it got rolling. His agents denied at Jackson Hole that they ever had any intention of seeking firm commitments from his fellow governors. It sounded like Lyndon Johnson saying in 1966 he never had had any plans to campaign—and it was believed exactly as much. Romney himself did not attend, having been obliged—conveniently or otherwise—to stay in Lansing with a foot-dragging state legislature.

Romney's failure to attend, on balance, probably was a good thing; it saved him embarrassing questions about his lack of support. More important, it relieved him of a comparison that he as a Presidential hopeful might have found even more embarrassing. At the opening session in West Yellowstone, at which all the Western governors wore cowboy outfits, the entrance of Ronald Reagan, as tall in the saddle as in his grade-B movie days, reduced all the other governors to bit players. He was, said McCall, right out of American folklore, and tourists and television cameramen alike fell over each other getting him in focus. Politicians, too, took note when the word got around that one F. Clifton White, mastermind of the Barry Goldwater takeover in 1963-64, was in town, reportedly in the service of Reagan.

It was from this point forward that Reagan began to be regarded as a likely candidate. For all his denials—cowboy boot toeing the dirt, boyish smile, head shaking from side to side—Reagan was box office; he was from the most populous state, and no matter what Nixon could say or do, he was the emotional heir of Goldwater. Reagan already had opened the door to the skeptics by announcing he would be California's favorite son in 1968. Ostensibly, the decision sought to avoid a divisive state primary and thus send a united and influential delegation to Miami Beach in 1968. But then Reagan said he would permit his name to remain on the Oregon primary ballot, and heads nodded knowingly. He could not conscientiously ask that it be removed, he explained, because to have it stricken under Oregon law, a man had to say he would not accept the nomination. And having agreed to be the California favorite son, Reagan said, such a statement would be dishonest. Translated loosely by those who had heard all the variations before, this meant: "I'm not ruling out anything."

Among those at West Yellowstone and Jackson Hole who were watching and listening were Nixon agents Bob Ellsworth and Pat Hillings. They kept their ears open and did little active lobbying. They didn't have to do much; the governors were doing fine for Nixon on their own, with their disposition to remain uncommitted to Romney. If the governors did not get together in a stop-Nixon bloc, the only roadblock would be the primaries—the primaries and a hard-charging Reagan eroding Nixon's carefully nurtured Southern base.

About the only intelligence that blurred the picture of a thriving Nixon operation was a rumor that after a splashy beginning as chairman of the Nixon-for-President Committee, Gaylord Parkinson was on his way out. After setting up his jazzy headquarters in Washington, with big blowup pictures of Nixon and an N-shaped lightning bolt for an emblem, "Parky"

207

had set about creating Nixon organizations in the first primary states. He had gone to New Hampshire like a cheerleader, trying to pump his gung-ho spirit into staid Yankee Republicans. "Parky was a salesman," one of his cohorts told me later, "but he came on a little strong for them. He went up there once to meet a group of old Republicans, and all he talked about was young people and pizzazz." Soon backs were up, not only in New Hampshire but in other states where loyal Nixon supporters were eager to work on Nixon organizations—but their own way. "He was a great one to come up with plans," another Nixon insider said later, "but when it came to execution, he didn't have it." Nixon, an issue man, began to lose patience too with Parkinson and his "pizzazz." He was suspicious also that Parkinson might be keeping an oar in with Reagan back in California.

What to do about Parky became more and more of a problem. Momentum in politics as in football can be a definite plus, and Nixon was building momentum. The dumping of his national chairman would precipitate unfortunate publicity and work against the image of inevitability that the Nixon campaign was trying to encourage. Then fate intervened. Dr. Parkinson's wife, seriously ill, underwent major surgery. Parkinson informed Nixon he would have to leave. The search began immediately for someone to step in so that the change could be achieved with a minimum of disorder and adverse speculation about organizational troubles within the Nixon campaign.

Stans asked Bob Ellsworth to take over as executive director of the committee, with another more prominent Republican as chairman. The search in late July or early August settled on former Governor Henry Bellmon of Oklahoma, one of his state's all-time vote-getters, popular among the GOP governors and a longtime good friend of Peter Flanigan. Bellmon had been called in by Flanigan on some of the early 1967 Nixon strategy meetings. He knew where the Nixon campaign was going, who was involved in it and where work had to be done. Unlike Parkinson, Bellmon came on distinctly soft sell; Nixon had known him since 1960, when Bellmon served as his Oklahoma chairman and helped him carry the state with ease.

But there was at least one major drawback concerning Bellmon too. He didn't want the job. He already had begun preliminary work for another campaign of his own—for the United States Senate in 1968 against the formidable senior Senator from Oklahoma, Mike Monroney. Bellmon also argued that he was not the best man; he didn't know the national political scene and wasn't familiar enough with national issues. Flanigan persisted and Bellmon resisted, until finally Nixon himself called. Bellmon relented, but informed Nixon he could not serve beyond November if he had any hopes of beating Monroney.

The negotiations over a successor to Parkinson did not really slow the Nixon operation because Ellsworth and others had been doing the real spadework all along. Bellmon was to be a front man of sorts, with special lines to the Republican governors. And that was the way it worked through the fall of 1967. Meanwhile, without fanfare, Nixon's latest law partner and confidant, John Mitchell, was beginning to move inexorably into the political sphere. His initial emergence did not square with his later image as a tyrannical, protective power-seeker; actually he started as another lieutenant in the field. Yet in his first outing in Presidential politics, he demonstrated his penchant for organization—the meat and potatoes of the successful candidacy. While Parkinson was ruffling feathers in New Hampshire, Mitchell was resolutely building a tight Nixon group in the second primary state, Wisconsin. In the 1950's, he had helped develop the state's borrowing system by drafting legislation establishing its borrowing agency. Now, the man who had become head of that agency, Jerris Leonard, was planning to run for the Senate as a Republican. He joined forces with Mitchell in 1967 and with a group of political veterans who had put Governor Warren P. Knowles in the statehouse for two terms. A Milwaukee lawyer and Mitchell associate named John MacIver, hard-working, astute and personable, was appointed chairman of the Wisconsin Nixon-for-President Committee, and by late July a full-scale organization was unveiled, staffed by forty-two experienced campaigners. The plan, dull stuff on paper but vital to a winning campaign, was to have chairmen in each of the seventy-two counties, the ten Congressional districts and about fifteen or twenty of the largest cities and towns. The Milwaukee public relations and advertising firm of McDonald-Davis-Schmidt Inc. geared up a sophisticated advertising campaign centered on Nixon's foreign policy experience. Though as matters developed this organization never had a real challenge, it was an impressive political force in its thoroughness and professionalism. Mitchell in his first outing had managed to tie up the key Republicans in Wisconsin. In the succeeding months, he was to launch similar operations in most other states, drawing in almost always the influential and effective members of the local Republican establishment. It was true that he was planting seed in the political soil that Richard Nixon had been preparing ever since 1963, but his administrative talents nevertheless were impressive.

Organizational work was going forward now not only in the primary states but in those that did not have primaries, in the fashion of the Goldwater operation of 1964. But because Nixon knew he had to dispel his "loser image" he purposely helped focus public and press attention on the primary states. It was time to be less coy. In a series of individual interviews with political reporters from the leading newspapers, he began finally to discuss his likely candidacy openly and to stress the importance of the primaries. He told Warren Weaver in late July that "winnability" was his chief problem. "More than the others, I have to win every primary," Nixon said. "Rockefeller, Percy and Reagan are in an enviable position. They can sit back and see what happens. I can't." If he failed to demonstrate in the early primaries that he was the strongest Republican, he said, he would get out, rather than hold on and work for a deadlocked convention. "I'm not going to the convention as a second- or third-string candidate to sit on a clump of delegates and try my hand at brokering," he told Weaver. "By that time, assuming I decide to run, I'll either be in or out. . . . As far as I'm concerned, I'm going to get the nomination if I prove I'm the strongest candidate. If I can't demonstrate that, nothing else I do is going to mean anything."

Those remarks certainly seemed to be laying it on the line. But they were the kind of comment political reporters of late had come to expect from Nixon; candid to a degree that sometimes seemed self-destructive. Nixon aide Steve Hess and David Broder, in their 1967 book, *The Republican Establishment,** observed accurately: "Nixon has, in one sense, compounded his problem. In making himself more accessible to reporters, he has also made himself more visible, and what is perceived is Nixon the Manipulator, the man of technique, not of substance. It is Nixon's habit, for example, on his cross-country campaigns for congressional candidates, to brief the reporters aboard his plane about the political background, personalities, special issues and special problems of the district or state he is about to enter. The briefings are extremely useful to the press; were he not a politician, Nixon would make a superb political reporter, for his insights are shrewd, his information encyclopedic and his gift for summary and exposition exceptional. But . . . Nixon is not content to be admired. Rather than let the reporters discover for themselves how he adapts his basic speech to the situation, he goes on to say, 'Now, this is a pretty conservative district, so you'll notice I don't bear down as heavily on . . .' or, 'The Democratic incumbent here has been a very good Congressman, so I'm going to have to stay away from personalities and concentrate more on . . .' "

Nixon had demonstrated this same self-damaging candor to me in his remark that when he occasionally makes a favorable comment about the opposition "it's a device, of course, to show I'm fair-minded."

There is always a great temptation, in dealing with a public figure who so obviously stands a wary guard over his own image and who regards the press—even now—as an adversary, to practice amateur psychoanalysis on him. This is particularly so with Nixon, because his irregular afflictions of candor do not square with the cautious demeanor he usually shows the press and public. Whenever a more relaxed, more humorous, less partisan Richard Nixon has shown himself in the past, the appearance has sparked another round of comparisons between "the old Nixon" and "the new Nixon." This has happened so often over the years that Nixon-watchers have been obliged to go on to "the new, new Nixon" and beyond in discussing the changes.

* New York, Harper & Row, 1967.

The man himself says he deplores all the talk about new Nixons. "There's been no significant change," he told me in 1966. "People go through that psychological bit nowadays. They think they should always be reevaluating themselves. I fight the battles as they come along. That sort of juvenile self-analysis is something I've never done." Yet it seems to those who have watched and listened to him closely since his 1960 and 1962 defeats that self-analysis has been one of his practices to the point of preoccupation, and a practice that has contributed to his later political success. In a particularly revealing interview with James J. Kilpatrick in the *National Review* in late 1967, Nixon himself offered the best analysis anyone has given of his recent, and excessive, candor.

"The old label clings," wrote Kilpatrick, "like an outworn bumper sticker: Tricky Dick." But rather than discount the liabilities of his two earlier defeats, he went on, Nixon "talks of them with the detached interest of a baseball fan appraising his club; good field, no hit. He sees himself critically, as a man studies his mirror image for blackheads and ingrown whiskers. His purpose is to acknowledge the defects, and to do what he can about them." Then it was Nixon talking: "All right. They still call me 'Tricky Dick.' It's a brutal thing to fight. If anyone takes the time to check my public record fairly—and it's all there, the votes I cast, the speeches I made, the things I wrote—he'd have to conclude that on the great issues of the past twenty years, my record is clear and consistent. Look at my record on civil rights; and then look at Lyndon's. But I've been in this game long enough now to know that few voters have the time or inclination to study a record. The carefully cultivated impression is that Nixon is devious. I can overcome this impression in one way only: by absolute candor."

It was as if he were saying, "Okay, starting tomorrow morning at eight o'clock—I start telling the complete truth." Nixon in recent years has practiced this antideviousness technique so pointedly—and obviously—that it became a standing joke not only among the press but among some Nixon staffers. As the campaign of 1968 approached and all during it, Nixon killed his listeners with his candor. And as usual he was not satisfied with the *act* of candor; he always had to hang a clear label on it, for those who might miss the fact he was being untricky. Hardly a speech or an interview went by without repeated phrases like "to be perfectly candid," "speaking quite frankly," "putting it bluntly," and so on. What followed was not always candid, frank or blunt, but for those not familiar with the substance of what he was discussing, the *impression* was likely to be one of candor. (Nixon used the same technique to combat charges that he never dealt in specifics. "Let me be quite precise," he would say, and then go off into generalities.)

Candor, of course, has its limits, as George Romney soon learned in an episode that was to have a catastrophic impact on his already floundering campaign. On the last day of August, Romney appeared on a Detroit television show. Still plagued by his image of fuzziness on Vietnam, he was asked: "Isn't your position a bit inconsistent with what it was, and what do you propose we do now?" Romney responded: "Well, you know when I came back from Vietnam, I just had the greatest brainwashing that anybody can get when you go over to Vietnam. Not only by the generals, but also by the diplomatic corps over there, and they do a very thorough job. And since returning from Vietnam, I've gone into the history of Vietnam, all the way back into World War II and before. And, as a result, I have changed my mind . . . in that particular. I no longer believe that it was necessary for us to get involved in South Vietnam to stop Communist aggression."

This statement, which went unnoticed and unreported for several days until the TV interviewer alerted newspapers, in itself might not have been so damaging coming from someone else. With the credibility gap of the Johnson administration ever widening, and with the civilian's normal mistrust of the military, it was believable that an attempt to brainwash a visiting politician from the opposition party would be made. What hurt was that Romney was admitting that the brainwashing worked, and in the context of his already muddled image as a thoroughly confused man on Vietnam, that too was readily believable. The "brainwash" quote itself was bad enough; what made it cataclysmic for Romney was that it summed up perfectly the public unease about him; it was a convenient catchall phrase with which to dismiss this dogged, somehow irksome man who would not go away. Later, in the early days of the New Hampshire primary, reporters traveling with Romney amused themselves during dinner by writing a theme song for him, to the tune of "Something Stupid," a currently popular ditty recorded by Frank and Nancy Sinatra:

> I know I stood ahead of all until I went and dropped the ball
> By talking too much.
> I tried so hard to satisfy the press' request to clarify
> Vietnam and such.
> And then I went out in the cold to try to get a little vote or two;
> I had to go and spoil it all by saying something stupid like
> "I'm brainwashed."

But it was no joke for Romney. He dropped sixteen points in the Harris Survey. The largest newspaper in his state, the Detroit *News,* ran an editorial demanding that Romney "get out of the presidential race" in favor of Rockefeller as a result of the "brainwash" remark. It showed, the paper said, that Romney apparently was unable to adequately organize and coordinate "a purposeful campaign" or to "articulate specific goals." It noted that Romney had repeatedly supported the Vietnam War in the two years after his Saigon visit and asked, "How long does a brainwashing linger?" Romney called a press conference in Washington, brushed off the *News'* editorial, insisted he was talking about "LBJ-type brainwashing, not Russian-type brainwashing," and vowed to press on. Nixon, busy writing magazine articles based on his travels, said nothing.

The new Nixon-for-President chairman, Henry Bellmon, had plenty to say, however. "Mr. Romney has shown weaknesses that in a Presidential campaign he would find damaging," he told reporters at a Washington press conference. For specifics, he cited the "brainwash" statement. He was one of the governors on the same trip, Bellmon said, and he "did not come back with the feeling Mr. Romney expressed. I believe we were fully and factually informed. There was no indication we were misled or brainwashed in any way." It was a telling blow to Romney's position, but Bellmon was not applauded by his new

214

boss for administering it. Such comments were a violation of "Parkinson's Law." "Ray Bliss called me too and chewed me out," Bellmon said later.

Bellmon's remarks came on the occasion of a meeting of the Republican National Committee at which the Nixon strategy board had resolved to put on a good front, to impress influential GOP officials his campaign was humming. Bellmon and Ellsworth ran a large hospitality suite with plenty of liquor, campaign buttons and literature, and pretty girls to hand them out. It was as if election year already had arrived and Nixon was the nominee. Friendly Congressmen and other prominent Republicans were assigned to each of the 100 members of the national committee, to sell them on Nixon with favorable polls and newspaper columns, and generate the idea that Nixon was on his way. And at around the same time, Bellmon and Ellsworth made a pilgrimage to Gettysburg to ask General Eisenhower to speak out for Nixon. He declined to commit himself, although in a review of all the potential candidates he left little doubt in Bellmon's mind that eventually he would be for his old Vice President. Eisenhower's early endorsement would have been helpful, but it wasn't vital.

Everything was pointing now toward the first primary, in New Hampshire. Romney was a setup, and New Hampshire was the place to knock him over, and in so doing strike the first blow against Nixon's loser image. At another meeting of the strategists, the field of prospective local leaders was scanned and it was decided this time to bypass all the former governors and factions. Picked was a twenty-eight-year-old lawyer named David J. Sterling, a state legislator and weekly newspaper columnist who could devote full time to the campaign, mobilizing young Republicans and particularly his colleagues in the state legislature.* New Hampshire was a small state, always favorable to Nixon in the past, hawkish on the war, and essentially old-line Republican. The plan would be to commit all the regular party people, leaving Romney to scramble for support; Nixon would be presented not as some grubby supplicant, but as the worldly heir apparent.

* Shortly after the inauguration of Richard Nixon in 1969, David Sterling lost his life in an auto accident in New Hampshire.

The early New Hampshire polls already indicated Nixon to be far ahead of Romney. If it turned out to be just the two of them, the Nixon strategists had no worries. There remained the possibility, however, that Reagan, under pressure from aides in Sacramento, might permit his name to go on the ballot there and in later primaries. Any serious splintering of the vote could dilute the impact of Nixon victories, casting doubt on whether he really was a winner again. Shortly after the 1966 elections, Goldwater had gone to see Reagan at Nixon's specific request and reported back that Reagan wasn't interested in the nomination. Nixon himself had met Reagan in California in late July. Reagan reaffirmed that he would be a favorite son in California, and Nixon pledged he would not challenge him. Nixon in an interview with David Broder expressed fears of Reagan's clouding the primaries and then emerging the winner in a brokered convention. "If I came out as the choice of a backroom meeting, people would say, 'The voters didn't want him but the bosses did.' "

Romney, meanwhile, was still in there pitching, this time on a month-long self-education tour of urban problem areas—again with the press in inquisitional pursuit. The highlight of the trip was a confrontation between George and Lenore Romney and a few hundred hippies in a park in San Francisco's Haight-Ashbury, with the bearded and sandaled love children asking Romney what he would do about Vietnam. Romney promised to send them copies of his Hartford speech!*

Of greater concern to the Nixon camp, understandably, was word that Reagan was planning some travel of his own, and not to Haight-Ashbury. The California governor, with former Sacramento aide Tom Reed beating the bushes ahead of him, made a "sentimental journey" back to Eureka College in Illinois, his alma mater, and then went on to Columbia, South Carolina, and Milwaukee, drawing huge crowds at each stop and setting Republican cash registers ringing. In each state Nixon was

---

* The Romney urban tour was best summed up by Jon Lowell, then of the Detroit *News*, as Romney's plane came in over New York City. "There are eight million stories in *The Naked City*," Lowell proclaimed, mimicking the standard close of the prominent TV series of the day, "and we're covering the dullest."

strong, and those on the Reagan staff who were dreaming of the White House were encouraged. But so far, at least, it was no more than fund-raising, and Reagan clung to his contention that he was just another favorite son.

Although all this activity made some Nixon backers nervous, their leader kept to his controlled schedule. He made his first major foreign policy speech of the year in New York in mid-September, charging that the Johnson administration's credibility gap existed abroad as well as at home and calling on the nation to "speak with a new candor"—much as he was doing on the campaign trail. Nixon also had finished by now two major magazine articles on which he had been working during the summer. They were published in October, one on "Asia After Vietnam" in *Foreign Affairs* and the other in the friendly mass-circulation *Reader's Digest,* on crime. The Vietnam piece enhanced his rating with academics and came in time to be a fundamental paper in the Nixon administration's early bid to lower unilateral American commitments in Asia. He made a strong if somewhat wishful case for development of a Pacific community of nations that would take the leading anti-Communist role in Asia after the Vietnam War was ended, an "emergence of Asian regionalism" with Japan at the focal point that would give the United States a chance to get out from under in the area, though retaining considerable influence.

While still locked into the Cold War rhetoric of the 1950's that remained his personal point of reference, Nixon wrote: "One of the legacies of Vietnam almost certainly will be a deep reluctance on the part of the United States to become involved once again in a similar intervention on a similar basis. The war has imposed severe strains on the United States, not only militarily and economically but socially and politically as well. Bitter dissension has torn the fabric of American intellectual life, and whatever the outcome of the war the tear may be a long time mending. If another friendly country should be faced with an externally supported communist insurrection . . . there is a serious question whether the American public or the American Congress would now support a unilateral American intervention, even at the request of the host government."

The *Reader's Digest* article, also polished and well reasoned, projected the domestic Nixon as more conservative. Although when taken as a whole, the article recognized the need to attack social problems in the black slums, the bulk of it was a hard pitch for repressive police measures: "While attacking the problems with urgency we must await the results with patience. But we cannot have patience with urban violence. Immediate and decisive force must be the first response."

At one point, Nixon lapsed into the simplified rhetoric that was more in keeping with his campaign style: "Our judges have gone too far in weakening the peace forces as against the criminal forces. Our opinion-makers have gone too far in promoting the doctrine that when a law is broken, society, not the criminal, is to blame." (Or, as George Wallace was putting it at the same time: "It's gettin' nowadays that a policeman gets hit over the head and before they can get him to the hospital, the judge is orderin' that the man who hit him be turned out of the jailhouse and back on the street to hit somebody else.") Shortly after publication of the *Reader's Digest* article, Nixon in a speech on the same subject struck more balance between repression and social rehabilitation. "While adequate police forces are part of the answer to the short-range problems," he said, "the long-range problems will not yield to superior force alone. . . ." But the basic image that emerged was that of a man committed to what increasingly was coming to be known in the catchphrase as "law and order."

While Nixon's writings thus were keeping his name prominently in print, two other Republican prospects, Nelson Rockefeller and Ronald Reagan, suddenly were becoming the subject of some most unlikely speculation—that they might somehow be brought together on the same "dream ticket." In mid-October the National Governors' Conference, in its endless search for the better watering hole, chose the Virgin Islands for its annual spectacle, with Rockefeller and Reagan the star political attractions. To get there, the governors cast taxpayers' criticism aside and chartered the S.S. *Independence* for what will go down in the annals of political junketing as the Granddaddy of Them All. Governors, their wives, children, staff aides, political hangers-on and reporters took over the cruise ship for, as they say, nine fun-filled days and nights. From the tip of the ship's stern—from whence came noontime strains of steel band rhythms while the governors and guests lunched on Bloody Marys and lobster—to its bow—where the duly elected swingers danced and drank each night away in the ship's bar—it was a gas. As Rockefeller and Reagan came aboard at the Manhattan pier, *Time* was on the stands with a cover picture of the two governors as possible Republican running mates. That, and Romney's sliding fortunes, put Rockefeller in the spotlight as the ship sailed out of New York harbor. Reporters corraled him on the ship's sun deck and asked him about the *Time* cover.

"I wouldn't be human if I didn't appreciate a nice remark," Rockefeller told them, "but I'm not a candidate, I'm not going to be a candidate, and *I don't want to be President.*" The newsmen weren't sure they had heard him correctly. Was he saying flatly he didn't want the job? "You heard me loud and clear," he said. Did he mean that if nominated by the Republican Party, he would reject the nomination? "I *said* [this time with some irritability] I don't want to be President."

Although Rockefeller had indicated repeatedly that he wasn't going to be a candidate, this was something else again. Word of the comment buzzed through the ship. Agnew, his draft-Rockefeller drive seemingly scuttled, refused to quit. "That's pretty definite," he acknowledged, "but I still say if he's drafted it would take a pretty emphatic individual to turn down a genuine draft. Indeed, I can't conceive of it." Nixon, in Washington to talk to Republican Congressional leaders, agreed. He said he had no doubt Rockefeller would take the nomination if it were offered to him.

Romney, of course, was heartened by Rockefeller's statement. In fact, he had met with Rockefeller on the ship and had asked point-blank whether, in spite of all that had been said, he wanted to run. Romney was facing the fact that his campaign was foundering, and the question was his way, one Romney insider said later, "to keep Rocky honest. In effect, George was saying, 'I'm giving you your excuse for walking away from me. The best way for me to make sure you're sticking with me is to offer it to you.' " At that point, clearly, Rockefeller wasn't taking.

Rockefeller's disavowal of interest was not the only temporary lift for Romney's spirits on the Virgin Islands cruise. There also was the melodrama called "The Night Marvin Watson Sank the *Independence*." In a scenario right out of an old Marx Brothers movie, Lyndon Johnson attempted an arm-twisting ploy on Vietnam that had Romney cavorting around the ship gleefully proclaiming, "I told you so!" In two past governors' conferences, Romney had balked against a resolution supporting the President on the war. Like the Senate's Tonkin Gulf resolution, he had argued, it amounted to a "blank check" for whatever action Johnson cared to take. Now, because conference rules required a three-fourths approval of any proposal, the twenty-one Republican governors aboard the *Independence* (out of forty-two) could easily block any Democratic-proposed Vietnam resolution.

As the ship plied the blustery Atlantic and Romney lobbied hard against the approval of another "blank check," a message from the White House came over the ship's radio to former Governor Price Daniel of Texas, newly appointed by Johnson to be his goodwill ambassador to the governors. The cable, from Presidential political aide Marvin Watson, instructed Daniel to strong-arm the Republican governors to back a Vietnam resolution, and particularly to put heat on Republican Governor James A. Rhodes of Ohio by asking him whether "he is now running out on his former position" of support. The message was taken by the ship's radio operator in the early hours of the morning, typed and delivered in a sealed envelope to Daniel. Sometime before daylight, a press aide to Governor Reagan, an old Washington newshound named Lyn Nofziger, somehow obtained a copy of Watson's telegram and turned it over to his boss. Reagan informed his Republican colleagues of the discovery, and Nofziger was commissioned to tip off the press. This he did that night while the governors frolicked at a costume party that could have been part of an old Carmen Miranda musical. A duplicating machine in the ship's pressroom soon was grinding out the "secret" cable wholesale, while reporters en masse elbowed their way past undulating governors and partners in the ship's bar to get Republican comment. Romney, a graduate of a Washington dancing club in earlier days, was going Latin on the dance floor, in a huge straw slouch hat, native beads and bright multicolored tropical shirt.

"I think it brings into the open the type of service rendered by the Office of Emergency Planning [Daniel's office]," Romney crowed when asked about the cable. He wished Daniel and Watson "luck in their new jobs"—assuming they would get the ax for their gaffe—and said the incident was another example of "news manipulation, snow job, hogwash and attempts at brainwashing." And he trotted off gaily with his partner, the wife of Governor Daniel Evans of Washington. Reagan, sitting with his wife at the edge of the crowded floor, blithely sipping crème de menthe through a straw, declined to say how he had got hold of the telegram. After years of being the other man in the movies, he clearly was a hero in this reel and was enjoying it immensely.

As Republicans rushed to have their observations transmitted ashore through the press, Democrats were escaping everywhere but over the side. The President's chief ally, Governor John Connally of Texas, locked himself in his cabin and gave instructions to the ship's phone operator not to disturb him. Elizabeth Carpenter, Mrs. Johnson's press secretary, hustled round the ship trying to persuade reporters they were overplaying the story, but it was beyond even her talents at press agentry. Daniel, on learning the cable had been purloined and leaked, telephoned Watson to advise him. Asked later what Watson had said when he heard the news, Daniel replied: "Keep up the good work." The upshot of the whole mad night was the scuttling of the Vietnam resolution, along with tentative plans (or, rather, tentative nonplans, as was the President's preference) for Johnson to fly to the Virgin Islands and address the conference there.

Although Romney and to a lesser extent Reagan emerged as the political winners in the episode, Nixon too had reason to be pleased. In torpedoing the Vietnam resolution and turning the case of the Watson telegram to Republican advantage, the GOP governors had demonstrated a unity for the party they had not been able to muster behind one of their own members as a Presidential candidate. At the same time, Nixon's agents aboard —Bellmon and John Sears—were able to confirm to him that the governors were staying loose. Bellmon, distinctly soft sell, kept the governors posted on how the Nixon organization was moving. He spent a great deal of time working on Rhodes, who still was inclined toward a Rockefeller-Reagan ticket. The governors were not willing to jump aboard the Nixon bandwagon, but neither were they making any serious moves to ambush it.

While Romney and his gubernatorial buddies thus were cavorting to and from the Virgin Islands, Nixon was using the time out of the spotlight for some preliminary reconnoitering in the first primary states. In speeches in Laconia, New Hampshire, and Waukesha, Wisconsin, he reiterated his determination to stick to his hard-line position on Vietnam. There might be movement in the country generally toward a more dovish attitude, but it wasn't evident in Republican circles, and that's where the GOP nominee would be chosen. The Gallup Poll for October showed Nixon still the choice of the Republican rank and file, with 42 percent of all those polled, compared to only 18 percent for Rockefeller, 14 percent for Reagan and 13 percent for Romney. And for the first time, Nixon bested President Johnson in a two-man test, 49 to 45 percent, with 6 percent undecided.

There seemed to be no end to Nixon's rising fortunes. During a television interview in Oregon, he let slip a bit of family news that also did his political aspirations no harm—daughter Julie and General Eisenhower's grandson, David, were engaged to be married. ("The next move," said one cynic in the press corps, "is for Tricia to bag George Gallup's grandson.")

The Virgin Islands cruise marked the end of the preliminary shadow-boxing for the 1968 campaign; although Romney may not have known it yet, he was out on his feet. While he laid plans for a Romney-style handshaking, moral-fervor blitz of New Hampshire starting shortly after the first of the election year, Nixon sat back, surveyed the opposition, and contemplated his next moves like a chess player closing in patiently on checkmate. The polls in the state showed him to have a huge lead, the kind that Romney on his own could not hope to close; the only threat was an unforeseen blooper by Nixon, and the best way to avoid that was to say as little as possible. This, pure and simple, was the Nixon strategy for New Hampshire: show the flag, ignore Romney, project the Elder Statesman and let the sure victory roll in, sweeping over the troublesome loser image once and for all. (A Harris Survey in December, 1967, while showing Nixon far ahead of all other Republicans, noted that 56 percent of those polled felt "he has lost too many elections.") Romney thus had been made to order for the Nixon strategy: an experienced candidate who never had lost. Beyond that, the longer Romney stayed in, the longer Rockefeller— pledged so completely to Romney—would have to stay out.

After a year of the most dogged, punishing testing of the political temperatures, Romney finally lowered himself into the water in mid-November, in a press conference in Detroit that packed all the surprise of a Russian election. He would take his campaign into every corner of New Hampshire, he said, and would win. Almost at once, however, the emptiness of this optimism again was demonstrated. In early December, the Republican governors—whose candidate Romney had hoped and expected to be fully a year earlier when they had met at White Sulphur Springs—convened again in Palm Beach. Romney himself was not there, finally having gone off on his long-delayed trip to Europe, the Soviet Union and a Christmastime visit to South Vietnam. But his chief agent, Nelson Rockefeller, was on hand to make yet another try to shake the indecisive liberal-moderate majority to action. Right behind him were Nixon's men—Bellmon, Ellsworth, Sears—reminding the governors of the catastrophic results of a stop-Goldwater effort in 1964. They drew from many governors a pledge that if the former Vice President appeared to be on his way to winning the nomination, they would not be part of a similar stop-Nixon drive.

Finally it was time to unveil some muscle. The Nixon camp did so in Governor Tim Babcock of Montana, a conservative who had been thought to be a Reagan man but who had been committed secretly to Nixon for at least two months. Babcock told reporters he was perfectly willing to go along with Nixon if he could demonstrate he could win in the first two primaries. If so, Babcock would have no part of a stop-Nixon drive, in favor of Reagan or anybody else. Rockefeller tried to hold the line, calling Romney "one of the great campaigners" who by "going to the people of New Hampshire in an exciting way" could pull an upset. Most other liberals and moderates weren't buying it.

"It's beginning to look like we'll have to reconcile ourselves emotionally and ideologically to Nixon," said Governor Tom McCall of Oregon, who had been boosting Rockefeller as an alternative to Romney.

Governor John A. Love of Colorado, also considered a moderate, reflected the success of the Nixon operation. "If Nixon wins the first two or three primaries," he said, "and someone calls a meeting to draft Rockefeller as a stop-Nixon drive, that would be a destructive thing. . . . Rockefeller should be called on to run only if a deadlock develops after two or three ballots." And Governor David Cargo of New Mexico, who was under strong pressure to come out for Romney but who was suggesting that a stop-Nixon effort be organized behind Rockefeller, said of the moderates' apparent reconciliation toward Nixon: "It looks that way. There's no fight. There's nobody who will get up and say we've got to get behind Romney"—and he frankly included himself.

Rockefeller didn't help either when, in an impromptu talk with reporters on the terrace of the old Breakers Hotel, he allowed that while he didn't think a Rockefeller draft was a possibility, he would "have to face it" if it happened. The remark spurred McCall and the chief advocate of a draft-Rockefeller effort, Spiro Agnew, to new hope. Nixon, though, had good reason to be pleased with the work his men had done in Palm Beach. If the governors didn't join in a stop-Nixon "cabal"— there wouldn't be much in his way once he disposed of Romney in the early primaries.

While the Palm Beach meeting thus drifted in typical indecisiveness, Nixon went about his business. Former Congressmen Ellsworth and Don Jackson shortly afterward held a significant meeting at the Mayflower Hotel in Washington with Nixon supporters on Capitol Hill, a group that grew steadily all through 1968. Nixon himself inched closer to candidacy with a major speech on the domestic crises of the cities and race, telling the National Association of Manufacturers in New York that "after this decade of opening doors, we need a decade of preparing people to walk through these doors. After a decade of revolution, we need a decade of reconciliation." The country had listened "too long to the extremes of the new left and the old right," he told them. "America needs today to hear the voice of the broad and vital center." And Richard Nixon left no doubt in the minds of his audience that his was that voice.

The speech was the kind that would be made in a general national campaign, or even as a President already in office, not in a do-or-die party primary. Clearly, Nixon was looking far ahead. With Romney seriously damaged, Rockefeller clinging to his no-candidacy pledge, and Reagan playing a waiting game, Nixon already could see—to borrow that unfortunate phrase from the lexicon of Vietnam self-deception—a light at the end of the tunnel. But in this case, the rays really were peeking through. The task was to proceed cautiously through the tunnel, eschewing the temptation to break into a wild sprint, and thereby risk a cave-in that would snuff out the light—probably, for a two-time loser like Nixon, forever.

10

Burying the Loser Image

WHILE Richard Nixon now concentrated single-mindedly on the Republican Presidential contest about to start, a historic wrenching was under way in the ranks of the Democratic Party that was to have a more profound impact on his future than any strategy he had planned for undoing George Romney in the approaching first Republican primary in New Hampshire. With Lyndon Johnson resolutely committed to major American involvement in a stalemated ground war in Asia, the unthinkable was being thought by dissident Democrats: dump him. Through the summer, in centers of antiwar sentiment like Wisconsin, California, Michigan and New York, they had been toying with a variety of possible ballot-box protests against Johnson, but these were local, issue-oriented musings. It was not until a young New York reformer, Allard K. Lowenstein, a feverish sampler and catalyst of campus thought, began to conceive of stringing all the local efforts together behind a national candidate that the idea came into focus of actually denying the Democratic nomination to a sitting President.

Lowenstein, a close friend of Senator Robert F. Kennedy of New York, discussed the prospects periodically with him during the spring and summer. Kennedy, the first Democrat regarded to have a Presidential future who spoke out against the Vietnam

War, shared the growing despair about it but was immobilized by his personal relations toward Johnson. Although he disliked immensely the man who had succeeded his brother, John F. Kennedy, in the White House, and although he was increasingly convinced that Johnson was leading the country toward disaster in Vietnam, Robert Kennedy felt he himself could not make the challenge. He was a captive of the entrenched reputation that he was "ruthless," and of his own obsession that a personal effort to replace Johnson as the 1968 Democratic nominee would be written off merely as a vendetta. Knowing Kennedy felt this way, Lowenstein needled him about running but did not ask him outright. Kennedy was sympathetic with his friend's efforts to find a winning anti-Johnson candidate, but unconvinced they would get anywhere. Had Kennedy agreed then to take on Johnson, the cataclysmic events of 1968 undoubtedly would have been quite different. The man Lowenstein finally persuaded to run, Senator Eugene J. McCarthy of Minnesota, never would have been approached at all; the antiwar forces would not have been split in the grueling primaries; Lyndon Johnson might have been chased out of the race with a resounding defeat in New Hampshire, or he might not have withdrawn at all. The impact on Richard Nixon also might have been quite different.

Might-have-beens, however, were a cheap and plentiful commodity in 1967 and 1968, and the controlled and professional nature of the Nixon operation did not waste time on them. The fact was that Kennedy misgauged the intensity of the antiwar protest. He let himself be deterred from an early, direct challenge of Johnson by his own excessive concern that his feud with the President was an unworthy motivation, and would be politically damaging. The decision was a catastrophic one. Lowenstein moved on to others—retired Army General James M. Gavin, proponent of the "enclave" theory for holding critical base areas in Vietnam while negotiating; former Ambassador John Kenneth Galbraith; Senator George S. McGovern of South Dakota; finally, McCarthy. The Minnesotan at first told Lowenstein he thought "Bobby should do it," but he finally acceded. McCarthy was deeply disturbed about the war itself, but beyond that, about what it was doing to American values, to

American perspective toward the rest of the world, and above all to the ability of the people to exert an impact on policy. His candidacy, announced on November 30, was an effort to dump Johnson and end the war, but at the same time it was a test of the system's capacity to respond to and accommodate public sentiment for basic shifts in the nation's direction. "I am hopeful," McCarthy said at a press conference in the Senate Caucus Room, "that this challenge . . . may alleviate to at least some degree this sense of political helplessness and restore to many people a belief in the processes of American politics and of American government."

McCarthy could not have known as he uttered those words how successful he would be, for a time anyway, in achieving that broad goal. But in cutting down Lyndon Johnson, and in so doing restoring confidence among millions that the system still could be moved by citizen action, he would clear a path to the White House for Richard Nixon, a man he viewed—as did Robert Kennedy—with a mixture of contempt and ridicule. It was not a path without pitfalls, but Nixon with the self-discipline and caution that had marked most of his actions and words since 1964 would prove equal to its negotiation.

Talk of dumping Lyndon Johnson, however, and interest in McCarthy's effort to do it, were subordinated to the Nixon-Romney contest as the 1968 New Hampshire primary began. The idea, most said, was just too far-fetched.

Romney, still determined he would turn things around once he was able to get directly to the voters, plunged in first. He had come back from his world trip with his already battered image damaged even more, as a result of a story from Vietnam that painted him—unjustly, those who accompanied him insisted—as an insensitive bumbler. On Christmas day, he visited the wards of American wounded and was accused, at least by inference, of campaigning among them and using them as props. Jonathan Moore, who had been Romney's State Department escort on the famous "brainwashing" trip of 1965, accompanied him again and was mightily impressed by Romney's ability to cope with the world leaders he met en route, and particularly Soviet Premier Aleksei Kosygin in the Kremlin. But such performances were in private, and when George Romney performed in public, something too often went wrong.

Actually, his campaign in New Hampshire was well conceived and well implemented. Had he come into the state without all that had happened over the previous year, he might have made it close. The young and savvy campaign team of David Goldberg—he of the 1964 Lodge upset—and John Deardourff, a former Rockefeller researcher and tactician, built a network of "home headquarters" in towns throughout the state, and Romney in January worked them with the persistence of a missionary. No group was too small to send him bounding from his campaign bus through the snowbanks and into a supporter's living room, there to pound away his favorite theme that "moral decay" had eaten into the very fiber of the American spirit. The intensity of the man, and his sincerity and good will, came through in most of these parlor gatherings, but always in the context of what the people of New Hampshire had read or heard about him over the previous year. Now he was the guy who didn't know when he was licked. One day in a small town, Romney walked into a bowling alley and decided to try his luck at duckpins. He failed to knock down all ten, so tried again, and again, and again, and again, until only one pin was standing. Bristling, he gritted his teeth and persevered against it, as the press and townspeople watched. Amusement among the crowd turned to embarrassment. By actual count, thirty-four rolls later, Romney finally knocked this last pin down! That was the way it was with George Romney, and those who heard or read that story were likely to nod their heads knowingly and smile.

Yet on the critical issue of Vietnam, Romney delivered in mid-January one of the most reasoned and straightforward speeches given by any candidate up to then or afterward. He unveiled a plan for a "guaranteed neutralization" of Vietnam and Southeast Asia that included a call for an "internal settlement" between the Saigon government and the National Liberation Front. Romney's audience, at Keene State College, sat soberly and listened to this long speech without interruption. When he finished they gave him sustained and enthusiastic applause. Coming at the end of his third day of campaigning in the primary, Romney derived a tremendous lift from the response, which got even better when a student tried to rile him by asking: "Were you brainwashed this time?" Romney shot back: "I know I wasn't given the full facts when I visited South

Vietnam in 1965, and that's what I referred to. I know this time I dug into it and I got the picture, and I gave it to you here tonight." But it was much too late.

One night around this time at Romney's headquarters motel outside of Manchester, the candidate sat on his bed and talked optimistically with his campaign manager, Len Hall, a savvy veteran who knew the campaign was going nowhere. "Len," Romney said, "we're really coming up now. We're a little behind, but I think we can go ahead." Hall said nothing. He returned to Washington and asked Fred Currier, Romney's own pollster in Detroit, to take a special reading. Hall wanted to be sure, and he wanted the result to have particular credibility, coming from the man whose polls had guided Romney to political success in Michigan.

A preliminary reading of the next Currier poll showed no significant improvement for Romney at all. Also, complicating the picture now was the threat of a write-in for Rockefeller. The New York governor early in January had made a special trip to New Hampshire to urge his old supporters to stick with Romney, but the polls indicated a residue of strength for him. A Rockefeller write-in not only would deny Romney votes but conceivably could push Romney back to a third-place finish. Hall and Jonathan Moore, armed with the preliminary reading, went up to New Hampshire for another meeting with the candidate and staff. "We haven't moved, George," Hall told Romney. "And we have this Rockefeller problem. We have to consider the possibility of getting creamed." Romney took the word soberly. If the trend continued, somebody added, "we'll have to consider whether we want to pull out to avoid complete humiliation." Staff aides, expecting the dogged Romney to explode at the very suggestion, were surprised that instead he nodded his assent.

Romney, though now facing the possibility that his labors of more than a year might have to be ended prematurely, plodded on, as if hoping by his sheer presence and zeal to pound his way into the hearts of the New Hampshire voters. He rose before dawn to shake hands with factory workers on mornings so cold that less hardy newsmen accompanied him in shifts; they wore earmuffs and ski masks while the candidate stood hatless for an hour or more, beaming at each half-awake worker as he rushed past. Meanwhile, Nixon pointedly left the field to him, occupying himself with a leisurely trip to Virginia and Texas, non-primary states, where organizations already were operating for him. He went also to Oklahoma, the first state to select all its delegates to the national convention. There, too, though it was regarded potential Reagan country, he was in good shape, with Bellmon running for the Senate and Governor Dewey Bartlett friendly. Bartlett kept Oklahoma's twenty-two delegates uncommitted in the hope of luring party stars to fund-raisers, but eventually Nixon won fourteen of them.

All through January, while Romney persevered in frigid New Hampshire, Nixon took his sweet time moving formally into the Presidential starting gate. It seemed at times he was determined, for personal as well as tactical reasons, to hold off the plunge as long as he possibly could. In several interviews, he referred to "these miserable primaries" that cost so much and sapped so much energy from a candidate. It was, of course, more than the physical grind. The primaries were a threat; a candidate had to be seen and he had to say things, and when that was the case, anything could happen. The clear intent was to minimize the possibility of a Nixon goof. Also, Nixon felt that in 1964 both Rockefeller and Goldwater were overexposed in tiny New Hampshire. With the polls showing him so far ahead of Romney—some now had him ahead by four to one or more—all Nixon had to do was, in his favorite sports parlance, "eat up the clock." The New Hampshire race certainly was on his mind through January, but he demonstrated remarkable self-control in staying away for nearly a month while his opponent grabbed all the hands and all the headlines. (At a question-and-answer session at Washington and Lee University in Lexington, Virginia, Nixon was asked whether he thought black militants H. Rap Brown and Stokely Carmichael "had crossed the line of treason." No, he replied, he didn't think the constitutional definition of treason applied to Brown "and Stokely Primary.")

Right to the last day of filing for candidacy, the Nixon operation was a study in control. With only three hours to go before the books closed, young Dave Sterling strolled into the office of Secretary of State Robert L. Stark in Concord and presented a

231

petition bearing 808 signatures for Nixon, well beyond the 50 required from each of the state's two Congressional districts to qualify. Stark sent Nixon a telegram in New York "notifying" him of Sterling's action and giving him ten days to indicate whether he wished to have his name kept off the Republican primary ballot. Stark did not hold his breath waiting for a reply.

The answer came two days later in a most unorthodox—and most self-assured and confident—way for a major public figure to launch a campaign for the Presidency of the United States. Nixon's efficient and ever-growing staff, bankrolled through the diligent efforts of Stans, Flanigan and Co., had been preparing 150,000 letters from the candidate announcing to New Hampshire households his intent to run—about 85 percent of the total. Mailed earlier, they were reaching their destinations at about the time on February 2 that copies were handed to reporters at Nixon's New York campaign office. The letters, in a nice public relations touch, thus broke the big news first to the important voters involved, stressing how critical their role was in the American elective process for 1968. Nixon, recognizing they were "keenly aware of their special responsibilities, of the broad influence of their votes," told them that "in 1968, your responsibility is greater than ever." The nation, he wrote, faced choices "beyond politics . . . peace and freedom in the world, and peace and progress here at home, will depend on the decisions of the next President of the United States. For these critical years, America needs new leadership. . . ." The newly declared candidate stressed his experience ("During fourteen years in Washington, I learned the awesome nature of the great decisions a President faces") and made a virtue of his being out of public office ("During the past eight years I have had a chance to reflect on the lessons of public office, to measure the nation's tasks and its problems from a fresh perspective. I have sought to apply those lessons to the needs of the present, and to the entire sweep of this final third of the 20th Century. And I believe I have found some answers."). It was a strong and confident beginning, but if the voters of New Hampshire drew from the last phrase an expectation that they would hear those answers in more than sweeping generalities, they were to be disappointed. Eating up the clock did not call for specifics, especially on the one issue about which most voters wanted specific answers—Vietnam.

George Romney also wanted to hear some of those specific Nixon answers—indeed, desperately needed to hear them, in the hope he might find an issue or a comment that would knock Nixon off his self-constructed pedestal. Romney welcomed Nixon's entry as a chance "to engage in a public discussion with him on domestic and world problems and opportunities." There would be fat chance of that; Romney already had challenged Nixon to debate him, and Nixon had grandly turned the bid aside as helpful only to the Democrats. Nixon intended to ignore Romney if he could, letting what damage already had been inflicted on his foe sink in. A poster on the cool Nixon going up around the state was clear enough, without mentioning the frenetic Romney: "You can't handshake your way out of the kind of problems we have today. You've got to think them through—and that takes a lifetime of getting ready."

So cool and low-profile was Nixon's New Hampshire campaign that he literally slipped into the state under cover of darkness to launch it. The night of February 1, when the letters had been mailed, with speechwriters Buchanan and Price and Dwight Chapin he boarded a plane from New York to Boston. There Nick Ruwe met them, drove across the state border and on to Nashua for the night. The owners of the small hotel didn't even know Nixon was coming; the party arrived about midnight, had a drink, dispersed and went to bed. A press conference was scheduled for early afternoon of the next day, and Nixon wanted to be well rested for it. The modus operandi, in sharp contrast to the way Nixon had punished himself in 1960, was one that was to be followed with Prussian discipline not only in New Hampshire, not only in all the other primaries, but throughout the general election campaign itself.

Nixon used good judgment in arriving in New Hampshire a night early. The next day was rainy and miserable, fogging in airports throughout New England. That morning, from New York, Mrs. Nixon, Tricia and Julie, Nixon buddies Bebe Rebozo and John Davies, and secretaries Rose Woods and Shelley Scarney, later of the White House staff, set out in two cars. In

233

less than an hour, the second car broke down. All the passengers except Davies piled into the first and proceeded, while Davies stayed with the second car and all the luggage. Reporters from all over the country were grounded short of their destination and straggled in. One large group chartered a bus at LaGuardia Airport and arrived barely in time for the afternoon press conference, which Nixon obligingly had delayed a few hours.

The candidate was composed and confident as he stood before microphones in the meeting room of the Manchester Holiday Inn. "Gentlemen," he began, "this is *not* my last press conference." Good-humored laughter on both sides demonstrated how deftly Richard Nixon in five years and more than three hundred press conferences after that famous "last" one had handled the "press problem" growing out of his 1962 tirade. The objective in New Hampshire was to bury Nixon's loser image, and characteristically he laid that fact out immediately. "I've given consideration to this problem, 'Can Nixon win?' " he said. "I want to be quite candid about it. . . . There is no one in this room or in the nation more interested in seeing the Republican nominee win this year. . . . The Republican Party must nominate a man who can win . . . [and] a man who can do the job. Those who have lost elections in the past have come back to win. . . . I believe I am better qualified to handle the great problems of the Presidency than I was in 1960. I recognize I must demonstrate to the American people . . . that I can win and that I can do the job. I am prepared to meet that challenge. I have decided that I will test my ability . . . in the fires of the primaries, and not just in the smoke-filled rooms of Miami Beach. . . . I believe I am going to win the New Hampshire primary, come out the decisive winner of the primaries, go on to win the nomination, and if I do that, I believe I can defeat Lyndon Johnson."

Nixon acknowledged that the polls showed him far ahead, but he insisted the outcome could be "much closer than the surveys indicate." (Press corps graduates of the Nixon School of Political Tactics allowed themselves a smile at the mentor's ability to deliver this self-serving prediction with a straight face.) It was not true, either, that he would be in New Hampshire only six days, and that his pace would be leisurely. He planned an "all-out, very intensive campaign," he said. (The grads smiled again.)

Nixon actually spent about twenty days in the state, but he carefully limited his exposure. When speeches and rallies took place, they were vigorous and well planned, but the overall impact—intentionally—was low key. The candidate was not to be burned out; he was to be presented almost as though he already had been nominated by his party, and was tuning up for the real campaign in the fall.

Basic to this strategy was to ignore Romney, and by ignoring him, to downgrade him. Asked about Romney's challenge to debate, Nixon quickly slipped into his unifier's cloak. "The great debate of 1968," he said with due solemnity, "should be betweeen the Republican nominee and Lyndon Johnson. The only winner of a debate between Republicans—as we learned in 1964—would be Lyndon Johnson." Listening to Nixon make a response like that one was like watching Ted Williams hit one out of the park in the old days. The pitch came right through the strike zone and he dispatched it effortlessly. Everyone in the room knew Nixon was playing the front-runner's game strictly by the book, that he wanted no part of a debate that just possibly could produce the Nixon misstep that Romney so desperately needed. He was so transparent, yet so good at it.

There also was an opportunity in the press conference to make points against Rockefeller. Did he expect a challenge from the New York governor at the convention? "Any realist," Nixon replied, "knows Governor Rockefeller could become a candidate at a later time. So, for that matter, could Reagan or Percy. But if any of these men are to become candidates, it's a very long chance for them, unless they are willing to enter the primaries. I believe the decisive winner of the primaries will and should be nominated. I believe his ideas and ability to cope with the issues should be tested in the fire of the primaries and not just simply kept in the grandstand and submitted to the tender mercies of the kingmakers at the convention." Another fat pitch belted out of the ball park.

That night at the Highway Hotel in Concord, Nixon held what for him was most rare—a party for the press. A bartender dispensed drinks as the candidate circulated through the small ballroom, shaking hands, renewing acquaintances, holding forth among clusters of newsmen. Finally he jumped onto a chair and gave a short informal talk.

He had not been responsible for the terrible weather that day, Nixon assured his guests. It reminded him of an official state visit he had made to Morocco as Vice President. There had been a severe drought, but the day he arrived it poured. That night, at the state dinner, he was toasted grandly as "The Man with Green Feet." It was a great compliment, a translator informed him. It meant "wherever you walk, grass grows." Nixon grinned broadly as he delivered the punch line. The faithful at a party rally might have roared at that one, but there were only polite titters from the reporters—and more than one grimace. Later that night, after Nixon's departure, a fierce competition erupted in the hotel bar to set this new disclosure to music. Finally, this lyric won out as the early Nixon campaign theme, to the tune of "The Wearing of the Green":

> Oh, your name is Richard Nixon,
> You're the newest ever seen,
> You're speaking on the issues
> But your feet have turned to green.
> You're the party's elder statesman,
> There's no place you haven't been,
> But who will buy a used car
> From a man with feet of green.

The writing of this song was not an act of press hostility toward Nixon. Ersatz campaign songs have been a traditional time-killer on the trail; there would be others, about Nixon and the other candidates. It probably was fair to say that Nixon's stock with the corps of national political writers never was higher. That is not to say he was a favorite; but there was little sentiment to "get" him. Whether or not the press had indeed "learned a lesson" from the way it treated him in 1960 and 1962, there had been an impact, and Nixon for his part did his best to be cordial.

Part of the new emphasis on "candor" was to be greater access to the candidate and his activities. Nixon said himself at the press party he would be available for interviews and briefings along the way, and the press would be kept informed of his whereabouts at all times.

It came as a particular jolt, then, when reporters learned the next morning that Nixon had slipped out of the hotel unannounced at an early hour and had been driven to the nearby town of Hillsboro. About ten New Hampshire college students and an equal number of farmers and townsfolk, handpicked by the local Nixon committee, were brought into the Hillsboro Community Hall for an "entirely unrehearsed" discussion with the candidate. Using the courtroom of young Dave Sterling's father, District Judge Walter Sterling, Nixon answered questions from the citizen panelists as a hired camera crew recorded the scene on television tape. No reporters were present.

When a Romney aide learned of the exercise, he tipped off the press. The Nixon staff was chagrined but defensive. The discussions were to be excerpted for use in later TV commercials in the state. It had been decided to do them secretly, Bob Ellsworth said, to keep the panelists "as free from being examined, inspected and reported on as possible." Pat Buchanan expressed concern that reporters might "inhibit those people," and hence they were excluded "so that people would feel at ease."

There, on the very first day, the pledge of an open campaign had been found wanting. Because credibility had been a particular Nixon problem, and because as the Republican candidate he would hope to capitalize on Lyndon Johnson's "credibility gap," the disclosure was a bona fide gaffe; not of the dimensions Romney needed to get back into contention, perhaps, but enough to put the press on alert, and to revive some of the old suspiciousness. The staff and the candidate did not budge, however, from the basic position that the press was to be excluded. The next day, reporters were transported by bus to the hall, where they had to remain outside while uniformed guards admitted the citizen panelists for more taping sessions.

What had happened that first weekend, especially exclusion of the press from the Hillsboro tapings, was no inadvertence. The writing press, conditioned to old traditions of campaigning, had been under the impression that when they sat before

Richard Nixon in his opening press conference on Friday afternoon, they had been in on the start of his drive for the Presidency. They were only half right. They had witnessed only the visible, secondary segment of a carefully conceived and controlled two-track campaign.

Months earlier, Len Garment, Nixon's law partner, had recruited two experts in the art of television advertising and showmanship. Their names were Harry Treleaven from the J. Walter Thompson agency in New York, a summer neighbor of Garment's, and Frank Shakespeare, a refugee from high-level internecine combat at CBS. The three of them, with later recruits, masterminded a revolutionary second track over which Richard Nixon could be presented directly to the electorate without the risks entailed in exposing him on the first, traditional track.* That track was too hazardous, mined as it always was with the unexpected and patrolled so diligently by those shabby reporters who always were watching and then scribbling things, harmful things, in their little notebooks.

The first, traditional campaign track obviously could not be abandoned, but with deftness it could be used as a façade behind which the second track—controlled, insulated presentation of the candidate on television, in his best moments and at his best angles—could operate. In the primaries, the regional target areas offered ideal laboratories for testing and refining the second-track campaign, and the tapings in Hillsboro consequently were just as much the "start" of the Nixon Presidential campaign as the candidate's press conference the afternoon before. One condition was vital, however: the monitors of the first track, the reporters, could not be permitted to monitor the second. That would spoil everything.

In the Nixon campaign of 1968, television was to carry the message unfiltered by the press wherever that could be arranged. Putting the candidate on film precisely the way his media managers wanted him was well worth risking some flared reportorial tempers. Simple arithmetic governed: How many voters read newspapers and how many watched television? And

---

* For a detailed and devastating inside account of how this second track was created and implemented, see *The Selling of the President 1968* by Joe McGinniss (Trident, 1969).

how many believed what they read, as opposed to what they saw with their own eyes? All that appeared on the TV screen in a campaign commercial, of course, was not all that was involved. But with professionalism in the candidate and expertise in his media men, the average viewer could not very well sort out the spontaneous from the staged. Not that Nixon's actual *performance* was staged; the questions and the answers in the Hillsboro tapings were spontaneous, but by selecting the panelists and being able to excerpt the most useful exchanges and discard the others, it was not quite all that met the eye. What was done in New Hampshire was continued with refinements throughout the year; pretty soon the press became accustomed to the routine and stopped squawking. And in the process, they covered the comings and goings of the candidate and reported on a side of the campaign that relatively few voters ever saw, while being excluded from or minimizing the side that, to millions of voters, was the "real" campaign—inside the radio and TV studios of the nation. That campaign was tremendously expensive, but the Nixon treasury from the start could pay the bill. Stans organized a fat-cat Republican version of Lyndon Johnson's "President's Club" called "RN Associates," in which 1,000 contributors laid $1,000 each on the line for a gold lapel pin bearing Nixon's initials. It was a status symbol in the Nixon camp to wear the pin that had pumped a cool million dollars into the campaign at the outset of 1968.

In New Hampshire, it was not exposure, but overexposure, against which Nixon was guarding. He was exceedingly popular in the state; on that Saturday afternoon after the first Hillsboro taping, he drew about 2,000 persons to a public reception at St. Anselm's College in Manchester. The affair was patterned after a very successful event in the 1962 California race designed to capitalize on the candidate's "celebrity" status, "the Dick Nixon community reception." Lines were roped off, and the crowds waited patiently to meet Dick, Pat, Tricia, Julie and the most recent family acquisition—David Eisenhower. Julie and David together provided most of the sex appeal—she innocent and vivacious, he innocent and unassuming. His tousled head of hair and open expression quickly won the hearts of the Republican faithful—and, from the accompanying press corps, the nickname "Howdy Doody." (At one point Nixon stopped shaking hands and informed his fans that he had another appointment, but since they had been kind enough to come out, he would stay awhile longer. The crowd applauded—and reporters snickered. They had been told earlier that Nixon's next event was several hours away. By such minuscule fibs was his credibility gap with the press sustained.)

That night, before a packed house of 1,300 at the Highway Hotel, Nixon delivered what came to be "The Speech." Though in ensuing weeks and months he scribbled away at its contents on his yellow legal pad, it remained relatively constant all the way through November. What the country needed, he said, was "leadership that recognizes that the real crisis of America today is a crisis of the spirit." What Lyndon Johnson offered was to "continue what we have been doing for the last five years for another four years. Shall we continue?" Nixon asked. "The only answer is, when the strongest nation in the world can be tied down for four years in the war in Vietnam with no end in sight; when the nation with the greatest tradition of respect for the rule of law is plagued by random lawlessness; when the nation that has been a symbol of human liberty is torn apart by racial strife; when the President of the United States cannot travel either at home or abroad without fear of a hostile demonstration, then it is time America had new leadership!" The peroration was delivered with fist-pounding emphasis, and the crowd of already convinced Nixon supporters gave him thunderous applause. He neither sounded nor acted like a loser, nor was he treated like one. NIXON'S THE ONE, the red and white signs proclaimed, and he basked in the acclaim and in the reality that here at last, after six years on the shelf, he was back in the "arena" he looked upon as the only real testing place of the public man.*

Long before Nixon had announced his candidacy, one of his

---

* "Nixon's the One" was a prized brainstorm of the Nixon media men, because it suggested he was the man who was right for everything, without saying specifically that he was right for anything. In that light, the slogan really did capsulize the Nixon campaign strategy. In contrast, his opposition proclaimed from New Hampshire billboards: ROMNEY FIGHTS MORAL DECAY. Of which one Romney staffer once complained, "He doesn't sound like a Presidential candidate; he sounds like a toothpaste."

close associates told me one night that when the time came for another try, Nixon would enter the New Hampshire primary but would "speak to the country." In other words, instead of conducting the customary provincial campaign, he would use the first primary as a base, soliciting the support of New Hampshire voters but always speaking to a national constituency and running as though he were in a general election against the Democratic President. That was the way it turned out; having dropped into the state for three days, Nixon took off immediately for Wisconsin, Oklahoma, Colorado and Indiana in the next week, providing the personal spark to organizational efforts in all those states.

Although New Hampshire was the first primary, the second, in Wisconsin, was regarded as the key; if Nixon lost in New Hampshire, Wisconsin would be the point of no return; if he won, he could polish Romney off in Wisconsin, build up momentum and nip Reagan before he really got started. Reagan would be on the ballot in Wisconsin, the first of the three primaries in which all likely prospects were listed unless they specifically withdrew with an affidavit disavowing candidacy. Though Reagan did not plan to campaign, a Reagan committee was buying television time for a filmed documentary about him.

During Nixon's visit to Wisconsin, the candidate made the kind of slip that could have unsettled his smoothly functioning operation. The capture of the intelligence-gathering ship *Pueblo* by North Korea in the Sea of Japan had become an international incident, with the Republicans demanding strong action from the Johnson administration. Nixon himself showed restraint, though deploring the lack of protection for the ship when seized. There was considerable speculation about whether the ship had been in international waters or within the twelve-mile territorial limits claimed by North Korea. In a press conference in Green Bay, Nixon was asked whether, if the *Pueblo* actually had violated North Korean waters, he thought it would be proper to apologize to obtain release of the eighty-three crewmen. If there had been a violation, he said, the United States "could consider" apologizing; admitting that the ship had been in North Korean waters would be "a small price to pay" for return of the surviving crew members.

This was the same Richard Nixon who, in the 1960 Presidential campaign, had sharply attacked John F. Kennedy for suggesting the United States might apologize for the U-2 spy plane incident that shattered a planned U.S.–Russian summit conference in Paris. Reminded of the U-2 affair, Nixon said he saw no reason to have apologized for the U-2 because that spy plane, sent over the Soviet Union during the Eisenhower administration, had not violated any law on air space in existence at that time. In the *Pueblo* case, he said, had the ship been in North Korean territorial waters, it would have been a violation of international law.*

Nixon at Green Bay also sought to differentiate between the U-2 and *Pueblo* incidents by saying the North Koreans knew for several days that the *Pueblo* was off the North Korean coast, whereas there was no advance Soviet knowledge of the U-2 overflights. The second point clearly was not so. American government officials acknowledged in 1960 that a number of U-2 flights had been made and that the Russians knew of them but kept quiet because, at that time, they did not have a fighter or an antiaircraft missile capable of reaching the height at which the U-2's flew.

Here was a clear political misstep by Nixon, and a blatant effort to slough it off. It might have been expected to jar Nixon's confident and cool game plan, but it did not. Pat Buchanan, doubling as press secretary, sought to persuade reporters they had no story, and he largely succeeded. As matters turned out, Nixon's willingness to consider apologizing to get the *Pueblo* crew back did not hurt his campaign one iota, because only two or three reporters wrote about it. When they attempted to obtain further clarifications from him he brushed them aside, noting—accurately—that the question of territorial violation still was under State Department review. In contrast with the Romney "brainwashing" remark, which struggled its

* In the U-2 affair, a number of the planes had been flying over the Soviet Union until one was shot down in May, 1960, and its pilot, Francis Gary Powers, was captured, tried and sentenced to a ten-year jail term. He was freed in February, 1962, in exchange for the Soviet spy Colonel Rudolf Abel. The United States at first denied, then admitted, responsibility for the flight.

way to the surface and was played into a *cause célèbre*, this Nixon gaffe withered and died for lack of reportorial interest and pursuit. And whereas the "brainwash" statement threw the Romney campaign into a panic, the Nixon operation proceeded on schedule and on course. After the candidate's first nine-day swing, Robert B. Semple, Jr., of the New York *Times* compared the Nixon campaign to "a great ocean liner. The whole thing is stately, dignified, proud and—above all—slow. . . . But the Nixon campaign vessel, however comfortable it may be, is no ship of fools. Behind its dignified exterior and stately course lies a series of cold political calculations." It was irrefutably true; a story made the rounds in New Hampshire that the Nixon strategists actually were becoming concerned that the efficiency of their operation was giving it a bad image of coldness. One of them even professed to be pleased when a minor mix-up demonstrated that they were, after all, human.

Although the appearances of the candidate were carefully and rigidly programmed, efforts were taken to persuade the press that the man himself was not. Staffers scoffed at the recurring "new, new Nixon" talk, insisting that he was the same individual he always had been; it was just that reporters and the public were beginning to perceive him in his proper light. Constancy was the byword. In a television interview in Green Bay that first week, Nixon fielded the "new Nixon" question thus: "To the reports that there's a conscious change, I'm not aware of it. . . . So far as I'm concerned I can only be as I am. I have to present my views as I believe them, and if it takes basically putting on an act in order to be a successful candidate for President, I'm not the man." The point was it did not have to be an act. Nixon long ago had demonstrated that he had a quick mind, and that it was politically attuned; in conversation, he seemed to race ahead, anticipating challenges and spearing them. When the same interviewer in Wisconsin asked him why youth should support him, he said: "I happen to think I bring a certain competence. . . ." Then, with only the slightest pause: "That, of course, is a self-serving statement that candidates have to make, rather shamelessly . . ." If Nixon learned anything at all from his past, it was that the press had the capacity—and often the willingness—to shoot him down. He had a way of saying self-serving things, and it had earned him the nickname Tricky Dick. Anticipating that reaction, it didn't hurt to spear his lapses himself before somebody else did; in fact, it could be a plus.

In saying he was not aware of "a conscious change," Nixon always made clear he was not denying he had matured over the years. Discussing his 1962 run-in with the press, he said in Green Bay: "I feel as time goes on in 1968 I'll have a better press. Perhaps I've learned something. . . . Perhaps in this respect there is a new Nixon." The "growth" argument actually was a standard response to the "new Nixon" speculation as far back as 1960. During his campaign against John Kennedy, Nixon was asked by CBS commentator Walter Cronkite whether he resented "talk of there being a 'new Nixon.'" He replied: "No, not particularly. I think our people generally like to appraise their public servants and to detect, if they feel it is justified, any changes that indicate growth or change that they might approve. Now, as far as I'm concerned, when people say there is a new Nixon, that must mean that people who did not like the Nixon that they knew before, now like the one that they know now. Now I happen to believe, myself, that perhaps many of those who discover the new Nixon may not have known the old one; but seriously, may I say this: we all change . . . [in eight years] I have learned a lot, and it is very possible that I certainly do convey a different impression today than I did previously, because if I hadn't learned, I wouldn't amount to too much. So, I will concede that I have changed, and I hope for the better."

Eight years after having said that, it would have been difficult to dismiss the "new, new Nixon" talk of 1968 on grounds that people who didn't like either the "old Nixon" of the fifties or the "new Nixon" of 1960 now liked the third version, or that they may not have known the earlier two. Nor was it simply a matter of conceding that he, like everybody else, had changed as he got older. The implication of the "new, new Nixon" label was not that he really had changed, but that he really hadn't—that he just tried to make it look that way. Nixon's acknowledgment to James Kilpatrick that he had to be absolutely candid to dispel the "Tricky Dick" appellation risked feeding the "new,

new Nixon" talk as much as reducing it. Outward evidences of change—the fact he was more relaxed, wittier, more tolerant of criticism, more candid—were not particularly good arguments when the indictment was that the man changed his outward appearance to meet criticism, yet inwardly remained the same.

The debate on the "new, new Nixon" drove reporters to their typewriters one late night on the Nixon press bus in Wisconsin. The inadequacy of "The Man with Feet of Green" as a campaign theme song was apparent, so they produced a replacement, to the tune of "There'll Be No Changes Made," that lasted through the early primaries:

> There's been a change in my address and a change in my fee,
> But there will never be a change in me.
> My wife won't be different, her name is still Pat;
> Rocky's a switcher, but I'm not like that.
> There's been a change in my hairline and a heavier beard,
> But I'm so much like me that it's almost weird;
> That honest expression, that same open face—
> I've got the stuff to lose the race.
> There'll be no changes made.

There was, of course, no earthly reason for Nixon to make any visible changes, in himself or in his campaign strategy. He continued, no matter what Romney did, to remain far ahead in the polls. When the Michigan governor, increasingly frustrated, began to hit harder and more directly at Nixon, the former Vice President went blithely on his measured way. With less than a month to go in the primary, Romney started to needle Nixon on Vietnam, calling him a "me-too" candidate and referring to "the Johnson-Nixon policy on the war." But Nixon wouldn't bite. Even when Romney made his elaborate proposal for the guaranteed neutralization of Southeast Asia, Nixon dismissed it with a few words as something to think about after the war was over.

Meanwhile, in his own ranks too, Romney seemed to be getting shoved aside. On Saturday, February 24, Rockefeller sang his praises at a fund-raising luncheon in Detroit, then fell into the same old go-around with reporters on his own availability for a draft. Pressed hard, Rockefeller conceded he would accept one if it came, but tried his best to indicate he didn't expect it would, and that he still backed Romney. Not surprisingly, his statement of availability smothered his disclaimers in reports of the exchange, chilling the Romney camp.

The mood of those in New Hampshire who knew the score now was one of undisguised gloom. An amateur write-in for Rockefeller was under way despite the governor's own efforts to stop it, and was bound to cut into Romney's vote. Rockefeller's Detroit statement certainly didn't help any. More important, Len Hall had received from pollster Fred Currier the final readout on his last New Hampshire survey. It was, as anticipated, disaster—something like Nixon, 75 percent; Romney, 10 percent; Rockefeller, 8 percent and gaining. On Monday afternoon, Hall met in his Washington headquarters office with Bill Johnson, Romney's state campaign manager; Jonathan Moore; and Larry Lindemer, a key Romney aide from Michigan. They discussed the poll again and made a phone call to New Hampshire that yielded corroborating intelligence: not only would Nixon inundate Romney, but noncandidate Rockefeller might also pull more votes as a write-in. That did it. For the first time, the Romney strategists now discussed explicitly the idea of pulling out. There would be four advantages to that step. First, it might save Romney, a proud man with an admirable record, from extreme personal and political humiliation. Second, it might preserve to some degree his voice in the party on issues. Third, it might deprive Nixon of a clear-cut victory with which to dispel his loser image. And fourth, it would clear the path for some other moderate or liberal Republican—presumably Rockefeller—to take up the challenge before it was too late. Also, there was the question of money. Currier's polls showed Romney badly beaten not only in New Hampshire but also in Wisconsin, where an estimated $400,000 was budgeted. What with his lagging campaign, there barely was enough money to finish New Hampshire.

The decision was made to lay the facts before Romney and make a recommendation. The fact that he had not exploded earlier, when the subject had been broached just tentatively, encouraged the strategists that he might go along. Hall called Dick Van Dusen, whose judgment Romney trusted, and asked him to accompany Romney from Detroit for an "important" meeting in Boston the next night, Tuesday. All he told Van Dusen and Romney was that the top strategy board had a "proposal."

On the same Monday afternoon, John Deardourff sat in his office in the Romney headquarters in Concord and surveyed the scene candidly for three reporters who were old friends. As he proceeded then and later at dinner to assess the situation a full two weeks before the primary, it began to dawn on the reporters that what they were hearing was more like postmortem after a crushing political defeat than a preelection progress report. Deardourff recited not only grim poll statistics that indicated how hopelessly behind Romney was, but breakdowns on specific "intensity" questions that measured his appeal. The response was infinitesimal, to the point that even after all he had done and said since November, 1966, there was no firm public knowledge of who Romney was! One last-ditch idea being considered was to ask Rockefeller to come into the state; in effect to carry Romney across the finish line on his back. The thought was that at least the New Yorker might be able to channel the Rockefeller write-in vote into the Romney total.

The next morning, the same reporters sat in the Hanover law office of Bill Johnson and got the same gloom-filled picture. At one point a question was asked: "Is there any chance you might just pull out?" Johnson paused, then said, as if dismissing the idea, ". . . When you're lying awake in bed at night and you can't sleep, a lot of things go through your mind." Two days later, he apologized to the reporters and told them he had been working at his desk on a draft announcement of that very step when they had walked in, but he had been committed to secrecy.

On Tuesday night, Romney arrived in Boston to do a long radio interview heard widely in New Hampshire. In it, he sought to downplay Rockefeller's statement of availability for a draft and insisted he would win in New Hampshire. From the radio studio he went to the Ramada Inn for the meeting. Also present were Hall, Johnson, Van Dusen and Romney's press secretary, Travis Cross. Moore and Lindemer, after having

247

dinner with Hall at the Treadway Inn in Harvard Square, awaited the outcome. The bad news of Currier's polls, which always carried great weight with Romney, was laid squarely before him, together with the grim recommendation. Romney listened soberly, then said he wanted "to sleep on it." Again, given his dogged nature, this reaction was taken as a positive sign. After Romney had left the room, the aides turned to the job of writing a draft statement. Moore at this time joined the group, and he, along with Hall and Johnson, were strongest for the pullout. Van Dusen and Cross, unhappy but realistic, went along. Hall phoned Max Fisher, Romney's good friend and money-raiser, in Acapulco, where Fisher was vacationing. Fisher confirmed the glum picture on campaign funds. (Later, he denied he had been consulted, but others in the room when Hall called insisted he had been.) Hall also broke the news to George Hinman, Rockefeller's top political man, in an early-hour call. Romney hadn't definitely said he would quit, but it was clear Hall had little doubt now that his candidate would bow to the realities.

Early the next morning, with only a few hours' sleep, Moore arrived at Romney's room for breakfast, armed with a typed text. When he got there, however, he found that the governor had written his own. Moore suggested that there was a particular "opportunity" in acting at once; the Republican governors were meeting in Washington the next day and the withdrawal could be cast in the form of a report to them on the commitment Romney had made more than a year earlier at White Sulphur Springs. He had pledged to them, if they would give him time to demonstrate what he could do, he in turn would inform them if he couldn't make it. That way, the governors still would have time to get behind another candidate.

Romney liked the idea. If the ball were thrust into the hands of the governors, they might run with it, they might move finally on consolidating behind some other candidate. There had been and continued to be much talk about whether Romney should specifically urge that they back Rockefeller, the logical choice. But all the speculation over the last year that he really was only a stalking horse for Rockefeller had greatly irritated Romney; to ask the governors now to back Rockefeller would only seem to confirm that speculation. Besides, he reasoned, if he did so, the other governors would be boxed in. They would ask: "Is he giving us the ball, or isn't he?"

Undeniably also, one of the participants said later, there was "some exasperation, some pique, even suspicion" on Romney's part after Rockefeller's remarks to reporters on his own availability Saturday in Detroit. But this was not a key element in his decision against specifically urging Rockefeller on the other governors. George Romney, a man of quick temper, is also a man of good will who cannot sustain genuine anger against anyone for long. He took the decision to get out, according to all who were there at the time, without alibi or lament.

When it was clear he would step out, somebody said: "Who's going to call who?" It obviously was a bit of news that would not sit well with all those who had worked so long for Romney. The governor decided to take the hardest chore for himself. "I'll call Lenore," he said. (Others took the news harder. Two young Michigan aides on their own decided to stay in New Hampshire, like a couple of Huks, and fight from the caves. They announced *they* would mail out all of Romney's unused literature and thereby encourage a groundswell of support for him. The Concord *Monitor* gave the story page-one play, and one of them, racing back to the room at the Highway Hotel, called the other and told him about the publicity windfall. Through the hotel's paper-thin walls, he was heard exclaiming the fantasy of the year: "Hey, we might pull this out yet!")

At the Ramada Inn that morning, and on the campaign bus to the airport, Van Dusen and Moore, using Romney's draft as a base, wrote the final statement. The plan was to fly to Washington, where Romney would make a late afternoon report to his fellow Republican governors. As calls went out to the staff, the word leaked to the press—first to the Detroit *News* and then the wire services.

Nixon was engaged at the time in one of his very few old-fashioned, multistop tours of small-town New Hampshire. While he was speaking in midafternoon to about 300 citizens in the Knights of Columbus Hall in Milford, speechwriter-press aide Pat Buchanan got a call from a newsman friend. At about the same time, Mike Wallace of CBS heard the news from his

249

office, and both Buchanan and Wallace stood at the front of the podium waiting for Nixon to finish. As Nixon took the last applause and stepped down, Wallace tried to get to him, but Buchanan and Dwight Chapin, Nixon's personal aide, hustled the candidate into a washroom just to the rear and closed the door. Inside, Buchanan told Nixon: "Romney's pulling out of the race!" "What?" Nixon said. "At a five o'clock press conference," Buchanan told him. Nixon decided at once that his only response was to make none until he had heard what Romney had to say. He would proceed with his last two stops as if nothing had happned.

By now all the reporters in the caravan had heard the news and were bunched outside the washroom waiting for Nixon. He finally came out with Buchanan and Chapin, trying for all the world to look as if he knew nothing. Wallace was the first one to get to him, and he "told" the candidate about the reported pullout. Nixon feigned surprise—though it was clear he just had been briefed by Buchanan. "I don't believe it," he said. ". . . I don't comment on rumors." Then, as the political world buzzed around him, Nixon blithely proceeded to sign five autographs for a young boy. Then he went to a shopping center and to another hall for two more campaign talks, delivering them calmly and without haste, before returning to the Holiday Inn in Manchester in time for Romney's televised press conference. During each talk, Buchanan and Chapin would be burning up the phone lines for information, then would climb into the candidate's limousine and give him the latest details en route to the next stop. It was in itself a remarkable demonstration of Nixon's self-control under stress.

A further demonstration not seen by reporters occurred at the motel when Romney went on the air. One wing was confiscated by Nixon and his staff; security police barred all newsmen. Nixon disappeared into a room down the hall, presumably to watch the press conference. Actually, he did not. Apparently feeling himself too emotionally involved to make a clear judgment on Romney's performance, he instructed several of his aides—Buchanan, Ray Price, Rose Woods, John Sears—to watch and then report to him. This they did at a long postmortem at which the development was carefully assessed.

Though reporters clamored for a statement, it was nearly an hour before Nixon released one. Declining to appear personally, though the press was demanding to see him, he sent down this brief observation: "Governor Romney has waged an energetic and vigorous campaign. I am sure that, as one of the nation's outstanding Republican governors, he will play a major role in Michigan and in the nation in assuring the Republican victory in November which is so essential to provide the new leadership America needs."

There was no crowing in the statement, partly because it would have been tactless, but also because Nixon and aides weren't sure they had much to crow about. It was, in retrospect, an unprecedented victory—probably the first technical knockout in the history of Presidential politics—and in a single swipe it cleared away much of Nixon's loser image. It showed, one aide tried to convince Nixon, that he was so strong his opposition was "afraid to get into the ring with you."

Yet Nixon at the outset was disappointed, and worried. Knowing he was far ahead in the polls, he felt deprived of a certain, smashing victory in the primary, and also in Wisconsin. Now the press would be saying Nixon may have lost his loser image, but he still hadn't beaten anybody. Beyond that, the Nixon staff was suspicious at first that Romney's withdrawal was part of a coordinated scheme to bring Rockefeller into the race, and there always was a chance of a sudden switch in the public mood. As long as Romney remained in, and an easy mark in later primaries, Rockefeller would be neutralized; the Nixon strategists knew that George Hinman had been traveling around the country, and they had reports he was telling friendly Republicans that even if Romney were to win all the primaries, he could not be nominated or elected, but Rockefeller could be. It now depended on whether Rockefeller moved quickly to fill the vacuum.

The preliminary Nixon fears proved unwarranted. Quick checks with the Republican intelligence network around the country indicated the pullout was not part of any elaborate scenario to bring Rockefeller in immediately. Nixon read that fact, rightly, to mean that Rockefeller was holding a weak hand, and knew it. "The pullout turned out to be good for us," one

251

Nixon aide said later, "in that it forced Rockefeller to show his cards, and he didn't have any."

It was true. Rockefeller was boxed in; it was too late for him to get into New Hampshire actively and hope to catch Nixon there; and if he did contest New Hampshire, he would be put on the ballot automatically in Wisconsin, Nebraska and Oregon. In Wisconsin, Nixon already had one of his strongest organizations humming, and Nebraska was solid for the former Vice President. Only in Oregon, whose Republican primary Rockefeller had won in 1964 and whose governor, Tom McCall, was eager to back him, could Rockefeller reasonably hope to beat Nixon. The trick was to stay out of New Hampshire, Wisconsin and Nebraska and yet go into Oregon—a trick, Rockefeller finally determined, that could not be pulled off. The trick not only was to avoid the "wrong primaries" but to make no move that would panic those states, particularly in the South, that were remaining uncommitted or were supporting favorite sons as a holding action. As long as conservative Republicans were able to dream that they had a choice between Reagan and Nixon, they might straddle, but if it ever appeared that the hated Rockefeller was becoming a realistic threat, they would shelve their dreams and sign on with Nixon. The Rockefeller strategists may not ever have appreciated the potency of this attitude; Nixon did, and as time passed he came to welcome a Rockefeller candidacy as a means of establishing himself as the "centrist" candidate between the New Yorker and Reagan. If, by the same token, Reagan should come on strong, he could reasonably expect the Rockefeller support to come his way eventually to prevent a Reagan nomination.

Rockefeller, however, for all his protests of noncandidacy in early 1968, had not been idle. His man Hinman, as the Nixon camp knew, had been testing the political waters around the country long before Romney withdrew. Rockefeller was being kept informed through Hinman of draft activities in his behalf in Oregon, Maryland, Colorado and Washington State, and he wasn't objecting. "He doesn't say no," Governor Agnew, still trying to draft Rockefeller, said in an interview in his Baltimore office in mid-February. "I just tell him how many people are interested, and he indicates it's very flattering." (Agnew, while singing Rockefeller's praises, went out of his way to emphasize he was not trying to organize a stop-Nixon cabal. "I like Nixon," he said. "If Rockefeller can't be brought in, he may well be my choice.") Another governor to whom Hinman talked was Tom McCall. Sometime in January, McCall had flown down from Portland to meet Hinman at the San Francisco Airport, where for about three hours they discussed the chances of a draft, the Oregon situation and Rockefeller's own attitude. That attitude, as Hinman painted it, was the same privately as it was publicly—no candidacy, but susceptibility to a genuine draft.

As long as Romney was in the picture, of course, it was agreed that Rockefeller could not move. And now that Romney was out, the timing was all wrong. Nixon, confident Rockefeller could not catch him in New Hampshire with only two weeks to go, seized the initiative. "Let me make one thing quite clear," Nixon said. "I'm not issuing a challenge. I'm not belligerently saying, 'Now, Governor, either come in or stay out.' " But in effect that was precisely what he was doing. Of Romney's decision, Nixon said pointedly: "I take no pleasure, no gratification in seeing him have to make this decision. I admire men who get into the arena. Some of the others have not." And also: "He [Rockefeller] may think that his purposes may be better served by a draft. He may think that it would be better for the king-makers at Miami to select the nominee. . . . I would trust that Governor Rockefeller would get in and answer questions on Vietnam. It would be very interesting. . . . I think he has every reason not to answer them up to this point because he is not a candidate, but if he becomes a candidate, he could do so." Wouldn't a Rockefeller candidacy be divisive? Nixon was asked. Not, he said, "if Governor Rockefeller conducts himself in the primary campaign as I have conducted myself in this one." By focusing on Johnson instead of each other, he said, "We would make the case against Johnson in a double-barreled way that otherwise would be made in a single-barreled way."

Actually, it already had been assured that more than one barrel would be aimed at Lyndon Johnson. Alabama's George Wallace by now had launched his third-party Presidential campaign, using LBJ as his favorite target. Having capped in California an impressive campaign to place his name on the ballot in all fifty states, Wallace was stalled only temporarily by a family tragedy. In January he had taken his wife, Lurleen, fighting a losing battle against cancer, to Houston for special treatments. They stayed in a gaudy motel across the road from the hospital, Lurleen undergoing the treatments as an out-patient as George waited nervous and immobilized. But he was raring to go; two weeks later in a Washington press conference he announced his candidacy, insisting Lurleen would not have it any other way.

All the while, of course, Gene McCarthy already had been making the anti-Johnson case quite well in the Democratic primary in New Hampshire. Until Romney's abrupt withdrawal, McCarthy's lonely, low-key effort against an absentee candidate had been playing second fiddle to the Nixon-Romney race. With the drama sapped from that one, the press army that had invaded the state to cover the Republican war looked around for more stimulating action. In McCarthy, they found it to a degree few had expected.

While Nixon tried unsuccessfully to lure Rockefeller into New Hampshire, McCarthy's candidacy, along with the state of the Vietnam War, unrest at home and a champing Robert Kennedy, set off a bizarre set of circumstances. As they unfolded, there seemed at times to be only one constant—Richard Nixon. And when the chaos of the next three months was through, he alone of the contenders would remain politically unsullied.

11

The Mad Month

RICHARD NIXON was correct in gauging that
Nelson Rockefeller was in a bind. At the meeting of Republican governors at which George Romney announced his withdrawal, Rockefeller held a round of discussions with fellow
governors and emerged on March 1 just where he had been.
Any way he looked at it, getting into the primaries against
Nixon would cut the party up, and himself too. "The party
must decide who it feels can best represent it and who it thinks
can best command the confidence of the American people,"
Rockefeller intoned in a stiff formal statement. "The Republican Party has two objectives: it wants to remain united; it
wants to nominate someone who can get enough independent
and Democratic votes to get elected. I am not going to create
dissension within the Republican Party by contending for the
nomination, but I am ready and willing to serve the American
people if called."

To no one's surprise, he was not called. A write-in drive for
Rockefeller in New Hampshire, weak and unsanctioned, produced scarcely the whisper of a summons. The real contest in the
state now was on the Democratic side, although there too only
one active candidate was on the ballot. But that candidate,
Gene McCarthy, was far from the only active Democrat. A
triumvirate of regular New Hampshire Democrats, obediently

rising to the defense of Lyndon Johnson, had set about to shoot this mosquito of a challenger with a cannon. The three, Governor John W. King, Senator Thomas J. McIntyre and Bernard J. Boutin, a former Kennedy and Johnson sub-Cabinet member, began by flatly predicting that McCarthy, campaigning on an antiwar platform, would be lucky to get 10 percent of the vote.

Next, they allowed themselves an exercise in heavy-handedness of which Johnson himself might have been proud—the circulation of numbered "pledge cards" on which registered Democrats were asked to sign their loyalty to the President on the dotted line. Portions of the cards were to be sent directly to the White House to let Johnson know—and, McCarthy immediately inferred, record—who still loved him. As the days of winter limped on, and McCarthy and his ever growing army of college students smothered New Hampshire with their low-key demand for an end to the war, King and Company realized that in Lyndon Johnson they were selling an exceedingly unpopular commodity.

In the last days of January and the first of February, at the time of the Vietnamese New Year, or Tet, a momentous event occurred that was to have unforeseen political ramifications. The enemy in South Vietnam launched a devastating series of attacks on American installations and personnel, including a temporary siege of the American Embassy. With this Tet offensive, Johnson's men in New Hampshire embraced rank jingoism, wrapping the President in the flag and labeling McCarthy as a man whose criticism gave "aid and comfort" to the enemy. As his own readings indicated increasingly that McCarthy was on the rise, King took to charging in print and on radio that a McCarthy victory would produce "dancing in the streets of Hanoi," and Boutin sharply adjusted his prediction. By early March he was saying anything less than 40 percent of the vote against an absentee candidate would be disastrous for McCarthy. Clearly, King and Company could see what was coming, and were hedging their bets.

Nixon, now deprived of opposition and consequently also of the spotlight, saw too that Johnson was in trouble and sought to capitalize on that fact. Although he had a clear field in the New Hampshire primary, around-the-clock teams of women volun-

teers manned special phones in the Highway Hotel headquarters in Concord and mailed out thousands of pieces of
campaign literature. There was to be no letup; Nixon wanted
an overwhelming vote, and according to finance chairman Stans
later, spent about half a million dollars for it in New Hampshire. By word of mouth to the press, Nixon's aides sought first
to build up the threat of write-in opposition from Rockefeller
and Reagan and thus be able to claim a greater victory. "New
Hampshire becomes a very significant race with a massive, well-
financed write-in for Rockefeller," Nixon insisted. "He has the
money and the men to do it." But the strategy didn't take
because it was clear Rockefeller wanted nothing to do with an
amateurish, eleventh-hour write-in that was doomed before it
started. Next, on a radio show in Hanover the day after Romney withdrew, Nixon argued that the primary still could be
"very significant," by "testing whether Nixon or Johnson gets
the most votes." In a state with 149,000 registered Republicans
to only 89,000 Democrats, and in a primary in which the Republican now was virtually unopposed and the Democrat absent
and under siege, this gambit didn't take either.

By this time, the focus on McCarthy had turned New Hampshire into a political battleground on Vietnam. Nixon, while
still peddling his hawkish views, was not satisfying some of his
older counselors who believed he had to put daylight between
himself and Johnson on the war. It was necessary, they insisted,
if he hoped to emerge from the primaries as anything more than
a me-too candidate whose ability to beat Johnson would be
severely questioned in and out of party ranks. At one of the
staff's periodic strategy meetings in New York not attended by
Nixon, Herb Brownell, the former Attorney General in the
Eisenhower administration, insisted that Nixon had to say
something stronger. He had to say he would end the war. "Ike
did it in 1952," Brownell argued. Others at the meeting
thought it was a terrible idea, one that would break the cocoon
of generalities Nixon had spun about himself to retain his
flexibility in the developing and uncertain Vietnam situation.
It was such a bad idea, in fact, that some younger aides who
ordinarily would have counseled Nixon against it didn't bother
to do so, assuming that the candidate himself, as a political

expert, would see how wrong the advice was and would reject it out of hand.

A few days later, however, on March 4, Nixon was in Hampton, New Hampshire, delivering a speech full of old-fashioned patriotism, when he suddenly told the audience: "If in November this war is not over, I say that the American people will be justified in electing new leadership, and I pledge to you that new leadership will end the war and win the peace in the Pacific." The Brownell view apparently had got to him, and had been bought.

As the crowd broke into warm applause, reporters raced to telephones. In the earlier speeches, Nixon had indicated his belief that a Republican administration could end the war, but this was the first time he actually had pledged to do it in such specific terms. The news was flashed around the country, and reporters traveling with Nixon began to press him harder than before on just how he intended to fulfill his pledge. Democrats took up the cry; if Nixon had any answers that would end the war, he was bound by basic decency to offer them to President Johnson so that no American troops would die needlessly between then and the start of a new administration in January.

But Nixon, aware he had blundered, retreated. "People ask me, 'What will you give North Vietnam?'" he said in an interview in the New York *Times.* "Let me tell you why I won't tell you that. No one with this responsibility who is seeking office should give away any of his bargaining positions in advance. That's why I will not be tied to anything Johnson has said except the commitment. Under no circumstances should a man say what he will do in January. The military situation may change, and we may have to take an entirely new look." Like George Romney, Nixon wanted to avoid being trapped by unforeseen developments; unlike Romney, he was determined to keep his mouth shut and avoid a full discussion of Vietnam. He had no "magic formula," he acknowledged. "I'm not trying to be coy or political. It's an objective [ending the war]. It's vital to get out in an honorable way. Any man who ran for office and didn't present himself this way shouldn't present himself to the American people."

For all this, pressure from the press continued. As the primary approached, though, Nixon was losing the spotlight even more to the onrushing McCarthy. As King, McIntyre and Boutin stepped up their personal attacks on McCarthy's patriotism—and raised their predictions of his total vote, thus revealing their growing concern—the scent of upset filled the New Hampshire air. Nixon sought again to make a Nixon-Johnson referendum out of the race, but few were interested when a David-Goliath struggle was taking place entirely within Democratic ranks.

On primary day, March 12, a typical New England blizzard hit the state. McCarthy's student army intensified its efforts to get out the vote, and in one of the wildest, most joyful political nights in years, gathered at the Sheraton-Wayfarer Inn in Manchester to watch the returns. Almost from the first word, it became clear that McCarthy was making history; if he had not brought a sitting President down, he had shaken him severely. The final figures gave McCarthy a staggering 42.2 percent of the Democratic vote to 49.4 percent for Johnson, and twenty of twenty-four convention delegates.

On the Republican side, as expected, it was Nixon by a landslide, 84,005 votes or 79 percent, to 11,691 write-ins for Rockefeller or 11 percent. Nixon, bypassing the traditional victory hoopla, had returned to New York, and shortly before 9:00 P.M. he issued a bland, cool statement from his Park Avenue headquarters. The New Hampshire vote, he said, meant "we are going to win in August, and that America is going to get a new leadership in November." He called the vote "the first referendum on Lyndon B. Johnson," and renewed his thinly veiled challenge to Rockefeller. The New York governor's small write-in vote, Nixon said, indicated "the people of this country this year don't like absentee candidates" and that "the results should indicate to him that it would be very hazardous to stay out of the race." His own total vote, Nixon said modestly, "will impress those who have been waiting to find a winner." After six years under the shadow of his loser image, Nixon's first night as a certified winner again was marked by amazing aloofness and self-control. Rockefeller, asked for his reaction, dismissed the primary as not very significant. "There was no competition," he said.

Thus it was on to Wisconsin, where Nixon had a powerful organization revved up, but where again he was destined to play second fiddle to another McCarthy-Johnson confrontation, this time with the President's name on the ballot. Nixon was not aware of it then, but while he and his aides sought ways to extract some positive dividend from their investment of about $600,000 in the Wisconsin primary, still another development was unfolding on the Democratic side that was to have more impact on Richard Nixon's drive for the Presidency than anything he said or did in Wisconsin. After months of tortured soul-searching, Robert Kennedy—the heir apparent of the man who had beaten Nixon in 1960—was about to risk all in the 1968 race.

Nixon, for all his talk about political realism, is a man who spends much time in his own past. Though he denies this, he is forever referring in public and private comment about this or that place, or this or that person, involved in one of his past victories or defeats. Already noted here as an illustration of his penchant for reliving the past were his return to the Moscow park where he held his highly beneficial "kitchen debate" with Soviet Premier Khrushchev and his earlier call at the Khrushchev flat. And in that past, no one group of people looms greater than the Kennedy family. A Kennedy denied him the Presidency in 1960; a Kennedy, in Nixon's own reasoning, denied him the governorship of California in 1962 as a result of the Cuban missile crisis; now, in 1968, another Kennedy was about to block his path again.

Richard Nixon would confess in private that he had great admiration for John Kennedy, for his style and easy manner. What he did not confess, but what showed often in defensive comments, was that he held John Kennedy and clan in awe; the kind of awe that a scrambler displays toward the rich who always have been rich, as the Kennedy boys had been. The Kennedys in turn viewed Nixon on a scale that ran from amusement to contempt. Arthur Schlesinger noted in his book *A Thousand Days** that those who argued in 1960 that there wasn't much difference between Kennedy and Nixon drove Kennedy crazy. "The contention that he and Nixon were two peas in a

* Houghton Mifflin, 1965.

pod exasperated him," Schlesinger wrote. "He said that this was the fashionable cliché of the campaign. And he obviously feared that it might have some impact. I think, moreover, that he felt personally insulted by it, for he considered that there was no one he resembled less than Nixon. . . . 'He has no taste,' Kennedy said with contempt. On issues, he added with disarming candor, 'Nixon is about as far advanced as I was ten years ago.' " (As noted, Nixon in turn has no great admiration for Schlesinger.)

Robert Kennedy essentially shared his late brother's view of Nixon, though in one way he was like Nixon—often ill at ease in public, in small political or social gatherings. But Robert Kennedy brazened out his discomfort, whereas Nixon would willingly impale himself on the trite and obvious if it could get him through cocktail party discourse. Meeting Robert Kennedy in a small group, or alone, one might spend silent minutes staring down at his shoes with him; an awful awareness would creep in that unless someone came up to break the trance, the impasse could go on for hours, because Kennedy would prefer sweating out the uncomfortable silence to mouthing some inanity. Richard Nixon, by contrast, was visibly tortured by small-talk silence. He preferred to make an observation about almost anything that came into his head, rather than stand there groping. As a result, he kept up a constant chatter about where he had just been, where he was going, when was the last time he had been where he was, who the local Congressman was, how much he had won by last time, etc. If it wasn't political statistics, it might be the local sports team, complete with names of stars and their feats. A Lord High Executioner directed to dole out the maximum punishment to Robert Kennedy and Richard Nixon would have had an easy chore: just put them alone in a room together.

Robert Kennedy entered the race for the Democratic Presidential nomination mainly because the Vietnam War finally overwhelmed him, persuading him to put his political future on the line to stop it. He moved too because he became convinced Lyndon Johnson would do nothing significant to combat racial injustice and unrest in the nation's cities. But Kennedy also ran because he began to see as inevitable Nixon's nomination as the

Republican candidate. As long as he could rationalize that his own candidacy would split the Democratic Party, he desisted. But during and after the New Hampshire primary, Kennedy was able at last to convince himself that the party already was split; there was no valid rationalization left for inaction. Kennedy's prime target as a candidate, beyond any doubt, was Lyndon Johnson. But even if Johnson could be brought down, Nixon would be well positioned to become the next President. And that, in Robert Kennedy's mind, would be a disaster.

Having turned aside the siren call of Al Lowenstein in the summer and fall of 1967, Kennedy had felt for some time he could oppose Johnson on the war and still stay out of the race. But the Tet offensive of late January and early February, 1968, so jolted him that he put his uncharacteristic caution behind and jumped in. After months of meetings with his advisers, Kennedy about a week before the New Hampshire primary decided to run; in a meeting in his office on March 5 with his brother, Senator Ted Kennedy, and old Kennedy hands Fred Dutton and Kenneth O'Donnell, he actually considered announcing before the New Hampshire vote. It was agreed, however, that such a move would appear to be pulling the rug out from under McCarthy; it would look "ruthless," that label that always had haunted Robert Kennedy. So he waited. But not long enough; the day after McCarthy's "victory," Kennedy blurted out to a reporter at Washington National Airport that he was "reassessing" his position. As a result, once again he was called "ruthless" and charged with trying to capitalize on McCarthy's feat. This catchphrase pursued Robert Kennedy throughout his dramatic, ill-starred dash for the Presidency.

Nixon, as a man who had labored long under the "Tricky Dick" label, knew the potency of catchphrases. He deftly made use of the "ruthless" label against Kennedy, referring to him almost always as "Bobby," painting him as the spoiled little rich kid who would commit any deed to get what he wanted. It always was done in a lighthearted way, in the context of a commentary on the hopelessly bickering Democrats. But listening to Nixon, one often had the feeling there was nothing he wanted less than to come up against the Kennedy clan again. One Nixon insider insisted later, however, that Nixon would have welcomed running against Robert Kennedy because his candidacy would have scared the Deep South and helped Nixon pull votes from Wallace. As for any personal intimidation or superstition Nixon may have felt about facing the brother of the man who had beaten him for the Presidency, this insider shrugged off the idea. "Nixon's view," he said, "was, 'a different year, a different man.' "

Kennedy formally became a candidate on March 16, the Saturday after the New Hampshire primary. His move came, as already noted, as the weight of the Tet offensive in South Vietnam shattered long-held American illusions about "progress" in the war. On the very day of Kennedy's announcement, yet another incident occurred in a small Vietnamese hamlet called My Lai 4, in an area of Quong Ngai Province known to Vietnamese as Song My, but to Americans as "Pinkville" because it was a Viet Cong haven. Kennedy did not know about what happened there and was never to know, but other Americans were told twenty months later that on that day, American soldiers massacred old men and women, children and babies. It was a report of brutalization that shattered the moral underpinning beneath traditional American righteousness, and the basic American justification for being in Vietnam. When the story was publicized, it had a profound impact on American public opinion; had Kennedy known of it and made use of it in the ensuing campaign, the course of the war and of the 1968 political campaign might have been much different.

Kennedy entered the race too late to get on the ballot in Wisconsin. There it would be McCarthy against Johnson on the Democratic side and Nixon against Reagan on the Republican side, with neither Johnson nor Reagan campaigning personally. A Reagan Committee in Wisconsin had been working for several months, and had touched base with Reagan aides in California, but was making little headway. His supporters were staking much on a special documentary about the governor that was to be shown on television the final weekend. Nixon, knowing Reagan posed little threat, was looking ahead to Rockefeller, who, in spite of what he had said about not contending for the nomination, now was meeting with moderate and liberal party leaders and edging ever closer to open candidacy. With Kennedy further splitting the Democratic ranks, it was reasoned, the Republicans could have a contest and still remain strong enough to win in November.

The Rockefeller strategy was clear: to avoid the remaining important primary in which Nixon would be favored, Nebraska, then run in Oregon, where Rockefeller would have his best chance. Nixon, in Portland for some fence-mending three days after the New Hampshire vote, insisted that if Rockefeller entered the Oregon primary he would be the favorite, having won there in 1964. A loss for himself in Oregon, Nixon said, would not finish him, but if he defeated Rockefeller there, he would have the nomination assured. It was classic political hedging, by the master himself.

Rockefeller, after weeks of indecision, appeared in mid-March to be ready to become a candidate. But timing was a key. Nebraska, like Oregon, now conducted a "free-for-all" primary. That is, any public figure deemed by the secretary of state in Lincoln to be a candidate would have his name placed on the ballot, and could remove it only by filing an affidavit saying he was not a candidate and did not intend to become one. Thus, it appeared necessary for Rockefeller to make his announcement after March 15, the Nebraska deadline, but before March 22, the Oregon filing deadline. That way, Rockefeller could avoid Nebraska but be entered in Oregon, where he could make an all-out effort to derail Nixon.

Nixon aides had been working diligently to have state officials in Nebraska extend the deadline and thereby list Rockefeller's name the moment he announced. But the Nebraskans were adamantly opposed. Kennedy's lieutenants, at the same time, decided at the eleventh hour that their man would enter in Nebraska, and they somehow persuaded the state officials the deadline did not apply to Presidential candidates. Kennedy's announcement therefore, on March 16, though one day after the deadline, automatically placed his name on the Nebraska ballot. Having done this, the Nebraskans also had to bow to pressures from the Nixon camp to hold open the Republican list for a few more days, pending Rockefeller's expected declaration of candidacy, now set for March 21.

There is reason to believe that before this development, Rockefeller indeed had planned to announce on that day. Most of his close advisers, including faithful Governor Agnew of Maryland, awaited his nationally televised press conference with warm anticipation. Agnew in fact was holding a press conference when Rockefeller came on television, and Agnew had two TV sets brought in so all could watch. Newsmen and photographers packed the New York Hilton ballroom as Rockefeller strode in. The event had all the trappings of the start of a Presidential campaign; New York Republican hangers-on applauded and cheered lustily for the man they were sure now was about to become their candidate. An electorate that already had been jolted by three unexpected developments in three weeks— Romney's withdrawal, McCarthy's success in New Hampshire and Kennedy's candidacy—should have been prepared for anything. But it was not; even the authoritative New York *Times* a day earlier had reported Rockefeller would run. Consequently, the audience was stunned and Agnew publicly humiliated in the presence of the press in his own office when Rockefeller stood before the television lights and announced that a "realistic appraisal" of the 1968 Republican picture had convinced him the party did not want him to contest Nixon in the remaining primaries.

A "considerable majority" of the GOP leadership appeared to want Nixon, Rockefeller said. "It appears equally clear that they are keenly concerned and anxious to avoid any such divisive challenge within the party as marked the 1964 campaign. It would therefore be illogical and unreasonable for me to try to arouse their support by pursuing the course of action they would least want and most deplore."

An active primary candidacy by him, Rockefeller said, would serve only to cancel out the tremendous advantage of unity the Republicans now had, in light of the Democratic split. Doubtless bearing in mind his own low party standing for having failed to support Goldwater in 1964, Rockefeller obviously did not want to be tagged with the "spoilsport" label again. "How should a responsible Republican act in a period of such crisis?" he asked. "I cannot believe that the Republican retort to the Democratic scene should be: 'Any din you raise, we can raise higher.' I honor the right of open dissent and the rigor of honest debate as vital marks of democratic life. I have been known to take pride in combat for political principles. But I do not believe that the way to compose perilous national division is to create more partisan division. For the Republican Party, this is particularly true, for it is—even in full unity—a minority party. Its deep discordance could only mean its sure impotence. The serious service of the nation demands that this party dedicate all its strength to the constructive and the creative. This means: the study of national issues, the design of imaginative programs and the quest of meaningful unity."

Such words, had they come from Nixon, would have been taken as self-serving, since he was himself the candidate of party unity. From Rockefeller, they marked a giant step away from the folly of 1964. Whether he would have made them had he been able to avoid the Nebraska primary and almost certain defeat there at Nixon's hands is another question. Also weighing on Rockefeller was the condition in the nonprimary states. Many convention delegations in the South and West, officially still uncommitted, were staying so only as long as they could permit themselves the fancy of a Reagan candidacy. An overt challenge to Nixon by the dreaded Rockefeller probably would have persuaded hundreds of conservative delegates to abandon the Reagan dream for the reality of Nixon as a necessary move to block Rockefeller. This one constant—that Nixon occupied the centrist position between Reagan and Rockefeller and thus would be the beneficiary of the fears on each flank—made Nixon's nomination a virtual certainty, barring an unforeseen blooper, long before the convention in Miami Beach.

Rockefeller's statement that he had learned the party didn't want him to contest Nixon in the primaries was accompanied by a reiteration that he stood "ready to answer any true and meaningful call" from the party. But he added: "I expect no such call. And I shall do nothing in the future, by word or by deed, to encourage such a call." They were words he soon would regret having uttered.

Nixon himself, only a few blocks away at the Hotel Pierre, had expected Rockefeller to enter. As was the former Vice President's rather unusual custom on such occasions, he did not watch Rockefeller's television press conference, but instead assigned Buchanan and Chapin to do so and report to him. He was astonished when they told him what had happened, but soon offered the analysis that Rockefeller's entry would have pinned everything on the Oregon primary, with the stakes too high. If Rockefeller had entered again, Nixon told his aides, "we could lose something or win everything. Rockefeller could win something or lose everything." In other words, he felt one defeat for himself after five primary victories would not be as damaging to him as a defeat for Rockefeller in his first and only primary test.

For the second time in three weeks, Richard Nixon appeared to have scared off a major foe. For a man who had yet to shake his loser's image with a victory over an active opponent, he was doing all right. "Governor Rockefeller has set an example for all Republicans to follow," Nixon said. "I believe when we get to Miami, the decision will be in my favor." The only barrier to his nomination now, Nixon said, would be "my own mistakes," and it was clear he had no intention of making any.

Almost at once after Rockefeller's spectacular no-go decision on March 21, Nixon moved in. Sears, in Alaska helping to obtain a statement of endorsement from Governor Walter J. Hickel, phoned Nixon immediately and urged that Agnew be fielded on the first rebound. Ellsworth went down to Baltimore, where the head of the Draft-Rockefeller effort still was recovering from the personal humiliation of the Rockefeller decision and how it had been conveyed to him. Ellsworth found Agnew to be personally embittered. A meeting was arranged between Nixon and Agnew in New York for March 29. For two hours the two men talked, and each came away strongly impressed with the other. Afterward, Agnew told reporters he still believed Rockefeller would be the party's best candidate. He acknowledged, however, he was "discouraged" by Rockefeller's actions and was looking Nixon over carefully. "I am not ready to announce any support of Mr. Nixon at this time," Agnew said. "I have high regard for him. He's the front-runner." Nixon said nothing publicly, but aides noted from that point that their boss occasionally would remark how impressed he was with this fellow Agnew.

It really was not surprising that Dick Nixon and Ted Agnew would hit it off. Both were Horatio Alger beneficiaries of the

American Dream; boys of humble beginnings who had parlayed hard work and fealty to party and nation into public prominence beyond their wildest expectations. To Nixon, struggling son of a struggling grocer, Agnew's upward climb had all the right ingredients: son of a Greek immigrant, conditioned to self-sacrifice by the Great Depression; diligent law student; company commander in Europe in World War II; hard-working insurance claims adjuster; manager of a chain of food stores; trial lawyer; Baltimore county executive; successful underdog candidate for governor; Kiwanian, Legionnaire; loyal, active Republican.

For the moment, though, it was enough that Agnew had been the most outspoken advocate of Nelson Rockefeller among the governors; alliance with him would help assure Rockefeller's inaction, and might provide a very useful link to the other governors. Agnew, though a freshman, had made a very favorable impression on most of his colleagues at the governors' conferences. He was straight-talking and tough-minded. In coming out for Rockefeller so openly, Agnew only was recognizing what the other more reluctant governors knew—that the New Yorker was the class of their league; that if anyone had the right to carry the governors' banner, it was Rockefeller. Agnew could be a useful man for Nixon to have in his corner—not in any really leading role, of course, but as a symbol of party unity.

Perhaps fortunately at this juncture, Nixon found himself crowded off the front pages of the nation's newspapers, and off the television screens, by a political phenomenon that now was sweeping across the country like a great uncontrollable spasm: Robert Kennedy, freed of his self-doubts, was running pell-mell against the personification of the nation's discontent—Lyndon Johnson.

In such unlikely places as Kansas, Georgia, Alabama and Tennessee—places where patriotism was thought to mean unquestioning loyalty to the Commander-in-Chief in time of war and where the Kennedy name was supposed to be suspect—the brother of the late President generated wildly receptive crowds with a free-swinging and at times careless attack on Johnson. Part of the stimulus was the personal Kennedy aura, to be sure, but it certainly also was the emotional unleashing of pent-up public disenchantment, even hostility, toward the overbearing man in the White House. Kennedy entered the race marked by many as a usurper of McCarthy's success in New Hampshire, but in these first days he managed to cast Lyndon Johnson as the usurper of all that had been started by John F. Kennedy, and as the betrayer of the power Johnson had inherited.

There was in Robert Kennedy's stump manner, when he talked about Vietnam, a ringing evangelism. Like a sinner who had repented and been converted to the faith, he acknowledged his own misjudgments as a member of the national administration that first had enlarged the war. Then he preached fervently and urgently that it was better, having erred, to recognize error and correct it than to continue it. To audiences and a whole country that similarly had struggled with their consciences over Vietnam, the Kennedy catharsis was both relevant and emotionally appealing. "Past error is no excuse for its own perpetuation," he said at Kansas State University. ". . . The course we are following is deeply wrong. . . . I am concerned that, at the end of it all, there will only be more Americans killed, more of our treasure spilled out, and because of the bitterness and hatred on every side of this war, more hundreds of thousands of Vietnamese slaughtered; so that they may say, as Tacitus said of Rome: 'They made a desert and called it peace.' I don't think that's satisfactory for the United States of America. I do not think that is what the American spirit is really about. I do not think that is what this country stands for."

In this and similar pleadings, Kennedy triggered fervid responses among his predominantly student audiences; the stridence of voice and style awakened recollections of that earlier Kennedy who had exhorted the country to start moving again, to recapture its sense of pioneering, adventure and idealism. And on top of that, there was the shared dislike and mistrust of Lyndon Baines Johnson, whose arrogance and arbitrariness offended the public tolerance far more deeply than Johnson himself realized. Richard Nixon, too, railed against the excesses of Johnson, but in a partisan framework; though fellow Democrat Kennedy strove constantly to escape the oversimplification that his opposition was a personal thing, the public belief that it was personal encouraged those who also had a personal dislike for the President to embrace Kennedy. Many, of course, also embraced his view that the war was a disaster that had to be stopped, but in those early days of the Kennedy campaign, it seemed at times that the words spoken, their meaning, did not matter nearly as much to audiences as the intensity and aggressiveness with which they were uttered. Like Kennedy himself, many had held in their hostility toward Johnson; now, with Kennedy giving vent to his own feelings, their feelings likewise spilled out. Nixon had criticized Johnson, but with caution and deference, always tempering his remarks with assurances of support in pursuit of the war; Kennedy's criticism swept over any such restraint.

Frank Mankiewicz, the Senator's press secretary, knowing of Kennedy's long soul-searching before finally entering the race, attributed the excesses of the first days to "the free-at-last syndrome." If it was true for Kennedy himself, it appeared to be true for many in his audiences as well. Richard Nixon, for all of his exhortations about "new leadership," never touched this vein of discontent quite so deeply as Robert Kennedy did, partly because what Nixon was offering, certainly on the war, was not very new. Kennedy managed to project by personality as well as oratory a fierce challenge to all that Lyndon Johnson seemed to be; Nixon, though of the opposition party, seemed himself more like Johnson—the operator, wheeler-dealer, Tricky Dick. Had Kennedy been nominated by the Democrats, Nixon —not the Democratic candidate—might have been carrying Lyndon Johnson and the war around his neck in the fall campaign. But that did not happen, and Nixon eventually was able to enlist many of the discontented, though never with the fervor or depth of commitment that Kennedy drew.

In a Presidential year when the route to success obviously was the tapping of discontent, Nixon had to share not only the hard sell—with Kennedy and George Wallace—but the soft sell as well—with Gene McCarthy. McCarthy, having demonstrated the effectiveness of his approach in New Hampshire, continued his campaign of quiet rage against Lyndon Johnson in Wisconsin. There, with a built-in army of antiwar students from the University of Wisconsin and other liberal schools in the Midwest, and with one of the most aggressive adult protests against the war, McCarthy was in more familiar territory. He did not have the advantage of having the New Hampshire triumvirate of King, McIntyre and Boutin working against him in Wisconsin, but even a more sophisticated Johnson team could not stem the tide against the President there. The Johnson headquarters in Milwaukee was barren of people and spirit, and a scouting trip into the state by the best Democratic political doctor in practice, then Postmaster General Lawrence F. O'Brien, diagnosed the illness quickly and realistically.

The genesis of O'Brien's Wisconsin trip was itself a commentary on Johnson's political sickness. He went not at the President's request, but because one loyalist Democratic Congressman, Clement J. Zablocki, asked him. Zablocki, who could read the dire signs, urged O'Brien to come see for himself, to fire up the lagging regular Democratic troops and, hopefully, get the message back to the President about what deep trouble he faced in Wisconsin. But although O'Brien came and saw, and did his best to paint Johnson as a man who "did not betray his trust" after John Kennedy's death, he was not the ideal man any longer to convey the message to Johnson. In the suspicious climate that existed through late 1967 about the possible attempt of Robert Kennedy to depose Johnson—a prospect about which Johnson apparently was convinced but O'Brien (rightly at the time) was not—O'Brien's stock, as an old Kennedy man, had fallen. The President increasingly had looked to his fellow Texan Marvin Watson as his political wise man. Watson shared Johnson's trust and, unfortunately for the President, his ignorance about national politics. It was one of the great myths about Lyndon Johnson that he was the consummate politician. When it came to Congressional politics, he had no peer; in dealing with politics outside of Washington, he was a babe in the woods. His incredibly inept bid for the 1960 Presidential nomination, when he thought his Senate leadership and cronyism with other Congressmen could deliver delegates, was a clear example; so was his neglect and misunderstanding of the role of governors in grass-roots politics, demonstrated in the revolt of the Democratic governors at White Sulphur Springs in 1966. In turning to Watson, he was contributing to his own demise. It was Watson, not O'Brien, who felt New Hampshire was safe enough to entrust to King and Co. Watson perhaps thought by engineering the New Hampshire victory himself, his political standing would climb with Johnson; whatever the reason, O'Brien was not consulted, though his background as a New Englander, as well as a national politician, was obvious. New Hampshire had been a disaster, and now Wisconsin loomed as an even greater one. As the primary approached, all signs pointed not simply to a moral victory by McCarthy—a good showing— but a clear majority and a clear rejection of Johnson, whose name this time was on the ballot.

McCarthy, now riding the crest of his New Hampshire upset, and his loyal student ranks stiffened by the effrontery of Kennedy to move in on him, found in Wisconsin an even more congenial atmosphere for his low-key campaign against Johnson. The state already had an antiwar bias; the University of Wisconsin had been a hotbed of early protest against Vietnam, and Donald Peterson, Democratic chairman of the Tenth Congressional District, was a leader in the original "dump Johnson" effort that had brought McCarthy into the race. The state's two liberal Senators, William Proxmire and Gaylord Nelson, declared themselves neutral; so did the most popular at-home Democrat in the state, Attorney General Bronson LaFollette, and two of the three Democratic Congressmen. Watson and the Democratic National Committee, unable to find any notable Wisconsin Democrat to head the Johnson campaign, finally drafted a young Pentagon economist from the state, Leslie Aspin, and sent him home to see what he could do. In addition to O'Brien, other Johnson administration stars were dispatched in the late stages—Vice President Humphrey, Secretary of Agriculture Orville Freeman, Housing Secretary Robert C. Weaver, Attorney General Ramsey Clark, even consumer adviser Betty Furness. They might as well have stayed home; Humprey failed even to fill a small hall.

To add to Johnson's woes, there also was the fact that Nixon was virtually unopposed on the Republican side. The perennial, Harold Stassen, was entered, but nobody took him seriously except himself. The effort for Reagan never got anywhere, in spite of four showings of the Reagan documentary on television on the final weekend. Consequently, there was little incentive for Republican voters to stay in the GOP column. In Wisconsin, they may cross over and vote in the Democratic primary, and with anti-Johnson sentiment high, the indications were they would do just that—vote for McCarthy to humiliate Johnson. Nixon, with about $600,000 already committed to Wisconsin and an impressive professional and volunteer operation already humming, went into the state for about seven days, with a twofold purpose: to fire up the troops for the November effort and to discourage an anti-Johnson crossover that would diminish his own vote. Deprived of a live opponent, Nixon was reduced to running against Johnson and against his own performance in New Hampshire. Neither would be easy, but the Nixon organization, working originally on the premise that Wisconsin could finish off Romney, already had massive telephone and door-to-door canvass operations ready to contact an estimated 400,000 households. It would proceed as planned, with the message that the best way to hit Johnson was not by crossing over for McCarthy, but by demonstrating the demand for a Republican—Nixon.

Hit Johnson. That was the fuel that ignited all the campaigns. In playing on the growing discontent in the country, and in using Lyndon Johnson as a whipping boy, Nixon in fact was being outdone in both the hard sell—by Kennedy and Wallace— and the soft sell—by McCarthy. But it did not really matter. All the competition was outside Republican ranks; within, Nixon stood alone. Though he campaigned in Wisconsin, he broadened his activity now to building bridges and smoothing relations. While in Wisconsin he conferred with Governor Knowles and announced plans to visit with all the other twenty-five Republican governors before the convention. "I am thinking—as I really have before—in terms of November," Nixon said confidently. Then, presumably, he would have Lyndon Johnson all to himself, except for side snipings by Wallace.

Yet there was one cloud, at least in the view of some of Nixon's strategists. He had been saying that only a mistake could stop him, and by his own yardstick, Nixon had made one in New Hampshire—his "pledge" to "end the war and win the peace in the Pacific." Although Nixon had tried to back off the statement, the press continued to ask him about it. With the mem-

273

ory of Romney's running inquisition on Vietnam clearly in mind, the Nixon camp feared that this misstep could hang on and generate more trouble. Perhaps the candidate's advisers were overstating the danger, but the Nixon operation of 1968 was supersensitive and superefficient. Loose ends had to be tied up; no potential for difficulty could be left unattended.

The need to take some action had been underlined about two weeks before the Wisconsin vote when the New York *Times* ran a story reporting that Nixon's old foe Rockefeller was privately contemptuous of the Nixon "pledge." It said: "Mr. Rockefeller has said privately that he believes Mr. Nixon made a major tactical blunder in saying he had plans to end the war without disclosing these plans. . . . When he has been alone with friends, Mr. Rockefeller has scornfully mocked Mr. Nixon by patting his suit pocket and saying that he keeps a peace plan there while hundreds of Americans die each week in Vietnam."

The account irritated Nixon strategists no end. The "pledge," some of them informed the *Times* subsequently, had been "misrepresented." Nixon never contended, they said, that he had a "plan" to end the war, and he repeatedly had said there were no "magic formulas or push-button solutions" to peace in the area. All he was saying, they insisted, was that he believed a new administration would have the capability to settle the war. They pointed to Nixon's general observations that the Johnson administration had put undue emphasis on the military aspects of the war and had neglected the political and diplomatic possibilities. Nixon himself granted interviews to reporters to underline his position, particularly that more assistance could be solicited from the Russians to resolve the Vietnam impasse. He seemed to have great confidence in his own persuasive powers with them.

Still, the concern lingered that the "pledge" held a potential for trouble. Accordingly, as the Wisconsin campaign approached its end, Nixon assigned his speechwriters to work on a Vietnam speech that would pull him back to a less vulnerable posture.

On March 27, the Nixon headquarters announced that a nationwide radio talk on Vietnam had been scheduled for the next Sunday night, March 31. Asked directly about reports that he would wait until he was his party's nominee before spelling out how he would end the war, Nixon insisted again he had "no gimmicks or secret plans," and he added pointedly, possibly with Rockefeller's gibe in mind: "If I had any way to end the war, I would pass it on to President Johnson." Then, after a campaign speech in Milwaukee on March 28, Nixon headed back to New York to concentrate on the Vietnam speech, which now—at least within the Nixon camp—had grown to some tactical importance.

For two days, Nixon and his speechwriting team considered what the candidate could and should say about Vietnam that would reduce the pressure on him to say how he would fulfill his "pledge" to end the war. What was in the works was an elaboration of Nixon's old theme that greater political and diplomatic energy be turned loose on the problem of a settlement, particularly by persuading the Soviet Union that a continuation of the war was not in the best interests of an East-West détente. Also, the strong McCarthy showing in New Hampshire and anticipated stronger showing in Wisconsin suggested to some Nixon strategists that there was no political capital in trying to out-hawk or even me-too Johnson. Perhaps it would be a good idea to begin to paint Nixon as less rigid on the war; with Rockefeller taking himself out, the only apparent threat for the nomination was Ronald Reagan, who had the same propensity for scaring people that Barry Goldwater had demonstrated in 1964. As a card-carrying anti-Communist from his House and Senate days, Nixon could modulate his Vietnam views a bit without having to worry about a conservative backlash.

Nixon would have preferred not having to make this sort of speech. He knew what had happened to Romney when he was drawn out of his self-imposed silence on Vietnam. Nixon was confident, of course, that he could discuss the war on his own terms and still withstand the newsmen's probings, but it would have been much safer if he had never had to make such a speech. One can imagine the temporary relief, then, with which the Nixon camp on Saturday received word that President Johnson had just requested nationwide radio and television time to make a major speech. With rumors circulating widely that American military men were requesting another large manpower transfusion for Vietnam, Nixon obviously could not make pronouncements about the war only two and one half hours before the President was to speak. Nixon's radio talk was canceled, in deference to the President's plans.

Before heading back to Wisconsin for a final public reception in Milwaukee on the Sunday before the primary, Nixon gave an interview to the Associated Press in which he reflected on the phenomenon of his political return. "I start with one proposition," he said. "Had it not been for events, I would have been dead." He was talking about events of the preceding four years, and particularly the Goldwater debacle that had opened the way for a unity candidate. But he might as well have been looking into his overworked crystal ball. Another event was about to explode on the election-year scene that would dwarf all those that had come before, and would for a time at least inject new imponderables in the drive for the Republican nomination that had been all but won by Nixon.

After three years of steady, even stealthy, escalation of the American commitment in Vietnam, Lyndon Johnson's radio-television speech on Sunday night, March 31, was to be the occasion of a major change in policy. All through the month of March, while the myth of his political invincibility was crumbling around him in New Hampshire, in Wisconsin and in the wake of the Robert Kennedy meteor of emotionalism, Johnson was undergoing a private agony that for a man of his pride was particularly bitter. Frustrated on the battlefield in Vietnam, jolted by the Tet offensive into facing the reality of stalemate, sniped at from the Senate and the nation's campuses, Johnson was spent. His best military minds were telling him in the aftermath of Tet that they could use another 206,000 American troops for Vietnam, a figure that would bring the American presence there to more than 714,000. Even with that number, he knew there was no assurance—perhaps no likelihood even—of "success." Nobody seemed to know just what that word meant anymore; there had been so much careless and extravagant talk, much of it spread by Johnson himself; there had been so much dissembling and self-delusion about what the Saigon government was and could be; there had been so much jingoism and legal gymnastics in what the American commitment really was, and what the goal was. The Vietnamologists had laughed when

Senator George Aiken of Vermont suggested that the United States "declare the war won, and go home." Yet that simple step would not have required any more self-deception than the rhetoric that defended stalemate as "denying the enemy victory" and urged more of the same as a way to "win the hearts and minds of the people."

Caught on this treadmill, Lyndon Johnson had turned to one of the men he most trusted through the years. He had made Clark Clifford, one of Washington's most successful lawyers, his Secretary of Defense.* Clifford, though generally knowledgeable about the war and a firm supporter of the President's policy, underwent a personal crash program to educate himself about its management and objectives. As the head of a special task force to examine the validity and wisdom of the huge new troop request, Clifford soon discovered to his surprise that there was a significant body of influential men in the government, including the Pentagon, who had basic doubts about the war policy. There was, in fact, what one administration official called "a nest of hidden doves" in the Pentagon that included such ranking men as the No. 2 civilian, Deputy Secretary of Defense Paul H. Nitze.†

This group and others outside the Pentagon were appalled not only at the size of the troop request, but at its implications for the future. Mobilization of the reserves would be necessary; new taxes would be required; pressing domestic demands, already pared down, would have to be cut to the bone or shelved altogether. And tactically, Hanoi could cancel out the American troop increase by stepping up infiltration. The call for 206,000 troops was a call for more of the same across the board on Vietnam. The argument raged within the Clifford task force, with the new Secretary of Defense at the outset merely probing, lis-

---

* Johnson, presenting his version of these events in a television interview shown in February, 1970, sought to downgrade the influence of Clark Clifford, and to emphasize the role of Secretary of State Dean Rusk, in constructing the policy change described on the next pages. Like other Johnson explanations during his Presidency and after he left the White House, this one did not square with the recollections of others and did not noticeably narrow the Johnson credibility gap.

† For a full, perceptive inside account of the momentous events of this period, see *The Limitations of Intervention* (David McKay Co., Inc., 1969) , by one of the "hidden doves," Undersecretary of the Air Force Townsend W. Hoopes.

tening to both sides, asking questions that to some of the sophisticates seemed too elementary. But is was the old story of bringing a fresh mind and a fresh perspective to a debate; it began to dawn on Clifford that the military was engaging in open-ended thinking, with no firm awareness of where the war was going. Considering the political limitations imposed on the use of American power and the growing dissent in the country, it became clear to Clifford that the Johnson administration should stop chasing the phantom of "victory" and take the turn toward negotiations and disengagement.

Other leading Presidential aides were reaching the same conclusion. United Nations Ambassador Arthur J. Goldberg, utterly frustrated in New York, in mid-March wrote Johnson a long memorandum urging that he halt the bombing of North Vietnam as a means of bringing Hanoi into direct peace talks.

The day after Johnson received the Goldberg memo, the same day Kennedy announced his candidacy, Johnson is said to have told his chief Vietnam advisers at the White House: "Let's get one thing clear. I'm telling you now I am not going to stop the bombing. Now I don't want to hear any more about it. Goldberg has written me about the whole thing, and I've heard every argument. I'm not going to stop it. Now is there anybody here who doesn't understand that?"

The outburst silenced those upon whom it descended in the Cabinet Room, but it did not end the doves' groping for a way out. They were assisted, finally, by Johnson's chief speechwriter, Harry McPherson, a youthful-looking, soft-spoken Texan who as it turned out also was a "hidden dove." McPherson proposed a compromise in a memorandum to the President: as a means of enticing Hanoi to the negotiating table, the American bombing could be cut back to an area just north of the demilitarized zone, where most of the targets threatening American troops and operations were located. At the same time the President could offer a complete bombing halt if Hanoi would give assurance that pressure in the DMZ and against the major cities of South Vietnam would be withheld. Johnson, in the face of evidence gathered by Clifford that maintaining the status quo could lead only to more frustration, astonishingly bought the compromise. McPherson, already assigned to write a speech for delivery on nationwide television on March 31, incorporated language announcing the basic and critical change in Vietnam policy. But the President was to surprise McPherson and the nation with an ending of his own. With his wife off to the side in the studio, Lyndon B. Johnson faced the American public that did not seem to want him anymore and told them he was deescalating the war. He outlined the limited bombing halt and then, with a glance at his wife, proceeded into the startling conclusion:

"With America's sons in the fields far away, with America's future under challenge right here at home, with our hopes and the world's hopes for peace in the balance every day, I do not believe that I should devote an hour or a day of my time to any personal, partisan causes or to any duties other than the awesome duties of this office—the Presidency of your country.

"Accordingly, I shall not seek, and I will not accept, the nomination of my party for another term as your President."*

The Democrats were most immediately affected. Suddenly their party leadership was there for the taking. Senator McCarthy was making a speech in a hall in Waukesha, Wisconsin, when some young backers came running down the aisle shouting the news. Senator Kennedy got word from John Burns, the New York Democratic chairman, and a New York aide, Dall Forsythe, aboard his plane as it parked at the terminal at John F. Kennedy Airport after a flight from the West. For both McCarthy and Kennedy, the news was a mixed blessing. It removed an opponent, but it also removed a target. Vice President Humphrey, in Mexico City, knew he soon must enter the ranks against these two as the heir apparent of the party regulars. He was as aware as the next man of the depths to which Johnson's political stock had plunged, and that he would have to run as his own man. But if he did not know then, he would shortly

---

* Lyndon Johnson, in another televised postmortem on this period in December, 1969 insisted he had decided long before the New Hampshire primary that he would not seek reelection. The activities on his behalf in the two primary states, however, painted an entirely contrary picture. Johnson's obvious efforts to rewrite the history of his White House years in the most favorable light cannot erase the fact that he had political forces working in the field in March, 1968, and they were taking a drubbing.

learn that being his own man would not be as easy as it once had been.

On the Republican side, Richard Nixon, having conducted another of his highly successful public receptions in Milwaukee in the afternoon, was heading back to New York on his chartered Boeing 727 when Johnson spoke. Thoroughly composed, he was ready with a comment when his plane landed. "This is the year of the dropouts," he said. "First Romney, then Rockefeller, now Johnson." Nixon acknowledged he had not expected Johnson to pull out. He rated Kennedy the new Democratic favorite, with Hubert Humphrey moving in quickly as the candidate of the administration. "I'd be very surprised if President Johnson lets Bobby Kennedy have it on a platter," he said.

Almost at once, though others did not at first sense it, Nixon could see the old familiar shadow of Nelson Rockefeller creeping up on him again. "The Democrats are a divided party," he said, "but our game could change, too. . . . Rockefeller will have to determine whether, after withdrawing from the race, he will enter it again."

Lost in the pandemonium was the staff concern about Nixon having pledged to end the war. Now that the President had ordered a bombing halt, with peace talks an imminent prospect, the course required of Nixon the Patriot was clear. It was, not surprisingly, identical to the course best suited to Nixon the Candidate. The morning after the Johnson speech, he announced he was imposing a moratorium on himself on the Vietnam situation, at least until there was some evidence of the bombing halt's effect on the start of peace talks.

"In light of these diplomatic moves, and in order to avoid anything that might, even inadvertently, cause difficulty for our negotiators," Nixon the Patriot said, "I shall not make the comprehensive statement on Vietnam which I had planned for this week." He did permit himself, however, to urge the Johnson administration to recall "the lesson of Korea, when most of the U.S. casualties were sustained after peace talks began," and to warn against any settlement "that would encourage further aggression by its weakness." Nixon was not exactly suggesting the prospect of a sellout, but those Democrats who were accustomed to holding every Nixon phrase up to the light had some reason to feel they saw a hook in that one. "This is a time for both hope and realism," Nixon went on, "a time to explore every avenue toward settlement, but at the same time to keep on guard against the temptations of a camouflaged surrender." That last phrase surely wasn't going to make them happy at the White House. More important politically, Nixon wouldn't have to make that speech on Vietnam after all.

The Wisconsin primary on April 2 was rendered anticlimactic by the Johnson withdrawal; it nullified any threat of a large Republican crossover into the Democratic column to vote against the President. Nixon won 79.4 percent of the Republican vote, even exceeding his New Hampshire performance of 79.1 percent. The Reagan absentee campaign, concluded with four television showings of the special documentary on his life, could do no better than 11 percent. The film was distinctly hard sell, opening with footage of Reagan's swearing-in as governor of California and flashbacks to 1958 and 1962, when the man he beat, Governor "Pat" Brown, had polished off two Republican giants, Senator William F. Knowland and a man named Richard M. Nixon. But Nixon's loser image was dissipating now, and fast. On the Democratic side, any thought that Johnson's pullout might generate a groundswell sympathy vote for him was buried under a solid McCarthy victory: 412,100 for him, to only 253,700 for Johnson and 46,500 write-ins for Kennedy. Johnson had vowed he was through, and from Wisconsin the response definitely was not, "Say it ain't so, Lyndon."

The President, in coupling his withdrawal with his first pullback in Vietnam, could not have known the windfall he was handing Nixon. In the guise of the national interest, Nixon not only held his tongue about Vietnam through the preliminary wrangling over a site and agenda for the peace talks, but held it right through the November election. From start to finish, the justification was the same: to spell out his own plans on Vietnam would jeopardize the talks, or would tie his own hands as a peace negotiator if he were to be elected President. Though the country was being rent by the paramount issue of the war, the front-running Republican candidate—and, later, the Republican Presidential nominee—steadfastly declined to tell the American people what he would do about that issue if they sent him

281

to the White House. He spoke often and loud in the safe generalities about "orchestrating" economic, diplomatic and military policy, but he refused to go beyond them. Press conference questions about Vietnam were deftly smothered with this mumbo jumbo, and before long the questions did not come anymore, or they came without the press' customary tenacity. When George Romney tried to punt on first down, the ball was slammed down his throat; now Richard Nixon, ever reminding the press of his past unpleasantness with them while assuring them all was forgiven, faced hardly any rush at all.

The sanctuary that Johnson's March 31 speech and subsequent actions gave Nixon on Vietnam was not the only significant impact they had on the former Vice President's candidacy. When the first shock of the Johnson pullout had passed, Nixon realized, as had McCarthy and Kennedy on the Democratic side, that he suddenly had been denied his prime target. For fully four years—during the 1964 "salvage" effort of the Goldwater campaign, in the 1966 Congressional comeback drive and since—Richard Nixon had been riding high on the back of Lyndon Johnson. Although Nixon's own comeback strategy required a softening of the partisan image that had made him the darling of Republicans and the demon in Democratic eyes, he still had the wherewithal to wield the ax when necessary. In 1965, in trying to bail out gubernatorial candidate Wayne Dumont in New Jersey, Nixon had swung it against Vietnam critic Professor Eugene Genovese with such old-time zest that even some of his supporters winced. But when it came to railing against Lyndon Johnson, Nixon—or practically any other speaker for that matter—had carte blanche.

After Johnson's first year in the White House, during which he masterfully led a country numbed by the John Kennedy assassination through some of its most uncertain days, the veneer had worn off. The Lyndon Johnson known to Washington in his Congressional days—able, astute, but also domineering, calculating and crude—stood up, and he was fair game. All the old epithets—wheeler-dealer, operator, arm-twister—could be trotted out against him without undue explanation; the man's reputation had prepared the way, and as Johnson increasingly dissembled on how deeply he was committing the nation in

Vietnam, he became not only disliked but disbelieved. He was an easy mark; so easy that even the man they called Tricky Dick could have at him with effect.

At first it was thought that Nixon would be ineffective against Johnson because Nixon had a credibility problem of his own. But Nixon was last year's operator and Johnson was this year's; Nixon, whatever else was believed about him, was generally considered too straight to have turned his public prominence to private fortune. He had entered public life a relatively poor man and had left that way. Not so with Johnson; in the course of his Congressional years, he and his wife had amassed a considerable fortune through ownership of radio and television properties in Texas, some of which benefited from decisions of the Federal Communications Commission. No wrongdoing was established, but it was the nature of the Johnson reputation—as it often is with public men—that none had to be for the public to assume the worst.

Thus Richard Nixon had in Lyndon Johnson the basic ingredient that made his post-1964 menu for party unity so palatable to so many Republicans. When the party fortunes were at their lowest in 1965, Nixon appreciated that the debacle had been fashioned not by the strength of Lyndon Johnson, but by the almost unprecedented weakness of Barry Goldwater as a Presidential candidate. Voters were not simply apathetic toward Goldwater; they were scared of him. Lost in the avalanche of anti-Goldwater votes was an already considerable and growing apathy toward Johnson. In extensive public opinion polling in the fall of 1964, I found that apathy existing side by side with fear of having Goldwater in the White House. One answer repeatedly came to inquiries about voters' preference for Johnson: "He's the lesser of two evils." Nixon knew this, used it to advantage for others in 1966 and expected to use it again to put himself in the White House in 1968. And now, with one straightforward, totally unexpected sentence, it was all gone.

Or was it? A lot now depended on whether, as Nixon had predicted, Vice President Humphrey would move forward to pick up the administration mantle. If he did, Nixon could saddle him with Johnson; not with the personality, but with the policies. This prospect, on the surface at least, was more promising for McCarthy and Kennedy than for Nixon. Their fight was chiefly against the Johnson policy on Vietnam, and there seemed to be no way Humphrey could avoid carrying that policy on his back into the campaign for the Democratic nomination. Without Johnson, running a campaign attack would be more difficult for Nixon now, but not impossible. The war, after all, was not the only issue; Democratic dissent still could be exploited. In Cincinnati several days after the President's speech, Nixon played on the opposition's confusion. "A divided Democratic Party cannot furnish the unity that America needs," Nixon said, "and above everything else, we need a united United States today."

And on the domestic front, racial unrest had raised temperatures and lowered tolerance to new levels. The code phrase "crime in the streets" that had been coined to encourage white backlash in the Goldwater campaign of 1964 now was refined to "law and order," and it was both more respectable and more effective as a political slogan. This clearly was not a good year for liberals, for those who believed in assuaging trouble in the streets with new assurances of equal treatment to increasingly militant black Americans, and Hubert Humphrey most certainly was one of those liberals. In that respect, he was even a better target for Nixon than Johnson was.

A lot had happened on the racial front since Richard Nixon last had run for President. John Kennedy had scored a political coup among black voters in 1960 by calling the wife of Dr. Martin Luther King with sympathetic words when Dr. King was jailed for demonstrating in Georgia. Then King was considered a militant by whites; now, his Gandhian nonviolence was losing favor among blacks. King himself was pressing to maintain a place of leadership in a black movement turning more and more away from integration toward separatism—and, in some instances, violence.

In his struggle to show that his nonviolent way remained valid and effective, King four days after Johnson's withdrawal was in Memphis leading a demonstration in support of a strike of black sanitation workers. The night before, he had rallied his forces with one of his patented speech-sermons that concluded with these words: "Like anybody, I would like to lead a long life. Longevity has its grace. But I'm not concerned about that now. I just want to do God's will. And he's allowed me to go up to the mountain. And I've looked over, and I've seen the promised land." Now, the next early evening, King was leaning over the balcony of his motel room when a rifle shot from a bathroom across the back alleyway snuffed out his immensely useful life.

With that shot, the issue of "law and order" was elevated to equal standing with the Vietnam War as a determinant of American votes in 1968. The shot, fired by a white man against one of the great nonviolent black leaders in American history, set off a wave of black violence and riot, and on its heels a flood of repressive thought, oratory and reaction against the black man and his aspirations in the nation. It was a flood whose headwaters had been navigated openly for years by George Wallace; now, much more deftly and subtly, Richard Nixon found in the repressive mood one more vehicle for continuing his drive for the White House. He did not have Lyndon Johnson to kick around anymore, but he had "law and order," and in his fashion he would make the most of it.

12

Without Johnson to Kick Around

MARTIN LUTHER KING'S violent death, in the cause of maintaining nonviolent protest as an effective weapon in the black revolt, ignited an immediate riot in Washington, D.C. The nation's capital, the first major American city to attain a black majority, broke into smoke and flame hours after the deed, and the sorry spectacle of federal troops guarding the Capitol building and the White House itself was flashed by television to every corner of the country. The riots of previous years in Watts, in Newark and in Detroit had been much more severe. But the outbreak in the Washington black ghetto, in some cases only blocks away from these national symbols of self-government, brought the black revolt as never before to the awareness of that significant segment of the country that still wears its Americanism on its sleeve. For that white, middle-class segment, the spectacle of the Capital City under siege, finally, was too much.

Nor was Washington the only scene of rioting. It broke out in black sections of several other big cities as a torn and tense nation, whites and blacks, bid good-bye to Dr. King. Presidential politics ground to a halt; most of the nation's political leaders, Richard Nixon among them, flocked to Atlanta for the simple, moving funeral of the champion of nonviolence. And when it was over, the candidates, sensing the emotional exhaus tion of the nation, went into seclusion. For some, like Robert Kennedy and Eugene McCarthy, the hiatus lasted only a few days. For Nixon, it stretched to more than two weeks, during which time he addressed in private the problem with which the others were publicly groping: how to give focus to a campaign now deprived of the prime target, Lyndon Johnson, and how to conduct that campaign amid the deepening racial unease spread by Dr. King's assassination.

"Richard Nixon," wrote Mary McGrory in the Washington *Star*, "has hung out the 'Do Not Disturb' sign on the door of his campaign. It is understandable. These are terrible times for a man who intended to conduct a bland and stately campaign against an unpopular incumbent." Actually, the respite was a welcome one for Nixon. Running against phantom opposition in his party was tolerable as long as he could swing out at Johnson in the other party. The situation had enabled him to act as though he already had been nominated, and was running against the President. Now he would be spinning his wheels while the Democrats decided whether their candidate would be Kennedy, as Nixon thought, or Humphrey. Correctly, he did not consider McCarthy a real possibility. But having run under the threat of opposition from Nelson Rockefeller in 1960 and ever since, Nixon now was looking over his shoulder again. The New York governor's brother, Winthrop, was saying in his state capital of Little Rock that Nelson would be a candidate after all. "I feel he did not make it adequately clear that he is a candidate and would happily accept the nomination if elected at the convention," Winthrop said. "I think you will find that Nelson will be active this summer."

Nixon and his strategists took that prediction to heart. During the King assassination moratorium, which lasted sixteen days for Nixon, unusual attention and effort were directed toward a speech the candidate was to make on April 19 before one of his favorite forums, the American Society of Newspaper Editors in Washington. Six weeks earlier the invitation had come in, and the staff seized it as an opportunity to strike a major blow against Nixon's loser image before a group that always had been friendly to him. Maybe reporters didn't care for him, but editors were impressed.

Price, Buchanan and Garment discussed the best way to display the Nixon wares. A full-blown speech on foreign policy was the most obvious approach, but then Johnson pulled out, Nixon's moratorium on Vietnam was declared, and the need to say anything substantive about the war was obviated. Since the ASNE hosts had invited Nixon to choose his own format, why not a panel of editor-questioners? By now this technique had been honed to a near-science in Nixon's staff-produced sessions with local voters, taped for local television. The innovation had been a smash hit in New Hampshire and again in Wisconsin, and it showed Nixon at his most confident, knowledgeable, expansive and relaxed. Nixon agreed to the idea, and particularly so when the Nixon staff learned that Rockefeller also would be on the program, one day before Nixon's appearance. It was an ideal opportunity, without having to risk face-to-face debate, to have Nixon compete with Rockefeller.

"We guessed that the governor would come up with a ponderous speech ponderously read," one of Nixon's aides told Bob Semple of the New York *Times*. "The Q-and-A format, preceded by brief introductory remarks, seemed an appropriate mechanism to contrast the styles of the two candidates. If Nixon could successfully handle a broad range of questions tossed at him by a panel of respected editors, it would, we thought, show that Nixon had the equipment to be a successful campaigner and Rockefeller did not."

In much the same way that a President is briefed for a White House press conference, the Nixon staff proceeded to draw up a series of memoranda on the key questions their man likely would face from the editors. For about a week leading up to the appearance, he studied them. Then, the weekend before the session, Nixon went to Washington, took a room at the Sheraton-Park and began to make his final notes. He shut himself off from all but a few of his closest aides and crammed for that appearance in the same way he had prepared for examinations at the Duke Law School.

The preparations were well worth the effort. Nixon was a smash success. Not only was he loaded with facts with which to turn back all questions; he conducted himself with a good-humored self-assured flare that awed the editors. They had heard from

Rockefeller the day before at lunch, and true to the Nixon staff's prediction, he had delivered a ponderous speech ponderously. It was, actually, a very well-reasoned and impressive survey of the nation's urban needs, coupled as always in Rockefeller's case with a long-range—and expensive—program to meet those needs. The editors listened attentively and, for the most part, silently. Nixon, by contrast, put on a show for them. He was funny: "I was surprised when Romney got out, when Bobby Kennedy got in, when LBJ got out. And I was surprised when Rockefeller got out . . . if he did." He was spirited: he expected Kennedy to be his opponent, and although some thought he had lost the debates to John Kennedy in 1960, "I will debate him with everything I've got." He was candid: on the Vietnam peace talks, he didn't have all the facts so he wouldn't criticize. He was statesmanlike: he would remain silent on the war "as long as there is hope for successful negotiation." The President should have "a free hand to negotiate an honorable peace. . . . As far as I'm concerned, I'm not going to do anything to undercut him until he's had a chance to bring it about." The editors interrupted him repeatedly with applause; as they left, many remarked on the contrast between the performances of Nixon and Rockefeller, and many wrote favorable commentaries in their papers.

The Nixon forces were ecstatic. "I think the last two days may have decided the nomination," Ray Price said afterward. "We got Rockefeller out in the open," said another aide, "and we beat him. . . . Rockefeller came down with winner written all over him and we came down to face a group of people who had branded us losers. Who's the winner now?"

Having thus "disposed" of Nelson Rockefeller, Nixon embarked on an eight-state western swing to talk to Republican governors and other leading Republicans and—hopefully—to start closing the door on the other undeclared opponent for the nomination, Reagan. At each state capital, in Minnesota, North and South Dakota, Wyoming, Montana, Nevada, Oregon and Idaho, Nixon told local reporters he was "fact-finding, not arm-twisting." The facts he was finding were very encouraging. Most of the governors, though favorably inclined toward him, were leading uncommitted delegations to Miami Beach to avoid splits, and this approach fit in nicely with Nixon's; if it prevented him from having a hard convention majority on paper, it also reduced the possibility that Reagan could demonstrate enough out-of-California support to get his candidacy off the ground. Bob Ellsworth, who had taken over the Nixon campaign from Bellmon, spread the word that the Reagan forces were raising a small fortune to make a strong showing in the Nebraska primary and then to stop Nixon in Oregon. They would spend about $350,000 in Oregon alone, he said, and Reagan himself was preparing to go into the state, where as in Nebraska his name would be on the ballot.

Oregon now was emerging without doubt as the last obstacle in Nixon's way to the nomination. If he were to be stopped, it would have to be there, not at the convention as some pipe dreamers thought. Only if opponents could demonstrate that he still was a loser would the party, so much in his debt and so comfortable ideologically with him, turn him down. Going into New Hampshire, the burden of proof had been on Nixon, and there and in Wisconsin he had come through. He would again in Nebraska, of that the Nixon forces had no doubt; it was Fred Seaton's state and had been the one bright light in Nixon's camouflaged candidacy of 1964. But in Oregon anything could happen. Rockefeller had beaten Goldwater there in 1964, and a big write-in effort had been started for Rockefeller there this year, before his sudden TV pullout. But the burden now was on the other side. If nobody could convince the party, somehow, that Nixon still meant defeat, he would be nominated.

That he was indeed still a loser was a conviction held deeply and with gnawing distress by Nelson Rockefeller. In announcing on March 21 that he would stay out of the primaries and make no active bid for the nomination, Rockefeller—like Robert Kennedy in the days before he entered the Democratic race—had been persuaded by hard fact, at the expense of his personal desires. But also like Kennedy, Rockefeller had not taken into account the unpredictability of tomorrow; no sooner had he pulled back and left the field to Nixon than Johnson himself had withdrawn and had created an entirely new situation. Many Republicans and other voters who felt confident Nixon could beat the skidding Johnson were not so sure he

290

could survive a Kennedy bid for restoration. It might be neces, sary, some Republicans thought and some told Rockefeller, to fight charisma with charisma, liberalism with liberalism, and that meant Rockefeller against Kennedy.

Rockefeller's March 21 decision already had slammed the door on the remaining primary tests against Nixon in Nebraska and Oregon. But it might yet be possible to bring the party to its senses before the Miami Beach convention. In contemporary American politics, public opinion was king, and those who measured it were oracles. Rockefeller in 1966, with one of the most imaginative (and costly) media campaigns in political history, had attacked public opinion, bent it to his will and scored an upset comeback for governor. Starting as a candidate with whom the lowliest Republican office seekers in New York shunned association, Rockefeller spent a fortune in radio, television and newspaper advertising and built himself into a winner again. His media brain trusters hammered away on his achievements in one of the nation's toughest jobs, and on his experience. They stressed his incumbency—he had the job, he knew what had to be done. "Governor Rockefeller for Governor," all the ads and commercials said. And it worked. Why, then, couldn't it be done on a national scale? No matter how the delegates to the Republican convention felt personally about Rockefeller and Nixon, they wanted to win this time, and they read the polls as everyone else did. The primary route was closed, but if the electorate could be assailed in such a way, and in such strategic places, that his standing in the polls could be driven upward, until they said clearly that Nelson Rockefeller was the only Republican who could best the Democratic candidate, wouldn't the convention be compelled to act accordingly?

Nelson Rockefeller thought so. And so, on April 30 in Albany, after having taken himself out of the Presidential picture only forty days earlier, he thrust himself back in. "I do this," he told a press conference, "because . . . the dramatic and unprecedented events of the past weeks have revealed in most serious terms the gravity of the crisis that we face as a people. . . . In the new circumstances that confront the nation I frankly find that to comment from the sidelines is not an effective way to present the alternatives. . . ." He reiterated he would steer clear of the primary-election states, making no write-in effort. He made no reference to the central role of public opinion polls in his strategy, but it soon was to become obvious.

At the time Rockefeller made his television announcement, Nixon was in Harrisburg, Pennsylvania, to confer with one of the Republican governors less inclined toward him, Raymond P. Shafer. The former Vice President watched in his room at the Holiday Inn Town. Afterward, he told reporters: "I think I'm going to win. If I'd been advising Governor Rockefeller, I'd have told him to enter the primaries to prove [his] argument that he's more popular with the voters and I'm preferred by the bosses. Now he's appealing to the bosses and I to the people."

That last sounded a bit like the old Nixon, but on balance the former Vice President took the news of Rockefeller's entry with the cool of the new Nixon. He said it was "helpful to have another active candidate, even at this late date," and he was "glad to hear that he intends to address himself to the issues. That kind of a campaign will not divide the party. It will unite it at Miami."

In Harrisburg, Nixon's talk with Shafer, the fifteenth governor with whom he had met since entering the race, produced no tangible results. Shafer was uncommitted, and Nixon said he honored that position and would not attempt to raid the Pennsylvania delegation. But, he added, "if an effort is made from another's direction, we would have to react." In other words, if Rockefeller moved in, so would Nixon.

The Rockefeller entry came at a most propitious time. Massachusetts Republicans were going to the polls on the same day, supposedly to rubber-stamp the selection of Governor John A. Volpe, a Vice Presidential hopeful, as their Presidential favorite son. The Nixon forces, who had been dangling the Vice Presidential bait in front of Volpe, regarded his favorite-son status as a holding action for them. But when the results were in, the winner was not Volpe but Rockefeller, on a write-in. He received 30 percent of the vote, to 29.5 percent for the embarrassed Volpe and 25.8 percent for Nixon on write-ins.

The outcome, though a surprise, precipitated no change in the Nixon strategy. Nixon was ahead and Rockefeller had to catch him, and there were no more primaries open to the new candidate, except on write-ins in states where Nixon's organization was strong. While the Rockefeller machine busied itself for a siege of the public opinion surveys, Nixon proceeded on schedule to complete his string of unbroken—and uncontested—primary "victories." In May there were three to pick up: Indiana on May 7, Nebraska on May 14 and the big one, Oregon, on May 28.

In Indiana, overshadowed by the first Kennedy-McCarthy confrontation on the Democratic side, Nixon used this extremely conservative and extremely provincial state to test positions to be used in the new circumstances, with no Lyndon Johnson to attack. Nixon's managers had latched onto the law-and-order issue early in Indiana, turning out bumper stickers that said, simply but suggestively, FEEL SAFER WITH NIXON. The pitch was criticized by the national press as subtle backlash, and was quickly dropped. Nixon himself found that the code phrases of New Hampshire and Wisconsin—that "some of our courts have gone too far in weakening the peace forces as against the criminal forces"—were more than good enough; they were among his biggest applause-getters in Indiana, where as in those two earlier primaries his audiences were overwhelmingly white.

On the war, the Kennedy-McCarthy fight gave Nixon an opportunity not merely to maintain his own moratorium but to make a virtue of it. "Let's not destroy the chances for peace with a mouthful of words from some irresponsible candidate for President of the United States," he said in Evansville. "Put yourself in the position of the enemy. He is negotiating with Lyndon Johnson and Secretary Rusk and then he reads in the papers that not a Senator, not a Congressman, not an editor, but a potential President of the United States will give him a better deal than President Johnson is offering him. What's he going to do? It will torpedo those deliberations. It will destroy any chance for the negotiations to bring an honorable end to the war. The enemy will wait for the next man."

When, on May 3, Johnson announced that after long wrangling the enemy had agreed to Paris as the site for the talks, Nixon called the news cautiously "the beginning of a long, hard road" to peace. "In my view," he said righteously, "no Presidential candidate, of either party, should say anything or do anything to

293

destroy the fragile hope that has arisen today." Kennedy and McCarthy, locked in an increasingly bitter struggle for leadership of the antiwar movement, were of course not about to desist from criticism. And Richard Nixon was of course not about to start. His patriotism continued to serve his political strategy well; still without having said what he would do about Vietnam, Nixon four days later rolled up yet another impressive vote in Indiana. With the excitement all on the Democratic side, he received 508,000 votes, compared to only 328,100 for Kennedy, 238,700 for the Humphrey stand-in candidate, Governor Roger Branigin, and 209,700 for McCarthy. Nixon ran without significant opposition in a state that was staunchly Republican in national elections, but still the turnout contributed more evidence to the case against his image as a loser.

Already in some states, that evidence was being converted into new Nixon support. Nixon's chief delegate recruiters—Ellsworth, Richard G. Kleindienst (a member of Goldwater's Arizona Mafia in 1964), Sears and McWhorter—were fanning out around the country, conveying the message of Nixon's strength and popularity among party leaders and at state conventions. Key Republicans were recruited to line up their local troops. In Michigan on the very day of the New Hampshire primary in which Michigan Governor George Romney was to have been a principal, Ellsworth persuaded the State Senate majority leader, Emil Lockwood, to be the Michigan Nixon-for-President chairman. While Romney straddled the fence, refusing to come out for Rockefeller, Lockwood got nineteen of Michigan's twenty state senators to sign a pro-Nixon petition. (Though Nixon eventually received only four of Michigan's forty-eight first-ballot votes at the convention, many of the other forty-four—which Romney kept as a sentimental favorite son—probably would have gone to Nixon on an early ballot.)

In Nebraska just one week after the Indiana primary, there was some slippage, but nothing serious. All the establishment Republicans—Governor Norbert T. Tiemann, Senators Roman Hruska and Carl Curtis and the state's three GOP Congressmen—were on the Nixon team. The Reagan film was unleashed again, and the California governor's vote doubled his Wisconsin showing, up to nearly 23 percent. Much was made of the

Reagan absentee "surge," but the fact remained that Nixon, himself campaigning in the state for only two days in the last two weeks, again had been a landslide winner, with 70 percent, while write-ins for Rockefeller were negligible. The near-inevitability of Nixon's nomination now was beginning to creep into the awareness even of those who least wanted to recognize the fact. Wishful thinking, in and out of the Reagan camp, conjured up prospects, however, that reality could not. Speaking of this phenomenon, Ward Just wrote in the Washington *Post* that Nixon "must be America's only major political figure who can win seventy percent of a state's vote and still have the analysts talking about his opponent's twenty-three per cent."

There now remained only Oregon. Nixon moved into the state confident that in its May 28 primary—the last in which he was entered, since Reagan's favorite-son status ruled out California on June 4—he would score the decisive victory. For the first time since Romney had bowed out in New Hampshire, Nixon faced at least the semblance of real opposition. But it was only a semblance; though there were tales of great amounts of money pouring in for Reagan, and the documentary film was updated to provide more timeliness and fire, the quasi-candidate himself did not go into the state. Rockefeller, having squandered what could have been a significant write-in effort backed by Governor McCall, also stayed out of the one primary state he had carried in 1964. The man who had campaigned successfully then against the absent Barry Goldwater on the slogan "He Cared Enough to Come" could hardly hope to make any serious inroads in 1968 by staying away.

Yet the Nixon forces were prepared for the worst. "Oregon was the Armageddon," one of the chief strategists said later. "It was a fairly liberal Republican state, with a maverick reputation. It was the finish of the Stassen campaign in 1948; Rocky upset Goldwater and Lodge there in 1964, and earlier in 1968 he had had fifty thousand signatures on a petition urging him to run. And the Reagan people *were* throwing money around. This is where they were going to knock off Nixon."

They were not, of course, going to do any such thing. Unlike the man Nixon thought would be his Democratic opponent, Robert Kennedy, the former Vice President had been looking ahead and pointing toward Oregon. Kennedy, having plunged headlong into the Presidential race only two months earlier against an active foe, had to spread his forces thin and concentrate on the immediate; Nixon had the luxuries of no active primary opponent and plenty of time, manpower and money. While attempts of second-echelon Kennedy lieutenants to get an Oregon organization working were sputtering, Nixon as in all the other primary states had a solid machine staffed by experienced political men. Governor McCall hung back, and so did Senator Mark Hatfield, but Nixon's strength was in knowing and being able to enlist the less prominent party men. Early on, he had signed up the former Oregon secretary of state, Howell Appling, to head the campaign, and Maurice Stans made half a million dollars available for the effort. All this, and the momentum of his earlier overwhelming primary votes, made Nixon unstoppable in Oregon, particularly by any absentee candidate.

Using the same combination that had sustained him thus far—appearance of action and reality of leisure—Nixon served up a mix of personal and television appearances. In order to make capital of Rockefeller's "He Cared Enough to Come" slogan of 1964, Nixon spent the better part of the first week after Nebraska demonstrating that in 1968 he was the one who cared enough. He toured places like McMinnville and Hillsboro, southeast of Portland, Medford in the south and Pendleton in the sparsely settled northeast. Then in the final week, in his fifth visit to Oregon in six months, he returned to the Portland area and Klamath Falls, and wrapped up the campaign with a statewide telethon that drew an estimated 31,000 phone calls. The phenomenal response convinced Nixon he would do even better in Oregon than he had hoped. Until then, he had not been so sure; to prepare for the worst, he had said it was possible a combination of Reagan and Rockefeller votes would keep his total under 50 percent. Ellsworth in New York issued a poor-mouth statement that insisted his man would do well to get 34 percent, Rockefeller's percentage in 1964. An exceptionally strong showing, Ellsworth said, would be 40 precent.

But if Oregon was, as it turned out, the wrong state for Robert Kennedy—virtually all-white and virtually problem-free—it was

296

the right one for Nixon. Kennedy sought to arouse Oregonians about the plight of the nation's disadvantaged minorities and alert them to American youth's demand for change; Nixon deftly exploited a vulnerability in that demand—campus anarchy.

Although Oregon itself had some of the most activist campuses in the Northwest, Nixon was able to take this tack by focusing his fire on students clear across the country, in his own adopted city of New York. The day after the Nebraska victory, Nixon went to Pendleton and called on Columbia University to "rid the campus now" of revolutionaries. The place to begin a national drive against the use of force and coercion on campus, he said, "is with the anarchistic students at Columbia. . . . The eyes of every potential revolutionary or anarchist on an American campus are focused on Morningside Heights to see how the administration at Columbia deals with a naked attempt to subvert and discredit its authority and to seize its power." Although academic freedom required that a university be receptive to new ideas, he intoned, "academic freedom also dictates that the rationally committed stand up and resist the dictates of the emotionally committed."

In a primary campaign marked on the Democratic side by a frantic competition dominated by young activists, Nixon's effort seemed an oasis of calm and middle-aged good sense. The candidate himself seemed to embody both characteristics. He was the most relaxed man in his entourage. The primary machinery was humming, and satisfied all was in order, he continued to look ahead. He spoke openly to reporters not about Oregon but about the convention, and not about winning it but about what he would do when he had won. Selecting his running mate was the first and most important decision, and he tossed many names out. Not surprisingly, some were those of favorite-son candidates or others who had a grip on a state delegation—Romney, Reagan, Rhodes, Percy, Shafer and a man named Agnew, from Maryland. David Broder of the Washington *Post* talked to Nixon on May 16 and wrote among other things that Nixon had his eye on Agnew. The former Vice President had met the Maryland governor recently, Broder wrote, and had been impressed by his views on urban problems and by his high standing with other governors. The following day, Don Irwin of the Los Angeles *Times* ran down a list of names and added: "And a man who has gained ground in recent months because of his strong stand on the cities, Governor Agnew of Maryland."*

There were a few bumps along the way for Nixon, but nothing serious. The traveling press by now had generally accepted the fact that the candidate simply was not going to break his moratorium on Vietnam. In a meeting with the American Association of Editorial Cartoonists, however, his old assailants questioned him sharply. And when he resorted to the old dodge that he could not spell out his Vietnam plans for fear of hurting the Paris talks, one irate cartoonist asked him: "How could you stand up and ask us to vote for you when you don't want to be specific?" Nixon replied righteously: "If there is a chance we can get the war over before this election, that is much more important than anything I might wish to say to get you to vote for me." Well, what were the sharpest points of difference between himself and Rockefeller? "To point out differences would create difficulties in putting together Republican unity. I'm not going to take him on even if he takes me on." Earlier in his introductory remarks, Nixon said he had begun to believe all the talk about a "new Nixon" until he saw the latest Herblock cartoons. "It's the old Nixon," he cracked. After his artful dodging on Vietnam and Rockefeller, others present agreed—and they weren't being facetious.

It was true that Nixon did not take Rockefeller on directly in Oregon, but he did strike a few glancing blows as primary day approached. On a plane trip from Portland to Klamath Falls, he released a statement that insisted without naming Rockefeller that "no cozy courtship can substitute for a direct open appeal for votes" in Oregon. "This is not the year, and these are not the times, for absentee candidates," Nixon said. "The crises

---

* At a press conference in Baltimore around this time, Nelson Rockefeller, sitting next to Agnew, the supporter he had humiliated in his first decision not to run, suddenly apologized publicly for "having gone the wrong way at the psychological moment. . . ." Agnew, startled, replied: "No apologies. . . . I don't accept the apology, as I don't think it's necessary at all. I don't think many people realize what a candidate for President has to go through." Whereupon Agnew announced he would go to the party convention as a favorite son, thus denying Rockefeller a state he otherwise may have had.

facing us both at home and abroad are too serious for those who ask the mandate of leadership to send out proxies to explain their views and ask for support." This last was an obvious reference to an eleventh-hour dispatch of old football hero Y. A. Tittle to Oregon for Reagan and a more publicized cross-country dash in Rockefeller's behalf by Mayor John Lindsay of New York. Lindsay dutifully traipsed around Portland shaking hands, spreading glamor—and raising suspicions among canny Republicans that he was campaigning more for Lindsay-in-'72 than for Rocky-in-'68. The visit inspired some enterprising strategists—never identified but certainly no enemies of Nixon—to draw up a newspaper ad that said: "He Cared Enough to Send Mayor Lindsay—So Write In Lindsay." Few did, but the message concerning Rockefeller's own lack of interest came through clearly.

The clincher for Nixon was the final media push. All winter and spring, the media-oriented campaign had been experimenting, shooting film of extemporaneous, press-barred "town meeting" panels, judiciously exposing but never overexposing the "real" Nixon just "being himself." Now came the tour de force. The candidate prerecorded a documentary-style film called *Nixon Now* that cost an estimated $100,000 and ran for thirty minutes on nationwide television. Excerpts from the four previous primary campaigns and from the meet-the-people panels were shown. The focus was away from the past and Nixon-the-loser; *Nixon Now* was Nixon-the-rehabilitated-winner.

Then came the ninety-minute telethon, with daughters Julie and Tricia among the girls taking phone calls. Underhand pitcher Bud Wilkinson sorted them, served up the fat ones and openly marveled at the answers. It was both the informed Nixon and the folksy Nixon, an unbeatable combination in Oregon. Billy Graham, the candidate's old friend and adviser, was in town drawing bigger crowds than any of the candidates in a Portland ball park, and on the telethon Nixon mentioned that fact; obviously he had a realistic perspective on things. In Oregon, playground of hunters, he told his TV audience he favored a state-by-state approach to gun control legislation. He relied on Senator Hruska of Nebraska for advice in this field, he said, and was convinced the most effective way to control the sale of guns was to stop crime. (Relying on Hruska, the champion of the gun lobby in the Senate, for advice on gun controls was a little like asking an old Tammany Hall precinct captain what to do about electoral reform.)

On primary day, while McCarthy on the Democratic side worked the Portland streets and Kennedy flew to California to get a jump on the approaching primary there, Nixon relaxed in his Benson Hotel suite and saw reporters. As one of those to be granted a private interview, I had carefully prepared for it. Knowing how logical Nixon's mind was, and hoping to make the best use of the time allotted, I wrote in my notebook the major questions to be asked, taking care to have one follow logically upon the one before. The aim was to use as little time as possible asking questions, thus leaving more for the candidate's answers and hopefully obtaining a cohesive and flowing view of his positions and plans.

As I was ushered into the living room by Dwight Chapin, Nixon came over, shook hands and invited me to sit on a sofa while he settled into a comfortable armchair, feet propped up on a coffee table. He was smiling, cordial and remarkably relaxed and buoyant for a man about to face probably the most critical point to date in his comeback. We made general conversation for several minutes, and then I asked my opening question. Nixon, nodding, answered it straightforwardly and precisely, then proceeded to go on to its logical extension, covering not only the second question I had written down, but the third and fourth and fifth. At first I just sat there nodding and taking notes, but as he moved inexorably along, embracing in his answer my next questions in turn, I could not suppress a smile. It seemed to unsettle him somewhat, and I finally said: "Mr. Nixon, I believe you've peeked at my notes. I've written down my questions and you've answered most of them already." He stopped, a baffled look coming over his face. "Oh, no," he said, with obvious sincerity, "I wouldn't do that." Realizing he had taken me seriously, I hastened to assure him I had only been jesting. The assurance seemed for a moment to embarrass him, and then he laughed self-consciously.

Nixon's answers were most revealing about his campaign and his own approach to it. "Haunting this campaign," he said at one point, "is the specter of 1960." This man who insisted he was a fatalist, who had no time to waste reexamining the past, who had put his 1960 defeat behind him, was admitting what any casual observer knew to be the case: in one hand as he campaigned in 1968 was a 1960 road map, marked with all the pitfalls.

"One-half of one percent per precinct made the difference then," he said, "so we can't go with just good people. . . . We don't want to be saddled with first-rate second-raters. . . . We have to go with the best, really first-raters. In 1960, I was really going with the [Eisenhower] administration team, plus some of my own. Now we have an entirely new, fresh team. And we have a good mix." He reviewed the list, together with his own descriptions, as though he were reading from some confidential credit rating: Pat Buchanan, "conservative in the responsible sense"; Dr. Martin Anderson, a Columbia University economist, "right of center"; Richard Whalen, military specialist from the Georgetown Center of Strategic Studies and author, "modern *Wall Street Journal* center."

The question that had opened the interview, and had triggered his free-flow response, suggested that he had conducted a mistake-proof campaign in the primaries now ending. Was it all carried out according to plan?

"It's been a campaign that couldn't possibly be planned ahead," Nixon said. "I remember at a National Security Council meeting once, President Eisenhower said, 'Planning is absolutely vital. Plans are useless.' It's been that fluid. I look at this campaign as a war. We were planning for Romney and eventually Rockefeller, but those plans turned out to be useless. So we had to run as if we were pointing to November. I began talking against President Johnson, but then he was out. A basic speech doesn't change much, we all know that, but we've had to shift emphasis. The moment Johnson got out, Vietnam went on the back burner. [It had, of course, been there all along, as far as serious discussion by Nixon was concerned.]

"We didn't set out in advance and plan what to do, but we had a young organization that was fluid—not so rigid that we got caught with our pants down when things changed. The primaries have been good for us. We tested our organization, and I

301

got out to the small towns I'll have to miss in the final. [That's how he always referred to the general campaign, and when he used the expression, without explanation, it had the effect of signaling to his listener that he knew he was talking to another insider in the game, another pro. He often uses the language of the political pro in such interviews, in contrast to his public speeches, which are filled with parenthetical explanations that sometimes suggest his audience has just been parachuted into their seats from Mars.]

"We also tested techniques—the telethon, TV spots, press backgrounders, always with Q-and-A. We put a great deal of emphasis on this, and we'll be emphasizing it more. I like the give-and-take. It helps me. . . . In 1960, there was a frenetic quality about my campaign. Promising to go into all fifty states. We aren't going to make that mistake again. I've learned that the candidate should take time to think. Every three weeks I go to Florida for a few days. That's how I keep the tan." And he gestured toward his face, wonderfully bronzed and suited for color TV. "I take some of the boys with me, and we mix it: on the beach for a while, and then hours of going over ideas." (One of "the boys" told me later that going to Florida was more calculated than Nixon made it sound. "We kept going back to Florida mainly so he could keep that tan," he said.)

Speechwriting was one of the main activities in Florida, the candidate went on. "I don't say I do all the writing. They do a lot, and I edit. The slowdown gives me a chance to do creative work. [Nixon also likes to use that expression in interviews, and to call himself an intellectual.] We've already had more major speeches in 1968—breaking new ground—than in 1960 in the final. By the time we get to the convention, we'll have a good bank."

By participating in the researching of a speech, Nixon said, he was able to deal more effectively with the subject matter in public. "The moment you read something good somewhere, you can figure that in the next press conference someone will ask you about it," he said. (And in his mind the press conference—televised—was the real arena, the real test of a man's ability to survive.) "In 1960, I felt the big speech was the most important and I had to be up for it. Meeting committees and politicians was next, then press conferences, and then TV. Now we've reversed the order. Now television and the press conferences are the most important, and that's why I won't do them on the run."

The primaries, and his effective use of television in them, Nixon said, had produced a measurable change in the public's and the press' attitude toward him. "When I started, the first question always was, 'How can you destroy your loser image?' I get less of that now. And the second question was, 'How about TV?' The primaries helped me show I can cope with it."

With the primaries finally behind him, he said, he would concentrate on the nonprimary states, speaking to convention delegates, seeking support but not firm commitments. "I hope to get second-ballot strength where there are favorite sons, and first-ballot strength where there are not. I won't ask for commitments—but my people may. I find commitments beginning to come in. But I'm not going in hard. I want to win in November, and I don't want any blood splattering. None of that—'Get aboard, it's now or never.' We'll welcome people aboard any time they come."

In the remaining time before the convention, Nixon said, he would continue to go to Florida for three days every two or three weeks, and would take a long rest just before the convention, to do some heavy reading. "I'm basically more of an intellectual than I ought to be," he offered. "I want those ten days just to read and think. After the convention, the luxury of that will be gone." And what would he read? "No politics. No mysteries either. Some good philosophy that makes the mind work."

As I left, I didn't know much more about the workings of the mind of Richard Nixon, but I did come away with one very clear impression—that the man was on top of events and knew it. The axioms of Eisenhower to the contrary, Nixon had drawn up a game plan and had followed it to the letter. He adjusted to circumstances where necessary, but essentially he adhered always to the basic element of that plan: sharply control the exposure and the comments of the candidate in public and on television, and hang on. Developments, if anything, cemented the game plan; on the Democratic side, divisions enabled Nixon to attack not only the political ghost of Lyndon Johnson but all factions fighting to succeed him; on the Republican side, Romney's pullout, Rockefeller's vacillation and Reagan's timidity only underlined Nixon's strength. In the remaining time up to and through the Republican convention, and on through the general election campaign itself, the same game plan would apply.

The night of May 28 in Oregon, the final stop on the primary road for Richard Nixon, was triumphant. As the returns came in, even the highest expectations of the Nixon strategists were surpassed. Rockefeller fizzled completely, getting barely more than 4 percent of the vote; Reagan could do no better in his neighboring state than he did in Nebraska and wound up with 22 percent. Nixon swept all the rest, more than 73 percent of the vote in what was to have been his toughest test. The ballroom on the lobby floor of the Benson was jammed with workers and well-wishers. John Ehrlichman's balloons hung from the rafters and a jazz combo swung out, to the glee of the young straights in the Nixon camp. John Eisenhower, David's father, announced the results and led the cheers, and then the candidate himself came in, throwing his arms up over his head in the swift motion that always looked as though Bonnie or Clyde had unexpectedly jammed a heater into his ribs and told him to reach for the ceiling.

It was the story of Nixon's life, however, that even a Kennedy in travail provided more genuine excitement and interest than a Nixon in victory. As the Nixon celebration geared up, Robert Kennedy, back from his day of campaigning in California and already informed that he had lost his first election, pushed through a mob scene in the Benson lobby just outside the Nixon ballroom. His wife, Ethel, pregnant, was crushed in behind him, but stayed close as the faithful shrieked their undiminished support and encouraged him to continue. The curious pushed in to gawk at how a Kennedy reacted to losing, and he reacted very well. In a talk to his Oregon workers, Kennedy blamed nobody but himself, thanked the state's voters for being fair and then dispatched a congratulatory telegram to the victorious candidate—a studied gesture underlining Gene

McCarthy's own failure to do the same for him when Kennedy had beaten him in Indiana and Nebraska.

As far as is known, no word—spoken or written—passed in the Benson between Kennedy and Nixon, who had told laughing Oregon Republicans the night before he thought that on the Democratic side it would be "Bobby by a hair or two." It was another example of Nixon's political crystal ball going foggy, but nobody noticed, or cared, on the Republican side that night. Being a prophet was important when one had little else going for him. Now it was not. Nixon had received 70 percent or more of the Republican vote in six states, and for all practical purposes he had captured the Republican Presidential nomination.

While Robert Kennedy and his entourage in Kennedy's seventh-floor suite held a sort of defeat party, quiet and full of reciprocal shorings-up, Richard and Pat Nixon and friends— John and Barbara Eisenhower, Howell and Jane Appling, Bebe Rebozo—dined and held a sort of victory party, about as quiet, in the Benson's excellent London Grill. The Republican convention still was more than a month away, and of course anything could happen, but the Nixon team knew where it had been and where, in the intervening time, it was going. The loser image had been reduced to the barest shadow by a sweep of the primaries; the risks of exposing the candidate to the voters had been minimized and surmounted. Now all that remained to finish the job, while Ronald Reagan stalled and Nelson Rockefeller thrashed about in search of the Holy Grail of the Nixon-can't-win public opinion poll, was to commit the party pols. Among them, the atmosphere always had been receptive or at least resigned to Nixon. Now finally was the time to start locking some doors and collecting the keys.

13

Locking the Last Doors

FOR all the supreme confidence of Richard Nixon and his strategists, they had not gone into the final primary in Oregon without considering the possibility that he might for some reason be upset, or at least be undermined by a strong showing for Ronald Reagan. Right after the Wisconsin primary, delegate-counter John Sears had written the candidate a detailed memorandum pointing out that if somehow all did not go well in Oregon, the threat in terms of solid delegate strength then would come not from Rockefeller, but from Reagan, probing what then would be a soft underbelly of conservatism in the Southwest and South. As a result, a specific "escape rope" was tied to the Oregon plans—an immediate post-primary tour of the conservative "Sun Belt," starting in Phoenix with a visit to the shrine of Barry Goldwater, down through John Tower's Texas and on to Atlanta for a most critical meeting with the major Republican leaders in Dixie. If Nixon did stumble in Oregon, the swing would afford an opportunity to identify and shore up sagging support and to head off Reagan incursions. If Oregon was a success, then the trip would enable the high-riding Nixon to pay his dues in these conservative bastions quickly and relatively inconspicuously, while the nation's political attention was riveted on California and the final Democratic primary between Kennedy and McCarthy.

306

This latter course turned out to be the modus operandi. The Reagan threat was still present in the conservative belt, but it had been severely weakened by the Oregon outcome. Therefore Nixon would direct some of his attention not only to delegate-wooing in the Southwest and South, but also to Nelson Rockefeller's efforts to have the polls indicate he was the strongest Republican candidate. Rocky's strategy was simple: pour a fortune in advertising and candidate exposure into key cities and states. Then poll them and produce the results to show he clearly was the people's choice. The plan, drawn up by the Jack Tinker and Partners advertising agency in New York in consultation with Rockefeller speechwriter and adviser Emmett J. Hughes, focused on thirteen "Northern Tier" states plus Texas, covering 60 percent of the nation's population. One estimate of advertising included 377 pages in 54 newspapers in 40 cities and 462 television spots a week, on 100 stations in 30 cities; at a cost of $3,000,000.

As the month of May had advanced, and Nixon was busy nailing down Nebraska and Oregon, Rockefeller had been gearing up his blitz against the polls and doing some low-key delegate-chasing of his own. Boxed in by the sometimes latent, sometimes overt hostility toward him as the man who had cold-shouldered the party nominee in 1964, Rockefeller had to be careful how he handled his strongest arguing point—that Nixon, like Goldwater in 1964, could not win. In personal meetings with state delegations, he was limited by the realities to stress the positive—his own vote-getting record in New York and his ability there and presumably elsewhere to attract Democratic voters and independents. Unspoken but always in mind was the argument that if Kennedy was to be the Democratic nominee, the liberal Rockefeller would have the best chance against him. That case, however, was weakened by Kennedy's loss in Oregon.

At the same time, Rockefeller's well-financed staff was aggressively in pursuit of the negative—the effort to prove Nixon still was a loser, and Rockefeller the only Republican who could win. A program of intensive private polling was laid out for the large cities in seven major states where Rockefeller hoped the delegate situation remained somewhat fluid—Pennsylvania, Maryland, Ohio, Michigan, Illinois, Minnesota and Kansas. At

307

the same time, field representatives led by the astute John Deardourff, who had labored against impossible odds in behalf of George Romney in New Hampshire, took their own soundings. They urged party politicians to hold off on commitments until the Rockefeller polls were completed; it would be important to these politicians to know what a Nixon candidacy would mean in their own states, for the Presidential candidate and for all those lesser office-seekers whose fate might be tied to the top of the ticket.

The Rockefeller camp was confident that the polls would bear out its contention that only the New York governor could deliver victory to the Republicans in 1968. And to document that contention, Rockefeller's publicity was concentrated heavily in those key areas where the pollsters would be making their measurements. Full-page newspaper ads, signed by influential citizens, proclaimed Rockefeller as the problem-solver, with both head and heart, who knew urban problems and how to harness big government to cope with them. If Nixon's own tactics had brought use of radio and television to a new peak of refinement, Rockefeller's bold plan for poll-shaping broke new ground in the field of public opinion.

With all this in mind, Nixon left Portland the morning after his Oregon triumph and flew to Phoenix to speak at a fund-raiser for Senatorial candidate Goldwater, to confer with Arizona's Republican Governor Jack Williams, and in general to pay homage to the party's right wing. On the steps of the State Capitol, he also found time to observe that the current interest in public opinion polls amounted to an "obsession" that made no sense. "The idea that we are going to determine America's future by a few pollsters is ridiculous," he said. In an interview with Semple of the New York *Times,* however, Nixon made it clear he understood what Rockefeller was up to, and that two could play that game. "The polls—that will be the drill down in Miami," he said. "Rocky will come in with figures showing he can run better against the Democrats in such-and-such a state, and we of course will say that's not true. There will be polls flying all over the city."

The pilgrimage to Phoenix, where Goldwater already was solidly in his corner with sixteen deliverable delegates, was a success, as was the next stop in Dallas, where favorite-son John Tower was prepared to hold the bulk of the 56-member Texas delegation for Nixon. In Dallas, the candidate managed to touch all necessary bases by praising native son Lyndon Johnson for going along with Congress on budget cuts and on crime legislation. Then it was on to Atlanta, and the critical meeting with the Dixie GOP hierarchy.

Very early in the game, as far back as 1966, Nixon had realized certain developments in the South had to be prevented if he were to get the Republican nomination. One of them was an endorsement by Senator Strom Thurmond in South Carolina for Ronald Reagan. Such a decision could trigger similar actions by other key Republicans throughout the Deep South. Accordingly, Nixon had moved early to woo and eventually capture Strom, an old-line Dixiecrat who, seeing how South Carolina politics was going, had switched to the GOP in the Goldwater campaign of 1964. During Thurmond's first reelection campaign as a Republican in 1966, Nixon went into the state and spoke for him at a large and successful political gathering. Thurmond liked Nixon, especially his tough line on national defense and his reputation as a card-carrying anti-Communist. But on the past-performance charts, if ever there was a Ronald Reagan man, it would be Thurmond, in whose breast it was rumored not only beat an American heart but flapped an American flag. Yet Strom also was a politician with a strong sense of personal survival. That sense had led him in 1964 to change his party allegiance from Democratic to Republican, to support Dixie hero Goldwater and to put himself squarely in the vanguard of the emerging conservative Republican Party in the South. Though he won reelection as a Republican in 1966, Thurmond was realist enough to see the damage Goldwater's lemminglike approach to politics in '64 had wrought on his new state party. Also, there now was the threat of inroads from George Wallace. Thurmond wanted no repeat performance; although he thrilled to the old Decoration Day platitudes of Ronnie Reagan, he was vulnerable to the argument that only Nixon could unify the party and keep the Dixie GOP in good health.

In the courtship of Strom Thurmond, the key figure was

Harry Dent, then the Republican state chairman in South Carolina and the man closest to Strom. Though the GOP national committeeman from the state, Drake Edens, wanted Nixon, he was not strong enough politically to deliver Thurmond. But Edens was a conduit to Dent, who was. Through Edens, the small Nixon organization of 1966 began to woo the state chairman. It so happened that on the occasion of Nixon's visit to Columbia for the Thurmond affair, a minor tragedy occurred in the Dent household. In their rush to get to the hall, the family dog somehow was run over by a car. Dent and his children were depressed by the incident. As soon as the Nixon agents learned of it, they told their leader, who wasted no time dispatching another dog to the Dent family. By such simple gestures are political friendships sometimes cemented and alliances forged. The demise of the Dent dog of itself did not, of course, open the way to the capture of Thurmond, but Nixon's response was an indication of the ardor of his pursuit.

The actual annexation of Strom began in March, 1968, when Nixon went to the South Carolina Republican convention. By this time Dent was an ally and direct talk with Thurmond was in order. Kleindienst, who now was directing the Nixon delegate hunt, along with John Sears and Fred LaRue, met with the Senator at a hotel across from the State Capitol and got down to cases. Thurmond delivered a long and frank monologue on what he needed to see in a nominee he could support. The emphasis was not on trimming on civil rights, nor on changes in the Supreme Court, nor on the selection of the Vice Presidential candidate, but on the subject dearest to his heart—national defense. He said he did not expect to be satisfied on civil rights by a candidate who had to run nationwide, but if that candidate could support him on national defense he could go along. It is not clear whether the specific subject of the antiballistic missile (ABM) system was mentioned at this juncture, but it didn't have to be; everyone present knew the ABM was dear to Thurmond's heart. He had just written a book on national defense and other subjects called *The Faith We Have Not Kept* that indicated how important he thought an ABM system was to the nation's survival, and in the next weeks, Nixon dropped the Senator a note or two telling him what a helluva book he thought it was. The two men talked several times on the phone, and by the time Nixon arrived in Atlanta to meet the Republican chairmen of the thirteen Southern and border states, he knew pretty well that he had Thurmond in camp.

On May 31, at the Marriott Motor Hotel, the state chairmen asked Nixon not for a veto on his choice of running mate, but for assurances that federal patronage in a Nixon administration would flow to the Republican Party in the South. In the Eisenhower administration, some of the chairmen noted pointedly, that flow was promised but didn't occur in nearly the scope anticipated. Would Nixon play ball? As a veteran of the Eisenhower administration, he knew how tough patronage could be to handle with a Democratic Congress. But John Mitchell, attending with Nixon, came down strong on giving assurances to the Southerners, and Nixon acquiesced.* Knowing that many hearts present really belonged to Reagan, Nixon did not push too hard. He merely urged the chairmen not to commit their delegations for anybody else until they had given him, as the man who had risked the primaries, a fair shot at the convention. Most agreed.

Extracting this promise from the chairmen had the effect of keeping Reagan on ice, since only with a Southern base could he hope to move out with any success. "The burden of proof," said Georgia chairman G. Paul Jones afterward, "is on the Reagan people. Up to now Nixon's main problem has been the question of whether he can win. He has always had tremendous support because he has worked so hard for us. But the Oregon results suggest that this man is also a winner." James E. Holthouser, Jr., the North Carolina chairman, lined up with Nixon, and the chairmen of four other states said they were "leaning" toward him. "You can feel the tide when it starts to run," Holthouser said, "and you can feel this is Mr. Nixon's year."

Mitchell claimed 300 or more of the 348 Southern and border delegates represented by the thirteen state chairmen. "With what else we've got that's a great surplus over the 667 needed,"

---

* Less than a year later, when the Nixon administration was in its first months, howls of discontent already were being heard from the Dixie chairmen. LaRue, at this time working in the White House, busied himself with assuaging them, and eventually Dent was moved in as the chief political contact, taking over from Sears.

he said. "The ball game for all intents and purposes is over. And the people who work for Reagan are realists. Mr. Nixon has great rapport in the South over the years anyway. The people here all like Ronald Reagan, but they love Dick Nixon." Actually it was just the other way around, but they had decided after loving a loser in 1964 they'd prefer a possible winner they just liked.

Mitchell finally had begun to take hold now as the campaign manager. Ellsworth had proved unable to move to the head of what essentially was the Nixon Mudge inner circle; the law firm's political nucleus had ganged up on him, and had complained about him to Nixon. Mitchell, contrary to the popular impression, did not elbow his way into the command; Garment, wanting to keep the campaign in the law firm, turned to Mitchell. At first Nixon had not been convinced that a man with no tactical political experience would do, but Mitchell's ability to line up all the Republican powers in Wisconsin and elsewhere soon removed the candidate's doubts. Together, Nixon and Mitchell would make an ideal team: Nixon the political tactician and Mitchell the ironhanded implementer.

More disturbing at the Atlanta meeting than any Reagan threat was the specter of George Wallace, which several Southern chairmen testified was hanging darkly over the struggling young GOP in the Deep South. Immediately after the meeting, Nixon called Thurmond in South Carolina and asked him to fly into Atlanta. Thurmond agreed, and the two men met the next day, June 1, with Nixon trotting Strom out to give the state chairmen confidence that he meant to defuse Wallace and honor the South's patronage desires. Afterward, on the way back to the airport, Nixon is said to have given Thurmond some assurances in return. He would order a start on some antiballistic missile system, and that was what Old Strom wanted to hear. The Senator went back to South Carolina determined to bring the state, and the rest of Dixie Republicanism, safely into the Nixon corner. Three weeks later, after considerable pulling and hauling within the delegation, Thurmond announced that South Carolina's twenty-two votes would go for Dick Nixon at Miami Beach. They did, along with the bulk of the remaining Southern vote. "The book on Thurmond," one of Nixon's closest strategists said later, "always was that he was more interested in national defense than anything else. That was the reason he was strong for Nixon. . . . So nobody ever talked race to him. The idea was to talk national defense."

From Atlanta, Nixon and Mitchell went on to Key Biscayne for a major stocktaking. About ten other key aides attended, including Haldeman, Ehrlichman, Ellsworth, Buchanan, Price, Sears and Chapin. It was here finally that Mitchell emerged, in the phrase of one of the participants, as "El Supremo." He had been easing into that status by virtue of his authoritarian take-charge manner and by the obvious confidence Nixon, not usually one to delegate top authority, placed in him. "In an eight-hour discussion of all aspects of the campaign," another participant recalled later, "the operating premise was, 'The nomination is ours.' " Earlier plans to engage in diligent dele-gate-wooing in the nonprimary states were shelved because Nixon agents around the country concluded it wasn't necessary. Haldeman reported there were some calls from party leaders suggesting that "we could better use our time elsewhere." Nixon could not leave the field entirely to the intensive Rockefeller drive, but he could not appear either to be clashing head-on with him. Debates against Rockefeller, already being suggested, were of course out of the question. Yet it would not look good if Nixon went underground; it would leave him open to charges of backing into the nomination. Finally it was decided he would simply start the fall campaign early; that is, he would maintain his visibility by making selected visits to seven or eight key industrial states that would be battlegrounds against the Demo-cratic candidate, and where he would have a fighting chance—California, Ohio, Illinois, Pennsylvania, New Jersey among them.

In addition to making plans for the preconvention period and for holding the line at the convention, the Key Biscayne meeting began to look ahead to the general campaign. Poor communications between Nixon and Lodge in 1960 had led to many contradictory statements; this time, a politically astute Nixon man would be assigned to the Vice Presidential candi-date to watch out for bloopers and improve coordination. Sears was selected to shuttle between the two campaigns. But as things turned out, this was a luxury the Nixon campaign could not afford, and Sears was sentenced to spend all fall with the Vice Presidential entourage.

After the Oregon primary, Nixon was doubtful that Robert Kennedy would be the Democratic nominee. But he was confident that against Kennedy or Hubert Humphrey—he ruled Gene McCarthy out, no matter what—he would win. "If it's Bobby it will be a contest between men, and if it's Hubert, a contest between policies," he told Bob Semple. "Bobby and I have been sounding pretty much alike already, and we can't hold his feet to the fires of the past. But Hubert—Hubert can be portrayed as the helpless captive of the policies of the past. There is a honeymoon with Humphrey now, but it will be over by September. Humphrey will be to Johnson what Stevenson was to Truman. You remember back in 1952 when Stevenson acknowledged that there was a mess in Washington, but said that he could clean it up. Humphrey will have to admit the mess too. We'll hang that around him hard."

Kennedy, however, was not out of it yet. While Nixon was making his pilgrimage to conservatism through Arizona, Texas and Georgia, Kennedy was staging an all-out effort to bounce back in the California primary. After having refused to debate McCarthy all spring, he agreed in this last outing, because now he was the one who needed the confrontation against the man who had defeated a Kennedy for the first time. Like millions of other Americans on the night of June 1, Richard Nixon watched the one-hour debate on television, sitting in his Key Biscayne villa. And like millions of other Americans, he was not overly excited about it one way or the other. But it did at least deprive McCarthy of his Bobby-Won't-Debate issue and dispelled the notion, held by many McCarthyites, that if only their man could get Kennedy in the same room with him, McCarthy would demolish him.

Kennedy, buoyed by great crowds that had turned out for him in California after the Oregon drought, poured it on in the final day. As the Nixon strategy session went forward a whole continent away on June 3, Kennedy raced desperately up and down the length of California, determined to make every last minute count. Like Nixon, he too was media-conscious, but a good part of his appeal was how people reacted to him in the streets, not how he reacted to a TV camera. The final day therefore was scheduled to demonstrate that appeal once more in the three main population centers of the state—the San Francisco–Oakland Bay area, Los Angeles and San Diego—each of which also could assure him maximum free television exposure. Kennedy flew in his chartered jet from Los Angeles to San Francisco for a motorcade through Chinatown and lunch at DiMaggio's on Fisherman's Wharf, then back to Los Angeles, through Watts and Venice to Long Beach, on by plane to San Diego and back to Los Angeles. It was media politics of a sort, since TV cameras followed him everywhere on the streets. But it was vastly unlike Nixon's easy-does-it, preserve-the-candidate approach, and it took its toll. At the final rally in a hall at the El Cortez Hotel in San Diego, Kennedy barely finished his speech, hurried off and sat with his face in his hands at the top step of the stage. The media politics of Nixon did not permit such things to happen to the candidate, and certainly not to be seen by the public.

The next night, a refreshed and victorious Kennedy appeared before his joyous campaign workers in the ballroom of the Ambassador Hotel, and as he then walked off through a pantry area, it was about 3:13 A.M. in Key Biscayne, Florida, and Richard Nixon was asleep. So was his speechwriter and sometimes press aide, Pat Buchanan. Buchanan's phone rang. It was Julie Nixon and David Eisenhower calling from New York. They had been watching on television and had heard: Robert Kennedy, like his brother before him, had been shot in the head. Buchanan immediately called Nixon; by now he too had heard. Once again the fate of a Kennedy had cast a shadow over Nixon's own career, injecting uncertainty about what lay ahead. He canceled all activities for the next two weeks; visits to state conventions were shelved, along with the plan to devote the remaining preconvention period to tours of the major marginal industrial states. The Nixons went to New York for Robert Kennedy's service at St. Patrick's Cathedral, occupying seats in one of the VIP sections. There, on either side of the flag-draped casket, sat all the others who had been featured players in the

315

bizarre political year now plummeted to its starkest hour—the candidates: Governors George Romney and Nelson Rockefeller, Vice President Hubert Humphrey and Senator Eugene McCarthy; the set-piece villains they attacked: Secretary of State Dean Rusk, Chairman of the Joint Chiefs of Staff General Earle G. Wheeler, and the man each of the candidates sought to replace, Lyndon Johnson. Probably no event other than a funeral service could have brought them all together in one place, except perhaps the inauguration of a new President, and it was not until that happened nearly eight months later that they all were together again.*

Nixon spent the post-assassination moratorium between Key Biscayne and New York conferring with party leaders (including Vice Presidential hopeful Senator Mark Hatfield of Oregon, a dove on Vietnam, who endorsed Nixon despite the candidate's nonposition on the war). Only a few days earlier, the problem had been how to fill the time between then and the convention, how to look active without risking a public misstep. Now inaction was a virtue, and beyond that, the late-starting Rockefeller, also forced to the sidelines by Kennedy's death, had to give up valuable time. During the interlude, Rockefeller's staff prepared speeches and television commercials designed to move their man into the void as the one candidate who understood and had rapport with Kennedy's constituency of blacks and blue-collar workers. The claim without doubt had validity among the blacks, and they often turned out in force for him, but Nelson Rockefeller lacked the boyish charisma and suggestion of restored dynasty that had given Kennedy's campaign much of its emotional allure.

When he resumed campaigning a week later, Rockefeller faced an electorate that already had been too thoroughly buffeted by oratory and tragedy to be capable of wildly enthusiastic response. Rockefeller campaigned long and hard, speaking urgently and with the ring of experience, his broad smile and winking, squinting eyes greeting voters across the land. But the effort lacked an inner drive. "Everybody on the staff knew,"

---

* On January 20, 1969, McCarthy did not attend the actual swearing-in of Nixon on the U.S. Capitol steps, but he was on Capitol Hill and stopped by at the new President's traditional post-inauguration luncheon to wish him well

said one Rockefeller aide later, "that win or lose, they had cushy jobs waiting back in New York. The trouble was Rocky wasn't hungry enough for it, and neither were the people around him." Asked at one point what the lavish campaign was costing, Rocky replied: "I hate to think." (Yet there was always one economy the man observed. To others, the expression was, "Thanks a million," but Rockefeller always said, "Thanks a thousand—fella.") In the multimillion-dollar advertising blitz, the emphasis was heavily on urban problem-solving; one TV spot showed a young black American, just back from Vietnam, walking through a ghetto, while the voice of the concerned narrator spoke of how Governor Rockefeller was striving to give him the real chance he deserved from America.

All this activity caused the Nixon camp only moderate concern. The same self-control that the candidate had displayed all year had been infused in the staff, and the strategy of unflappability did not waver. At the Minnesota Republican convention in Duluth the weekend after the Kennedy funeral, Nixon's representatives came face to face with the Rockefeller blitz, measured its impact as formidable in that state, and backed away from a showdown. As Rockefeller spoke to the delegates, his aides circulated the latest Minnesota state polls, showing him beating either Humphrey or McCarthy in Minnesota and Nixon losing to both. In a state party requiring 60 percent of all delegates for endorsement of a candidate, Nixon lieutenants feared they might fall short. So instead of pushing for an endorsement, they used their influence to have the convention conduct an unofficial straw poll—which Nixon won, 681–595, over Rockefeller, with 45 votes for Reagan. Then Nixon, advised by Ellsworth of the team's inability to muster the 60 percent, spread a blanket of reasonableness and party unity over the whole show with a telegram urging the convention to express its views "in a harmonious way." Thus Nixon emerged with no endorsement, but with no black eye either, while the Rockefeller camp, which desperately needed a breakthrough of some kind, missed out. "Although we didn't want anybody to vote against us," one Nixon lieutenant noted later, "we'd tolerate it, so we'd have that support once we got the nomination."

Rockefeller missed out, too, at the annual Republican Gover-

317

nors' Conference in Tulsa the same weekend. Once hopeful of having as many as nineteen or twenty of the twenty-six GOP governors in his corner, Rockefeller flew in and out of Tulsa with only one somewhat hazy endorsement, from Governor Raymond P. Shafer of Pennsylvania, to show for his trouble. While Nixon lieutenants Ellsworth and Sears floated unobtrusively and confidently around the fringes, watchful for any sign of slippage, Rockefeller sought to put the best possible face on a bleak outlook. He didn't really want outright endorsements, he insisted, just agreement by favorite sons to hold on. Endorsement by a large gubernatorial bloc, he said, would only release some delegates to Nixon then being denied him by their allegiance to favorite sons. What he wanted, Rockefeller said, was to strike a "delicate balance." It was pure fantasy, and no doubt he knew it. All the fight—if there had been any—had gone out of the liberal governors long before.

Even old Rockefeller allies Romney and Agnew were making pro-Nixon sounds now. Agnew particularly talked of the need for a candidate who would show firmness in dealing with racial unrest and rioting, and of his inclinations toward Nixon as that man. The Maryland governor was particularly critical of the recent Poor People's March on Washington and the encampment of Resurrection City on federal property near the Lincoln Memorial. Agnew remarked at one point that many Cadillacs had been seen parked near the encampment—a remark he obviously saw as simply a recitation of fact, but which appalled party liberals as racial innuendo.

In addition to eroding Rockefeller's gubernatorial strength, Nixon was nibbling away at the New Yorker's Nixon-Can't-Win theme. To counter Rockefeller's poll-oriented blitz, Nixon produced surveys by his pollster, J. E. Bachelder of Princeton, New Jersey, challenging Rockefeller's main pitch—that only he could beat the Democrats. The Bachelder polls, in the key industrial states of New Jersey, Pennsylvania, Ohio and Illinois, showed Nixon winning in all four and Rockefeller in only three. In the three in which Rockefeller ran ahead, the survey acknowledged, he was stronger than Nixon, but that was a fact the Nixon camp could afford to release. It lent a note of integrity to the polls, and party pols who read the results knew that winning states was what counted in the electoral college system, not the margin of victory.

Rockefeller, after having stayed out of the primaries, needed more than simply an edge in the polls to make his point against Nixon. That was how the sentiment in the GOP required it; unless Nixon was a sure loser the party was inclined to go with him. Because of this fact, shifts in the prestigious Gallup Poll favoring Rockefeller slightly really didn't make much difference. In May, the poll showed both Nixon and Rockefeller beating Humphrey, Nixon by 39 percent to 36 percent, Rockefeller by 40 percent to 33 percent. But in June, both fell behind, Nixon by 36–42, Rockefeller by 36–39. That Rockefeller's trailing margin was less was no persuasive point for his nomination.

Making little real headway in the major polls, Rockefeller sought to apply heat on Nixon from other angles. In Chicago, he labeled the former Vice President as head of "the leadership that failed eight years ago" and a man given to making "belligerent prophecies on this tragic war." And, as always, a loser. Recalling 1960, Rockefeller would say: "He carried Illinois until he got to Chicago, and then he lost the state. He carried Pennsylvania until he got to Philadelphia, and then he lost the state. He carried New York until he got to New York City, and then he lost the state." And later, when a heckler shouted, 'Nixon's the one," Rocky shot back: "That's right, he's the one, he's the one who lost it for us in '60!" On Vietnam, Rockefeller urged more imaginative efforts to start productive negotiations in Paris. But Nixon, in his inimitable way, disposed of such pleadings as faintly inimical to the Paris talks. "I'll not say anything that the enemy might interpret as offering a better deal," he said with appropriate righteousness.

As Rockefeller thrashed about with little success to show for his expenditure of money and energy, payments on political promissory notes continued to come in to Nixon. The Illinois primary gave him an estimated fifty of fifty-eight delegates; state conventions in New Mexico, Montana and Washington, with a total of fifty-two delegates, delivered another thirty-four, and there were Strom Thurmond's twenty-two. Still, Rockefeller persevered.

On June 24 in Atlanta, where he had about as much chance of making serious inroads into the Republican delegation as Stokely Carmichael, Rockefeller tried to pin George Wallace on Nixon. Nixon's Southern campaign coordinator, former Congressman Howard "Bo" Callaway—the man who outpolled Lester Maddox for governor of Georgia in 1966 but not by enough to keep the election out of the Democratic state legislature—had goofed. He had gone before the Mississippi Republican convention and suggested, or so it was reported, that Wallace should join the GOP. Rockefeller called on Nixon to repudiate Callaway, who insisted all he had said was that since Wallace like the Republicans wanted to get the Johnson-Humphrey administration out, "maybe we can even get George himself on our side, because that's where he ought to be."

Nixon refused to be suckered in. At an airport interview in New York, he straight-armed the Rockefeller thrust and went on his way. "I don't want it [Wallace support], and from what I've heard he's in it to stay. From what I've read, Wallace's support is in the direction of the racist element. I have been in politics for twenty-two years and I have never had a racist in my organization. . . . Congressman Callaway's statement may be subject to misunderstanding. What he was trying to say was that people who want a change in the United States should not waste their vote on a third-party candidate. I believe that. I believe a vote for Wallace on the right or, shall I say a peace candidate on the left, is a wasted move." About three weeks later in Philadelphia, as his foes talked darkly of a Nixon-Wallace deal to avoid a stalemated election going into the House of Representatives, Nixon said flatly that "under no circumstances would negotiate with Mr. Wallace, nor would Hubert Humphrey. He accused Wallace of "cultivating a myth" that the Alabamian would be strong enough to force the election into the House; he might win Mississippi, Alabama, Louisiana and possibly Georgia, Nixon said, but "as far as the Congressional votes in those states are concerned, they'll all vote for Humphrey because they're all Democrats."*

* This and other flaps cast Callaway as a lightweight in the Nixon inner circle Mitchell in the campaign at one point wanted to fire him, but Nixon demurred Nevertheless, Callaway's shortcomings were key factors in his failure to land job in the Nixon administration later.

On July 1, Senator John Tower came out from under his favorite-son disguise and openly endorsed Nixon, as Reaganite and Rockefellerite hearts sank. "Dick Nixon already has about fifty delegates more than the six hundred sixty-seven he needs for nomination," Tower said. "He's already over the top, and this is cream on the cake." Both of Nixon's foes needed help from the favorite sons to keep Nixon within hauling range, and Tower's move unsettled their pipe dreams. With Thurmond and Tower thus nailed down on the South's flanks, Nixon leisurely and confidently made the rounds of Republican governors and other party leaders in the Northern industrial states, like a visiting chief of state on a goodwill tour. In Cleveland he conferred with enigmatic Governor Jim Rhodes, sitting tight on a bloc of fifty-five out of fifty-eight Ohio delegates, and came out of the meeting reporting that Rhodes had urged him to consider New York Mayor John Lindsay as his running mate. Nixon already had said that the constitutional requirement for Presidential electors to vote for only one man from their state had ruled out fellow New Yorkers Rockefeller and Lindsay. But he didn't mind repeating the suggestion; it made fairly clear to any discerning party politician that if Rhodes was boosting Lindsay for No. 2 with Nixon for ideological balance, he must have written off Rockefeller's candidacy.

Nixon went on to Chicago for a meeting with 200 delegates from nine Midwestern states, and thence to Philadelphia, where he met his first black group of the year. For two hours, with basketball star Wilt Chamberlain in tow, he conferred privately with twenty-eight leaders of local antipoverty, job opportunity and educational programs, including two members of the city's Black Coalition. Afterward one of them, Stanley Branch, said of Nixon: "The man leveled. If he was jiving, he fooled me. But I think he was straight." And from that carefully cloistered confrontation with black America, the candidate went over to Annapolis for a meeting with the Maryland delegation and dinner with a man who had grown increasingly distant from black America after riots in Baltimore, and increasingly closer to Richard Nixon—Spiro Agnew. "That guy Agnew is really an impressive fellow," Nixon told one aide afterward. "He's got guts. He's got a good attitude."

In mid-July, President Eisenhower contributed his endorsement. The old general had suffered still another in the series of heart attacks that had plagued his later years, and for days at a time through the summer his death was believed to be imminent. During one of his recovery periods, Nixon had visited him and reported afterward he was making remarkable progress. A few days later, speaking from his bed at the Walter Reed Army Hospital in Washington, Eisenhower termed Nixon "a man of great reading, a man of great intelligence, a man of great decisiveness . . . [and] great experience [whose] nomination and election in this year's election would serve the best interests of the United States." A film cameraman was permitted in the room to record this event for later use.

All was going according to plan. Next, there was a quick visit to California, a massive "Welcome Home, Dick" reception in Los Angeles, and a retreat to the Newport Beach home of an old friend, Federal Judge Thurmond Clarke, to start writing the candidate's acceptance speech. That was how confident Nixon was—and with good reason. The retreat continued at Montauk Point, Long Island, where Nixon sequestered himself in a five-room cottage with only his valet, Manolo, with him. "We heard from him this morning," an aide told newsmen one day. "He called my bungalow and said, 'Bring me some more yellow pads.' And then he hung up."

In still another demonstration of his confidence, Nixon dispatched a letter to about 300 Republican leaders soliciting their "advice" on the selection of a running mate. Three questions were asked: Who would make the best Vice Presidential candidate to provide geographic and philosophic balance? Who would be the best campaigner in person and on television? Who is the best qualified to be President?

While these preparations proceeded, the political calendar moved along. Now, as in 1964, the annual National Governors' Conference intruded itself into the campaign scene, this time in Cincinnati and this time with the tables turned. The talk was not about a stop-Goldwater effort with Nixon playing Iago to George Romney's Othello, but with Rockefeller and Reagan under scrutiny as a possible stop-Nixon coalition. But there was no sense of desperation that such an improbable marriage of opposites required.

While Democrats, scarcely six weeks after Robert Kennedy's assassination, dishonored themselves with discussions about the possibility of suiting up thirty-six-year-old Senator Edward M. Kennedy to save their collective skins, the Republican governors settled into the realization that they had been had again. Rockefeller alternated between inflating Reagan's delegate strength, thus suggesting that Nixon was slipping in the South and could be stopped, and deflating Reagan personally. The Californian continued to insist he was not an active candidate for anything. This view was taken with all the seriousness it deserved, in light of the fact that Reagan's Cincinnati visit was a stopover on his way to meet Southern delegates in Birmingham. Nixon lieutenants, meanwhile, stood around, talked to governors and looked like a menagerie of Cheshire cats. This was one National Governors' Conference that Nixon was not going to stumble over.

About the most excitement generated occurred when a bodyguard for Governor Lester Maddox of Georgia brushed against a man in the headquarters hotel lobby and felt he was wearing a gun under his jacket. The man was seized and disarmed, amid reports that his target had been Reagan. By now, after Kennedy's death, President Johnson had ordered the Secret Service to guard all Presidential candidates, including George Wallace and Reagan. The watchful presence of these plainclothesmen was a constant reminder of what kind of year it was, and what emotions were loose in the country as the first of its major political parties made ready to choose its standard-bearer.

14

Miami Beach: A Coronation

Now at last it was time for the Republican Party's quadrennial extravaganza to begin. Miami Beach, once predominantly a winter haven for the wealthy and ostentatious, over the years had become the year-round haven for the merely comfortably well-off and ostentatious, and the convention-going and ostentatious. Where other cities were consumed by national political conventions, Miami Beach by its sheer crassness absorbed this one. Delegates took over most of the major and many of the minor hotels along the 200-block beachfront, and although they engaged in all the customary imbecilities of political conventions, they blended into the scenery with chameleonic ease.

Assignments of hotel space constituted a tipster's sheet on the opening odds: Nixon at the spanking new Hilton Plaza in the center of activity; Rockefeller far up the strip at the Americana, out of touch with the mainstream action; Reagan at the less imposing Deauville, closer to the Nixon camp and always in its shadow. The most outlandishly ornate and transparently veneered of the major hotels, the Fontainebleau, functioned as the convention and press headquarters. There, as bleached, bronzed blondes in their fifties stuffed themselves with only partial success into bikinis and parked themselves beside an Olympic-sized pool defiled by washed-off suntan oil, the GOP held its platform hearings on what was wrong with the country.

For nearly a week before any of the candidates arrived in town, the party under the languid direction of Senate Majority Leader Dirksen took hour after hour of wearying testimony on what the platform ought to say. In past conventions, and notably in 1960 and 1964, the platform debate had offered foes of the front-running candidates, Nixon and Goldwater, their last opportunity to stir a row that might conceivably have opened the way to an upset. In both previous conventions the tactic had failed. In 1960, Nixon dashed off to New York and made his "Treaty of Fifth Avenue" with Rockefeller on platform concessions long since forgotten. In 1964, the Goldwater-dominated platform committee ran roughshod over the forces of William Scranton. Now, in 1968, Nixon passed the word that there was to be no fight over the platform. "He felt it didn't mean a damn thing," one campaign aide said later. "He always said that nobody remembers what's in a platform after it's written. He declined to let it become a battleground. It just wasn't worth fighting over."

Nixon, along with the other candidates, sent statements to the platform committee indicating his general positions on the major issues of Vietnam, law and order, urban problems and the economy. But he did little pushing. With Dirksen running the show and with the bulk of committee members on Nixon's side or amenable to his candidacy, he didn't have to. Dirksen had remarked facetiously before the hearings opened—and after a feeble challenge from the governors to have one of their own chair the committee—that he was going to "write the platform on my portable" before arriving in Miami Beach. Later, he insisted that "my impish tendencies were on the ascendancy and my tongue got a little waggish." But nobody was too sure, when the bland platform emerged, that he hadn't been telling it the first time like it was.

Amid much fanfare that at last he was about to break his self-imposed silence on what should be done in Vietnam, Nixon lifted the lid only slightly in his platform statement. The Paris negotiations, he said, "must be waged more effectively." At the same time, greater efforts had to be made to shift the burden of the fighting back to the South Vietnamese. As better-trained and better-equipped South Vietnamese were phased in, he said, "American troops can, and should be phased out. This phasing-out will save American lives and cut American costs. . . . It is a cruel irony that the American effort to safeguard the independence of South Vietnam has produced an ever-increasing dependency in our ally. If South Vietnam's future is to be secure, this process must now be reversed." These words did in fact provide a strong indication of the direction in which Nixon then was thinking about the war, but he smothered them in justifications for not committing himself. In addition to his oft-repeated concern about tying the hands of American negotiators in the Paris talks, he said, he didn't want to talk himself into a corner with Hanoi. "These [talks] impose limits on what a Presidential candidate can responsibly say," Nixon insisted, "not because of what the American people might think, but because of how Hanoi's negotiators might interpret it. . . . Anything he might say, any differences he might express, would be taken by Hanoi as indicating the possible new direction of the next administration."

In another platform statement, on law and order, Nixon showed no such restraint: "The people of this country want an end to government that acts out of a spirit of neutrality or beneficence or indulgence toward criminals. . . . Poverty, despair, anger, past wrongs can no longer be allowed to excuse or justify violence or crime or lawlessness. We must cease as well the granting of special immunities and moral sanctions to those who deliberately violate the public laws—even when those violations are done in the name of peace or civil rights or anti-poverty or academic reform."

This last was very strong language, not too far removed from Reagan's remarks to the platform committee on the same subject: "We must reject the idea that every time a law is broken, society is guilty rather than the lawbreaker. It is time to restore the American precept that each individual is accountable for his actions."

The Nixon and Reagan statements both were applauded enthusiastically by the committee. A third, delivered by Mayor Lindsay, was received with marked coolness. "The war on crime," Lindsay said, "will require both intelligence and perspective. It will not be solved by simplistic cries for law and order. It will not be won by ill-founded attacks on the Supreme Court to please narrow constituencies. We should not be stampeded into primitive solutions: clubs, guns, tanks. These are instruments that cannot work in America; peace cannot be imposed in our cities solely by force of arms. The root cause of most crime and civil disorder is the poverty that grips over thirty million of our citizens, black and white. . . . If we are to eliminate crime and violence in this country, we must eliminate the hopelessness, futility and alienation from which they spring." It was one of the most thoughtful speeches of the convention, but it was as much out of step with the prevailing mood as it would have been had it been delivered in San Francisco in 1964.

The final version of the platform, after only relatively minor skirmishing, tossed the Nixon opposition some small, insignificant bones, and its potential as an eleventh-hour battleground experienced a quiet death. On Vietnam, both the Nixon and the Rockefeller viewpoints were clearly seen: ". . . We pledge to adopt a strategy relevant to the real problems of the war, concentrating on the security of the population, on developing a greater sense of nationhood, and on strengthening local forces. It will be a strategy permitting a progressive de-Americanization of the war, both military and civilian."

On crime at home, it was law and order, with only the slightest softening: "We must re-establish the principle that men are accountable for what they do, that criminals are responsible for their crimes, that while the youth's environment may help to explain the man's crime, it does not excuse the crime. . . . while demanding protection of the public peace and safety, we pledge a relentless attack on economic and social injustice in every form."

As already noted, Nixon had planned all along to soft-pedal the platform hearings. He had observed after the Oregon primary that "the polls . . . will be the drill down in Miami," and he had not been mistaken. Well before most of the delegates or any of the candidates had arrived, in fact on the very morning the platform committee first prepared to convene, "the drill" began—in a crashing avalanche of Rockefeller's hopes.

In its editions of Monday morning, July 29, the Miami *Herald* printed the final preconvention results of the prestigious Gallup Poll. After all Nelson Rockefeller's breakneck traveling, exhorting and spending—all aimed at affecting the public opinion surveys incontrovertibly in his own favor over Nixon—Gallup found that the one Republican who could win was—Richard Nixon! Based on interviews during the previous week, the poll showed Nixon running two percentage points ahead of Vice President Humphrey and five ahead of Senator McCarthy, with Rockefeller merely tying Humphrey and edging McCarthy by a single point!

Members of the platform committee, aides of the candidates, newsmen scanning the front page of the *Herald* slipped under their doors at the Fontainebleau, scarcely could believe their eyes. But there it was:

Nixon	40	Rockefeller	36
Humphrey	38	Humphrey	36
Wallace	16	Wallace	21
Undecided	6	Undecided	7
Nixon	41	Rockefeller	36
McCarthy	36	McCarthy	35
Wallace	16	Wallace	20
Undecided	7	Undecided	9

The poll lifted the Nixon camp into a state of absolute euphoria and plunged the Rockefeller forces into the deepest gloom. Since Rockefeller had chosen to live by the polls, the results surely meant he had died by them. It was a mortal wound, self-inflicted. And John Mitchell was right there to give the dagger a twist.

"Experience in the primary elections," he said, "has shown that Richard Nixon runs far ahead of the polls when it comes to the actual election count. We, therefore, tend to discount the polls generally. But since it was Governor Rockefeller's suggestion that particular attention be given to public opinion surveys this year, additional interest must be centered on the Gallup

Poll, which long has been looked upon as the most respected of the national polls." Despite the clear Gallup results, he said, "we anticipate there will be a separate series of gadgeteered polls, seeking to prove a specialized point of view. We predict that these will have no effect on the nomination."

The reeling Rockefeller forces were quick to oblige. Hoping somehow to plug the gaping wound, they did indeed spring loose two of their specialized polls. One suggested that Rockefeller ran considerably stronger than Nixon in nine key states, Rockefeller winning all nine for 226 of the 270 required electoral votes and Nixon only five for 152 votes. The other indicated that Rockefeller was widely preferred in key Congressional districts in Michigan, Ohio and New Jersey. Both surveys were feebly transparent, as was George Hinman's characterization of the Gallup Poll as "just a head count." The truth was, the Gallup results were an unmitigated disaster for Rockefeller. Something better than what Mitchell not too inaccurately had called "gadgeteered polls" was needed.

In short order, it appeared. Gallup's major competitor, Louis Harris, released his final preconvention survey, and the results from Rockefeller's point of view were good. He clearly ran ahead of both Humphrey and McCarthy, and Nixon clearly trailed both. The Harris figures were:

Rockefeller	40	Humphrey	41
Humphrey	34	Nixon	36
Wallace	20	Wallace	16
Not sure	6	Not sure	7
Rockefeller	40	McCarthy	43
McCarthy	34	Nixon	35
Wallace	19	Wallace	15
Not sure	7	Not sure	7

The Rockefeller convention forces, heartened by the Harris results, frantically reproduced them and during the night slipped them under the doors of delegates and newsmen. But it was not enough. Even in the event delegates and the press believed Harris over Gallup—and few indicated they did—the whole thrust and impact of the Rockefeller campaign-by-polltaking had been irretrievably compromised. In order to make a significant dent in what essentially was an anti-Rockefeller convention, the governor needed categorical evidence not simply that he ran ahead of Nixon, but that he was a sure winner and Nixon a sure loser. Although the reigning cliché insisted that Nixon's strength ran "a mile wide and an inch deep," most delegates were of a mind to go along with him unless they were shown *conclusive* proof he couldn't win. Long before either poll appeared, many had expressed resentment at the notion they could be swung so easily one way or another by public opinion surveys. These politicians, perhaps even more than the general public, had come to put great stock in the polls. On a personal basis, however, many balked at the idea that the performance of the huge American electorate could be measured with such certainty by a sample of a few thousand voters. Thus, the conflicting findings served not only to undermine each of the two specific polls but to discredit polltaking generally among an audience that was emotionally very willing to see polltaking discredited.

Just as George Hinman had sought to take the curse off the Gallup Poll result by calling it a "head count," Nixon agent Herb Klein quickly labeled the Harris figures "incredible" and suggested that Harris as a pollster had an unreliable record. "To be on the low end of a Harris poll usually means to be on the high end of an election vote," he told a press conference at the Hilton Plaza after the Harris Survey was released.

For the polltaking business, the fiasco was the nadir of what had been a steady erosion of public confidence all through the stormy, unpredictable year. No one was more aware of this fact than George Gallup, Jr., running the show while his father was abroad, and Harris. "I was under tremendous pressure to explain why we differed," Gallup Jr. told me later. "Harris called me and suggested we could iron things out by showing the sequence [timing] of the polls. I jumped at the chance."

In what surely was one of the most amazing exercises in this year of the unexpected, these two fierce competitors quickly put their heads together and produced a joint statement that for many befuddled readers only added to the polls' credibility crisis. Their "seeming differences," the two pollsters said, were "not as dissimilar as they might appear to the public at first glance." The fact that Gallup's poll was taken between July 20 and 23 and Harris' between July 25 and 29 was one explanation of the different results, they said. Another was "normal sampling fluctuations." And then, to the astonishment of the Nixon forces, Gallup Jr. agreed with Harris that Rockefeller as of the latest survey was running stronger. Considering all the recent polls together, the two public pulse-takers said, Rockefeller had a clear lead in a three-cornered race with Humphrey and Wallace, whereas a Nixon-Humphrey-Wallace election would be very close. Herb Klein summed up the situation well when he observed: "It looks like they've got a pollsters' protective society organized."

Gallup Sr., when he learned what had happened, was disturbed. His son, in his zest to lance the troublesome controversy, had accepted Harris' data without question. It was not that there was any clear reason to doubt the Harris results, but that as a matter of operating policy a professional pollster stands behind only his own data, and can vouch only for what he produces himself. "It wasn't my intent to say the Harris figures were correct," Gallup Jr. told me. "It was a gesture of friendship in a sense. It came out of all the harassment, not as a master plan to protect the polling industry."

That Gallup Jr. and Harris would be deeply concerned about the reaction to their "seeming differences" in the Nixon-Rockefeller polls was hardly surprising. Although they had refined their techniques and had built an impressive record for accuracy, the pollsters always were haunted by the big miss—the prediction of Gallup and others in 1948 that Thomas E. Dewey would beat Harry S Truman. That failure, according to Gallup Sr., resulted when polling was in its relative infancy; the pollsters, he says, stopped interviewing too soon and missed a late swing to Truman. Since 1948, the polling business had labored diligently to move itself out of that shadow. Efforts at refinement were accompanied by a vast growth in public opinion polling itself; although there seemed to be an unshakable disposition to speak disparagingly about polls, hardly a major politician would take a serious step anymore without commissioning or consulting polls. The politicians' thirst for information about voter attitudes, and the public's less self-serving craving for prophecy, produced a multimillion-dollar offshoot of the news business in which Gallup and Harris were only the most prominent names.

Gallup, one of the industry's pioneers in 1935, long had restricted himself to "public" surveys for about 120 American newspapers that bought his service. Harris, after a fling at private polling for John F. Kennedy and other clients, also moved into "public" polling in 1963. With them came an army of polltakers who sold their wares to politicians or other private clients—old-timers Archibald Crossley and Elmo Roper and his son Bud, John Kraft, Oliver Quayle, Joe Napolitan, John Bucci, Fred Currier and a string of others around the country. Some lesser-known private pollsters doubled in commercial surveys, running what are known as piggyback polls, in which political questions are added to surveys basically intended to determine marketing preferences among specific economic groups. Although most political pollsters frown on this practice, contending it damages the credibility of all sampling, the public was in no position to separate piggyback polls from the rest; when one poll of whatever kind was wrong, all polltaking suffered.

A lingering and paradoxical skepticism thus clung to the public view of polling. On the one hand the notion that the polls somehow were a wild guessing game became a cliché repeated by some of the most sophisticated voters. Yet many of these same voters felt the polls were so thoroughly believed by others that they undermined the public's incentive to vote, or they stampeded the electorate into what the polls earlier had indicated. The pollsters call this idea "the bandwagon theory" and flatly reject it, pointing to Exhibit "A"—the Dewey-Truman race. If polls caused stampedes, they note, Dewey as the front-runner from start to finish would have been an easy winner.

It is the pollsters' contention that they do not "predict" elections; they merely measure public opinion as it is at a given moment. Harris has called polltaking "single snapshots at one point in time of a constantly moving picture"; in 1968, the picture moved so swiftly that the polls were bound to show large fluctuations from one week to another. But the pollsters are well aware that others, especially professional politicians, are convinced the polls are shapers of opinion. "Polls have no measurable effect on voters," Gallup told a group of newsmen at Princeton in advance of the 1968 election, "but I've never met a politician who didn't believe they did. Every single candidate believes he has to have some kind of poll he can pull out of his pocket to show that he's ahead." This observation, while accurately sketching the intensity of the politician's interest in polls, does not give him adequate credit for versatility. Candidates who adopt an underdog role (Romney in New Hampshire) like to flash surveys showing themselves behind but gaining, and those who fear they're so far ahead that their supporters may lose interest (Nixon in New Hampshire) like to quote polls showing they're in a tight race.

Going into 1968, the ambivalent public attitude toward polls was of particular concern to the established pollsters because it beclouded a remarkably good record for accuracy since the 1948 failure. Gallup in sixteen Presidential and Congressional election years after the Truman-Dewey race had been off an average of only 2.7 percent, and only 1.5 percent in the seven elections between 1954 and 1966. In the Kennedy-Nixon cliff-hanger of 1960, Gallup had Kennedy by 51 percent, compared to his actual vote of 50.1; in 1964, he gave Johnson 64 percent and the President received 61.3; in the 1966 Congressional elections, he gave the Democrats 52.5 percent and they got 51.9. Harris, as a private pollster for John Kennedy in 1960, says he was right in thirty of thirty-three states, and in his first national election effort, 1964, also came up with 64 percent for Johnson. In due time in 1968, both Gallup and Harris—working with their reputations squarely on the line—would emphatically vindicate themselves, but when their split over Nixon and Rockefeller strengths broke at Miami Beach, the public was ready to dismiss the polls as mumbo jumbo.

A year earlier, the Minnesota Poll, the well-regarded statewide survey of the Minneapolis *Tribune,* had asked voters whether they thought polls could be accurate if based on a sampling of 2,000 interviews (500 more than Gallup uses in most national samples). The response was 47 percent yes, 45 percent no, the rest undecided. One reason for this thin margin of public confidence probably is the almost invisible character of polltaking. The polls seem to materialize from nowhere; few citizens ever have been interviewed by a polltaker, or even know anyone who has been. In Gallup's system, only one American in about 133,000 is questioned. One interviewer in each of 300 sample units in the polling "universe" makes five "hits" or in-depth interviews of about thirty or forty minutes each, reading carefully prepared questions from a sheet, recording the answers exactly as given and forwarding them without interpretation for correlation and analysis by experts at Gallup's Princeton headquarters. The questions, before going out to the interviewers, are prepared for clarity and comprehensibility and pretested on live audiences in a Gallup laboratory called "The Mirror of America." Gallup and Harris in 1968 each had about 750 part-time interviewers who were paid about two dollars an hour and trained to elicit answers without leading or influencing the subjects. Usually the interviewers are middle-aged women of considerable formal education and an ability to win the confidence of subjects. Sometimes the same interviewer will work for two competing pollsters; if she is professionally disciplined, the pollsters say, it doesn't matter, because she is just a gatherer of data, not an interpreter of it.

Beyond the fact that most voters never are polled, public confusion and doubt about poll taking often result from failure to comprehend—and accept—the cornerstones of the enterprise: random selection and the laws of probability. Logic seems to argue against a system that in effect puts the names of 200,000 localities in a hat and pulls out 300, then sends a woman to each of the 300 places and has her ask only five individuals, whose addresses also are picked at random, what America is thinking. The pollsters insist that is the only way to guarantee a true sampling—one in which every American has exactly as much chance as any other to be interviewed. The figure of 1,500 interviews is based on experience and experiments with the law of probability that have established it as the optimum for getting accurate results with speed and economy. In any sampling made at random, a point is reached at which variations in the percentage of persons who take one position or another begin to level off. From that point on, increasing the size of the sample changes the ratio only slightly.

To those politicians and voters who are accustomed to thinking of elections in terms of voting blocs by age, race, ethnic origin and income, the random selection of targets also seems invalid. A city precinct may be selected, for instance, that has a black population far greater or smaller than the black population in the nation, or even in the particular city or state. It doesn't matter, the pollsters say, because it is a national sample, not a city or state one, that is being taken; in a truly random sample of sufficient size, the general racial, ethnic and economic composition of the electorate will be adequately reflected.

Poll-doubting voters are not generally aware, either, of the efforts taken by the more dependable pollsters to isolate not only persons registered to vote but those who probably will vote. Questions are designed to appraise a subject's level of interest and involvement, and to cull clues to separate the probable voters from the probable stay-at-homes. Also, refinements have been developed to pare down the critical undecided vote, which if too large can render a sample useless. Early practices of splitting the undecided vote down the middle or allocating it in proportion to the ratio of committed voters have been largely abandoned in favor of devices to draw out the undecideds. Subtle questions are asked to determine party allegiance and other leanings that give the analyst a fairly clear idea about how the subject is likely to vote. If these don't work, the individual is asked to fill out a secret ballot, which then is sealed in his presence. Such ballots usually are coded so that the voter can be identified, not by name but by sample area. On any particular question, the voter's intensity of feeling can be measured by asking him if he is highly or mildly favorable, or highly or mildly unfavorable, toward a person or policy position. Candidates buy private intensity polls to probe their own strengths and weaknesses so they can shore up their campaigns.

These refinements, however, have not been embraced by all pollsters. In addition to the continuing public skepticism about their business, there also existed in 1968 a considerable intramural concern that some polltakers themselves were undermining the industry's reputation. In a rare precampaign seminar for

335

national political writers at Princeton, Gallup, the veteran Archibald Crossley and others explained how polls worked and what the reporters should look for in evaluating their reliability. In the process, there was some sniping over methods of gathering and interpreting data by some of their colleagues. Fred Currier, the private pollster in Detroit who handled George Romney's account, held a similar session in Washington and warned the political writers to watch for interpretations that "go beyond the data." Some but not all of the criticism at Princeton was directed against Harris, on grounds that as the author of a column competing with the older, more prestigious Gallup Poll, he sometimes was overzealous in his presentation. Harris, on learning of the Princeton meeting, gave his side in another Washington session with the political writers. He considered himself, he said, primarily a reporter who used public opinion surveys to reach his conclusions. In the spring of 1968, at Gallup's suggestion, most of the leading pollsters or their agents met in Santa Barbara, California, to consider what they could do to improve their image and credibility. There, they carved the outlines of a code of ethics, agreed on greater standardization in polling practices and took first steps toward creation of a National Council on Public Polls. It was in this climate of industry concern that the Gallup-Harris fiasco broke on the eve of the Republican National Convention.

The whole episode sunk the polling business, in spite of all the advances in technology and sophistication and all the internal self-policing, into its greatest credibility crisis since the Dewey-Truman miss. It was nothing, however, compared to the political crisis now facing Nelson Rockefeller. If the Gallup-Harris statement bailed the polling industry out somewhat—which was doubtful—it did nothing at all for Rockefeller, though the collective, post-consultation conclusion was that he would run stronger than Nixon. What Rockefeller needed more than an edge in the polls, after having built his whole case on them, was their credibility, and that had been utterly compromised. In time, it could be—and was—largely restored, but Rockefeller had no time. In a few days, Nixon would be steaming into Miami Beach with nothing to bar his speedy and routine nomination. Rockefeller publicists, operating on the theory that the polls would be their candidate's strong suit, had rigged up floodlights that, when played against the side of the Fontainebleau and the delegation hotels at night, would proclaim, several stories high, the legend ROCKY CAN WIN. Even after the polling fiasco, the publicists continued to use the gimmick, obviously insensitive to the fact it now was a colossal self-mockery.

While the Rockefeller forces scurried around trying frantically to salvage the situation, Nixon continued to relax at Montauk. While depleting yellow legal pads, he soaked up the sun, maintaining the tan his television advisers felt was so important in persuading the American electorate to make an intelligent choice about the next President of the United States. Reporters assigned to Nixon did not see him for days on end, but they were told he still was busily at work on his acceptance speech and the decision on a running mate. Buchanan told me later that neither he nor Price saw the finished product until it was ready for duplication and release. Nixon, he said, dictated three full tapes to Rose Woods, requiring forty typewritten pages, then refined several drafts until he finally honed the speech to exactly what he wanted. "I write for a while on a yellow legal-sized pad," Nixon himself told reporters one day, "and then I talk what I have written into a machine. I play the machine back, and if something doesn't sound right, I revise it." Such insights into Nixon's intensive concentration on the speech conjured up the expectation of a great new visionary declaration. When the speech finally was delivered, it proved in many parts to be a patchwork of the same standard campaign speech he had used all spring and even earlier, in his precampaign oratory. It made one wonder just what he had been doing all those days at Montauk.

What Nixon had been doing, it turned out later, was staying out of the firing line for as long as possible—watching the scoreboard, which showed him clearly ahead. Also, he supposedly was fielding all the advice he had solicited from party leaders about the Vice Presidential nomination. Later, nobody seemed to be able to recall whether even one of the hundreds of letters that were said to be pouring in with suggestions had specifically urged the selection of Spiro T. Agnew. "Anytime you see R.N.

polling people," an intimate said later, "you can be pretty sure he's not seeking their opinion. He just wants to substantiate his own views. He's not the kind of man who comes to a situation without an opinion. In spite of all this searching and consultation, the fact we got who we did proves he wasn't coming at it with an open mind." Another insider told me: "Of course he had no intention of taking that advice when he asked for it. That's just Dick's way of making people feel they're involved in important decisions. It doesn't cost anything, and some people eat it up."

Reagan was the first of the featured players to arrive in Miami Beach, on the third day of the platform committee hearings. He had just completed visits to eight potential Reagan states, ending with a stop in North Carolina. The resident Republican power there, gubernatorial candidate Representative James C. Gardner, had told Reagan that unless he came out as a bona fide candidate, there wasn't anything the North Carolina delegation could do for him. The same kind of pressure for a flat declaration of candidacy came from the Florida delegation.* At a press conference, Reagan insisted he still was only a favorite son, but when asked whether he would become an "active, full-fledged" candidate once his name went before the convention, he replied: "At that point, you have no choice in the matter." Actually, he was destined not to wait until that point.

After appearing before the platform committee, Reagan returned to California to lead the state's 86-member delegation back to Sunset Strip East on Saturday. Arriving the same day was Rockefeller, flashing the irrepressible grin that had so unsuccessfully sought to camouflage so much political heartbreak in the long past. He would win, Rockefeller insisted, by eroding Nixon's strength, which he estimated at only 550 delegates, and then adding the slippage to his own total, which he placed at about 350, with 200 for Reagan. Rockefeller in fact

---

* Clif White later said he came at one point to within one vote of swinging the Florida delegation—a coup that could have started the slide to Reagan that Nixon strategists needed to avert. But the state chairman, Bill Murfin, with whom White and Clarke Reed, the Mississippi chairman, had been talking for months, was insisting on an informal unit rule. White thus faced, and lost, almost an all-or-nothing situation in Florida.

depended heavily on Reagan to do the eroding of Nixon delegates, and Reagan could not deliver. For if Rockefeller had a poll problem, Reagan had an ideology problem. He was, when you got right down to it, the Barry Goldwater of 1968. He had the rhetoric of the right to pull party conservatives from Nixon, but in attempting to put some daylight between himself and Nixon the centrist, he inevitably flirted with extremism, and the party pros had had enough of that in 1964. All the main conservative columnist-oracles—William F. Buckley, Jr., John Chamberlain, William S. White, Russell Kirk—were in Nixon's corner. So were the political embodiments of superconservatism, Goldwater himself and Thurmond. Reagan did not give his astute political lieutenant, Clif White, much to work with.

Even in the California delegation, in fact, strains were developing that were making it increasingly difficult to hold the line for Reagan as the favorite son. If he was going to run, some delegates insisted, he would have to declare himself. A caucus of the delegation was called Monday, and at its conclusion former Senator William F. Knowland reported that California now recognized its governor as "a leading and bona fide candidate for President." Ronnie Reagan, former movie actor, played the role of the drafted candidate to the hilt. Summoning up all his onstage shyness, he professed to having been bowled over by this spontaneous and unsolicited draft. Then he dashed off to confirm to all his Southern friends that modesty and state ties no longer prevented him from offering himself.

With news of Reagan's open candidacy still filling the news wires, Richard Nixon arrived from Montauk in the late afternoon. The arrival at the Miami International Airport was timed for a live network television pickup, and when the plane taxied to the terminal several minutes early, Nixon stayed aboard and waited. He came down the ramp finally like a visiting head of state, taking the welcome of his most prominent party backers and shaking some of the hands reaching across the ropes that held the crowd back. Security was extremely tight on the field, in the terminal and all along the route Nixon would take to his headquarters hotel. "This marks the end of one journey and, we think, the beginning of another that is going to lead us to a new leadership for this nation," he said woodenly.

Recalling he had made his original decision to seek the Presidency while staying in Key Biscayne in 1960, he noted: "So we see history repeating itself"—and Richard Nixon pointedly retracing still another personal milestone.

The candidate apologized for being late (though he had waited aboard for the TV pickup), but it seemed he had a small civic duty to perform in New York before leaving. He had gone to the U.S. Immigration and Naturalization Service office in lower Manhattan to be a witness for his faithful chauffeur-valet and cook, Manolo and Fina Sanchez, as the couple, Cuban refugees, received their citizenship papers.

Nixon, Mrs. Nixon, the two girls and David Eisenhower proceeded in a swift motorcade to the Hilton Plaza, as armed security officers stood watch at every overpass and a Marine Corps helicopter flew overhead. A huge crowd was packed around the entrance to the hotel; Nixon stepped eagerly into it, thrusting his hands over his head, waving the V-for-Victory sign. For him, it clearly always was that, and one wondered whether he ever was mystified by the college kids in all the McCarthy campaign pictures making the same V sign with their fingers. As the candidate worked his way up the hotel ramp through the crush, a multitude of colored balloons was released, climbing rapidly overhead. Always the balloons; it was the standard touch, worked out to a science by the advance team. First the balloons were filled with a gas, jammed into a huge truck van and the door slammed. Then, when it was opened, out they would fly. Nixon invariably displayed a look of astonishment and joy when they rushed out over his head.

The open declaration of candidacy by Reagan did not seem to disturb Nixon in the least. He was the man in the middle, and it was a comforting posture. The Reaganites hated the Rockefellerites and vice versa; Nixon was sure they couldn't get together. Any move by the convention to Reagan would send the Rockefellerites rushing to Nixon to prevent catastrophe; any move to Rockefeller would trigger the same reaction among the Reaganites.

While his desperate opponents raced up and down Collins Avenue visiting state caucuses, Nixon repaired to the plush penthouse of Miami Beach's newest hotel, a spectacular $300-a-day suite. Furnished throughout in gold, it had a large circular living room with a massive circular sofa and five gold chairs, and a bar and small serving area behind. Flanking the living room were two bedrooms with oversized twin beds in each. Nixon used one room, Mrs. Nixon the other. The candidate had a special telephone at his bed, another in the bathroom and a phone console on the other side of his bed, hooked up to his headquarters and to the convention floor through a network in the Hilton Plaza's solarium just above. There, John Ehrlichman, functioning as the Nixon director of convention operations, installed an elaborate communications post to link delegations on the convention floor to the candidate, to Mitchell, Ellsworth and other key aides. And to speed travel to the convention for the Nixon staff, Ehrlichman arranged a new wrinkle called "Nixon's Navy." The Miami Beach strip, a long thin island, is separated from the mainland by Indian Creek, a narrow inlet. Power boats of friendly fat cats were commissioned to ferry Nixonites across the inlet, where staff cars awaited, thus avoiding the horrendous traffic jam that existed along the strip most of the time. The ferry service itself was insignificant, yet it illustrated the Nixon staff's efficiency and devotion to detail.

Part of the Nixon strategy was to have the favorite sons, whose holding action Rockefeller now needed desperately, crumble into the Nixon camp one at a time. Tower had taken the leap even before the convention, and Thurmond had pledged to do so. The day before Nixon's arrival, Governor Dewey Bartlett of Oklahoma caved in, and Governors Louie Nunn of Kentucky and Agnew obliged as Nixon headed for Miami Beach. While Rockefeller urged other favorite sons like Rhodes of Ohio, Romney of Michigan and Senator Clifford P. Case of New Jersey to hold on, his forces tried to sell the idea that if Nixon could only be stopped on the first ballot, he would be finished. The notion was embraced by many members of the press who failed to reckon with two factors: Nixon's considerable second-ballot strength, when other favorite sons would fold, and his centrist position between the two "extremes"—Reagan and Rockefeller. The Nixon strategists obviously wanted to win the nomination on the first ballot and were

341

working diligently to do so. They were ready, though, to hang in beyond that for as long as it was necessary—until the Reaganites acknowledged once and for all that Nixon was preferable to Rockefeller, or the Rocky backers were ready to swallow Nixon rather than Reagan.

For all this, the Reagan action among the Southern delegations was disturbing the three Nixon lieutenants who were most wedded to the Southern strategy—Mitchell, Thurmond and Harry Dent. In Nixon's suite, they briefed him on the Reagan activity and warned that it was imperative that he tell the South again what it wanted to hear—about the pace of desegregation, about the Supreme Court, about the war, about the Vice Presidency. His opportunity would come the next morning, when special regional groupings of delegations would be ushered into his presence. Two of the groups would cover the South, and the second would include seven states he had a good chance to carry—Virginia, North and South Carolina, Kentucky, Tennessee, Florida and Arkansas. (Nixon eventually did carry all but the last, which went to Wallace.) Thurmond was given to understand the candidate grasped what the challenge was, and would acquit himself.

It had been the Nixon plan, in keeping with policy throughout the spring primary campaign, to end-run the writing press at the convention. There was to be no press conference by the candidate, although veteran political reporters argued openly with Klein that it was customary for seekers of the nomination to face the press at least once. Finally at one briefing, the usually mild-mannered and always highly respected political writer of the Washington *Post*, Dave Broder, rose and formally requested that Klein produce his candidate. Suddenly, what had been impossible became possible, and Nixon was ushered in on Tuesday, the morning after his arrival. It was an easy press conference for him: old questions on Vietnam and the same nonanswers, questions about why he was running again and why he thought he could win, about the Wallace threat and the Communist threat. He turned them all aside deftly and moved on to the real business of the day—meeting the regional groups, and especially the two from the shaky South. So much for the press, or so the Nixon camp thought.

It so happened, however, that a Miami *Herald* reporter managed to obtain a tape recording of what Nixon said to the second Southern group. That night, as the Nixons held court for all delegates in a grand, even regal reception full of decked-out Republicans who might have been in Miami Beach even if there hadn't been a convention there, the *Herald* hit the streets with the transcript. For a brief time all the playing it safe, keeping the candidate isolated from the press and gaffe-free, seemed suddenly stripped away.

Actually, most of what Nixon said in private he had said in public, except that he allowed himself a little more freewheeling hyperbole on themes dear to Southern hearts. Concerning what he called "some cockeyed stories that Nixon has made a deal" on his running mate, he told his guests: "I am not going to take, I can assure you, anybody that is going to divide this party." Heavy applause greeted the statement, for it meant to the Dixie group—rightly so—that their fears of Lindsay or Hatfield or Percy on the ticket were unnecessary. Next, he was asked whether he favored "forced bussing of schoolchildren for the sole purpose of racial integration." The problem, he said, exists in the North as well as in the South, and "I don't believe you should use the South as the whipping boy, or the North as a whipping boy. . . . I think that bussing the child—a child that is two or three grades behind another child and into a strange community—I think that you destroy that child. The purpose of a school is to educate. . . ."

On the role of the Supreme Court in this field, he also said what was expected of him: "I think it is the job of the courts to interpret the law and not make the law."

Asked about his support of federal open-housing legislation, Nixon appeared to be saying it was only a tactical move to preserve party unity: ". . . Conditions are different in different parts of the country . . . just like gun control [it] ought to be handled at the state level, rather than the federal level." But since Congress had passed an open-housing law, he said, the prudent thing at the time of the balloting had been to "vote for it and get it out of the way . . . to get the civil rights and open-housing issues out of our sight so we didn't have a split party over the platform when we came down here to Miami Beach.

343

. . . This is the party leadership position exactly. . . . Did they want to keep the issue on the plate? Did they want it on the fire? Did you want to have it come down here to Miami Beach and fight it out then?"

Nixon's long statement was really quite a remarkable political justification for supporting open housing. For any Southern listener who wanted to conclude that deep in the candidate's own heart he was against the idea, the response provided ample latitude.

The *Herald* story was to prove to be an embarrassment and somewhat of a problem during the fall campaign. At the convention, though, it served mostly to charge the batteries of the Rockefeller forces for a time—and to further convince Southerners who weren't at the meeting that Richard Nixon was all right. According to one Republican who attended the second Southern caucus, some delegates were concerned mostly that Nixon might pull a last-minute repeat of 1960—a prenomination pact with Rockefeller. Aides convinced the worriers that this time it wasn't necessary.

Goldwater, meanwhile, and Senator George Murphy of California were trying to put together their version of the "dream ticket"—Nixon and Reagan. According to Goldwater, he approached Reagan and Murphy sought out Nixon to arrange a meeting between the two principals, but Reagan balked, insisting he wasn't interested.

Wednesday, the day of the balloting, again found the action concentrated on the Deep South, with Clif White trying to nibble away at Nixon's strength in key states like Florida, Alabama, Mississippi and Louisiana, and Strom Thurmond busily shoring it up with assurances that Nixon "will not ram anything down our throats." It was such talk as this that gave rise to widespread belief later that Thurmond actually had a veto on the Vice Presidential choice; indeed, some Southern delegates said later that he had said as much in private caucuses. But here again, according to several Nixon intimates, it was more a case of Nixon's leaving the general impression with Thurmond that "things would be all right." If it made Strom feel better to think he had a veto power, then let him.

While Reagan and Rockefeller each continued his frantic

personal wooing, and accordingly flitted in and out of the public and the television eye all day, Nixon remained the isolated, protected monarch. He had selected this fellow Agnew to deliver his nominating speech, and aides were busy going over that, as well as screening the seconding speeches, especially one by Senator Mark O. Hatfield, said to be in the running for the Vice Presidential nomination. The main reason for asking Hatfield to second Nixon's nomination, obviously, was the fact he was one of the most prominent Vietnam doves in the Republican Party. Nixon was pushing the party unity idea as hard as ever; his own moderately hawkish posture already was established and he could afford to have Hatfield on the team—provided, of course, he didn't go too far.

When Hatfield submitted his draft, the Nixon image-makers, Frank Shakespeare, Len Garment and Bob Haldeman, along with political operative Bob Ellsworth, voiced concern that the Senator was pulling Nixon too far off his own course. They summoned Hatfield to the staff inner sanctum and questioned whether the seconding speech, in Hatfield's words later, "reflected Mr. Nixon on Vietnam or reflected me." Hatfield already had told the Nixon camp, in the framework of his possible selection as Nixon's running mate, that he was willing to run but would not consider it if he had to abandon his own position on Vietnam. "For one solid hour I was cooling my heels while they were reviewing my draft," Hatfield recalled. "Finally Ellsworth came out and asked me to walk the hall with him. He had some other wording and wanted me to review it. I looked at it and said, 'No.' It didn't agree with Nixon's own stated position and I told Ellsworth that. I got Nixon's statements out and Ellsworth agreed with me. A few words were changed, and it was worked out. I made it clear I was not going to get up there and give any generalities that didn't indicate my position. I told Ellsworth, 'If I'm to be helpful, I can't say things in such terms that people think I would abandon my viewpoints.' It was difficult enough to stand on my position on Vietnam and be supporting Nixon. If I was going to keep my influence with the peace groups I had to hold my position and give these people something to hang their support of Nixon on."

Hatfield's seconding speech, as delivered, did not overjoy the Nixon camp, and later there was speculation that the speech had killed his chances to be No. 2 on the ticket. Actually, he never was seriously in contention once Nixon had told the Southern caucuses that he was not going to select anybody who would split the party. That observation ruled out not only Hatfield but John Lindsay, who also never was in the picture despite printed pipe dreams to the contrary by the New York *Times*.*

Agnew's nominating speech didn't set the convention on fire either. The theme seemed to be that Richard Nixon had been there all along, and it was about time the party saw him. While the Nixon image-shapers were working overtime to play down their man's past, Agnew predicted to the convention that the people would vote in November "for a man who had the courage to rise up from the depths of defeat six years ago and make the greatest political comeback in history. When a nation is in crisis and history speaks firmly to that nation," Agnew concluded, "it needs a man to match the time. You don't create such a man; you don't discover such a man—you recognize such a man."

The nominating and seconding speeches, and the phony "spontaneous" demonstrations, rolled on through the evening's prime television time. Rockefeller by now had faced the music, but Reagan continued to work on the South. Clif White had reported to him at five thirty that afternoon that the vote would be close and that he had about thirty "possibly movable" delegates—enough to block Nixon's first-ballot nomination. "We can spend the next few hours going after them," White told Reagan. Throughout the evening, Reagan accordingly left the convention floor to meet with individual delegates and small groups in his communications trailer behind the hall, not to preach ideology at this late stage but to argue that Nixon still could be stopped.

The well-disciplined Nixon team, however, was alert, keep-

---

* Apparently in its eagerness to see a hometown boy make it, the *Times* for months before the convention had made Rockefeller seem to be a candidate on the rise. When the convention opened, the newspaper outdid itself keeping his prospects—and Lindsay's—alive long after they had been interred.

ing commitments firm and searching out weak spots themselves. They found one in New Jersey, where the favorite-son candidacy of Senator Case was awash in a flood of factionalism. Nixon had a staunch ally in Frank "Hap" Farley of Atlantic City, and with that wedge and the image of a rolling bandwagon, a split was engineered that turned out to be the first-ballot backbreaker.*

While this maneuvering proceeded, Nixon decided he needed some fresh air. He slipped down a back elevator to a basement garage with his Secret Service men and reporters Relman Morin of the Associated Press and Merriman Smith of United Press International. As they drove north away from the convention hall, Nixon talked animatedly about how both Rockefeller and Reagan had blown their chances by failing to take him on in at least one of the primaries, where a single defeat for Nixon might have stuck him for good with his old loser image. Because they didn't, he said, it was all over on the night of the Oregon primary.

The roll call confirming that evaluation finally got under way at about 1:20 A.M. Utterly confident of victory, Nixon, back in his suite, had agreed to admit a crew from CBS—Shakespeare's old outfit—to record the moment for posterity. The candidate sat alone in the center of the room, in front of the television set. He kept score on a pad, conducting a sort of running civics lesson for prospective son-in-law David, sitting off to one side. Behind on a sofa were Julie, Tricia and Rose Woods, and off to the other side, alone, was Mrs. Nixon. Aides, including Haldeman, Chapin, Garment, Shakespeare, Buchanan, Price and Ron Ziegler, who only recently had come aboard as traveling press aide, stood around.

The roll call went as expected, or better in a few states. The first, Alabama, resisted pressures for a Reagan sweep, and former Congressman James Martin delivered Nixon fourteen votes to

* "Hap" Farley was to be an unwitting contributor to one of the funnier political moments of the year later on when Nixon, speaking about the toastmaster of the annual Al Smith memorial dinner in New York, former Postmaster General Jim Farley, repeatedly referred to him as "Hap." As chuckles spread through the politically knowledgeable audience, one Nixon aide moved quickly to assure laughing reporters that Jim Farley "used to be called Hap"—a circumstance no veteran Democrat could recall.

twelve for the Californian. Wally Hickel came through next with eleven Alaska votes for Nixon to only one for Rockefeller. Barry Goldwater served up all of Arizona's sixteen for Nixon; Winthrop Rockefeller held Arkansas' eighteen as its favorite son, and Reagan kept all of California's eighty-six. Senator Peter Dominick delivered fourteen Colorado votes for Nixon, to three for Nelson Rockefeller and only one for Reagan; Nixon got four in Connecticut to twelve for Rockefeller, and nine in Delaware to three for the New Yorker. Then the first solid sign came: thirty-two out of thirty-four for Nixon in much-wooed Florida, with only one each for Reagan and for Rockefeller (from Governor Claude Kirk, or "Clyde" as the press called him, who was having his own personal Vice Presidential dreams). Without a break in Florida, Reagan was through. ("If it hadn't been for Strom and Goldwater putting the heat on," Clif White told me later, "Nixon never would have gotten the South.")

There remained, however, a slight question as to whether Nixon would go over the top on the first ballot without changes in votes after the first roll call. His own list showed 666 votes, one short of the majority required. The roll call ran through twenty more states, with a few variations in the estimate here and there, before the break came. Then Senator Case demanded that his New Jersey delegation be polled. Obviously, it was cracking; he needed the polling to smoke out the defectors on national television and possibly scare them off. The inevitability of Nixon was in the air now; a split in the forty-member delegation—twenty-two for Case and eighteen for Nixon—gave Nixon about ten more votes than the chart plotters had counted on. Nixon had his margin and then some, and he passed that intelligence on to David. There were satisfied smiles in the candidate's suite, but no tearing up of telephone books or dousing of heads with champagne. They had seen it all coming too long.

The roll call droned on with no more major surprises. Jim Rhodes, who had been sitting on fifty-five Ohio votes waiting for somebody to let him be a kingmaker, sat on them all the way, though by jumping aboard the bandwagon he could have hastened the climax by several states. It was not until the next-to-last state, Wisconsin, that Nixon went over the top. Governor Knowles was the one who finally put him over with thirty mandatory votes for the winner of the state's April primary. On the floor, around the Wisconsin delegation seated at the right front, cheers and victory yells went up as colleagues pounded the back of John MacIver, who had engineered the primary victory. Balloons filled the hall and a band blared the news that Richard M. Nixon had just been nominated as the Republican Party's 1968 candidate for the Presidency of the United States.

Up in the Nixon suite, there was applause and there were smiles, but again no unbecoming conduct. Nixon sat in his chair in the center of the room, and when he surpassed 667, his wife rose from her seat, walked over to him, patted him on the shoulder two or three times, and walked off. The nominee observed that he was pleased it had been Wisconsin, a primary state, that had put him over. Knowles and his workers there, he said, "deserved it"—the honor of making him the nominee. There was a phone call, which Nixon took himself, from Nelson Rockefeller. Rockefeller extended his congratulations, and then the two rivals exchanged small talk about their families, about how good it was to have them there at that historic moment, and about how fine they all looked on TV.

"You're good to call," Nixon said, finally, and hung up. "Nice of him to call," he said to his entourage, who had been listening in. "Good of him to call. . . . He couldn't have been nicer. . . . He said he gave me a good run. . . . He said Ron didn't come through as good as he thought he would." And then the victorious candidate lifted his eyes to the ceiling and down again, and broke into a mischievous grin.

Now the time had come to play the game of consult-on-the-Vice-Presidency. Most of the party leaders had been sent letters soliciting their advice, and the replies had been received and presumably filed someplace. Next would be the traditional smokefilled room. In 1960, having already made up his mind he would select Henry Cabot Lodge, Nixon had called in some three dozen party leaders, feeling certain their choice would be the same, let them say so, and then "acquiesced." This time it would take a bit more finesse, because the man on whom

Richard Nixon already had just about decided certainly would not spring automatically from any similar meeting.

That man was, of course, Spiro T. Agnew, who like himself had risen from humble beginnings and had proved in his own life, as Nixon was to say the next night in his acceptance speech, that the American Dream could come true. A big thing going for Agnew was his domestic posture. The Maryland governor, having survived a very difficult spring on the racial front, including a student revolt at predominantly black Bowie State College and riots in Baltimore, had emerged as hard-line on law and order. He had arrested 227 Bowie students for staging a sit-in at the State House and then closed down the school. After the riots in the wake Dr. Martin Luther King's death, he called in a hundred of the city's moderate black leaders and proceeded to castigate them publicly for failing to dissociate themselves from black militants. In a harangue whose choice of words provided a preview of what was to come more than a year later, Agnew blasted "ready-mix, instantaneous . . . circuit-riding, Hanoi-visiting . . . caterwauling, riot-inciting, burn-America-down type of leader[s]" and accused the moderates of having been "beguiled by the rationalizations of unity . . . intimidated by veiled threats . . . stung by insinuations that you were Mr. Charlie's boy, by epithets like 'Uncle Tom' . . . and of 'breaking and running. . . .'" About eighty of the one hundred blacks walked out on him, but others reacted differently to this new, suddenly turned-around Agnew. Buchanan, who shared that hard line, shuttled Agnew's statements in to Nixon, and they had their impact. "The boss thought this guy was a very tough guy," one aide recalled later.

Yet, on balance, Nixon regarded Agnew, from his Rockefeller association, as a liberal to moderate man who, coming from a border state, would be acceptable to all sections of the party. He was a second-generation American, an "ethnic," and Nixon liked that too. Nixon had no worries, either, that Agnew would upstage him. After several good talks with Agnew on the nature of the Vice Presidency, Nixon was satisfied that they shared the same view of what its occupant's role should be: what the President wanted it to be. "It had to be strictly a second-liner," another insider said later.

Also, at the time at least, Nixon judged that Agnew had the capacity to be President, if it came to that. And finally, in the key judgment, the nominee decided that Agnew would be the least divisive and would cost him least. "The Vice President can't help you," Nixon told close aides. "He can only hurt you." Polls were taken testing relative strengths of the prospects, and the appalling result was that every one of them reduced Nixon's pulling power. "Actually," one strategist said later, only half-kidding, "we wanted to run without a Vice President."

Having just about settled on Agnew in his own mind, Nixon set out to test his choice—not to throw it open—in three meetings with his staffers and chief backers. "The meetings were like the letters," one aide observed afterward. "To make everyone feel he was in on it." A considerable debate, however, already had been under way among the staff members, with the factions best illustrated by the positions of liberal-moderate speechwriter Ray Price and his conservative sidekick, Buchanan. The two young men had engaged in some heated verbal fights over the choice, each believing he was protecting the electability of Nixon. Price wanted somebody like John Lindsay to pull in the Northern industrial states, thus minimizing losses to Wallace in the South. Buchanan and many on the research staff, and also the dispassionate analyst Sears, wanted Reagan, as the man to cut deeply into Wallace in the South and free Nixon to campaign in the industrial North.

Buchanan early in the game submitted a memo to Nixon suggesting this latter division of campaign labors. The polls had Humphrey running about six points ahead at the time, with Wallace at about 18 percent, and most aides were of a mind that Nixon might have to take a chance on a running mate who might hurt him, but also could help him. When the polls started to turn around, however, Buchanan and others dropped the pro-Reagan sales pitch, agreeing that it would be foolish to take what one of them called "a high-risk strategy." Nixon himself rejected going either decidedly left or right on the Vice President; it would be divisive to his main theme of party unity. He would go down the middle with somebody who wouldn't offend anybody, and win the election by himself. He would handle foreign policy, so the second man ought to have some domestic experience, preferably as a governor. There was another reason, too, he didn't want Reagan or Lindsay. He told Buchanan and others he wanted no "superstars" who would outshine him, either on the ticket or later. Despite all the rhetoric about the importance of the Vice Presidency, Nixon saw the office clearly as a subordinate one, to be filled by a man grateful to have it, willing to take orders and carry out the most routine of chores.

Considerable debate ensued over which Republican best filled that requirement—in effect, of being an inoffensive political cipher. Senator Charles Percy brought all the disadvantages connected with Lindsay, without the advantages. Hatfield's Vietnam views were too dangerous. Dan Evans of Washington, never a serious contender, bombed out for sure with an unsatisfactory keynote speech. Romney could bring in a big state but he wasn't credible to the national press corps, so he wouldn't be credible to the voters. Howard Baker would be good but had only two years in the Senate. George Bush of Texas was too young, only a House member, and his selection could cause trouble with John Tower. Rogers Morton too was a relatively unknown Congressman. John Volpe was very strong, as an Italian Catholic and an Eastern governor not offensive to the South.

Perhaps the most surprising name on the list was that of the Secretary of Health, Education and Welfare in the Johnson administration, John Gardner. He was recommended, through Buchanan, by—of all people—the columnist laureate of conservatism, William F. Buckley, Jr. When Buchanan told Nixon of the recommendation, his reaction was: "Gardner? Buckley said that?"

Finally, there was Bob Finch. If there was one political man on the scene in whom Nixon had confidence and at the same time a close and warm personal relationship, it was Finch. But he was, after all, only a lieutenant governor.

The first group of conferees called in, in the early hours of Thursday, consisted of most of those who had been intimately involved in the winning of the nomination—in preparing the groundwork for the primary victories, in writing and researching, in the media magic, in delegate-counting and delegate-wooing. The list included Mitchell, Haldeman, Ellsworth, Kleindienst, Flanigan, Garment, Shakespeare, Klein, Stans, B chanan, Sears, McWhorter, LaRue, Rose Woods, Governors Hickel and Babcock, Senator Hruska, Mrs. Pat Hitt, Holton, Callaway, Glen Olds, Dick Moore, Wayne Hood, Congressman Clark MacGregor and Ed Nixon, brother of the nominee.

In this group, there obviously was more awareness of Nixon's own thinking, and consequently a more intelligent discussion within the framework of reality. Most said they preferred neither an ultraconservative nor an ultraliberal. Nixon, according to several participants, tried not to offer anybody's name, but when nobody threw in the one he wanted, he did, casually: "How about Agnew?" Most indicated they still didn't know much about him. Nixon remarked that Agnew had made a hell of a nominating speech, which he hadn't. "The only reason Nixon said that," one of the intimates said later, "was to give the guy a credential." But Nixon did not tip his hand. According to one insider, he ended the first meeting by summing up: "So your general advice is that I pick a centrist." Which is what he had in mind, anyway.

The second session was for party leaders in Congress and key states, plus a few governors. The list included: Senators Paul J. Fannin of Arizona, Hiram Fong of Hawaii, Jack Miller of Iowa, Karl Mundt of South Dakota and Thurmond; Governors Rhodes and Nunn; Congressmen Leslie Arends, Don Rumsfeldt, Sam Devine and John Rhodes; Presidential losers Tom Dewey and Barry Goldwater; former Attorney General Brownell, Illinois gubernatorial candidate Richard Ogilvie, Dent, Florida's Bill Murfin, Finch and—Dr. Billy Graham. The freeze on the Rockefeller wing and the liberal governors was obvious. Later, when Klein released the list to the press and proclaimed the nominee had consulted with a broad spectrum of the party representing every region, the irreverent Martin F. Nolan of the Boston *Globe* waved the list at Klein and asked him to point out the representatives of the liberal Northeast. Klein told Nolan with undisguised pique that the participants were men "who work in all sections of the country." The failure to consult the liberal bloc spread immediate speculation in the pressroom that Nixon for all his unity was proceeding on the Goldwater let-'em-eat-cake philosophy of 1964, which had told the Rockefeller wing, in no uncertain terms, to get lost.

Nixon conducted himself the same way with the second

group as he had with the first—soliciting views, listening, occasionally throwing out a name when nobody else mentioned it, like the name of Spiro T. Agnew. This meeting broke up at about 5:30 A.M. Goldwater recalls that as Nixon walked to the door with him, "he put his arm around me. 'Could you live with Agnew?' he asked. 'Hell, yes,' I told him, 'he's the best man you could have. He's been firm, and so what if he's not known? No Vice Presidential candidate ever is.' " Thus spoke the man who had picked one William E. Miller to run with him.

There was a break for a little sleep and then a third meeting with ranking party leaders: Dirksen, Gerry Ford, Tower, Ray Bliss, Senator George Murphy, Congressman Bob Wilson, Wisconsin chairman Ody Fish, Texas chairman Peter O'Donnell, Nixon floor manager Rogers Morton and, for the second time, Finch. Once again, Agnew's name surfaced only when Nixon suggested it.

It concerned Nixon that nobody in any of the meetings had volunteered Agnew, or even had picked up the ball once Nixon had offered his name. Though it now was late morning, he would have to have one more meeting. This finally was the meeting of decision. Six key advisers were called in: Mitchell Haldeman, Ellsworth, Tower, Morton and Finch. The last two it soon developed, were on Nixon's final list of four prospects the other two being Volpe and Agnew. Finch and Morton a times were asked to step out of the room. Finally, all six adviser were reassembled.

"Well," Nixon asked, "who should I take?" One of the group seizing this last opportunity, spoke up. "I think it should be Finch," he said flat out. "You know him, you know you car trust him, you know he can handle himself. And he doesn't have to be built up nationally." Mitchell, tight-lipped through this broke in. "You can't do it," he told Nixon. "It's nepotism." Mitchell obviously meant cronyism, but nobody missed hi point. Then Finch jumped up, red-faced and highly exercised "No, I won't do it!" he said with great emotion. "I won't pu myself through it!" Nixon also became agitated. "Bob, come i here," he said to Finch, motioning him into an anteroom. Th two friends walked in and talked for a few minutes out of ea shot of the others. Then, finally, Finch came out, calmed

Nixon, behind him and also calm, turned to Morton. "Call Agnew," he said.

Agnew was honestly surprised when he took the call in his suite at the Eden Roc. After a short talk with Nixon, he hung up, turned to his wife and said, simply, "I'm it." (And in the campaign to follow, he very often would be "it," as a result of some of his less diplomatic observations.) Ellsworth broke the bad news to Volpe and also to Hatfield, telling each at Nixon's instructions that his name had been given careful consideration. Other leading prospects were told the same.

Nixon then descended to the ballroom; it was approaching 1:00 P.M., and the reporters had been cooling their heels for nearly two hours, occupying themselves with guessing games about the identity of the running mate. Nixon mounted a low platform at the front of the room, looking into the battery of television cameras, and reported that his choice was "Governor Agnew of Maryland." Gasps of incredulity greeted the words. Nixon had spent all night arriving finally at his choice, and in that first honest reflex the press expressed its own, and what soon was to be the public's, judgment. Right then was born the question that was to dog the Nixon-Agnew ticket clear through November: "Spiro Who?" Nixon strode out without answering any inquiries, the room awash with shock. One of Nixon's more liberal aides, McWhorter, stood expressionless at the back of the room, his pale face reflecting his mood—and that of many of his colleagues.

Agnew was ushered in. Immediately he encountered a barrage of questions about his recent hard-line tactics toward civil rights demonstrators in Maryland. Already Nixon's choice was being interpreted by the press not as a safe middle-road decision but as an outright law-and-order payoff to the South and to Strom Thurmond for holding the line against Reagan, though Klein specifically denied that the South had been given a veto.

Agnew insisted he was "pro-civil rights" and was for its "implementation," not simply "the elaborate programming and distribution of money which is intended to bring about the equal opportunity and the justice that everyone talks about." And then he added the message that for all the later snafus would make him clearly in tune with the Nixon campaign: "I

355

expect fully that no civil rights can be realistically achieved without the restoration of order, without the abandonment of the condoning of civil disobedience."

Agnew said he would "welcome the chance" to run in what a questioner called "the Northern city ghettoes such as New York and Chicago." But as strategy would have it, he would not get much chance. One of his hopes, though, was to come true more quickly than he ever imagined or wanted. "The name of Spiro Agnew," he readily acknowledged, "is not a household name. I certainly hope that it will become one within the next couple of months." It did not take that long. One of the least remembered observations in the ensuing campaign was a report from Klein that the primary factor in Nixon's choice was his confidence that Agnew could take over the Presidency if necessary. Klein quoted Nixon as saying that if another man had to put "his finger on the button, I'd feel safer having his finger on it."

The Agnew selection predictably angered many in the party's liberal wing. After leading the Rockefeller draft effort for so long, he had gone over to the other side—ideologically as well as tactically—and now had been rewarded for it. An eleventh-hour effort was mounted to oppose the choice on the convention floor, and to get John Lindsay to be the standard-bearer. The Nixon forces headed it off by getting Lindsay to make one of the seconding speeches for Agnew—a welcome out for Lindsay. In their desperation, the rebels turned, cruelly, to the battered George Romney. He had dreamed of this convention as the one that would nominate him for President, and now they persuaded him to mark it by being humiliated as a losing Vice Presidential candidate.

As the roll call proceeded, Romney sat stony-faced in the Michigan delegation, his famous square jaw thrust out, listening to his lopsided defeat mount. He had the manner at first of a man who thought he just might win, but as the landslide built, and state delegations one after another confirmed Nixon's choice of Agnew, Romney broke into a broad grin and began to joke. As the roll call reached Utah, he lifted his hand and said, laughing: "There's a Romney in there. I'm going to get a vote." The delegation was polled and sure enough a Romney—his sister-in-law—came through for him. At the end, Romney rose and asked the convention to make Agnew's choice unanimous. It did, and he pledged to work for the ticket in Michigan. It was, for a man who less than two years earlier had been regarded by many as the front-runner for the Presidential nomination, a particularly sad ending.

All that remained now was Nixon's acceptance speech—that epic pronouncement on which the nominee had begun working during his last trip to California and which reportedly had taken the bulk of his time, thought and energies at Montauk. Yet when the cheers of the convention hall had died down on Thursday night, and the words came floating over the delegates' heads and into millions of living rooms across the land, they had a very familiar ring.

First there was a report from Mamie Eisenhower that the heart of her husband, as he lay critically ill in the hospital, "is with us. She says that there is nothing that he lives more for, and there is nothing that would lift him more, than for us to win in November. And I say, let's win this one for Ike!" Ronnie Reagan—"The Gipper" in *Knute Rockne, All-American* of years before—must have felt he had heard that line before. Much of what came next, reporters who had traveled regularly with Nixon indeed had heard before—sometimes in the very words, sentences and paragraphs of "The Speech" of 1966–67–68. Yet, now that the long hard road back was only one step away from triumph and vindication, it was vital that the self-proclaimed "centrist" candidate identify unmistakably the constituency that had brought him this far, and that he would need to carry him the rest of the way through this most turbulent of election years.

"As we look at America, we see cities enveloped in smoke and flame," Nixon said solemnly. "We hear sirens in the night. We see Americans dying on distant battlefields abroad. We see Americans hating each other; fighting each other, killing each other at home. And as we see and hear these things, millions of Americans cry out in anguish: Did we come all this way for this? Did American boys die in Normandy and Korea and Valley Forge for this?

"Listen to the answers to those questions. It is another voice,

357

it is a quiet voice in the tumult of the shouting. It is the voice of the great majority of Americans, the forgotten Americans, the non-shouters, the non-demonstrators. They're not racists or sick; they're not guilty of the crime that plagues the land; they are black, they are white; they're native born and foreign born; they're young and they're old. They work in American factories, they run American businesses. They serve in government; they provide most of the soldiers who die to keep it free. They give drive to the spirit of America. They give lift to the American dream. They give steel to the backbone of America. They're good people. They're decent people; they work and they save and they pay their taxes and they care. . . . And this great group of Americans—the forgotten Americans and others —know that the great question Americans must answer by their votes in November is this: whether we shall continue for four more years the policies of the last five years. And this is their answer, and this is my answer to that question: When the strongest nation in the world can be tied down for four years in a war in Vietnam with no end in sight, when the richest nation in the world can't manage its own economy, when the nation with the greatest tradition of the rule of law is plagued by unprecedented racial violence, and when the President of the United States cannot travel abroad or to any major city at home without fear of a hostile demonstration—then it's time for new leadership for the United States of America. [The 1,300 faithful who heard Nixon launch his 1968 campaign at the New Hampshire Highway Hotel on the night of February 3 surely knew where *they* had heard that before.]

"Look at our problems abroad. Do you realize that we face the stark truth that we are worse off in every area of the world tonight than we were when President Eisenhower left office eight years ago. . . . We all hope in this room that there's a chance that current negotiations may bring an honorable end to the war. And we will say nothing during this campaign that might destroy that chance. But if the war is not ended when the people choose in November, the choice will be clear. . . ." And more familiar phrases: ". . . To the leaders of the Communist world we say, after an era of confrontations, the time has come for an era of negotiations. . . . I am proud to have served in an administration which ended one war and kept the nation out of other wars for eight years afterward. . . . For five years hardly a day has gone by when we haven't read or heard a report of the American flag being spit on, and our embassy being stoned, a library being burned, or an ambassador being insulted some place in the world, and each incident reduced respect for the United States until the ultimate insult inevitably occurred. And I say to you tonight that when the United States of America falls so low that a fourth-rate military power like Korea will seize an American naval vessel in the high seas, it's time for new leadership to restore respect for the United States of America. . . ."

And these: ". . . Some of our courts in their decisions have gone too far in weakening the peace forces as against the criminal forces in this country. Let those who have the responsibility to enforce our laws, and our judges who have the responsibility to interpret them, be dedicated to the great principles of civil rights. But let them also recognize that the first civil right of every American is to be free from domestic violence. . . . If we are to restore order and respect for law in this country, there's one place we're going to have to begin: We're going to have a new Attorney General of the United States of America!" (This last drew a thunderous ovation, though nobody could seem to remember when any new President in a transition of parties in power ever had kept the old Attorney General.)

And still more from "The Speech": ". . . For those who are able to help themselves, what we need are not more millions on welfare rolls but more millions on payrolls. . . . Let us build bridges, my friends, build bridges to human dignity across the gulf that separates black America from white America. . . ." The lines were familiar, but they were effective; so effective, in fact, that the Nixon media men taped them and made extremely heavy use of them in the television campaign throughout the fall.

Yet there was at last, at the close, something new. Nixon spoke somberly of seeing a child who "hears a train go by. At night he dreams of faraway places where he'd like to go. It seems like an impossible dream. But he is helped on his journey through life. A father who had to go to work before he finished the sixth grade sacrificed everything so that his sons could go to college. A gentle Quaker mother with a passionate concern for peace quietly wept when he went to war, but she understood why he had to go. A great teacher, a remarkable football coach, an inspirational minister encouraged him on his way. A courageous wife and loyal children stood by him in victory and defeat. And in his chosen profession of politics first there were scores, then hundreds, then thousands and finally millions who worked for his success. And tonight he stands before you, nominated for President of the United States of America. You can see why I believe so deeply in the American Dream."

It was, for so important a speech, incredible corn, and on top of that, unoriginal, with heavy traces of Martin Luther King's famous "I have a dream" oration of the 1963 Civil Rights March on Washington. Yet Nixon delivered it with utter solemnity and sincerity, and from all appearances in the hall, it was taken in the same spirit by all the other believers in the American Dream who listened. Spiro Agnew, embarking on his campaign to become a household word, had said to the convention a few minutes earlier: "I stand here with a deep sense of the improbability of this moment." It was a sentiment abundantly shared by those who knew Agnew and those who did not, and by the millions who had seen or heard about Nixon's "last press conference" in California six years earlier, and had pronounced him politically deceased. Now, no longer could it be denied, or ridiculed or wished away. Once again, Richard M. Nixon was one of only two men who realistically would have a chance to be the next President of the United States.

15

The Master Plan

HAVING staked all and won on the premise that the Republican Party in 1968 would listen to the results of the Presidential primaries, Richard Nixon and his strategists now proceeded on the premise that the Democratic Party would not. And again they were right. It would, without doubt, be Hubert Humphrey on the Democratic ticket. From Miami Beach, Nixon and Agnew, after a stopover at President Johnson's Texas ranch for a briefing on the state of international affairs, went directly to southern California, where the campaign organization established a planning base at a resort near San Diego called Mission Bay.

From the start, Nixon made it clear his personal team would run the campaign, with headquarters in New York. Republican National Chairman Ray Bliss would stay on in Washington to attend to his "nuts and bolts," but that was all. Nixon spoke derisively in private of "those hacks" at the national committee and accordingly set his own course. That meant, of course, that the Captain Bligh of the Nixon battlewagon, John Mitchell, would be at the wheel, answerable only to the candidate himself.

Mitchell's reputation as an unsmiling martinet already was well established. Commander in World War II of the PT-boat squadron in which John F. Kennedy served, Mitchell ran an extremely tight, no-nonsense political ship. Younger members of the team got short, irritated shrift from him ("I never deal with junior officers," he said once), and senior officers of the line didn't fare much better. On one occasion, the former chairman of the Joint Chiefs of Staff, Admiral Arthur W. Radford, dropped by the New York headquarters to offer his help. He identified himself and a secretary informed Mitchell, but she was told to tell Radford: "He's too busy." Another aide, recognizing the admiral, personally ushered him into Mitchell's office and introduced him. "Oh, yes," Mitchell said, "I remember you. I was a commander in the Pacific in World War II." Silence. The aide, moving into the breach, diplomatically told Mitchell he was asking the admiral to perform this or that impressive-sounding but really window-dressing job. "Fine," the old commander said. And with that, he turned and went back to his desk, leaving Radford standing there without so much as a "Dismissed."

Nixon admired and needed Mitchell's toughness, but it was a blessing not without its drawbacks. Among elected Republicans, Nixon leaned heavily on his old friends in Congress, and many of them were treated as if they were just so many Admiral Radfords. And then there was the matter of Murray Chotiner. Nixon's old political war-horse had been poking around the operation during the spring, making a covert inspection trip of his own into New Hampshire in the early stages at the behest of campaign aides who had been under fire from Mitchell in New York. Mitchell was nervous about the cool approach that limited Nixon's exposure in the state while Romney raced around, and the advocates of the strategy needed a knowledgeable independent reading. So they took it upon themselves to tell Chotiner that Nixon wanted him to go up and check out the operation. Chotiner came back with a report to Nixon that all was as it should be. Mitchell didn't like that; he was not the kind who liked anybody poking around, or anybody going over him to the top. (Of the New Hampshire excursion, Chotiner told me later: "I came away with certain opinions." Murray Chotiner is a man who tells you he came away with "certain opinions" rather than telling you what he learned; he enjoys the image and the mystery of the inside agent.)

When Nixon wanted to move Chotiner into the New York operation, Mitchell was not enthused. Nevertheless, in the summer, Nixon told Chotiner to go down to Miami Beach for the convention. He was part of the post-nomination deliberations on Agnew (though his name did not appear on the list of participants released) and afterward went out to Mission Bay. Nixon moved him in as a special assistant to Mitchell, and Chotiner was assigned fourteen key states to monitor, including five of the "Big Seven." His job was to check on everything needed from campaign buttons to influential endorsements. Nixon retained a high regard for his old California friend's industry and attention to detail. Others on the staff were concerned that Mitchell, in his pursuit of the Southern and border states, was not giving sufficient attention to the pivotal industrial states. This was something Chotiner could do without publicity or fanfare—an important element because Nixon, for all his admiration of Chotiner, was aware of the man's poor public image as a political gut-fighter and fearful his presence could rejuvenate tales of the Voorhis-Douglas days and the "old Nixon." Mitchell didn't like it much. Chotiner moved into an office near Mitchell's at the New York headquarters on Park Avenue and, as is his style, plunged into his task. All fall Mitchell tried to find out what Chotiner was doing. Very insecure about his relationship with Nixon, Mitchell seemed to suspect Chotiner was waiting for the right moment to take over, and indeed other staffers had the same impression. Chotiner for his part did nothing to discourage that impression; he did what he thought needed doing and asked nobody. Captain Bligh didn't care for such insubordination from his unwanted first mate, but was too unsure of how he stood with Nixon vis-à-vis Chotiner to demand a showdown. Actually, Mitchell in his fretting did not take into account the political requirement that Chotiner be kept under wraps during the campaign.*

* Mitchell's concern over Chotiner's influence with Nixon continued even after the election. During the early days of the new administration, Mitchell, then organizing its political structure, was confronted with a request from Chotiner to be the new Republican national chairman. Aware now that Nixon could not afford to have Chotiner "out front," Mitchell and Haldeman agreed that Chotiner be moved into the national committee to run it behind the scenes. It may have been Mitchell's hope that Chotiner would get lost in the bureaucracy, but as soon

At Mission Bay, the game plan for running against Humphrey was hammered into final form. It included three basic issues: Vietnam, crime and violence, and inflation. Senator John Tower, chairman of Nixon's "key issues" committee, flew in, met with the nominee and reported that the campaign would concentrate on the "growing crime rate, growing civil disobedience and the causes for the restlessness among minority groups, the growing deterioration of buying power, inflation . . . and of course the involvement in Southeast Asia." What he did not spell out, but what was the substance of discussions between Nixon and his advisers, was that as the front-runner Nixon would avoid specifics on the key issues, particularly Vietnam. "The counsel was that he was not to spell them out in detail," one of the chief advisers on issues said later. "We had to be flexible. There was always the uncertainty of what Hanoi would do on the war, and there was Johnson. Nixon always was concerned that he'd pull a rabbit out of the hat. We knew he couldn't end the war, but we knew too he'd try a gesture sooner or later that might be interpreted that way. In the end, he did."

The emphasis on the crime rate, civil disobedience and restlessness among minority groups had, obviously, two purposes: to tap the general discontent among whites and to counter George Wallace with a velvet-glove version of the mailed fist with which Wallace saluted the white backlash. Nixon was not to mention Wallace head-on or get specific on this issue either, but by offering in outline a more respectable alternative, he

---

as the Californian was given a desk at the committee—on the quiet—he characteristically began to move in, and not so quietly. The chairman at the time, Ray Bliss, saw the ploy—rightly—as pressure on him to get out, but resultant publicity about Chotiner (some of it as a result of Murray's being too talkative) , and the displeasure of Rogers Morton, the man selected to replace Bliss, forced Chotiner to be shunted aside once again. Shortly afterward, Nixon had staff aide Bryce Harlow find a properly obscure hiding place for his old mentor. Knowing he probably could not then give him any job requiring Senate confirmation, he appointed him as general counsel to the Special Representative for Trade Negotiations. In that post, in an office only two blocks from the White House, Chotiner reaped the meager political fruits of his longtime diligence and loyalty. It was not until Nixon had been in the White House a full year that he felt he could permit Chotiner to "emerge." Then he appointed him as a special counsel to the President, in time to help with plans for the 1970 Congressional elections.

could give his allies in the South and blue-collar North raw material with which to lure Wallacites into the GOP ranks.

Finally, there was the prime reason for the overt decision to blur Vietnam and other key issues: a mood of supreme confidence that Nixon already had enough strength to win. The Gallup Poll that had buried Nelson Rockefeller, giving Nixon a 40–38 edge over Humphrey even before the Democratic fiasco in Chicago, reinforced that mood. Nixon surely would go up a few points, and Humphrey down, after the Democratic convention, and then Nixon would have enough right there to win in a three-cornered race. He just had to hold on to what he had. Thus, the same conservative attitude that had governed the primary period—campaigning "above the battle" as though Richard Nixon already were the nominee, as though he were in a dress rehearsal for the real thing—was projected for the fall campaign. Now, as the nominee, he would campaign as though he already had been elected—lofty, statesmanlike, not getting bogged down in detail, not stirring up clouds of controversy or trivia that might blur the Presidential image he had been building throughout the primaries.

"Image"—the word continued to dominate the discussions of Nixon insiders, and their heavy flow of memos and private polls. In the primaries, the big challenge had been to dissipate their man's loser image, and they had succeeded beyond their fondest hopes. Now, considering the growing public sentiment for change and the utter disarray in the opposition party, all they had to do was change the focus of their image-building; to take the product and keep it credible for about ten more weeks.

Accordingly, another key word, just as it had been through the primaries, was "control." And when that word entered the equation, the advertising and media image-makers entered right with it. They had been the architects of the strategy to keep Nixon away from the writing press in the primaries, and to serve him up on radio and television in carefully preplanned and often preedited doses, and it had worked. Now that the strategy in the general election was to be the same as in the primaries—to stress unity, to hold the ball, to kill the clock, Frank Shakespeare, Harry Treleaven and Company would be more important than the "issue" men like Price, Buchanan and

Richard J. Whalen, author of the best seller on Ambassador Joseph P. Kennedy, *The Founding Father*. John Mitchell, who more than ever now was the boss of the campaign, was not big on issues anyway. He was an implementer, and that was his strength with Nixon.

With some of the "issue" men, though, it was a source of irritation and conflict. They had hoped that once the primaries and the convention were out of the way, the political types whose main interest was holding delegates and party leaders, and who put increasing stock in the magic of the Madison Avenue boys, would move aside and let the advisers on matters of substance have their inning. Specific discussion of issues had been waffled long enough. A nominee for President should say what he would do if elected. But it wasn't going to be that way. Finally, Whalen, with illness at home, packed up and left. "What really does the man stand for?" the disgusted Whalen said to the *Times'* Semple at one point. Other Nixon insiders tried to smooth his departure, suggesting it was only temporary and that he would come back. But he never did, and the image-makers continued to ride high to the very end.*

The slicing of the Nixon fall budget, presented to the nominee by finance chairman Stans, made this fact abundantly clear from the start. According to Stans later, about $9,000,000 had been spent already to win the nomination, and another $24,000,000 would be spent in the fall—about twice Goldwater's budget in 1964. Of the $24,000,000, more than half would go for television, with heavy emphasis on the regional, hand-picked citizen panel shows that presented Nixon to his best advantage—relaxed, confident, informed, friendly, benign.

The actual cost figures outran Stans' first estimates, but in a phenomenal fund-raising job, he produced. The preconvention budget had started at $5,000,000 but nearly doubled, in spite of the one-sided nature of the campaign. For the fall, Stans told Nixon he would raise $20,000,000, but heavy television outlays raised that figure by another $4,000,000, making the 1968 Nixon drive for the Presidency by far the most costly in Ameri-

---

* Incredibly, after this history, the White House in the summer of 1969, in quest of an author to write the Nixon administration version of the events related in this book, approached Whelan. He considered the offer but finally turned it down.

can history. Stans worked the familiar lodes of the Republican wealthy and the general yearning for a Republican victory. He managed by the end of the campaign to have enough to pay all bills without resort to any special television appeal, or any eleventh-hour pitch to faithful fat cats accustomed to bailing out the party. The largest single fund-raising event was a network of twenty-two $1,000-a-plate dinners in mid-September, with Nixon speaking from New York on closed-circuit television. It brought $5,500,000 into the campaign fund and ruled out the necessity of borrowing a penny.

The plan for the $1,000-a-plate dinners was approved at Mission Bay. Stans immediately started phoning from there to find dinner chairmen. At the same time, he dispatched 10,000 letters to prominent Republicans asking each to give $1,000 to get the fall campaign started. "We made all our money plans at Mission Bay," Stans recalled later, when he was Nixon's Secretary of Commerce. "We met daily, and when I left, we had the fund-raising program ready to go. This gave us a terrific edge over the Democrats, who hadn't even picked their candidate yet, and were split. My approach as finance chairman was to free the candidate from any money worries whatsoever. Ours was by far the most expensive campaign ever, and I never once had to go to him to ask him to do anything to raise money." It was a statement nobody on the Democratic side could have made.

Another element in the campaign of control, and for Nixon a major one, was a tight rein on his running mate. Agnew had not yet said anything to inspire "the boss" to hitch up the leash, but after Nixon's 1960 experience with Cabot Lodge, the head of the 1968 ticket was taking no chances. Communications between the two entourages always had plagued Nixon and Lodge in 1960. Nixon felt afterward that if he could have got to Lodge fast enough, or could have had a political man screening some of his observations, statements like Lodge's "pledge" that there would be a Negro in the Nixon Cabinet could have been avoided.

The original 1968 plan called for John Sears to shuttle between the two entourages. In selecting Agnew, Nixon had in mind his dissatisfaction with Lodge, and he believed he had picked a man the second time around who could think for himself. At a cocktail party for the press at Key Biscayne right after the convention, he had said of Agnew: "There is a mysticism about men. There is a quiet confidence. You look a man in the eye and you know he's got it . . . Brains. This guy has got it. If he doesn't, Nixon has made a bum choice." Agnew's performance at a press conference immediately after his selection, Nixon said, indicated Agnew would display "poise under pressure" in the campaign. And later, on leaving Mission Bay, Nixon explained that "I wanted a candidate who could campaign nationally, not a sectional or a regional candidate, whose views at least were consistent with mine, so that I could entrust him with major responsibilities." But all that was before Agnew served notice that he would need a full-time monitor. In short order once the campaign began, Sears was sentenced to be tourmaster on the political equivalent of a two-month excursion to American Siberia. Herb Klein, as the chief press spokesman at Mission Bay, probably did not realize how accurate he was to be when he told reporters that Nixon and Agnew had discussed plans to build "the most closely coordinated dual campaign in America's political history."

The 1968 game plan confirmed at Mission Bay had an eye to 1960 in another respect too. Nixon long before had made up his mind he would not be locked into any foolish pledge to visit all fifty states, as he had then. There were seven key states in the coming election—New York, California, Pennsylvania, Ohio, Illinois, Texas and Michigan—with 210 of the needed 270 electoral votes. In 1960, Nixon had won only his native California and Ohio; in 1968, he and his strategists decided, he would have to take at least four, while holding the other states he had won in 1960. Thus, after making swings to each region—but not each state—in the nation, Nixon would concentrate heavily on the Big Seven, with the most extensive and expensive private polling operation in American political history, by Opinion Research Corporation of Princeton, constantly probing targets of opportunity. It would be up to Agnew to maintain the presence elsewhere, and especially in the Southern and border states vulnerable to George Wallace.

The focus on the Big Seven required steps to bind up the relatively few wounds inflicted on Republican leaders, predominantly liberal, in the primaries and at the convention. Nixon had decided against an immediate embrace in Miami

Beach after his nomination, preferring to solidify his position with the conservatives who were the backbone of his winning drive. His failure to consult the liberals on the choice of Agnew had raised eyebrows and sent typewriters clacking, but it avoided what very likely would have been an even bigger row, with a potential for a lasting split. Instead, he elected to let the Agnew choice sink in for a few days, for tempers to cool, and then he picked up the telephone in Mission Bay and began to apply the soothing syrup.

He called Rockefeller, Romney, Shafer and the other governors who had been aloof toward him—Harold LeVander of Minnesota, John Love of Colorado, John Chafee of Rhode Island (later his Secretary of the Navy), Dan Evans of Washington—and others outside the fold like Senators Chuck Percy and Jack Javits. Some came to Mission Bay—Senator Thruston Morton, Congressmen Clark MacGregor and Bradford Morse. The lines were going out to the liberals, and the doors were being swung open. Those who didn't come were promised a personal visit in a trip Nixon planned after his eight-day stay in California. Nixon had not forgotten his own mistakes of 1960, and he had not forgotten Goldwater's mistakes of 1964. He talked to Goldwater by phone, conferred personally with Reagan, and drew pledges of active campaign aid from each, though Goldwater would be busy seeking election to the Senate in Arizona (causing no grief in the Nixon camp). A bevy of "surrogate" candidates, who would tour the country in Nixon's behalf, came to Mission Bay for a seminar on what to say; they included Senators Hatfield and Baker, Governors Volpe and Hickel (both charter members of the Nixon Cabinet), Congressmen MacGregor, Morse, Donald Rumsfeld (Nixon's first antipoverty chief), William Brock and George Bush, and—the Ed Sullivan of the Nixon panel shows, Bud Wilkinson.

By the time Nixon left Mission Bay for his first fence-mending visits to the liberal governors, the whole package had been tied up: the kill-the-clock strategy; the issues that were to be alluded to but not really explored; the prime focus on TV image-making and the consequent isolation of the press; the money to pay for this most costly demonstration of media politics in history; the harnessing of Spiro Agnew; the concentration on the Big Seven; the extended olive branch to the liberals. It all looked so promising, so efficient, that the talk turned at a getaway press conference to the prospect that Mission Bay might be the next summer White House. Nixon dismissed the idea. "I don't like to be away from the action for more than three or four days at a time," said the man who a year later was to shift the whole White House operation to the West Coast for the summer and spend a record amount of time away from his Washington office in his first Presidential year.

Nixon's string of visits to the liberal Republican leaders was a resounding success. If they didn't really prefer him, they knew he was right about the need for party unity, so they fell quickly into line. For his part, Nixon made it easy by being solicitous of their views and their assistance. One of the first stops was in Michigan, to salve the sensitivities of the much-abused Romney. The governor, not one to bear a grudge, pledged full support to the Nixon-Agnew ticket. When asked how he squared that support with his personal competition with Agnew for the Vice Presidential nomination, Romney said with characteristic inelegance and self-deprecation: "What happened in Miami is similar to someone who had a little stomach tension and then gets a good big burp. . . . I think I enabled the delegates down there to have a good burp." Rhodes and Shafer also closed ranks quickly, and on one productive day in New York, Nixon bagged four of the party's most prominent liberals—Rockefeller, Lindsay, Javits and Massachusetts' Senator Ed Brooke.

After the tour, Nixon returned again to Key Biscayne to sit out the Democratic convention. He knew it made no sense for a candidate of one party to compete for the public's attention when the opposition party was choosing its nominee. In 1968 particularly, Nixon had no interest whatever in pulling the spotlight away from Chicago. He had said piously at Mission Bay he would have no comment on the Democrats until they had completed their convention, but about a week before it opened on August 26, Nixon met privately with Republican leaders in Illinois and told them: "Never has a party been more deeply divided. . . . They're going to split that party at the convention, whichever way they go. Let's get those that they leave behind."

Concerning the Democratic split, Nixon's crystal ball never

was clearer. The nomination of Hubert Humphrey was a fore-gone conclusion, but it was not to happen before all the dissident anguish and emotion built up against the Johnson-Humphrey leadership had exploded in headlines and on television screens across the land.

Trouble for the Democratic Party had been expected by politicians other than Richard Nixon, but few foresaw the degree to which the party would impale itself. The death of Robert Kennedy, in the greatest hour of his political recovery in California, had assured the nomination of Humphrey, yet it did not prevent a headlong plunge over the final cliff by the antiwar, antiregular forces of Gene McCarthy. Amid much other secondary jousting, the battle for the soul of the party was joined over a platform plank on Vietnam. The shattered supporters of Kennedy, now marching on their own or behind the stand-in candidacy of Senator George S. McGovern of South Dakota, collaborated with the McCarthy forces in hammering out a Vietnam plank that would call for a complete bombing halt in North Vietnam and a serious start to negotiations with all interested parties represented. Important in that effort also were those regular Democrats who wanted desperately to pull Humphrey out from under Johnson's bankrupt policy and personality. John Gilligan, the young Democratic candidate for the Senate in Ohio, was a leading arbiter. Johnson, though, applied heat through his loyal friend and lieutenant, Governor John B. Connally of Texas, and Humphrey, as Johnson's man, lacked the will and the conviction to break loose, to do as his chief advisers implored him—to become his own man. The antiwar plank failed by a 2–1 ratio, and Humphrey was hooked.

Connally won that one for Johnson, but he was personally unhappy because the convention had jammed through a resolution killing the unit rule for convention delegate selection and voting that perpetuated the autocratic party in the South. And some said his mood got darker later when he was summarily passed over as the Vice Presidential nominee.

The defeat of the antiwar forces delivered a major tactical advantage to Nixon. Humphrey now would run with the Johnson Vietnam policy on his back, making him an easy target. Not only that, Humphrey would be trapped on the issue and therefore not eager to bring it into the campaign. That suited Nixon perfectly. Had Kennedy lived and been the nominee, or Mc-Carthy, Nixon's free ride on the Vietnam issue likely would have been over. Either man would have backed him to the wall to say how he would end the war in Vietnam, and in the process would have converted the 1968 Presidential election into a clear referendum on Vietnam. Nixon might have won in such a test, but if he had, he probably would have had to tell the American voters exactly where he stood. Because neither Kennedy nor McCarthy was the Democratic nominee, Nixon was able to dissemble all the way to November on the single major issue before a nation choosing its next President.

There were, of course, other tactical windfalls to Nixon out of the Democrats' catastrophe in Chicago. As the fight over the Vietnam plank inside the Chicago Amphitheater became more and more emotional and hopeless, street protest in downtown Chicago intensified. McCarthy, determined to make his stand within the hall and nonviolently, had asked his supporters not to come to Chicago for the demonstrations planned by the radical-dominated National Mobilization to End the War in Vietnam. Its leaders billed the demonstrations as peaceful in intent and then went to considerable lengths to acquire the necessary city permits for use of public parks. But a combination of tactics, tempers, police stupidity and brutality soon turned peaceful assembly into confrontation. With the taunts of some of the more militant demonstrators penetrating the thin veneer of police self-control and tolerance, clubs started to swing and heads to bleed; as they did, hundreds of mild, nondemonstrating McCarthy and Kennedy supporters became outraged and, in the fashionable term, radicalized. What McCarthy at the outset had feared—that his fight would be misdirected out of the hall and into the streets—had come about.

The impact was politically devastating. Television, unable as a result of Mayor Richard Daley's restrictions to shoot the downtown street scenes "live," had to film the rioting and the police strong-arming on tape, process the tape and then run it on a delayed basis. Often the inflammatory tapes were shown repeatedly. Unfortunately, in the chaos, these facts of mechanics were lost on the home audience, leaving the widespread impression that all of downtown Chicago was one nonstop riot, raging simultaneously with the acrimonious histrionics going forward on the convention floor miles away.

At the Conrad Hilton, with violence exploding in the street outside, Hubert Humphrey prepared for the Presidential nomination he long had coveted. Millions around the nation watched with a mixture of awe and disgust as television conveyed the image of a political party committing suicide, but Humphrey, always the optimist, professed to be thrilled. When his nomination was assured on the first ballot, and the TV camera swung to his wife, Muriel, seated in the convention hall, the nominee walked over to the screen and—kissed Muriel's likeness.

In Key Biscayne, Richard Nixon picked up a phone and talked to the man who, along with Senator Edmund S. Muskie of Maine, would be opposing him and Agnew in the fall campaign. Nixon wished his opponent good luck, but he now knew, more than at any earlier moment in his long climb back, that the Presidency of the United States again was within his grasp, if only he could let nature take its course. The only man who could beat him now, it seemed abundantly clear, was Richard Nixon himself, committing a major political blunder. And this he was more determined than ever not to do.

Herb Klein stated the situation after the Democratic fiasco tersely and accurately: "They are going to be spending the next four weeks picking up the pieces. Meanwhile we will be ready to go next week with a unified party."

Not all the Democratic pieces were picked up by Humphrey. The Democratic candidate did not know it at the time, but as soon as the convention was over, and a disgruntled John Connally headed back to Texas, Nixon agents were camping on his doorstep. Just as they had fielded Agnew on the first hop after Rockefeller's March decision not to run, they began at once to woo Connally ardently. Fellow Texan and fellow conservative John Tower, Fred LaRue and other Southern Republicans applied their persuasive powers—and a spoken or implied promise of a major plum in the Nixon administration—and Connally played ball. He soon was instrumental in acquisition of oilmen in the Nixon hierarchy in Texas, and recruitment of other money men and politicians in this key state, largest in the South with twenty-five electoral votes. Nixon wanted to have a prominent Democrat in his Cabinet, and Connally as a former Secretary of the Navy would be the perfect choice to be his Secretary of Defense—if, that is, he could help Nixon carry Texas. Later in the fall, when Nixon talked of having a bipartisan Cabinet, Connally was the Democrat he planned to appoint to make it bipartisan. But it was not to work out that way.

By now, Richard Nixon's campaign machinery had been checked out for the Republican candidate's treadmill dash, and had been pronounced in top working order. Television, as Stans' budget and Shakespeare's plans had indicated, would provide the perfect isolation booth. Yet it was not politic to be all that obvious. Summing up what had been achieved as he left Mission Bay, Nixon had acknowledged that he planned to use television more effectively than he had in 1960, but he added: "I am not going to barricade myself into a television studio and make this an antiseptic campaign." Now, with the Democratic convention a shambles and the time at hand for Nixon to move out into the final drive, he had to demonstrate the truth of that statement. And, technically, he was telling the truth.

In September and October, Nixon would not lock himself in anywhere; what he would do in a sense was more deceptive. With his Madison Avenue cast in the van, he would apply in those two months all the lessons and techniques developed in his media-oriented two-track drive through the primary states to victory at Miami Beach. As in the primaries, the first track would be the traditional barnstorming campaign, augmented now with even more hoopla, balloons, cheerleaders, bands, screaming faithful and soaring, haranguing, partisan speeches. Show-biz promoters, like Tommy Walker at Disneyland, were signed on to assure professionalism. Behind this dazzling façade again would flow the media campaign—the subdued, carefully controlled exposure of the candidate on radio and television; the low-key presentation of the quiet statesman discussing issues in a format tailored deftly to him and particular segments of the electorate. Also, there would be the television spots, more than forty of them in at least three different categories: showing

Nixon himself; issue-oriented photo montages with Nixon as narrator; endorsements of Nixon by other prominent Americans. Prepared largely by Eugene S. Jones, the independent documentary maker who produced the award-winning *A Face of War* on Vietnam, they would flood the nation's television screens, inserted in everything from soap operas to time-outs during weekend football games. Nixon even would appear in one of *Laugh-In*'s quickie spots, without fanfare, asking, incredulously, "Sock it to *me?*"

Ever since the advent of television, of course, Presidential candidates had been working both sides of the street, campaigning from pavement and studio. But never before had electronic campaigning been used to so dominate a Presidential bid. Elaborately staged public rallies and transcontinental jet-hopping in the next two months would provide the excitement and the sense of motion that the American public had come to expect from its Presidential aspirants. Meanwhile, the media segment would function out of the spotlight, largely protecting the candidate from the physical ordeal, the tensions and the political pitfalls of traditional stumping—including hot pursuit by the accompanying press.

It was like the blitzing linebacker in football who barrels into the offensive backfield only to find that the quarterback, instead of passing as expected, already has handed off to a running back. Most of the American press, accordingly, would spend the fall of 1968 chasing the wrong play. And in an important innovation in press handling that was to have great tactical significance in the Nixon administration to come, Herb Klein would sit in the press box (the New York headquarters) and phone down overall strategy while young Ronald Ziegler carried the daily plays in from the bench. Ziegler was ideal for the role. Himself a pretty good football player at Xavier University of Ohio before transferring to the University of California, he was well trained to execute the plays given to him and not to be overly concerned with the philosophy behind them. Bright and properly wide-eyed as required in any political dispenser of the truth, young Ziegler had honed his talents for meeting the public as a tour guide at Disneyland. Upon graduation from California, he briefly was a press aide to Republican state legislators in Sacramento and then found a home in advertising and public relations. As a protégé of Bob Haldeman in the Los Angeles office of the J. Walter Thompson agency, Ziegler soon had some of the better accounts. When Haldeman managed Nixon's losing gubernatorial campaign in California, he brought in Ziegler, then only twenty-two years old, as a press aide to Klein. Ziegler kept his hand in by doing volunteer work in George Murphy's 1964 Senate campaign and in Finch's 1966 race for lieutenant governor.

Ron for all his boyish charm was sharp and capable. He had one major advantage that made him particularly valuable and particularly effective in his job; he was a card-carrying "flack"— a PR man. Unlike many newspapermen who, like Klein himself, switched over to handle a candidate's press relations and continued to think of themselves as newspapermen, Ziegler had no such hang-up. His loyalties, his purpose and his concept of his job were undiluted by viewpoints inculcated in many reporters-turned-flack by their early years in the press corps. He was not one who, like so many other press secretaries, would belly up to the bar with reporters and after a few drinks give out with the old "I used to be a newspaperman myself" routine. He never was torn, as some of his colleagues who had been reporters often were, between protection of his candidate and the public's right to know. That was journalism school stuff; on the field, it was "us" (the Nixon team) against "them" (the press). It was, for both sides, much the better arrangement. Unlike Klein, who liked to talk to reporters and editors about "our business"—a habit he continued in the Nixon administration when he became "director of communications"—young Ron, though sociable and likable if excruciatingly evasive, always knew which team he was on, and wanted it that way.

There were those in the press corps who looked down on Ziegler because he was merely a dispenser of the word rather than author of it. But in so doing, they underestimated his ability to perform that job extremely well from his boss' point of view, and the importance of a good performance in that job in the Nixon campaign. Insulating the candidate from a once-hostile, hard-to-control press corps, without causing an open revolt, was critical to the Nixon two-track campaign strategy. Ziegler, in his blue-suit, button-down, Wilshire Boulevard self-discipline, was what the situation required. Later, at the White House, he too extended his campaign function from insulation of the candidate to insulation of the President. Nixon and Klein both appreciated the tactical importance of having on the press firing-line a man who did not make policy; Ziegler always could shrug his shoulders, say he didn't know the answer to a question and offer to get it—and be believable. The fact was that on the big ones he *didn't* know. It was better for Nixon that way; anytime a tough question came up, Ziegler's innocence could buy time for the preparation of a careful response, if a response had to be made at all. And from all outward appearances anyway, Ziegler *liked* being the dispenser. There was none of that self-guilt in him that often infected former reporters who "defected" into public relations; he *was* public relations in all its flower.

Day after day through September and October, Ziegler would stand guard as the national press, in record numbers and at record cost, climbed aboard specially equipped jets to follow Richard Nixon the Barnstormer across the country and back again several times over. What they would see and write about in large measure was the sideshow, served up to a few hundred thousand voters a day at most, while Richard Nixon the Television Personality talked calmly and intimately to millions in their living rooms—unimpeded and with relatively few exceptions unmonitored by the press.

Reporters, in the year 1968, were mousetrapped, not only by the Nixon strategy but by events. Even if the major news organizations saw what Nixon was up to, and some did, they were operating in a year and in an explosive climate of violence and the unexpected; even more than in previous years, they had to cover the live body. After the assassinations of Martin Luther King and Robert Kennedy, the reporter who let any candidate out of his sight for whatever reason did so at his professional peril. Given these circumstances, it was a relatively easy matter for the Nixon media politicians to end-run the press.

The traditional campaign in itself was to be a considerable deception. The Nixon staff chartered three Boeing 727 jets, one for the candidate and staff, called the *Tricia,* one for the writing press (and paid for by them) called the *Julie,* and one for the radio and television newsmen and cameramen, still photographers, light holders and the rest of the American *paparazzi.* Except for a few pool reporters permitted aboard the candidate's plane each day, the press seldom would have an opportunity to speak to the candidate, with even the pool reporters restricted. Gone were the old days of a Presidential candidate mixing freely and often with reporters en route—an extremely valuable contact to newsmen attempting to gauge the man and his campaign. Press conferences would be few and stilted; statistics on Nixon's accessibility would be padded by what came to be called "press availabilities"—often hit-and-run confrontations at the base of his plane on landing, when local radio reporters would crowd around and ask simple questions Nixon had answered dozens of times before.

(On the only occasion I was a pool reporter on the *Tricia,* early in the campaign, fellow poolers Peter Lisagor of the Chicago *Daily News,* Tom Ottenad of the St. Louis *Post-Dispatch* and I wandered up uninvited before takeoff to say hello to Nixon in his private compartment. Nixon seemed a bit uneasy at the intrusion, but talked cordially and graciously with us for several minutes, telling about his plans for a short whistle-stop in the Midwest later on. When we returned to our seats, Lisagor set out to write a pool report to our colleagues on the press planes. Ziegler, sitting next to me, saw the pool report and offered to duplicate it on the *Tricia*'s copying machine. He went up to the front of the plane with the report—right past the copying machine into Nixon's private compartment. In a few minutes he came out again, gave the pool report to one of the staff girls and took his seat next to me. "Did you show our pool report to Nixon?" I asked him. Ziegler looked somewhat dismayed. "What?" he asked. I repeated the simple question. "Why, yes," he replied. "I thought he'd like to see it." "What right did you have to do that?" I asked him. "That was *our* pool report." Ziegler professed not to understand why I was exercised. After all, he was *not* an old newspaperman himself; how was he to know? He assured me that nothing in the report had been changed. That, I told him, was beside the point. While we appreciated his offer to duplicate the report, if he was going to run in and show it to the candidate we could do without his help. "Your point is well taken," the accommodating young press aide said. He assured me he would not make that mistake again.)

While the candidate thus ran for President wrapped in cellophane, his staff kept the traveling press docile with first-class seating and treatment on the specially equipped planes—including telephones that were plugged in whenever the tour was on the ground—and first-class hotel accommodations along the way. The staff also kept the press busy with routine and trivia. Speech handouts and position papers were ground out with maddening efficiency; something always was being spoon-fed to the press to keep the boys' typewriters humming and to keep them sufficiently occupied so they would not be driven to nag the candidate for not stating a specific position on Vietnam.

Although the reporters covering the barnstorming campaign were aware of the simultaneous media campaign, it proved extremely difficult for them to cover it. When Nixon would go into a city and tape a television talk or panel discussion with local hand-picked citizens, newsmen usually were barred from the studio. Local television interview shows sometimes were off-limits as well. Although reporters might be provided with transcripts of the interview the next day, by that time they were off to another city halfway across the country. The whole experience tended to have a lulling, even hypnotic effect on the reporter who covered Nixon for any period of time. For veterans of Presidential elections, it was Valhalla—up at a reasonable hour, late morning departure, perhaps one noontime appearance and another in the late afternoon, with the nights blocked out for TV tapings or study and rest. The Nixon campaign came to be called "The Country Club," and for good reason.

At his post-convention press party at Key Biscayne, Nixon had sat down at a piano and played, "Let Me Call You Sweetheart." It got a laugh then, but it really was the marching song of all those on Nixon's staff who had anything to do with the press. All were under specific orders to spread sweetness if not light, and they obeyed the orders. Having come this far, nothing could be permitted to happen in September and October that might upset or even intrude on the master plan drawn at Mission Bay.

16

Treadmill to a Cliff-Hanger

THE drive that Richard Nixon liked to call "the final" began from New York on September 3, jumped to Chicago, San Francisco, Houston and back East, all in the first week, running smoothly both in the streets and in the TV studios. Before takeoff, he reviewed his early itinerary and stressed his determination to meet the press' needs. Speeches would be scheduled in time to be published in afternoon and morning newspapers as well as shown on the morning and evening television shows, which meant few late-night affairs. With so many reporters covering him, he said, individual interviews were "not properly in the cards," but he would hold background sessions from time to time. "We want it to be an open campaign," he said, "just as we had an open convention."

The two-track Nixon strategy was invoked on the very first stop, Chicago, still recovering from the Democratic disaster of the week before. There were suspicions that the timing was intentional, to provide a contrast, but actually the Chicago visit had been planned long before. Nothing so important as the opening of the campaign could be left to last-minute improvisation, and when Nixon hit Chicago—at the lunch hour, of course—the results of weeks of preparation showed. A huge outpouring of backers, estimated by police at more than 400,-000, packed the downtown Loop area six deep or more, waving and shouting as confetti poured from office windows high above onto the nominee and his wife, perched in the back of an open car. Nixon, grinning happily, waving, his arms thrust over his head, shaking hands, received a remarkable greeting, pre-planned or not. It took him forty minutes to go nineteen short city blocks. With him were two recent backers of Nelson Rocke-feller, Thruston Morton and Ed Brooke, to demonstrate he had a unified party behind him. Many signs appeared to be hand-painted, but the similarity of the legends, like NIXON'S THE 1, AGNEW 2, betrayed their mass production.

That was the first track—visual contact and excitement for the writing press and the evening TV news shows. Nixon then retired to the Presidential Suite at the Sheraton Blackstone, where he remained all afternoon, resting and preparing for the second track that night. He had a long massage and then sat around, talking with aides, studying the backgrounds of the hand-picked panelists he would face on a $35,000 three-state regional TV hookup, and pondering what questions they likely would ask. The panel was selected carefully with just the right balance—one housewife, one businessman, one "ethnic," one Jew, one Negro, one Chicago newsman, one downstate news-man. The show was shown live from Studio One at WBBM-TV, the very place where Nixon in 1960 had debated John Kennedy for the first time—and lost. But this time the "opposition" was much softer. Nixon had no difficulty projecting his benign, statesmanlike image, fielding easy and familiar questions about "the new Nixon," Agnew, and law and order, while declining to make any partisan attack on the violence at the Democratic convention. The 300 faithful Republicans brought in as the audience applauded lustily after every answer. So did the im-partial moderator, adoring Bud Wilkinson. Despite Herb Klein's efforts, the press was barred from the studio by Shakespeare and shunted to another room, where they monitored the show through a window.

The next morning, before departing for California, Nixon held a press conference that gave the afternoon papers a new lead. Criticism of either the Chicago police or the demonstra-tors would not be helpful, he said. "What happened in Chicago

381

was not the agony of Chicago," he said with understanding sympathy. "It was not the agony of the Democratic Party. It was the agony of America. It could have happened in any other city." (He did not have to add, "Chicago papers and TV please note.")

In San Francisco there was another smaller motorcade through Chinatown. In 1962, on a similar tour, there had been a large banner greeting him in Chinese. Arranged clandestinely by the Woody Allen of Democratic politics, Dick Tuck, it had read: WHAT ABOUT THE HUGHES LOAN?—the anti-Nixon slogan of the California campaign, referring to a controversial loan to the Nixon family from financier Howard Hughes. This time, the efficient Nixon advance team made certain there was no such nonsense. At Santa Clara University that night, Nixon delivered his "forgotten Americans" speech and then was off to Houston. Wallace strength threatened to destroy Nixon's chances in Texas, but Nixon was wary about taking him head-on. "I will not mention Wallace," he told the pool reporters on his plane en route, "but I am going to frontally say what is the difference, what is the diametric difference between Nixon and Humphrey." And then, before 30,000 Texans at the Miller Memorial Amphitheater, Nixon borrowed the Wallace jargon. Noting that the Alabamian was saying there was "not a dime's worth of difference between Nixon and Humphrey," Nixon added: "There's not a dime's worth of difference between the policies Hubert Humphrey offers America and the policies America has had for the last four years." And again, he didn't say much specifically about the policies Richard Nixon offered America.

The intentional fudging, though following the script of the media boys and Nixon's own cautious, front-runner's approach, disturbed the two late recruits from the liberal wing, Morton and Brooke. Their concern spilled out at a press conference in Houston. "I feel sure," said Morton, a former national chairman and one of the GOP's most refreshing hip-shooters, "that our candidate is not going to let this heady wine [of large crowds] keep him from being definitive. It's awfully easy, when you've seen crowds such as we've had, to say, 'Well, is it raining out?

I'm not sure, it might be a drizzle.' This is something that—a trap that I think we fell into in 1948. It's not going to happen this time. . . . I just want to keep on warning everybody—Republicans from the county chairman level up—'not to sit on your duffs now, boys, and don't do what we did in 1948.' " Brooke echoed Morton's sentiments. Both men were politicians and understood the tactical use of trimming positions, but they told Nixon he might be going too far and generating a negative image that the Democrats could counter effectively. Anything that might tie Nixon to his past was dangerous.

Nixon later sought to counter the Morton and Brooke concerns, which had been spread by the press. "I have now taken positions, completely forthright positions, on one hundred and sixty-seven major issues in this campaign," he said, "more than any of the other candidates in the primaries and the final campaign. . . . I will continue to do so." One could just see some minion a day earlier poring over past speeches, plucking the "major issues," writing them down—on a lined yellow legal pad, no doubt—and numbering them as he went along. About a month later, the Nixon campaign released a crash-produced soft-cover, 194-page book called *Nixon on the Issues*. It included 227 subject headings in 42 categories. Among the "major issues" discussed were a Vietnam settlement, American prestige, the ABM, rebuilding NATO, the nuclear nonproliferation treaty, the *Pueblo,* Wallace, the Presidency, the Supreme Court and crime. And then there were these: East-West cultural exchange, the plight of Soviet Jewry, the Latin American heartland, the Nigerian civil war, "the American Dream," order, progress and justice, order and dissent, order and hope (three separate subjects), the Hill-Burton Act, credit unions, the cattle industry, retired military pay and fishing.

In Nixon's first foray into the South, Ed Brooke, the first black to be elected to the U.S. Senate since Reconstruction, dropped off the tour—not because Nixon was still trimming or, an aide insisted to reporters, because the entourage was moving south, but because Brooke had pressing business in the Senate. The official schedule for the first day, September 11, was a typical Nixon day on the campaign trail, 1968 version:

Departure: Press busses will depart from Nixon-Agnew Headquarters 450 Park Avenue (57th St. and Park Avenue), New York City.

10:15 A.M. EDT—Baggage should be at 450 Park Avenue for proper tagging and transporting to airport.

10:35 A.M. —Busses depart 450 Park Avenue enroute La-Guardia Airport, Butler Aviation Terminal.

11:15 A.M. —Arrive LaGuardia Airport—Butler Aviation—Board United Airlines #727 charters.

11:55 A.M. —Depart LaGuardia enroute Raleigh, N.C. Hot lunch will be served on board. Flying time 1:20.

Raleigh, N.C.:

1:15 P.M. EDT—Arrive Raleigh, N.C. Durham Airport.

1:30 P.M. —Depart airport enroute University of North Carolina.

2:00 P.M. —Arrive University of North Carolina, Chapel Hill.

2:35 P.M. —Arrive Phillips Hall Computation center for computer test demonstration conducted by Irwin Danziger, computer specialist.

3:10 P.M. —Depart University of North Carolina.

3:40 P.M. —Arrive Raleigh Durham Airport.

3:55 P.M. —Depart Raleigh, N.C. enroute Charlotte, North Carolina. Coffee and sandwiches on board: Flying time: 35.

Charlotte, N.C.

Hotel Headquarters: Whitehouse Inn, West Trade Street, Charlotte, N.C. (704-332-1121).

4:30 P.M. EDT—Arrive Charlotte Airport, Charlotte, N.C.

4:50 P.M. —Depart airport for downtown Charlotte.

5:10 P.M. —Arrive downtown Charlotte for rally.

5:20 P.M. —Mr. Nixon Remarks.

6:00 P.M. —Mr. Nixon Concludes. Depart enroute Hotel.

6:50 P.M. —Arrive Whitehouse Inn. Working Press Room—Senate Rooms E & F on the Mezzanine. Press Lounge—Senate Rooms A & B on the Mezzanine.

9:00 P.M. —Depart Whitehouse Inn enroute TV Studio.

9:10 P.M. —Arrive WBTV—Charlotte. Mr. Nixon will be interviewed by Ken Alvord, News Editor of WBTV, Charlotte, and Charles Whitehurst,

News Director of WFMY–TV. The program
will be shown on both stations at a later date.
NOTE: *Press will not accompany Mr. Nixon to
taping.*

10:45 P.M. —Taping concludes—Return to Whitehouse Inn.
11:00 P.M. —Arrive Whitehouse Inn. Overnight.

The presentation of the day's schedule here serves a purpose
beyond demonstrating the easy pace and the precise planning of
the Nixon operation. It shows how the candidate was able
largely to control the flow of news. Not shown was a morning
press conference with Javits and Lindsay in New York, providing party-unity headlines for the afternoon papers. Then, on
arrival in Charlotte, Nixon released a major policy statement,
for the evening radio and TV shows and the morning papers,
calling for postponement of Senate ratification of the nuclear
nonproliferation treaty, in the wake of the Soviet invasion of
Czechoslovakia. By the time Nixon finished speaking at the
Charlotte rally, most newsmen traveling with him had all the
raw material they could handle for the day, and were not
particularly concerned that they were excluded from a local
taped televison interview that night. Those who wanted to were
permitted as in Chicago to watch on closed-circuit TV, but not
in the studio. Use of Nixon's remarks was embargoed until the
following night, when they went out to North and South Carolina viewers. By that time, the reporters were off to Cleveland
and Indianapolis and had other stories to write. Not all were
able to tell their readers that Nixon in a closed Charlotte TV
studio had thrown a tremendous bone to the South—out of TV
range of Northern viewers.

In that TV interview, Nixon said he believed that the 1964
school desegregation decision of the Supreme Court was correct.
And he could not condone "freedom of choice" plans that
actually were a subterfuge to perpetuate segregation. But when
he was asked whether he agreed with the withholding of federal
funds to "bludgeon a local community into accepting an
agency's doctrine" (a classic of objective questioning), Nixon
replied: ". . . [to] say that it is the responsibility of the federal
government and the federal courts to, in effect, act as local

385

school districts . . . to use the power of the federal treasury to withhold funds or to give funds in order to carry [desegregation] out . . . that kind of activity should be very scrupulously examined and in many cases I think should be rescinded." In hard practice, though, the threat of withholding federal aid had been the only truly effective prod in the government's hands to gain compliance with the 1954 decision in many Southern school districts.

Senator Brooke, learning of Nixon's Charlotte criticism, said he planned to ask him about it. "I just wonder what he had in mind," Brooke said, "that would be more effective." So did reporters. When they sought a press conference for clarification from Nixon, they instead were put off by aides' explanations. It was a perfect example of how the pesky national press was being outmaneuvered and bypassed while the candidate pitched his message to a sectional audience.

The Nixon operation was not always able to skirt trouble, however. The problem of harnessing Agnew cropped up earlier than expected. On the popular Southern and Middle American issue of "law and order" and the dangers of the "permissive society" he was fine, but when he wandered into other areas, staffers held their breath. The first serious excursion concerned Humphrey, who had irritated Agnew by describing Nixon as a "cold warrior." While Nixon was preparing for his Southern swing, Humphrey already was encountering fierce and unmerciful heckling and picketing from anti-Vietnam students wherever he went. In Houston, Humphrey spied a headline on a story about Marine troop replacements and in desperation seized it to claim U.S. troop withdrawals were already under way. Immediately his own administration slapped him down, saying it wasn't so.

Agnew, talking to a small group of reporters in Washington, accused Humphrey of being "squishy soft"—of being "soft on inflation, soft on Communism and soft on law and order over the years." In calling Nixon a "cold warrior," Agnew said, Humphrey was mistaking "firmness for inflexibility." He and Nixon, he said, were "not going to be squishy soft as the administration has been" on crime and on "knowing your enemies." Humphrey, he said, "begins to look a lot like Neville

Chamberlain . . . maybe that makes Mr. Nixon look more like Winston Churchill." Asked if he was going to be the attacker in the campaign, Agnew replied: "I guess by nature I'm a counterpuncher. You can't hit my team in the groin and expect me to stand here and smile about it."*

The words "soft on Communism," immediately reviving memories of Joe McCarthy and the Red-hunting days of oratorical excess that for Nixon were better left unremembered, appalled the strategists on "the mother plane." It was a line that had to be dropped at once, and Agnew was so informed. On Capitol Hill, Republican leaders Dirksen and Ford said they didn't think Humphrey was soft on Communism, and in Rochester, New York, Agnew called a press conference and backed down. He hadn't really recalled the significance attached to the words "soft on Communism" in the past, he insisted. He meant nothing personal by them; they were just some words he happened to use. "If I left the impression that the Vice President is not a loyal American," he said, "I want to rectify that. . . . I said 'squishy soft' and I'm not proud of it."

There were, in short order, other words that Agnew just happened to use, and with each usage the men on "the mother plane" shuddered. In Chicago, in mid-September, he observed that "when I look out at a crowd, I don't see there a Negro, there an Italian, there a Polack. . . ." Called on the last phrase, he professed he didn't mean it to be a slur. And shortly afterward, on his plane en route to Hawaii, he walked down the aisle and saw Gene Oishi, an old Japanese-American associate from the Annapolis press corps, snoozing. Agnew inquired: "What's wrong with the fat Jap?" Those who knew Agnew in Annapolis assumed he was talking in the same tone of good-natured ribbing prevalent between governor and reporters around the State House, but others could not believe their ears. Some woke Oishi and told him what Agnew had said. The reporter at first sloughed it off, but on landing telephoned his

---

* In a TV interview in Nashville in October, 1968, Agnew said of the coverage his gaffe-filled campaign was getting: "Some people in the news media seem dedicated to the destruction of Agnew the candidate. . . . Some reporters are . . . attempting to portray me as some kind of political stumblebum. And I don't react kindly to that kind of treatment."

wife and told her, and she was furious. He finally agreed to let other reporters use the incident. When the account first appeared, at the bottom of a story in the Washington *Post,* one of Hawaii's Democratic Congressmen, Spark M. Matsunaga, also howled. That gave the story even wider publicity, and in the context of his earlier comments, Spiro—everybody was calling him Spiro now, or Spyro—was in hot water again.

At a luau on the island of Maui, Agnew—genuinely upset at the implication that he had meant the flip remark as an ethnic slur—discarded his formal speech and made an almost tearful apology before a crowd of several hundred Hawaiians. He recalled that his father was a poor Greek immigrant and he himself had borne the brunt of ethnic slurs as a boy. He likened his remark to harmless "locker-room humor." What has happened, he asked, to the "camaraderie that exists among men which allows them to insult one another in a friendly fashion?" Some reporters considered the apology the most effective speech of his campaign up to that point. He apparently had not grasped that the "fat Jap" remark could be taken by anyone as a slur. Later, in conversation with some reporters accompanying him, he said Polish-Americans kid among themselves by calling each other "Polacks" and then, with no detectable trace of humor, added: "Some of my best friends are Jewish!" Because of concern that the press was becoming anti-Agnew, a small informal get-together was arranged in Agnew's suite on Maui, but it disintegrated into heated arguments over a wide range of subjects, from the war, to the right of dissent, to what constitutes a slur. When Agnew again repeated his "locker-room humor" defense, Homer Bigart of the New York *Times* wagged his finger at his host and intoned: "Governor Agnew, one thing you must remember. Locker-room humor should never be equated with running for Vice President of the United States." Agnew sheepishly agreed.

In a speech on the island of Kauai, Agnew tried to pass off the "fat Jap" remark as an old statehouse joke, and said he hoped Americans had not lost their sense of humor. "I referred to him in certain slang they use themselves," he said. Oishi told his colleagues, though, he was not aware of ever having been called that before. On departing from Honolulu, Oishi put the whole incident into perspective. As the plane climbed, the pilot announced over the loudspeaker: "And out to your right you can see Pearl Harbor below." Oishi leaned forward and shouted into the ear of an Agnew staff man: "Bombs away!"

The irrepressible songwriters of the press and television had a field day with these Agnewisms. Charles Quinn of NBC wrote this one aboard the Agnew plane, to the tune of "Love and Marriage":

> Law and Order, Law and Order,
> Can't find Justice on my tape recorder.
> I believe in let live,
> But please don't let it be permissive.
> Japs and Polacks, Japs and Polacks,
> Want to keep them on their own blocks.
> Then the press grows shrewish,
> Though some of my best friends are Jewish.

Meanwhile, over on the Nixon plane, reporters were busy on this one, with Nixon supposedly singing to the chorus of "Can't Keep My Eyes Off of You":

> Squishy-soft on Communism, without much thought of realism,
> Ted Agnew's got a way with words, that Cabot Lodge did not.
> So cool it, Spy-ro, don't knock the Polack vote,
> And let the Jap sleep, he just got off the boat;
> You take the low road, I'll keep my moratoriums high . . .

Agnew did cool it pretty much after that. But there were other slips, like the time in Tennessee a reporter on a TV panel asked him why he wasn't going into more ghetto areas. "When you've seen one slum," Agnew said blandly, "you've seen them all."

The terrible press Agnew was getting, according to one insider, did not overly concern Nixon. "The manure wasn't sticking to him [Nixon]," this insider recalled later, "and Agnew was becoming pretty popular in the South." But the goofs bothered Agnew. He didn't like the image of a bumbler and a clown he was gaining; he didn't want to be a drag on the ticket, and he so told Nixon. He was especially sensitive because his Democratic counterpart was getting a very favorable press. Humphrey's running mate, Muskie of Maine, was proving to be the hit of the campaign—reasoned, low key, even Lincolnesque, some said. The contrast with Agnew was obvious and sharp. For a time it seemed as though the matter of the Vice Presidency might vie for public interest with the drab Nixon-Humphrey race, and indeed the Democrats did all they could to focus on Muskie and Agnew. On Sundays, when the Nixon and Agnew campaigns usually abandoned all pretense of motion and took the day off, Nixon would call Agnew, give him a pep talk and tell him not to worry.

Yet Agnew did worry. A speechwriter, Steve Hess, was assigned to take some of the spontaneity and resultant surprise out of his campaign, and at the outset Agnew was suspicious of the presence of a watchdog, though the basic strategy of holding on and protecting the ticket's lead in the polls also required caution from Nixon as well as from Agnew. "We spent a lot of time trying to figure out how to waste time," one staffer said later. "It was like a basketball game. We had lost the last time, so this time we scored a few baskets and used our ball-handling team. All those 'work weekends' in Key Biscayne—planes flying down there—just to sit around. Nixon was even going to the Olympics in Mexico City right in the middle of the campaign to kill a few days, but we decided it was too obvious."

Agnew, however, could not be blamed for feeling the reason he was being kept under wraps was his early goofs, because it *was* a major reason. The watchdogs were under orders to show Agnew in public in the industrial North just enough to spike rumors that the Republican Vice Presidential candidate had been kidnapped. One night the Agnew plane flew into Pittsburgh. There was a motorcade to the hotel and the candidate did not emerge again until six o'clock the next night, when he motored about fifty miles out for a speech and back again. When he departed Pittsburgh the next morning without having made a public appearance in the city, the local papers howled. The entourage went on to Youngstown, Ohio, for a rally in a movie theater, then to the Detroit Airport, where Agnew got into a car, drove about 300 yards to the airport motel, went inside and did not emerge until early evening. Then he was driven to a rally at Cobo Hall in downtown Detroit, and back to the airport motel.

The same day in Detroit, Hubert Humphrey had been campaigning like there was no tomorrow. Some of the reporters with Agnew complained that the candidate was being hidden. They began to pressure Agnew's press man, Herb Thompson, for a news conference or some explanation about what was going on. Thompson so informed a senior aide. Suppressing a grin, the aide replied: "Herb, you go tell those bastards that if they want to come along with us, there's good food and drink on the plane, and we'll drop down once in a while and get a night's sleep at a good hotel. Tell them that after the next stop we're going to get up in that plane and just fly around. If they want to come with the next Vice President of the United States, okay. Tell them we'll land after a while and then we'll all go into town and take a nap."

In the overall scheme of things, the "Agnew problem" was a relatively minor one. Agnew was working hard and doing the ticket some good where it counted—in the critical border states where George Wallace otherwise might take enough away to make Humphrey a winner. But every time Agnew goofed, it put pressure on Nixon to say something, and when he failed to submit to questions, it simply underlined his strategy of isolation. After his own remark on desegregation in Charlotte, and the Agnew "soft on Communism" slur, Nixon declined to hold a press conference. Ziegler, asked whether Nixon was "withdrawing from us," replied, "Not at all, certainly not." But, quite obviously, he was.

As often was the case when the press complained, Nixon did hold a press conference, several days after the Charlotte speech and the Agnew attack on Humphrey. In it, he backed off the Charlotte remarks somewhat, saying as President he would approve withholding of federal aid to recalcitrant school districts. What he had meant to say in Charlotte, he insisted, was that he approved such action in cases of local subterfuge to avoid integrating schools, but not simply as an economic tool to achieve integration "in a positive way through bussing and the like."

As for Agnew's remarks, Nixon noted that his running mate

had retracted the "soft on Communism" statement; he and Agnew would question the policies but not the loyalty of the Democratic candidates. Then Nixon tried to turn the whole incident onto the offensive. Humphrey's campaign manager, Larry O'Brien, had charged on a nationwide television panel that Nixon had been wooing the Wallace vote. He hoped, Nixon said, Humphrey "would show the same degree of statesmanship in perhaps getting Mr. O'Brien and some of his real hatchetmen to perhaps be a little more responsible in their statements." Far from wooing the Wallace vote, Nixon insisted, his aim was to woo black voters by offering policies to bring them into the mainstream of American economic life. The phrase "law and order" was not, Nixon said, a code phrase for racism. Actually, he noted, blacks suffer most from domestic street crime and hence would benefit most from "law and order." If there was any hanky-panky involving the Wallace vote, Nixon said, it was Humphrey's. He had received "reports from the South," he said, of collusion between Humphrey and Wallace to boost the Wallace vote in some Southern states. Such action sought to deprive him, Nixon said, of enough electoral college votes to win, thus forcing the decision into the Democratic-controlled House of Representatives.

That Wallace was a thorn to Nixon in the South there was no doubt. Yet the Alabamian's candidacy had its advantages too. Nixon could spout the law-and-order rhetoric and yet maintain his position as the centrist between Humphrey and Wallace. And tactically, Wallace provided Nixon with the perfect excuse for not debating Humphrey. Nixon had said during the primaries, in dodging debates with Romney and then Rockefeller, that he thought Republicans should debate Democrats, not other Republicans. He had no intention, however, of debating Humphrey as long as he remained ahead in the polls. The strategy of eating the ball did not call for anything so risky as a debate, with the possibility that a slip or a bad performance or a poor physical appearance might conjure up 1960 and the loser image again. Football fan Nixon knew that when you're ahead with time running out, you don't risk an interception with a pass. Nixon said he believed nationally televised debates between the two major candidates were in the public interest. But

Congress, which had to vote an exemption from the equal-time requirement of the Federal Communications Commission, would have to "work out an arrangement whereby we can have that kind of debate—not a three-way debate in any way. . . . I do not believe it would serve the public interest to build up any third- or fourth-party candidate by giving him equal time, and I would oppose that. . . ."

Humphrey, of course, wanted and desperately needed the debates—two-way or three-way. Trying somehow throughout September to get untracked from the aftermath of the Chicago convention and the strangling umbilical cord that tied him to Johnson, Humphrey was sinking ever deeper in the polls. But there were too many Republicans and allied Southern Democrats in Congress to get the equal-time matter off the back burner. So Nixon continued to treat Wallace like some pesky gnat, worth an occasional wave of the hand but nothing more—and certainly not equal status in a national television debate.

Nixon's desire to avoid a debate with Humphrey also was grounded in the simple fact that Humphrey's campaign was in dire financial straits, and Nixon, thanks to Stans' efforts, could buy TV time at will. So why give your opponent mass-audience exposure he could not buy on his own, with the additional possibility that he might beat you in debate? The Nixon answer, as it had been all through the primaries, was reliance on one-sided, controlled television. If you paid for it, you could do what you wanted with it. In city after city as he toured the country, Nixon starred in the unrehearsed but carefully staged local and regional "citizens' panels" in which selected patsies asked easy questions. With few exceptions it was, for Nixon, like Sandy Koufax pitching against a bunch of Little Leaguers. In some cases, because of scheduling difficulties, local panelists selected by the Republican organization and approved by Shakespeare and Co. were flown in to New York, put up in hotels and then ushered into the TV studio for the show. They were allowed to ask their own questions, but predictably most of the inquiries were pushovers for the veteran candidate.

Sometimes a newsman was placed on the panel to lend some semblance of authenticity to the show. But the one selected with few exceptions was a man whose specialty was something other than national politics. The only newsman-panelist with a national reputation as a political expert was the elderly dean of the California press corps, Earl C. "Squire" Behrens of the San Francisco *Chronicle.** Nevertheless, the news types selected did give Nixon some anxious moments. In his Philadelphia panel, a talk-show host and newspaper columnist named Jack McKinney sought to cut through the controlled atmosphere by ridiculing it and asking Nixon why, for nearly two years, he had not appeared on any of the uncontrolled national network panel shows. "I've done those quiz shows," Nixon replied, "until they were coming out of my ears." The audience of about 240 hand-picked Republicans cheered and applauded, and Nixon took the offensive. McKinney had blasted the citizen-panel format as offering no opportunity for following up questions, and the candidate invited him to proceed. The panelist obliged by criticizing Nixon some more for dodging and for "asking the voters to go to the ballot box with a wink and a smile" on the Vietnam issue. Nixon came back with his standard justification for saying nothing, and not surprisingly it carried the day with the ecstatic faithful in the studio audience.

Another reporter on the panel, from Camden, asked Nixon about the Professor Genovese flap in the 1965 New Jersey gubernatorial campaign. The candidate handled it neatly—he favored academic freedom, but no employee of a state university had a right to "call for" the victory of an enemy while he was on a government-owned campus. McKinney jumped on Nixon's words. Genovese had not said he "called for" a Viet Cong victory, he insisted. What he said was—but this time Nixon broke in; he quoted Genovese exactly, that he would "welcome the impending victory" of the enemy. McKinney insisted it wasn't the same. Nixon said he would leave it to the audience to decide. Afterward, McKinney told newsmen the show had been "very slick. . . . I don't think you can finalize a question with

* Behrens elicited a classic Nixonism by telling the candidate he had heard of "a gossiping campaign . . . that you are anti-Semitic." Nixon, after a long recital of his record—including his nomination by Richard Cardinal Cushing as "Man of Goodwill of the Year" for not raising the *anti-Catholic* issue in the 1960 campaign—offered: "Squire, you will note that I didn't go to the usual answer to that question that some of my best friends are Jews and that I have a lot of people on my staff who are. *That is all true.* . . .

an applause-getting technique. You just dissipate the questions." The media boys were overjoyed; all their careful planning and selection had nearly gone down the drain, but their star, whom they had treated like an inept robot to be protected from all serious confrontation, had bailed them out by being better under pressure than they had expected—and deserved.

Other newsmen tapped for later panels also squirmed at the control and the staging—and at Nixon's quick-wittedness. Detroit *Free Press* columnist Judd Arnett was frustrated in his attempt during the Michigan panel to get Nixon to agree to a television debate with Humphrey:

Arnett: "I happen to be of the opinion that we need a debate in this country, and I think that you and Mr. Humphrey should get at Vietnam and some other questions."

Nixon: "I think maybe Mr. Humphrey is having a great time debating himself."

Arnett: "You are prejudiced, Mr. Nixon. If you don't want to debate with the third-party candidate whose name shall not be mentioned, why don't you get your friends in the House of Representatives to pass a special law permitting you and Mr. Humphrey to debate?"

Nixon: "Have you ever looked at the membership on that committee? You know, it's always amusing to me when people say, well, now, why don't I get the Republicans to do something on a debate, or the rest. Let's remember that the Senate is two-to-one Democratic, let us also remember that the House is three-to-two Democratic, and anytime that Hubert Humphrey with his great influence on his side wants a debate, I would think that he would be able to get the Democrats to pass it. . . ."

Arnett wrote after his experience that while the panel was indeed unrehearsed, it reminded him of a sequel to *The Music Man*: "Instead of Professor Harold Hill, the con artist attempting to organize a boys' band in River City, we had Professor Richard Nixon, the Human Talking Machine, complete with diamond needle and amplifier. 'Come on in, ladies and gentlemen, and hear the recording of your choice. . . . Answers to questions asked a dozen times in other places by seven other citizens scared stiff. . . .' I do not know how we are going to do it, but some way we must smoke out Richard Nixon and make

395

him speak to the issues. There must be a debate and he could help arrange it. . . . This campaign is a farce, a mockery, a sham, a refutation of the existence of national communications. . . ."

For all the safeguards, however, the hand-picked panel approach wasn't foolproof against even the panelist without media experience. The Madison Avenue determination that there had to be a black face—one, not two—on the panel was a calculated risk that occasionally backfired. Or did it? In a show in Cleveland the black panelist, a YMCA official named Frank Kelker, jolted the candidate by telling him: "To be perfectly honest, Mr. Nixon, the Negroes are a little afraid of you. You have heard that. I know you have heard that." Nixon responded: "Let me make one thing clear—I'm not afraid of them. Let's be quite candid; that a lot of my good friends, my Negro friends and I, we talk about these things very frankly. We must have frank talks. That's what we need. I am glad you raised it quite as bluntly as this. But they say, 'Well, you're not getting enough of the Negro vote, and why should you, therefore, make any effort to go out and have programs that will help Negroes as well as whites, and so forth. Just forget them. Go after the white vote.' Let me tell you this, any man who goes in as President of the United States has got to be President of the whole country. I do not want to preside over a divided country. Go ahead as to why this attitude exists, and maybe we can find an answer."

His questioner stood fast. "I don't know why it exists," he said. "I want you to tell me why and what you are going to do about it." To this, Nixon served up his standard Negroes-have-the-most-to-gain-from-law-and-order answer, with the payrolls-not-welfare-rolls theme thrown in. The response didn't seem to satisfy the questioner, nor did it likely satisfy those black voters in the Cleveland area who were watching. But they weren't his constituency anyway. The answer did no violence to Nixon's "forgotten (white) Americans" who were the primary targets of his media campaign.

The same basic answer turned off black panelists elsewhere. Stan Sanders, a former All-American end at Nixon's alma mater, Whittier College, after appearing on a Los Angeles panel told reporters outside the TV studio: "Nixon's answers are not the kind of responses of people who are sensitive to change in the ghettos. . . . I didn't think he answered my questions about the black voter. I think he has written off the black vote."

Despite Nixon's protestation to the contrary, others thought so too. He made only two visits to black communities. One was a brief early-morning stop at a new shopping center site in North Philadelphia in late September, to see an example of blossoming "black capitalism." It was billed as a "rally," but when fewer than thirty local blacks showed up, mostly youths and shop owners, Ziegler said the stop had been planned all along only as an "education tour for Nixon."

From the black section, Nixon went out the same day to Philadelphia's white suburbs, and the large crowds suggested that this phase distinctly was not an educational tour for him. At one shopping center, he lectured his predominantly white audience: "You are fortunate people, but you know that in the great cities of America there is terrible poverty. There are poor people. There are people who haven't had a chance—the chance that you've had. You can't be an island in the world. You can't live in your comfortable houses and say, 'Well, just as long as I get mine, I don't have to worry about the others. . . .' This isn't going to be a good country for any of us to live in until it's a good country for all of us to live in." Having said that, Nixon then launched into his standard law-and-order speech, complete with descriptions of Washington, D.C., with the largest black population ratio in the country, as "the crime capital of the world . . . where secretaries can't go home after dark without fear. . . ." Later, in Detroit at the end of October, he went to a black community action center, but the visit was even less public than the Philadelphia "education tour." He talked only to the workers there.

Although the media campaign concentrated heavily on controlled use of television, radio also played a critical role. What may have appeared to be a throwback to pretelevision days actually was a careful implementation of some basic principles of the guru of the TV age, Marshall McLuhan. His book *Understanding Media* and other writings were staples in the Nixon media-politics strategy, for radio as well as television. In keeping with McLuhan's characterization of television as a "cool medium," or one that requires and stimulates participation by the viewer, the physical image of Nixon more than his specific ideas was the TV focus. But radio, in McLuhan's view, is a "hot medium" that requires less involvement from the listener and therefore more specific presentation from the "performer." Accordingly, on radio Nixon became extremely thoughtful, specific and benign. One radio presentation in particular, a speech on his concept of the Presidency in which Ray Price played a leading role, was a masterpiece in the use of "hot" media—laying out with precision and logic what the office could be, and should be, in the hands of the right man. Adopting a Presidential tone, completely devoid of the partisanship and haranguing normally associated with a political campaign, it amounted to a "fireside chat" by a man certain he soon would hold the office in question and clear in his own mind what he would do with it.

The tone was set deftly in Nixon's opening words: "During the course of this campaign I have discussed many issues with the American people. Tonight I would like to talk with you about a subject often debated by scholars and the public, but seldom dealt with directly in a Presidential campaign: the nature of the Presidency itself." Here, obviously, was a man bent on elevating the substance of political campaigning; taking time from the hurly-burly for a few quiet, contemplative moments of serious discussion—almost a seminar on the nature of leadership. In cold print, the phrases may appear unexceptional; in delivery, Nixon managed through them to convey great sincerity and conviction.

The radio talk presented *sotto voce* many of the same themes and allusions to racial conflict, crime, violence and public mistrust of government Nixon was shouting about on the stump and discussing animatedly on television. Here, he presented them in a careful context of scholarly concern. Of racial strife and of law and order he said: "The next President must unite America. He must calm its angers, ease its terrible frictions and bring its people together once again in peace and mutual respect. He has to take hold of America before he can move it forward. This requires leadership that believes in law and has the courage to enforce it; leadership that believes in justice, and is determined to promote it; leadership that believes in progress, and knows how to inspire it. The days of a passive President belong to a simpler past. . . . He must articulate the nation's values, define its goals and marshal its will. . . . he must lead."

He would lead, but not arrogantly, Nixon assured his listeners. "The President has a duty to decide, but the people have a right to know why. . . . Only through an open, candid dialogue with the people can a President maintain his trust and his leadership." In other words, he would be no Lyndon Johnson. "We should bring dissenters into policy discussions, not freeze them out; we should invite constructive criticism, not only because the critics have a right to be heard, but also because they often have something worth hearing. . . ."

And he would listen. "In order to lead, a President today must listen. . . . A President has to hear not only the clamorous voices of the organized, but also the quiet voices, the inner voices—the voices that speak through the silences, that speak from the heart and the conscience . . . the great, quiet forgotten majority—the nonshouters and the nondemonstrators, the millions who ask principally to go their own way in decency and dignity, and to have their own rights accorded the same respect they accord the rights of others." The "quiet voices" of the radio talk were, of course, Nixon's "forgotten Americans" of the stump speech—"the good people, who support their schools, their churches, who pay their taxes." But whereas the thunder about the forgotten Americans on the stump sounded ominously like backlash talk, the soft allusion to the quiet voices in this subdued radio chat was the essence of reasonableness, fairness and responsibility in the man who sought the Presidency— and who obviously was thinking deeply, even reverently, about what success would entail.

It was this side of the Nixon campaign, being played out in millions of American living rooms through September and October in contrast to the frantic gyrations of the hapless Hubert Humphrey, that may have had the greatest impact on the voters. In a country where people probably are subject to media influence more than any other people in the world, they nevertheless take great pride in their independence, their ability to think and decide for themselves. Never mind what the press might be writing about Nixon going into hiding, or refusing to debate. There he was on your television set, or talking calmly, confidently, knowledgeably on your radio. Reporters traveling with Nixon and trying to assess the campaign were severely handicapped because they usually did not have the opportunity to see this side of the Nixon operation and to gauge its impact. To a considerable degree, they covered one Nixon campaign in 1968, and the American people saw another. It was a strategy revolutionary in approach and scope, and masterful in execution.

Humphrey, of course, also had an extremely imaginative media program, but for a long time he didn't have the money to put it on the air. His tremendous troubles with the Vietnam issue and with street hecklers dominated all else in his news coverage. On September 18, Humphrey went to Boston, in one of the near-certain states for him, under the protective wing of Senator Edward M. Kennedy. Still he was clobbered. Massachusetts Democrats squeezed a very large crowd into a tight downtown intersection, but in the process created a captive audience not only for the candidate but for hundreds of irate college students. In Kennedy's first political appearance after the assassination of his brother Robert, they booed him and shouted "Shame on Teddy!" when he endorsed the man his brother had castigated for preaching "the politics of happiness and joy." Pressing on, Ted Kennedy sought to lecture the demonstrators. "If there has been one lesson in 1968," he shouted over the chanting, "it is that there is no room for anarchy" and that nothing is achieved "by shouting and screaming." But they ignored him. "Sellout! Sellout!" they yelled.

It was even rougher for Humphrey. Efforts to restrain the protesters with pointed references to Boston's favorite son, the late President Kennedy, and Humphrey-Kennedy efforts to create the Peace Corps and achieve a nuclear test ban treaty, were to no avail. Finally Humphrey turned directly to the hecklers bunched in front of him and said: "We will not move this country forward if it is plagued by those who deny freedom of speech, and who deny freedom of assembly to those who offer appeals to reason." To which the chanters responded, over and over again: "Bullshit!" Kennedy was so disturbed that he discarded his personal concern for security and rode with Humphrey back to the airport in an open convertible. En route to the next stop in the Midwest, Humphrey told newsmen: "We know it is going to happen. They will boo me, they will boo Teddy, they will boo the bishop. . . . The Goldwaterites were poor, misguided people. These people are intentionally mean anarchists. They do not believe in anything. This is the hard core. Take a look at them—filled with hatred, bitterness, bigotry. Look at their faces, filled with violence. They will never live long enough to run us off the platform because basically they are just cowards." It was brave talk, but Humphrey knew these people were hurting him badly. Chicago, while nominating him, had brought him to his knees, and now, nearly a month later, the war critics still wouldn't let him get up, no less start to run seriously. And at the same time, they blissfully ignored the man Humphrey thought should be their real target —Nixon.

What was even more maddening to Humphrey was that he wanted to take Nixon on, but couldn't get at him. In Springfield, Illinois, on the steps of the Lincoln home, he called for a confrontation "in the tradition of the Lincoln-Douglas debates." But he was talking to himself. "Mr. Nixon is having his own debate," Humphrey said. "I have a feeling the new Nixon and the old Nixon are going to go at it for some time, and we're going to see the real Nixon, and you're not going to like it." Listing a number of national issues including civil rights, farm problems and the nuclear nonproliferation treaty, Humphrey shouted at the end of each one: "Mr. Nixon, where do you stand?" It was good theater, but it wasn't budging Nixon. In exasperation, Humphrey called Nixon "the fastest-moving target I've seen, except a bevy of quail in the field. And I'll tell you, I'm a pretty good shot. I believe it's time Mr. Nixon came out of his storm cellar and gave me an aim on him." But Nixon wasn't coming out.

In Louisville, Humphrey came very close to calling Nixon the same thing he had labeled the Boston hecklers—a coward. He called Nixon "the man who campaigns without running—

who takes it easy and never makes a mistake—and either evades or straddles every major issue. . . . Is it confidence when he refuses to join me in a direct television debate on the issues—or is it something else? Is it confidence when he flees from invitations to answer questions on television news programs—he has not appeared on a national panel show since 1966—or is it something else?"

Nixon meanwhile continued to breeze around the country, basking in the universally large and sometimes huge crowds that had been generated for him by the astute hand of John Ehrlichman and associates. In Philadelphia, always a Democratic city, he clearly outdrew an earlier Humphrey visit. In Milwaukee, Sioux Falls, Boise and Seattle, the faithful turned out, increasingly more enthusiastic as they began too to believe they really had a winner in Richard Nixon. Occasionally, as at a rally in Victory Square in Seattle, he might be heckled by students shouting, "Hell, no, we won't go!" But all Nixon had to do was to tell the rest of the audience that he was listening to "the forgotten Americans" and "the good people who pay their taxes," and the cheers soon drowned out the chants. (Sometimes, "the good people" would start to chant "Dump the Hump! Dump the Hump!" It was confusing; that's what "the bad people" were saying, too.)

At times, the Nixon planners seemed to outdo themselves in their cleverness. In St. Louis, at a "Youth Wants to Know" forum, 3,700 high school students jammed the Kiel Opera House. The Nixon media boys were there to tape the best of it for later TV commercials. It went swimmingly for the most part. There were some boos when in answer to a question about why he wouldn't debate he said he wouldn't give Wallace a platform. But when a student asked him what the "new Nixon" had to offer young people, he turned the question deftly into the kind of fat pitch that made all the preplanning worth the effort. What the student actually asked him was: "Can we look to you for the ideas and understanding, the leadership as set forth in the New Politics?" Nixon blithely ignored the last phrase, the byword of the McCarthy campaign, and replied: "Well, that question raises the question that perhaps some of you are too polite to raise, and that is, is there a new Nixon? Is this just a façade that is put over a man who is really a man of the old politics? Does he really communicate with the young people? Does he care? And all I can say is this: You've got to look at the man and you've got to answer that question yourselves."

Citing changes in the country and the world since he first entered Congress in 1946, Nixon touched on what he had learned from associations with young people on his world travels, and what he learned from forums such as this one. "I believe that through this constant education that I have been receiving, by communicating like this with young people, that I know what the new world, the new generation wants," he said. From the St. Louis forum, however, Nixon's learning experience necessarily was sharply restricted to what the new white generation wanted. Although St. Louis had a black population of nearly 40 percent, there were only a few black students in the huge crowd. The organizers had seen fit to bus in students from sixty-eight school districts, most of them from the heavily white suburbs outside the city.

It was, without a doubt, the white vote that Nixon was after in border states like Missouri, Kentucky and Tennessee, through which he now was moving. With Humphrey running so very poorly, Wallace loomed as Nixon's chief foe in the Southeast and border states. Yet having used Wallace as his reason for spurning the television debates, Nixon could not take Wallace head-on. Nor did he have to. Again the virtue of being, or appearing to be, the "centrist" candidate was obvious. He could say all the things Wallace was saying about law and order, street violence, the Supreme Court's babying of "the criminal forces," excessive concentration of power in Washington and all the rest of the redneck litany, but with greater restraint. Next to the ranting Wallace, that was easy. Why throw your vote away on Wallace, who couldn't win, when you could get the essentials of what you wanted in the more reasonable, infinitely more respectable Nixon? It was a question that did not have to be belabored in the border states and Dixie.

Nixon's foray into the South was marked by one noteworthy clash with the press, one of the few in which he temporarily lost his cool head and showed a flash of the old Nixon and of his old animosity toward the traveling reporters. After the St. Louis

403

rally with the students, Nixon went on to Louisville for a party affair. During the day, the news had broken that Ambassador to the United Nations George Ball had resigned to help Humphrey. Ball had a wide reputation as having been the devil's advocate against the Vietnam policy in the Johnson administration, and his move carried strong implications for a possible new effort by Humphrey to move out of the Johnson shadow on the war. Reporters in the Nixon entourage tried manfully to gain access to Nixon for comment, but were turned away by Ziegler and the other press agents. That night, when Nixon was making one of his frequent after-dinner "private TV tapings" at a local studio from which they had been excluded, the newsmen even staked out all exits to confront him about Ball, but he brushed right by them. They were incensed, therefore, when, watching the local eleven o'clock news, they saw Nixon commenting on Ball in an "exclusive interview," excerpted from the "private TV taping."

The reporters went after the Nixon press aides in a bitter exchange about access to the candidate. They wanted to ask him not only about Ball, but also about a telegram from Humphrey asking Nixon to send a representative to confer with Larry O'Brien on a proposal for beating the equal-time requirement on debates. If the candidates arranged the debates themselves, the networks could cover them if they chose, or the debates could proceed off television. Did Nixon get the telegram? Had he replied? The reporters wanted the answers from Nixon.

That night they got nothing but a squirming Ziegler. The next morning, as the entourage prepared to leave the airport, Nixon walked over to the ramp of his plane for an impromptu news conference. He reiterated his position on not debating and called Humphrey's telegram "the first of a one-sided correspondence . . . the sort of kid stuff that somebody goes through when he's behind." He accused Humphrey of wanting a three-way debate to build up Wallace in the South, at Nixon's expense, and thus throw the election into the House. "He knows that he's running third in the South," Nixon said. "So he's trying to use Wallace to beat Nixon in the new South. He feels apparently that by having debates that maybe Wallace can win the whole perimeter of the South, which I otherwise might win, and I'm just not going to play that game."

From the crowd of reporters around Nixon, a television newsman suddenly suggested that perhaps Nixon was "relieved" to have Congress turn down the equal-time exemption and thus give him "a good way out." The candidate bristled, eyes ablaze. "You can put any words in my mouth that you want," he started, then checked himself. "But you see . . . no, no, I'm not complaining about it because you have that right." He seemed to be heading for the 1962 "last press conference" refrain all over again. "I've been perfectly forthright in this campaign. . . . I'm not afraid of anybody. I'm not afraid of any audience. I'm not afraid of any press conference. So that's the way it's going to be, and don't plant any words in my mouth to the effect that I believe that I don't have to debate Mr. Humphrey. I've done it before and I'll do it again and we'll win next time."

The exchange was a tense break in Nixon's strict let-me-call-you-sweetheart policy. He quickly regained his calm, and on the short leg from Louisville to the first stop, Chattanooga, he rode on the press plane, walking up and down the aisle, talking easily with individual reporters. The animals had got restless in their cages; it was necessary to throw them a bone or two.

Now, at September's end with little more than five weeks to go, the next Gallup Poll was in. It brought more bad news for Humphrey. Nixon was holding even at 43 percent, but Humphrey had dropped three points to 28 percent, while Wallace climbed two to 21, with 8 percent undecided. Nixon's failure to climb was not surprising to the insiders. Their campaign was essentially defensive—to hold on to what their candidate had. Still, with Humphrey having tremendous troubles with the Vietnam issue, the hecklers and money, Nixon might have picked up something somewhere. The Wallace climb was ominous, this late in the campaign. Nixon was ahead in every section but the South, and there he trailed Wallace, 31 percent to 38, with Humphrey at 24.

For Humphrey, the Gallup Poll only confirmed what he and his chief strategists already knew: he had to break out of Lyndon Johnson's embrace on the war, or forget it. The day before, he had been treated to his almost daily dose of humiliation when activist students of Reed College in Oregon walked out on him. And in Seattle, war protesters, led by a youth with a bullhorn, bellowed they were going to arrest him for "crimes against humanity." They called him a fascist and chanted "Dump the Hump!" until Humphrey, almost in tears, finally shouted back: "Knock it off!" and proceeded with his speech. The time, beyond all doubt, had come to move.

Drafts of a speech putting Humphrey on record for a bombing halt had been kicking around for many weeks, even as far back as the convention, when Humphrey was under pressure to "be your own man" before the nomination. Always in the way was the problem of Johnson, and beyond that the problem of Nixon, with his repeated warnings that nothing be said or promised about Vietnam that could undercut the talks in Paris. George Ball had conferred with Averell Harriman on the prospective Humphrey proposal, and shortly after he resigned from his UN post he flew to Oregon to give his sliding candidate assurances Harriman would not object. Ball, O'Brien and Senator Fred Harris finally persuaded Humphrey he had to call for a bombing halt. After much writing and rewriting, and much staff debating on what the speech would or wouldn't do, O'Brien and the national committee scraped up the necessary money and Humphrey went on nationwide television for half an hour on Monday night, September 30, from Salt Lake City.

"As President," the beleaguered candidate told the nation in the critical sentences, "I would be willing to stop the bombing of North Vietnam as an acceptable risk for peace, because I believe that it could lead to success in the negotiations and a shorter war; this would be the best protection for our troops. In weighing that risk—and before taking action—I would place key importance on evidence, direct or indirect, by deed or word, of Communist willingness to restore the demilitarized zone between North and South Vietnam. If the government of North Vietnam were to show bad faith, I would reserve the right to resume the bombing."

Finally, Humphrey had done it. But done what? The first sentence issued the long-delayed call for a bombing halt. The doves—O'Brien, Ball, Harris—got that. But the second imposed at least an implied condition and the third a prospect of resuming the bombing. The hawks—staff advisers Bill Connell and Jim Rowe—got that. It really wasn't all that bold a move. Apparently, though, it was enough to start bringing Democrats home. A pitch at the speech's end for funds to pay for the telecast provided an immediate barometer of its impact. The money and the pledges came flowing in, enough not only to pay for that night's telecast but to make the campaign treasury fluid enough to plan a second.

Nixon sought at once to exploit the Humphrey breakout from the Johnson policy. The speech, he said in Detroit, was Humphrey's "fourth or possibly fifth different position" on a bombing halt and could "very possibly" be interpreted by the North Vietnamese as "offering a concession in January that they could not get now." In another classic Nixonism, he suggested there was disagreement over what Humphrey actually had said; there still was time for Humphrey to escape leaving the impression, before it was too late, that he was sabotaging the American negotiators. "Because of the wide disagreement," Nixon offered, "he ought to clarify it and say he is not undercutting the United States position in Paris. I hope that Vice President Humphrey would clarify his position and not pull the rug out from under the negotiators and take away the trump card the negotiators have [the bombing halt]."

The Humphrey speech came for Nixon at a time his own party unity, constructed with such care and pride, was showing some mild signs of cracking. An editorial appeared in the *Ripon Forum*, the monthly publication of the young liberal Ripon Society, written and signed by Senator Hatfield, who had agreed to second Nixon's name and to be a surrogate candidate for him in the fall among peace groups, under certain understandings. Nixon, Hatfield had been assured, would be speaking out on such points as the need to broaden the base of the Saigon government and the Paris talks, de-Americanization of the war and greater nonmilitary emphasis in the pursuit of a settlement. But as the campaign progressed, so did Hatfield's disappointment. In exasperation, he finally wrote the editorial. Though it was couched in terms broad enough to embrace all candidates, Nixon clearly was the target.

"The Paris peace talks should not become the skirt for timid men to hide behind," Hatfield wrote. "In 1964 the American people—trusting the campaign promises of the Democratic presidential candidate—thought they were voting for peace, only to have their trust betrayed. Candidates at all levels are again expecting voters to accept their post-election intentions on faith, and they deal with Vietnam in terms of assurances not to 'sell out' our men in Vietnam and vague promises for 'an honorable peace.' This is not enough. In the democratic process, voters should not be forced to go to the polls with their fingers crossed; they should not be forced to rely on blind faith that the man they vote for will share their views on the most important issue of the election."

The Hatfield editorial might have created more of a stir if it had not appeared at the time of the Humphrey speech. That speech, for all its limitations, lifted a tremendous psychological load from Humphrey's shoulders. He began to campaign with his old bounce, and for the first time since Labor Day, the heckling fell off sharply. Humphrey had not exactly kicked Lyndon Johnson in the teeth, but for the first time he had shown some independence. Now he turned to the attack with zest, trying at every stop to remind good Democrats that the man he was running against was their favorite villain of old, Tricky Dick, and it was not too late to save the Republic from him.

Nixon, meanwhile, was more concerned about George Wallace than Hubert Humphrey. The border states and Southern states out of the Deep South were critical to the Nixon strategy. A big Wallace vote could deny them to him. Nixon had been determined not to mention Wallace or take him on frontally, but it happened anyway. In the most important staged panel show up to that point, Nixon appeared over a costly hookup from Atlanta to forty-eight television outlets in twelve Southern and border states. Again it was a newsman who provided the spark. Reg Murphy, editor of the editorial page of the Atlanta *Constitution,* asked him: "Vice President Humphrey has said that Governor Wallace is 'the apostle of hate and racism.' Agree or disagree?" Nixon at first seemed to beg off. "He's [Wallace] against a lot of things Americans are frustrated about," he said. "He's against the rise in crime. He's against the conduct of foreign policy, what's happened to American respect around the world. I'm against a lot of those things. The difference is, I'm for a lot of things, and that's what we need now. . . ." Nixon paused, as though debating whether to let it go at that. Then he went on: "We need policies at home that will go beyond simply saying that, 'Well, if somebody lies down in front of my Presidential limousine, it will be the last one he lies down in front of.' Now, look here. No President of the United States is going to do that, and anybody who says that shouldn't be President of the United States." Outside the studio later, Nixon told reporters that no man who would say such a thing "is even fit to be President."

The attack on Wallace, though strong and specific, turned out to be a quick, isolated raid rather than a change in battle plan. The next day, campaigning in South Carolina with Strom Thurmond, Nixon made no mention of Wallace. The closest he came was borrowing Wallace's "Stand Up for America" slogan to apply to Strom, whom he called "a man who has stood up for his state and will stand up for America. . . . I'm glad to stand with him today."

While Nixon thus worked one of the states Wallace hoped to take from him, Wallace was on a swing of his own that, if successful, could only benefit Nixon. On the day Humphrey made his bombing-halt speech, Wallace had flown into Chicago with his political Grand Ol' Opry show and had cut a noisy, sometimes tense swath through the surface and subsurface prejudices of the urban North. A short but lively eight-block motorcade through the Loop was punctuated by cheers of supporters and chants of "Wallace is a pig!" from angry blacks marching alongside his car. Wallace partisans distributed placards that said "Wallace, Daley and the Police," "I Worked to Buy My House," and "Don't Let Chicago Burn, George." But they couldn't find enough takers to exhaust the supply. Hecklers carried hostile signs, including one that said: "If You Liked Hitler, You'll Love Wallace." Though there was no violence, it seemed only an incident or an accident away. Wallace rode through smiling broadly, impishly, standing on the back seat of his open car, giving his little soldier's salute and saying, almost to himself, "Hi, folks."

The trip was aimed squarely at the white blue-collar backlash. Wallace killed most of the weekday afternoon in a second-rate Chicago hotel, then motored out to the tough, lily-white, blue-collar suburb of Cicero for a street rally at quitting time outside a large Western Electric Company plant. It clearly was "Wallace Country," and he regaled the crowd of several thousand with his standard pitch for law and order, defense of property rights, tougher handling of demonstrators and pressing on with the Vietnam War. There was an ugly moment in the crowd when a young girl bravely holding an antiwar sign had it ripped from her hands and torn up, while seething young toughs called her "New York Jew" and tried to talk each other into dragging her out. Wallace did not seem to notice, and the ugliness subsided.

The same mood prevailed the next days as Wallace toured Michigan, Pennsylvania and Ohio in search of the vote of the discontented white. The Wallace sideshow that had been so successful in the Deep South was transported North with no adjustments necessary. First there was Sam Smith's five-piece band twanging out "Cheatin' Heart," followed by two skinny, bleached blondes called the Taylor Sisters (Mona and Lisa!) leading the assembled in "God Bless America." Then a warm-up man named Dick Smith, an Alabama weekly newspaper publisher, would take the microphone and make a straight and hard pitch for money, as "Wallace Girls," dressed in red and blue blazers and dime-store hairdos piled high on their heads, circulated through the crowd with yellow plastic pails, for the take. Smith was, as hard as it may be to believe, a rough version of George Wallace, spitting out the same hate phrases and berating the ever-present hecklers. He would tell them, in Wallace's favorite phrase, that "you better have your fun now, because after November fifth, you're through!" Sometimes Smith's temper and invective would get the better of him, and he would end it with ". . . because after November fifth, we're going to do away with you!" Finally, as Mona and Lisa belted out the campaign song "Are You for Wallace?" the candidate would appear, the cocky bantam rooster in a tight blue suit, snapping off the salute, waving to the "acres and acres of folks," the cold eyes studying the crowd, seeking out the enemy.

410

It was just as it always was in Alabama, except the entourage was enlarged in the North to demonstrate the candidate's ties to the workingman. Brought along for the ride was a rag-tag collection of second- and third-echelon labor officials from Alabama and Georgia who did nothing but wave when introduced from the platform. They were right out of central casting, especially a doleful bruiser named Arnold Spurling, the head of a plumbers' local in Columbus, Georgia. When Wallace called his name, he would take one step forward and raise his arm over his head with all the aplomb of a professional wrestler taking the cheers of the crowd.

Having thus established his impeccable labor credentials, Wallace would launch into his standard harangue about how there wasn't "a dime's worth of difference" between the two major parties, about how they have tolerated the "anarchists and pseudointellectuals" and finally have "created a Frankenstein monster." All would be well "if we let the police operate the way they know how to operate." The crowd would cheer, needing no elaboration. If elected he would see to it that "the anarchists are taken by the back of the neck and put under a good jail." Sometimes the "anarchists" would respond by shouting "Sieg Heil!" and giving the stiff-arm salute, and it would rattle Wallace. But he was quick on the recovery: "I thought we got rid of the Nazis in World War II. I'm a disabled American veteran. I fought the Nazis and the Fascists in World War II."

Then he would to into the running-over bit: "I want the newsmen here to get what I say straight, because they been misquoting me. When I become President of the United States, and I come back here, and a bunch of anarchists lie down in front of my automobile, it's gonna be the last automobile they're gonna lie down in front of." The crowd would roar, and then he would point up at the hecklers and say, "If you anarchists don't believe me, I'm gonna come back and you just try me." Sometimes violence would break out in the stands, and Wallace would pounce on the opportunity: "Let the police handle it! Let the police handle it! They know what to do!" Often the hecklers were black, and Wallace would say to the crowd: "Look at them! You see who's causing the trouble? You

411

know what kind of people they are, and you're sick and tired of them!" The "acres and acres of folks" would shout their agreement. It was the sledgehammer version of the Nixon "forgotten Americans" pitch, but made mostly to Democrats rather than Republicans, and according to Gallup it was taking enough away from Humphrey to make Nixon a winner even in the East.

But then Wallace made his biggest mistake. In Pittsburgh on October 3 he unveiled—or, more accurately, unleashed—retired Air Force Chief of Staff General Curtis E. LeMay as his running mate. In a bizarre press conference at the Pittsburgh Hilton that came off like a Bob and Ray spoof, LeMay within a matter of minutes hung the same trigger-happy albatross around the Wallace campaign that had pulled Barry Goldwater down so quickly and emphatically in 1964. He was asked about his position on use of nuclear weapons, and as Wallace stood openmouthed and stunned at his side, the old Strategic Air Command bomber-in-chief proceeded to drop this verbal megatonnage:

"We seem to have a phobia about nuclear weapons. I think most military men think it's just another weapon in the arsenal. . . . The smart thing to do when you're in a war—hopefully you prevent it. Stay out of it if you can. But when you get in it, get in it with both feet and get it over with as soon as you can. Use the force that's necessary. Maybe use a little more to make sure it's enough to stop the fighting as soon as possible. So this means efficiency in the operation of the military establishment. I think there are many times when it would be most efficient to use nuclear weapons. However, the public opinion in this country and throughout the world throw up their hands in horror when you mention nuclear weapons, just because of the propaganda that's been fed to them. I don't believe the world would end if we exploded a nuclear weapon. . . ."

LeMay then proceeded to write off as "propaganda" reports that nuclear explosions caused permanent and hereditary damage to human and plant life. Citing tests at the Bikini firing grounds in the Pacific, he told of movies taken later that, according to LeMay's description, might well have been titled *Nukes Are Good for You:* "The fish are all back in the lagoons, the coconut trees are growing coconuts, the guava bushes have fruit on them, the birds are back. As a matter of fact, everything is about the same except the land crabs. They get minerals from the soil, I guess, through their shells, and the land crabs were a little bit hot, and there's a little question about whether you should eat a land crab or not." The rats on the atoll, however, were "bigger, fatter and healthier than they ever were before," he assured his flabbergasted audience. LeMay conceded that nuclear war would be "horrible," but said there really was no difference between being killed by a nuclear weapon or by a "rusty knife" in Vietnam. "As a matter of fact," he said, "if I had a choice I'd rather be killed by a nuclear weapon."

Wallace couldn't take it any more. Seeing his campaign disintegrating before his very eyes, he stepped in, desperately. "General LeMay hasn't advocated the use of nuclear weapons, not at all," he insisted. "He's against the use of nuclear weapons, and I am too."

The gray, steely LeMay wouldn't shut up. "I gave you a discussion on the phobia that we have in this country about the use of nuclear weapons," he said stiffly. "I prefer not to use them. I prefer not to use any weapons at all." But if he found it necessary to end the war? somebody asked. "If I found it necessary I would use anything we could dream up—anything that we could dream up—including nuclear weapons if it was necessary."

Wallace came in hard now. "All General LeMay has said, and I know you fellows better than he does because I've had to deal with you, he said that if the security of the country depended on the use of any weapon in the future, he would use it. But he has said he prefers not to use any weapon. He prefers to negotiate. I believe we must defend our country, but I've always said we can win and defend in Vietnam without the use of nuclear weapons. And General LeMay hasn't said anything about the use of nuclear weapons."

You could see now that all Wallace wanted to do was throw a sheet over his bomber friend and haul him away, but it had penetrated to LeMay finally that he had been led into an act of public self-flagellation. "Wait a minute now," he said, harshly, but without changing his stolid expression. "Let me make sure

413

you've got this straight. I know I'm going to come out with a lot of misquotes from this campaign. I have in the past. And I'll be damned lucky if I don't appear as a drooling idiot whose only solution to any problem is to drop atomic bombs all over the world. I assure you I'm not." But it was clear already Curtis E. LeMay was not going to be damned lucky.

The whole thing could have been a quick skit on *Laugh-In.* The setting was perfect. The wall behind LeMay and Wallace had been painted in a luminous psychedelic floral pattern, and there were doors high in the wall from which Secret Service men periodically popped their heads. One half-expected Wallace to turn to LeMay and tell him: "Say good night, Curt." For it was very definitely good night for the Wallace campaign. LeMay accompanied Wallace the rest of the day, and the general received a big hand when he was introduced in Indianapolis, at the foot of that grotesque city's grotesque war memorial. But no bigger than the hand Arnold Spurling standing next to him got when he stepped forward and gave his wrestler's greeting, showing a flash of white sweat sock as he raised his meaty arm. Wallace gave LeMay exactly the same opportunity to speak that he gave his good union friend Arnold, which was no opportunity at all. The general had had his say, and he knew it. Only the bubbling Mrs. LeMay, eyes aglow as she watched Wallace and listened to his oratory, did not seem to catch on. She rushed up to Wallace after he had finished and told him how great he had been. Wallace looked at her uncomfortably, as if discovering yet another reason for regretting his choice.

The LeMay debacle had an immediate and critical impact on the strategies of both Nixon and Humphrey. Wallace support began falling away rapidly in the industrial North, and whoever picked it up might collar the big blocs of electoral votes that could swing the election. Both Nixon and Humphrey had planned all along to work the key Northeastern states in the last weeks, but the opportunity presented by LeMay and his hot land crabs guaranteed an intensified effort.

On the heels of LeMay's selection, Nixon shot off a statement that said it all tersely: "We cannot put an irresponsible finger on the nuclear trigger and expect to avert the horror of a nuclear war." Campaigning in Flint, Michigan, a few days after

Wallace had filled a ball park there, Nixon asked a crowd of about 5,000: "Do you just want to make a point, or do you want to make a change? Do you want to get something off your chest, or do you want to get something done? Do you want to get a moment's satisfaction by your vote of protest, or do you want to get four years of action?" A week earlier, about half of the 16,000-member Local 599, United Auto Workers at the Buick works in Flint had participated in a straw poll. The results were Wallace, 49 percent; Humphrey, 39 percent; Nixon 12 percent. Nixon, now convinced that Wallace had peaked, was out to turn that around.

While Nixon thus tried to wean away Wallace votes in the North, his Republican friends in Congress were taking care of the nagging matter of the television debates. The Senate shelved the bill waiving the equal-time requirement for debates by Nixon, Humphrey and Wallace. The Humphrey forces, still feeling the money squeeze but desperate, reissued the challenge, selected the specific date of Sunday, October 20, and offered to split the cost for the necessary network time, or buy it all. The Nixon camp wasted no time responding. "The matter," said press aide Ziegler nervously, "has been closed by the Congress of the United States." He called the Humphrey proposal "just a phony deal and a publicity gimmick." Ellsworth put out a release suggesting it was all a plot to cause a Constitutional crisis. "Humphrey and his campaign manager [O'Brien] are well aware that he stands no chance in the popular election. However, they have clung to the minor hope that they could generate enough electoral votes for Wallace to throw the election in the House of Representatives. Their only chance was to get Wallace the greatest exposure on television." Ellsworth credited Senate Minority Leader Dirksen with blocking the debate bill, because he "saw through the cynical scheme and nailed it for what it was." The release ended with a variation on the Huntley-Brinkley sign-off: "Good night, Hubert. Good night, George."

Now, finally, the debate about which Richard Nixon had not been frightened was dead and buried. Humphrey continued to flail away at the idea, accusing Nixon of "evasion, avoidance and wobbling," and of trying to "hide out this campaign by relying on spot announcements and canned radio." The longer the silence from Nixon, the more frustrated Humphrey became. "Come clean like a man and debate," he challenged Nixon in Erie, Pennsylvania. In Scranton, he called him "Richard the Careful" and then, inevitably, "Richard the Chickenhearted." But it was all in vain. Nixon returned to Key Biscayne for a leisurely weekend of planning for his final three-week drive, and in a getaway press conference on October 15 he firmly turned aside the last pressures from newsmen for a debate. Asked about Humphrey's offer to buy time for a two-way debate, Nixon tried to sound willing but locked in by legalities. "I don't know how it can be done," he said. "My analysis of the law indicates that whether it's paid time or free time, a television network or station cannot put on two candidates without at the same time providing an opportunity to a third-party candidate and thereby fragment the two-party system." Well, he was asked, how about a two-man debate without television in a large hall with full transcripts printed by the major newspapers? He said he didn't consider such an arrangement would make "the best use" of the candidates' time, nor would it replace a TV debate, "where the people themselves can judge."

The answer, in addition to putting the final stake into the specter of the debates, provided a very revealing confirmation of Nixon's walking-on-eggs approach to the press as the campaign entered the homestretch. What he was saying, clearly, was that he didn't want his views filtered through reporters in such an important matter as a direct confrontation with his chief opponent. Nixon knew it and so did the reporters, so he went to great lengths to assuage them. His full answer bears repeating in this light:

"*I don't mean to downgrade the writing press,* but television changed campaigning, and I believe that a debate in which we are on national television, fully covered, where the people themselves can judge rather than having it judged by the press, *and I don't mean by that I think the press would be unfair, I* mean that every individual now likes to be his own judge. I think where the people themselves can judge, that's the kind of a debate I have agreed to, and that's the kind, if it is arranged, I will participate in, provided it's two men." (Italics added.)

416

Other answers in this rare press conference also revealed a studied attempt not to offend by this candidate who repeatedly had said that he was not going to play it safe. Asked whether he intended to leave open the option of increasing the bombing against North Vietnam if Hanoi stepped up its military activity, Nixon jumped in. "No, I am not going to say that," he insisted. "The immediate reaction to any statement of that sort is that we are waving the bombing around. And I am quite aware of how it would be played." And then, quickly: *"And I understand that, and I would not be resentful."* It was an addition that most reporters could translate easily—that Nixon understood how statements can be misinterpreted, not out of any intent to do him harm, but by honest mistake. But it was interesting that he felt he had to spell it out. (Also, in discussing Humphrey's increasingly more aggressive campaign style, Nixon commented: "I'm not going to engage in the kind of name-calling Hubert Humphrey is engaging in." Then he added: "Incidentally, *I'm not resentful of this* . . ." This man, who was considered in earlier years of defeat to have harbored such great resentment, was proving to be, in his determination to turn the other cheek, the most resentless Presidential candidate in history.)

Still another question, identifying Wallace as Nixon's "major opponent in some of the states you will be traveling in the next weeks," caused Nixon to break in—with apologies. "Only two, only in the next week," he said. "Let me make one thing—" and then he paused. *"I don't mean to correct you, understand,"* he said, correcting the questioner, "but in the final two weeks there are no states in which Wallace has a chance because they are all major states. . . ."

The format of the press conference itself was a typical exercise in Nixon's wary approach to the traveling news corps. Although his words were on the record, no cameras or recorders were permitted, thereby avoiding the permanent capturing of a flub. Nixon's yearning to have the people judge for themselves via TV clearly did not extend to such sessions.

The main purpose of the conference, it turned out, was to proclaim "Operation Extra Effort"—in Nixon's words, "the most intensive closing, the most intensive finish in campaign history" in terms of "people reached by radio and television, intensity of activity and speeches and issues covered." Not only was he going to nail down his own victory with this drive, but maybe win Congress too. "We're not going to play it safe. We're going all-out on the issues, the appearances, the activities between now and the elections." The final "blitz," Nixon said, would hit "the peripheral states" and then concentrate as never before in the seven target states.

Nixon's description of Operation Extra Effort was half right. In his two-track campaign, it was indeed all-out on the controlled media track. The Stans money tree was bringing in a final bumper harvest, and Shakespeare, Treleaven and the other media boys were pumping it into radio and TV spots, fireside chats and plans for a mammoth election-eve television extravaganza. A series of very impressive radio talks by the candidate, catching him at his most thoughtful, reserved and informed, was taped on major subjects from crime to the state of NATO and the state of American youth. Humphrey's media types, who also had planned a late-campaign drive, lacked money to buy TV time, and although their closing effort was impressive by past standards, it could not touch Nixon's. The second track of the Nixon campaign, the traditional in-person barnstorming, was something else again. In the first full week of the "blitz," Nixon averaged fewer than two public appearances a day. Reporters traveling with him on the Grand Divertisement had no trouble sorting out the appearance from the reality; to millions of television viewers, though, Nixon's windup may well have seemed to be "the most intensive closing, the most intensive finish in campaign history."

There was, however, at least one significant development in that first week of the homestretch. Behind the elaborately staged "victory" rallies, with the bouncing cheerleaders up front, the balloons and Dick Nixon telling the corralled faithful that "we're gonna sock it to 'em all over this country," there was a creeping concern. It was not yet fear, but it was moving that way. The Nixon camp was receiving intelligence that the old fixer, Lyndon Johnson, was getting ready to spring a surprise.

17

Near Disaster

ALL year, Richard Nixon had been cruising blithely above the battle; not mixing with the people—especially the blacks—not debating, not specifying what he would do to end the war if elected. And his opponents in their own travail could not touch him. It was maddening. Yet for all that, Nixon knew Lyndon Johnson, and behind the candidate's outward confidence had been a gnawing anticipation and worry that at the eleventh hour, Johnson would make some move in Vietnam that could cut him and his impregnable machine down. Inexorably now, it was happening, and neither Nixon nor his machine could stop it: Johnson was laboring frantically to arrange a deal with Hanoi that would bring Saigon directly into the stalemated Paris peace talks in exchange for a total halt in the American bombing of North Vietnam. The political impact at home would be devastating; the smooth, unflappable Nixon campaign juggernaut could be thrown out of kilter for the first time—and Nixon knew it. The panic among the men at the controls was slow in building, because Johnson was having great difficulties striking the bargain with Hanoi—and with his stubborn ally in Saigon, who feared any deal would be a sellout. But the makings of panic were there, and everybody at the command level of the Nixon organization was aware of it.

In the final three weeks the carefully insulated, programmed

Nixon campaign that had slipped steadfastly past one turbulent event after another all through 1967 and 1968 suddenly found itself forced off the resolute path of nonconflict to which it had been so purposefully committed. Before those last three weeks had run their course, the greatest weaknesses of the Nixon machine—its inflexibility in crisis and its inability to break out of its defensive, hold-the-line posture—would be laid bare by a series of unprogrammed bombshells. And in the end, it would be not so much political skill and planning, but luck and pure grit by a seasoned candidate determined to ride out the turbulence, that would carry the day.

The word, or at least the clear impression, that Johnson finally had worked out the deal to Saigon's satisfaction and was about to order the bombing halt hit the Nixon camp in mid-October. The President had been keeping the candidates advised by phone, and it is not entirely clear whether Nixon got first word of what was going on from him or from other sources in the government, but he did get a signal. In Kansas City on October 16, Nixon was about to speak before a large crowd in the city's old Union Station when he was called to a phone in an anteroom. Later, it was reported the call had been from Johnson, presumably to advise Nixon the negotiations on a bombing halt were approaching a decisive point. (Some Nixon aides observed with some bafflement much later that Johnson had been surprisingly considerate about keeping the opposition candidate posted. But that didn't stop the Nixon camp from being wary and suspicious at the time.)

The next day, in Johnstown, Pennsylvania, Nixon—seeing Lyndon Johnson's long arm reaching out for him—moved deftly if transparently to blunt the blow. "If a bombing halt can be agreed to in Vietnam . . . one which will not endanger American lives, and one which will increase the chances for bringing a peaceful and honorable solution to the war," Nixon said soberly, "then we are for it. And the one man who can make that determination is the President of the United States. Let's let him make that determination, and if he makes it, we will support him because we want peace, and we do not want to play politics with peace."

Ziegler denied Nixon had any inside information that the

United States was about to stop the bombing. Nevertheless, it was clear that in advance of such action, Nixon was carefully staking out a position that would keep his front-running campaign on an even keel. Nixon's pledge of support, Ziegler said, assumed that the two conditions—safeguarding American lives and advancing the chances of peace—would be met in any bombing halt. The "assumption" shrewdly left the door open for Nixon to criticize the bombing halt later on grounds that the conditions were not being met. "It put him in position not to be hurt," an insider recalled later.

Nixon repeated his pledge that night in Rochester before another full house momentarily marred only by a single loud heckler who kept shouting at the candidate. The man was removed by several police officers, to the roaring approval of the crowd. Nixon himself stopped speaking and, grinning, watched the man being hauled out. It was a far cry from the kind of mass heckling to which Humphrey had been subjected earlier in the campaign. "In our meetings," Nixon said proudly, "the cheers drown out the hecklers every time." It was true, but it was not surprising, since rally marshals always were alerted to be on guard against unruly-looking characters. For some rallies admission tickets were distributed, and only to the identifiable faithful.

Another reason the cheers always drowned out the heckling, it became clear the next day in Boston, was that only meetings at which cheers could be assured were held. Nixon already had written off Massachusetts but went to Boston ostensibly for another of his regional TV citizen-panel shows, to be beamed into New England. The Massachusetts Republican organization and Governor Volpe first considered a massive rally on Boston Common, then a smaller one in the Commonwealth Armory, but both ideas were dropped. The memory was too fresh of Humphrey and even Ted Kennedy being heckled by the large Boston-Cambridge antiwar student community. Finally, a day before Nixon's arrival, telegrams were dispatched to Republican leaders throughout New England to come to Boston for a pep rally in a secure ballroom at the Somerset Hotel. Traveling Nixon aides contended the armory rally never really had been scheduled and that the insulated New England GOP pep rally had been arranged "in the last week." But Volpe unwittingly spilled the beans. "They're very cautious," he told reporters, referring to the palace guard around the candidate.

Before the nearly 1,000 faithful who heard the pep talk at the Somerset, Nixon's words somehow seemed out of step with his pointed avoidance of the electorate in Boston. "There is too much hate—the young against the old, the black against the white, the white against the black," he told them. "Simply to allow the American people to vent that hatred as they vote for Nixon—to do so because they are voting against somebody else—that isn't enough. We don't want to win it that way. We don't want to back into this victory. We want to win it going away . . . and we want to be for something." And then the candidate went to his room, where he remained most of the time until he was driven to the television studio. After the show, he went straight back again, thus completing a stay in Boston of nearly twenty-four hours without once having shown himself in person to the voters. (During the New England regional television show, a panelist, Loring Swaim, asked Nixon why he had canceled his outdoor rally in Boston. "If this is to be, as you have said, the most intensive windup campaign that we have ever seen, why did you pass up that chance, and instead meet with party leaders?" Nixon replied with aplomb that "I had to find a way to get to as many people as I possibly could in this last two and a half weeks of the campaign," and he needed the time in Boston to record two radio talks. The answer, of course, sidestepped the question as to why he addressed the party leaders *instead* of going through with the scheduled rally.) *

On Saturday, October 20, Nixon flew about 1,600 miles—for one rally speech to an audience of 4,000 in an already solid Republican district in the Chicago area and another speech at an Eatontown, New Jersey, shopping center. Then, only two weeks from the election, he took Sunday and most of Monday

---

* The prohibition against reporters in the television studio for the citizen panel was carried to the ridiculous. In the audience at the Boston telecast were the parents of the AP reporter assigned to the Nixon campaign, Walter Mears. When the show was over, Mears sought entry to say good-bye to them. Security men barred him, and only when Mears caught the attention of John Ehrlichman inside was he admitted. Nixon made amends by personally greeting Mears' parents.

off, conferring with aides at his Fifth Avenue apartment and taping more radio talks.

Although Johnson still had not made the move of which Nixon was fearful, other signs were crowding in to disturb his reverie. The latest Gallup Poll showed Nixon still well ahead but Humphrey gaining: 43 percent for Nixon to 31 for Humphrey, with 20 percent still for Wallace and 6 percent undecided. The Harris Survey had Nixon ahead by only five points, 40 to 35, with 18 for Wallace and 7 undecided. As the gap narrowed, the specter of a Constitutional crisis grew. Nixon, knowing Humphrey would be the probable winner if the election were thrown into the Democratic-dominated House and no deal was made with Wallace, had called on Humphrey to agree that the winner of the popular vote be declared the next President. But Humphrey said he would "stand by the Constitutional process." Nixon said Humphrey's stand "is a clear indication that he cannot win the popular vote and his only hope of winning is to get Mr. Wallace enough votes in enough states to deny the electoral college vote to Nixon."

It was not just Wallace, though, but Humphrey himself, who was causing consternation in the Nixon camp now. Wallace votes in the key Northern states were falling away, and organized labor was making a monumental effort to bring them back home to the Democratic column. Nixon had to try to counter that. Chotiner for one was concerned that the campaign had gone overboard on TV, relying so heavily on the media boys who had not been through the rigors and tensions of a national campaign before.

In the view of some Nixon strategists, something very dangerous psychologically and tactically had happened. There were signs that what Republicans feared most—"the Dewey syndrome"—was developing. "All along we had our standing in the polls to protect," one of them said later. "We had to protect what we had. But a defensive posture was in conflict with our position as the 'out' party, which called for identifying problems and forcing the 'ins' to defend what they had done. We set out trying to save what we had, short of boredom. But the same thing seemed to be happening that happened with Dewey. He was so lofty in 1948 he lost his identity as the 'out.' Now Nixon, who had campaigned as though he already was President, already was 'in,' began to be regarded as the 'in.' And when he realized it, it was pretty late in the game. He had to break out of that, to go on the attack as an 'out' is expected to do, but when it was that close to the wire, he had to consider how far he could go. We were positioned in the middle between Humphrey and Wallace, where the strong feelings did not reside, and where most of the country was. Politically we had to play it day by day—who's hurting you more, Wallace or Humphrey, and who's hurting you where you are. We tried to play them off, tried to expand the middle a little where it counted."

Where it counted, perhaps more than anywhere else at this late stage, was Ohio. Although most blue-collar voters in the state were registered Democrats, Ohio was considered vulnerable to Nixon because many union members had a record of voting Republican in spite of their registration. Thus, when Wallace votes began to scatter in Ohio, the Nixon camp had strong reason to hope they could fall Nixon's way. It was this thinking that guided the strategy as Nixon headed for Cincinnati and a whistle-stop train tour through western Ohio the following day that would reveal the first outward signs of pressure.

In Cincinnati, suddenly, it was more like the old Nixon than at any time earlier in the campaign. Before 16,000 cheering faithful at the Cincinnati Garden in solid Taft Republican country, Nixon unloaded on Humphrey. He called him a "do-nothing candidate on law and order" and recalled a two-year-old Humphrey statement that had he lived in a slum as a youth, "I might have led a pretty good revolt." That kind of remark, Nixon said, constituted "adult delinquency not worthy of the Vice President of the United States. . . . There is no cause that justifies breaking the law . . . we will make sure that the wave of crime will not be the wave of the future."

The next day, on the Ohio whistle-stop, Nixon castigated Humphrey over a whole range of issues. At Middletown: "Mr. Humphrey's public record gives no indication that he believes there is a bottom to the well of the United States Treasury. He has built a public career of buying the people's votes with the people's money." At Dayton: "Hubert Humphrey . . . takes a lackadaisical do-nothing approach to law and order. For four years Mr. Humphrey has sat on his hands and watched the United States become a nation where fifty percent of American women are frightened to walk within a mile of their homes at night. . . . Freedom from fear must be restored to the cities and towns of America, and one of the first requisites is the defeat of Hubert Humphrey in November." At Springfield: "There's a mess in Washington. Let's clean it up. . . . When you clean up a mess, you don't turn to a man who helped make the mess." At London: "Whenever I begin to discuss the Supreme Court, Mr. Humphrey acts like we're in church. Mr. Humphrey's respectful silence [on controversial Supreme Court decisions on law enforcement] may stem from the fact that he has spent four years in Obedience School."

It was, indisputably, Law and Order Day on the rails across Ohio. At the final stop at the town of Deshler, one that Richard Nixon was to recall in an entirely different context on the morning after the election, Nixon told the crowd that pressed around his train in the gathering darkness: "In the forty-five minutes it takes to ride from Lima to Deshler, this is what has happened in America: There has been one murder, two rapes, forty-five major crimes of violence, countless robberies and auto thefts . . ."

In the press car, typewriters began clacking away. The lead written by Richard Dougherty of the Los Angeles *Times* was fairly typical: "It was the Richard M. Nixon of old Tuesday as the Republican presidential nominee whistlestopped through the towns and cities of Western Ohio heaping scorn on Vice President Humphrey."

Law and Order Day, and the very critical press accounts of Nixon's behavior, caused trepidation among the candidate's aides on the train and back in the New York headquarters. Governor Shafer and John Eisenhower, preparing for a Nixon visit through Pennsylvania, were aghast and so notified the Nixon camp. A strategy meeting was held by Mitchell the next morning; advice was flashed to Nixon to back off the tough law-and-order line. Mitchell, according to one account, thought what the candidate had said was fine, but the media boys had apoplexy. There had been a sharp difference of opinion in the first place about whether Nixon should go ahead with the tactic of hitting Humphrey so hard. Some aides felt that Nixon already was close enough to Wallace on the law-and-order issue to draw away slipping Wallace votes on that score. What he had to do, these aides argued, was to make himself more credible on gut social issues like social security, Medicare and the other traditionally Democratic vote-getters with which Humphrey could pull the drifters back in line.

"He had to convince the Democrats he was not a coldhearted Wall Street S.O.B.," one of the insiders at the Mitchell meeting said later. "He couldn't compete with Hubert in promising, but at least he could reassure them that he wouldn't take it away." And another said: "That kind of semantics was just knocking off Wallace. We had to campaign positively to get what he lost— campaign on jobs, minimum wage, et cetera. Instead, he talked about crime and law and order. It underscored the extent to which our campaign didn't foresee the opportunity to get a lot of lower-middle-class voters Wallace had drained away. But we didn't know how to get them. We were just thrashing out."

In Michigan and Pennsylvania the next two days, Nixon did in fact cool the harsh law-and-order pitch. He continued to hammer at Humphrey because there was the same Wallace fallaway going on in both states, but he focused his attacks mostly on other issues. With fear of a Johnson bombshell on Vietnam still hanging over his campaign, Nixon sought to contrast his own responsible position with a picture of Humphrey as a reckless and dangerous opportunist undermining the Vietnam negotiations. In an airport hangar rally in Saginaw, he accused the Vice President of having "the fastest, loosest tongue in the nation and the fastest switch of position ever seen in American politics. . . . I think the American people will question the peace-keeping capabilities of a candidate who week after week shows on every issue that he would rather switch than fight, rather spend than save, rather talk than mind his tongue on sensitive international matters. When a man is on all sides of the issue he creates a great risk of miscalculation on the part of our adversaries. . . . In this terribly important function of keeping the peace, you must remember that when there is miscalculation, when a potential enemy is not sure what you stand for, that's when the danger of war escalates."

The hard-hitting personal attack, and such labels hung on Humphrey as "the fastest and loosest tongue," recalled to some of the traveling press what Nixon had said specifically at Key Biscayne and even during the Ohio whistle-stop—that he was not going to engage in "name-calling" with Humphrey and was not going to "respond in kind." Did the switch indicate growing panic in the Nixon camp? Most assuredly not, Nixon aides were quick to tell anybody who asked. It was nothing more than part of the windup battle plan, aimed mainly at Republican workers who needed partisan firing up in the closing days. For the general public, one aide suggested, Nixon's series of ten nationwide radio talks was presenting the more thoughtful side of the Nixon campaign. Again there was the problem of sorting out the appearance from the reality.

The Michigan tour provided a special treat for the candidate. Waiting to greet him with George Romney at Saginaw were two heroes of the 1968 World Series, Al Kaline and Jim Northrup of the Detroit Tigers. There and in Grand Rapids, Nixon talked animatedly, small-boy-like, with the two sluggers, asking them about how they felt when they got crucial hits. At one point, a group of deaf mute schoolchildren were brought over to meet the candidate, who thereupon tried to let the kids know who his companions were. Pointing to them, then swinging an imaginary bat, Nixon would say: "Kaline . . . Northrup . . . Detroit Tigers? . . . World Series? Baseball?" The kids watched him with mouths agape.

The radio talks were not without their own bombast on occasion. While he was touring Pennsylvania, Nixon in a radio tape charged that the United States had "a gravely serious security gap" as a result of "policies which now threaten to make America second best both in number and quality of major weapons." The charge was reminiscent of the "missile gap" that John Kennedy had used so effectively against Nixon in 1960. The Johnson administration, Nixon said, had adopted "a peculiar, unprecedented doctrine called 'parity' [that] meant America would no longer try to be first. We would only stay even. This concept has done us incalculable damage." As a result, he warned, "by 1970 or 1971 we could find ourselves with a 'survival gap.' " The charge had the makings of a major issue, but Secretary of Defense Clark Clifford immediately released statistics on relative U.S.–Soviet strength that took the edge off. Besides, other things were developing in the realm of the Vietnam peace talks that soon would command all headlines.

Humphrey, desperately trying to make hay with Nixon's call for a delay in the nuclear nonproliferation treaty, seized on his opponent's "security gap" talk as a possible opening. Now he castigated the Republican candidate's call for nuclear "superiority" as an attempt to promote "an increasing militarization of American life and American foreign policy." Nixon countered a few days later by making an eleventh radio talk—only ten had been scheduled by the Nixon operation—in which he said he would as President press for enactment of the treaty and would seek "meaningful arms control agreements with our adversaries." The additional talk suggested that the "security gap" speech may have been excessive and needed softening, but Nixon aides denied it.

Nixon also announced suddenly that, for the first time in two years, he would appear the next Sunday night on a network panel show. Asked how come, he told reporters on his plane: "I never turn down ten million people." It was another sign that the Nixon camp was worried about the impact of a total bombing halt over North Vietnam. Nixon had, of course, been turning down TV audiences that size for two years, and the debates Humphrey had sought also would have attracted at least that many viewers.

The visible campaign meanwhile had moved into New York for the next to last weekend. The entourage was settled comfortably into the Waldorf-Astoria on Friday afternoon when Herb Klein and Ron Ziegler walked into the pressroom bearing a statement from the candidate that established beyond doubt the concern about Lyndon Johnson's expected Vietnam ploy that now gripped the Nixon command. It said:

In the last thirty-six hours I have been advised of a flurry of meetings in the White House and elsewhere on Vietnam. I am told that top officials in the Administration have been driving very hard for an agreement on a bombing halt, accompanied possibly by a cease-fire, in the immediate future. I have since learned these reports are true.

I am also told that this spurt of activity is a cynical, last-minute attempt by President Johnson to salvage the candidacy of Mr. Humphrey. This I do not believe.

It was a very cute trick, but very transparent—gaining publication of a rumor harmful to the opposition by publicly expressing disbelief in it. And true to form, Nixon was not content to draw public attention to the idea that Johnson was callously playing politics with the war. He had to say how pure Richard Nixon was for not taking political advantage of the rumor!

This latest suggestion of Presidential politicking with the Vietnam war is but one of many similar rumors and press speculations in recent weeks. I think it is only appropriate, therefore, to reiterate statements on this subject that I have repeatedly made in this campaign.

At no time in the campaign have I found the President anything but impartial and candid in his dealings with the major Presidential contenders about Vietnam. I know this has not been easy for him. Beginning long before the Republican Convention in early August, influential elements within and outside his Party have subjected him to intense pressure to contrive what he has aptly described as a "fake peace." It is to his credit that he has withstood these pressures.

The fact is, President Johnson is profoundly concerned about our half-million servicemen, including his two sons-in-law, in Vietnam. In every conversation I have had with him he has made it clear that he will not play politics with this war.

In foreign affairs the President must be our nation's only spokesman. The Paris negotiations are critically important and exceedingly delicate. At such a time I believe every presidential candidate should mind his tongue to avoid weakening our diplomatic hand by irresponsible comments on the matters at issue. This has been my position throughout the campaign. [But not, the observation clearly implied, Humphrey's.]

I have often said that all Americans will welcome a bombing halt provided it will, in the long term, save American lives and not cost

American lives. The President's adherence to this criterion has commanded our support. The protection of our fighting men, as he eloquently stated before the American Legion Convention six weeks ago, has demanded it. I have not been informed of any change in the President's position.

Progress toward a durable and honorable peace is far more important than any political campaign could possibly be. I will continue to do all that I properly can to facilitate the President's pursuit of an agreement that will save American lives and lay the foundation for stability and a just peace in Vietnam and throughout Southeast Asia.

Klein and Ziegler immediately were peppered with questions. Who were the "top officials" referred to? Who had told Nixon it was "a cynical, last-minute attempt" by Johnson to bail out Humphrey? "You've heard it at almost every stop," Klein replied. "I'm not referring to any particular individual." But the reporters had trouble recalling having heard it at almost every stop. Ziegler allowed at one point that members of the staff were concerned, but he wouldn't say which ones. Klein asked reporters why they were so concerned about who on the staff was concerned. "I'm concerned that you're trying to get a rumor in the paper by denying it," one of them replied. "We don't participate in that sort of thing," Klein said. Shortly afterward, Congressman Mel Laird, later to be Nixon's Secretary of Defense, came into the press room to take soundings about the impact of the ploy. He insisted that the rumor was everywhere that Johnson was about to pull a fast one, and he was surprised to be told that the reporters hadn't heard it.

Months later, a Nixon staffer told me of the incident: "It wouldn't have been proper for Nixon to make the accusation, but somebody else had to. There's a hole in the dike, or three or four holes, and the water is gushing through, and you can feel the thing swaying, but you know in three or four days the water pressure will go down if you can hold on. Elections do get out of hand. You can't control them, but we did a pretty good job. At the end it's like riding a tiger; you hold on."

What made Nixon's "defense" of Lyndon Johnson so interesting was that it was not simply the floating of a rumor to get it

430

printed. It was the way it sought as well to make Nixon a hero for dissociating himself from the "talk." More important, it revealed the high level of inner trepidation beneath the outward confidence and calm in the superefficient Nixon machine. "In the general we ran a much more mechanized show," one of the chief idea men told me later. "We had the armor out rather than the foot soldiers." Ten days from the end, the armor was creaking noticeably, and among those who noticed was Lyndon Johnson. He jumped on the Nixon implications as "ugly and unfair charges" and insisted he was as pure as the driven snow. It was hard to decide at this point whom not to believe.

That night Nixon made the last of his regional citizen-panel telecasts, this one beamed to most major states east of the Mississippi. He took pains to follow the staff advice that he make himself more credible to low-income Democrats. He said he favored a national standard in welfare payments by the states, and sought again to give assurances he was not recommending a new and costly arms race to keep the United States ahead of the Soviet Union in every weapon.

Now one of the last pitfalls was approaching. Nixon spent most of Saturday and Sunday, after a quick swing into New Jersey, preparing for his first network confrontation with a panel of reporters since 1966. The show was CBS' *Face the Nation* with Martin Agronsky and John Hart of CBS and David Broder of the Washington *Post* as panelists. It was a tough group, and Nixon, nervous and wary, knew it. For the full thirty minutes the three reporters went after Nixon as though they had been waiting for two years to get him on the spot. Nixon struggled to seize the upper hand but came off very defensive, sometimes patronizing and above all harassed; about ten times in the half hour he used the expression "let me make it very clear" or some close variation, like a debater concerned that his points might be missed.

The panelists were particularly rough with Nixon on the matter of the Vietnam bombing halt "rumors" and Johnson's countercharge. "I think President Johnson wants to bring this war to an end," Nixon said. "I think he'd like to have a bombing pause provided it isn't going to cost American lives, that it will save lives rather than cost them. I made that

431

statement and I would think that the President would be thanking, not attacking, me."

Agronsky was not satisfied with the answer on the "rumor." He asked Nixon: "Why, if you didn't believe it, did you raise it at all?" Nixon answered: "Because it seemed to me that with all the speculation that was going on, the speculation that there was about to be a bombing pause, and that it would be negotiated for political reasons, that it was important for the man most intimately involved—I would be the man I suppose that was supposed to be harmed by a bombing pause, although I am not sure that's the case, it was important for me to nail it once and for all. . . . My point is that I think we ought to be consistent on this and I think President Johnson has been consistent, I've been consistent. Mr. Humphrey ought to get in line, agree with his President for a change." It was quite a switch, accusing Humphrey of being out of line with Johnson only four days after having accused him of spending "four years in Obedience School." But the pressure was building now, and nerves and logic and memories were getting frayed on all sides.

John Hart was particularly persistent. Noting that Nixon had "confirmed" for the first time that a possible cease-fire was part of the negotiations, Hart asked Nixon whether he considered such a statement "rug-pulling" in the midst of the Paris talks. "Not at all," Nixon replied, with a trace of testiness. "Absolutely not, because after all, who has backed the President in this particular instance? I have. I am not the one that has even suggested we should have a bombing halt without conditions. That's Hubert Humphrey. I have been the one that is saying that the President is absolutely correct in saying we shall have a bombing halt provided it is going to result in saving American lives rather than costing American lives. That's a sound position. I back him up and I only wish that Hubert Humphrey now would button up his lip and stick with the President on this."

The last was an unusually tough remark coming from the "new, new Nixon." He followed it, in response to a question about a New York *Times* editorial accusing Governor Agnew of a conflict of interest involving a bank with which his state did business, by charging the paper with "the lowest kind of gutter politics that a great newspaper could possibly engage in." He called the charges "stale" and "inaccurate" and warned a retraction would be demanded "legally." (None ever was made, though the paper ran a story "clarifying" its position and in so doing taking much of the edge off its charges.) The interview continued that way, aggressive and combative, to the end, and although Nixon clearly was harassed, he persevered.

Contributing to the mounting tension now was the latest Gallup Poll. It showed Humphrey closing in even more; Nixon, 44 percent; Humphrey, 36; Wallace, 15. On the plane to Pittsburgh on October 28, Nixon attributed Humphrey's gain to "Wallace slippage" and professed not to be worried. "It finally came," he said. "Humphrey picks up a little more in the North, I'll pick up a little more in the South. Over all, it's a wash." As for the polls, he said, "Whatever Gallup shows as the final figure and whatever Harris shows as the final figure, I predict I will run three percent better than Gallup and five percent better than Harris."

Nixon's own optimism, and his outward high spirits and confidence, did not altogether sustain his team, however. The superefficient machine was showing more signs of unraveling. Bad advance work on Saturday had booked the candidate into a poor hall in Jersey City where hecklers were allowed to dominate, and had failed to generate the usual impressive crowd at another New Jersey stop. In Albany, Rockefeller produced his state employees outside the Capitol and they gave Nixon a mild reception that more than anything else conveyed Rockefeller's own coolness. In Cleveland on the final Wednesday of the campaign, there was a minor fiasco when local Republicans issued printed invitations, turned away young people who looked as though they might be hecklers, and wound up with less than half the 10,000-seat Municipal Auditorium filled. The usual balloons were there and the hand-painted signs, but many of the signs remained stacked among rows of empty chairs. For once the candidate could not intone about how "all over America record crowds are turning out. . . ." Instead, he rushed through his text and departed. "Somebody's going to hear about it in the morning," a ruffled aide said. "This is the last time the local committee will give out tickets." Reporters who tried to interview some of the young people denied admission were pushed away by police or by local Republican functionaries.

Nixon himself was becoming a bit more careless with his rhetoric than usual. When crowds would fail to respond adequately, he would raise his voice as if to coax the applause and cheers from them. After saying in Albany that it was time "to forget all the personality charges that have been hurled," in Pittsburgh he called his Democratic opponents "that disorganized rabble" who had staged the Chicago scene. At Marion, Illinois, he promised "jobs for everybody" in his new administration and in Rochester, Minnesota, seemed specifically to be promising one for Representative Albert H. Quie, a farm expert who introduced him. Quie, he said, "will be my Orville Freeman, if you know what I mean." Most listeners thought they did, but Nixon hastened later, when stories started moving that he already had tapped Quie to be his Secretary of Agriculture, to pass the word he had been speaking facetiously.

Now at last the blitz was on, in terms both of intensity of campaigning and of aggressive language. In shopping center rallies in suburban Detroit he repeatedly issued the "rabble" line; in Syracuse he charged that Humphrey "can't even control himself"; in a nationwide radio broadcast while he was in Cleveland, he charged that Humphrey "hopes for a Constitutional crisis to wheel and deal his way to power" and again challenged him to agree to back the winner of the popular vote. The challenge was understandable, in light of the estimate he now was getting from his brain trusters sitting in New York. "They didn't realize," said one of the traveling strategists later, "that the Wallace voters in the North were leapfrogging Nixon and going to Humphrey. The geniuses in New York were still telling Nixon he was going to win by three to five million." Had Nixon failed to win the popular vote, his challenge to Humphrey would have been an extreme embarrassment. The fact that he made it at all underlined in retrospect how wrong the New York "geniuses" were in those final desperate days.

On one issue, however, Nixon remained cautious of tongue—the war and a possible bombing halt. He kept walking a tightrope, repeating he would say or do nothing to harm the Presi-

dent's position if, as he noted warily in Cleveland, delicate
negotiations were taking place "as we understand they may be."
He knew, of course, that they were, and in a radio talk on the
previous Sunday he had sought more specifically than before to
carve out a position that would enable him to withstand the
political impact of a bombing halt. "These talks," he said,
"have entered a crucial phase. . . . An end to the bombing is
the highest trump card in our negotiators' hands. It should not
be wasted, or lightly played. Only the President can determine
whether the guarantees Hanoi offers in return are credible and
adequate, for only he has all the relevant information. My view
is this: If the bombing can be ended in a way that will speed an
honorable peace; if it can be ended in a way that will save
American lives rather than costing American lives, and *if the
President determines these conditions have been met by the
North Vietnamese,* then I will support his order to stop the
bombing." (Italics added.) That last was to prove a critical, and
politically masterful, phrase.

On Thursday, October 31, Lyndon Johnson at last dropped
the other shoe. The day had begun pleasantly enough for
Nixon. He had cast an absentee ballot in his New York apartment, along with his wife and their daughter Tricia, voting for
the first time. Nixon, upholding the sanctity of the American
ballot, declined to say how he had voted, but added, "I don't
mind if you speculate." Tricia asked him how to cast a crossover
vote—a strange question for the loyal daughter of a loyal Republican unity candidate for President—but when he began to
say, "What I'd do if I were you," she interrupted with, "Oh, I
know what I'm going to do." Nixon grinned and told reporters
admitted to the family scene: "Well, I can't tell the younger
generation what to do." It wasn't quite like the old gag scene of
Dick playing "God Bless America" on the piano while Pat
stitched stars on Old Glory, but it was close enough to bolster
the spirits of the good, forgotten Americans in the heartland
who were waiting patiently to vote for Richard Nixon.

The rest of the day Nixon worked on the speech he would
make at his final big Eastern rally, in Madison Square Garden
that night. At about six o'clock, or four hours before he was to
go on, the phone rang. It was Johnson, in a conference call to

435

all three candidates that confirmed Nixon's expectations—and fears. Agreement had been reached with Hanoi on broadening the Paris talks to include Saigon and the National Liberation Front. The broadened talks would start the day after the election, and accordingly Johnson had ordered a complete bombing halt to be effective the next morning. Nixon thanked Johnson for the advance word and hung up.

Shortly afterward, Johnson went on television and informed the nation. He did not present the news categorically as a deal, only that in light of the halt "we expect" there would be "prompt, productive, serious and intensive negotiations in an atmosphere that is conducive to progress." But it was enough to send a giant wave of relief, and of hope, sweeping across the nation—and to send shudders of impending doom through the more fainthearted in the Nixon camp.

For at least three weeks, American diplomats in Paris, Washington and Saigon had been working without letup to bring off the halt before the election. The recalcitrance of the Saigon regime had been the main stumbling-block. It saw itself being sold down the river for the Presidential aspirations of Hubert Humphrey, whose earlier call for a bombing halt had not washed well at all in Saigon. The secrecy of the probings, however, kept the conversations in Saigon to a very small group; some said later in fact that only President Nguyen Van Thieu had been consulted, and that his seeming concurrence was no concurrence at all. In short order, reaction in Saigon to the Johnson statement was to confirm that view. But Nixon did not know that as he left for Madison Square Garden, where Jackie Gleason and other Nixon supporters from the world of show business were entertaining 19,000 screened and assembled faithful awaiting the candidate's speech.

Despite the potential for political disaster of what Johnson had told him, Nixon cautiously hewed to his same line that the national interest demanded that he button up. He limited himself to expressing a hope that the halt would "bring some progress" to the peace talks and, pointing to Agnew sitting behind him on the stage, said: "Neither he nor I will destroy the chance of peace. We want peace."

Nixon aides took a bold, confident pose with reporters. The

halt had come too late, they insisted, to have any real impact favorable to Humphrey. The position that Nixon had carved out, they noted, anticipated the situation and required no last-minute adjustments. And that was the way Nixon played it. On Friday, November 1, in the first of a two-day swing through Texas, which John Tower was striving valiantly to save for him, Nixon made no substantive mention of the subject that by now was dominating the nation's headlines. As long as Johnson was trying to make progress in Paris toward peace, Nixon said in Fort Worth, "I'm not going to say anything to undercut him. Peace is too important for politics, and that's the way we're going to play it."

Others, however, already were planting the partisan seeds. J. S. "Tiny" Gooch, a local lawyer who introduced Nixon, said: "I hope this peace move put forward so forcibly last night really means something. I sincerely hope we're going to have peace, but I just can't help but believe that Hanoi would much rather deal with Johnson and Humphrey than with President Nixon." John Tower said the halt "raises questions" about why immediate cessation was required when the broadened talks were not to start until the day after the election. As for Nixon, he concentrated on Humphrey, calling him one of those "fuzzy thinkers" and "false prophets" who "profess to believe that keeping America strong is somehow being against peace." But Ned Kenworthy of the New York *Times* found Nixon "almost dispirited" in the delivery of his set speech.

But then, suddenly, on Saturday morning came the shattering word from Saigon: Thieu was not going to play ball. When others in his regime had learned of the bombing halt, they had revolted. There were emotional emergency meetings, and soon the wires were humming with the outcome, stated tersely by Thieu: "The Government of South Vietnam deeply regrets not to be able to participate in the present exploratory talks." Nixon at first handled the news warily. In a noon speech at the Austin Municipal Airport, he observed only that "in view of the early reports that we've had this morning, the prospects for peace are not as bright as we would have hoped a few days ago."

But Nixon knew now he had Johnson trapped in a major

political misstep; that a colossal windfall had come his way, just as it had begun to appear that Nixon's own master plan had been undone by a master counterstroke from the White House. As the Nixon entourage headed from Texas to California, where the final public rally of the campaign was to be held, the first move to capitalize on the sudden turn of events was made. Aboard Nixon's plane, Bob Finch pointedly briefed two wire-service reporters, Bill Boyarsky, then of the Associated Press, and Dan Rapoport of UPI. The Nixon camp had been surprised by the Saigon news, Finch said, because from what Johnson had told Nixon on the phone Thursday night, "we had the impression that all the diplomatic ducks were in a row" before making the announcement. The allegation did not have to be spelled out further—Nixon through Finch was charging that Johnson had jumped the gun on announcing the halt merely to provide political benefit to Humphrey. Finch insisted that his name not be connected with the statements, but it was clear to the reporters he was Nixon's emissary to them. In fact, when Rapoport asked Finch about a clarifying point, Finch went back to Nixon's private compartment and returned with the answer; Nixon obviously was involved in the Finch ploy all the way.

Now the political nerve ends really were being rubbed raw. Nixon on Sunday morning taped the *Meet the Press* panel and immediately underwent rigorous questioning about what Finch had said on the plane. Herbert Kaplow of NBC News hit him with it on the very first question.

Kaplow: "Mr. Nixon, some of your close aides have been trying to spread the word that President Johnson timed the Vietnam bombing pause to help Vice President Humphrey in Tuesday's election. Do you agree with them?"

Nixon: "No, I don't make that charge. I must say that many of my aides and many of the people supporting my candidacy around the country seem to share that view. They share it, I suppose, because the pause came at that time so late in the campaign. But President Johnson has been very candid with me throughout these discussions, and I do not make such a charge."

Kaplow: "Well, I was told about it on your campaign plane yesterday, and some other reporters were told about it by another one of your aides. Is it conceivable that they would put this out in disagreement with you?"

Nixon: "Oh, altogether conceivable. I know, for example, one of my aides who—so-called aides who made this statement is Lieutenant Governor Robert Finch. He completely disagrees with my appraisal of this. His appraisal of the situation around the country is that many people believe that the bombing pause was politically motivated and was timed to affect the election. I don't agree with him, but he is a man in his own right and has made this statement."

If Nixon did not believe at this point that there was political timing in the bombing halt, he should have been shipped forthwith to the Smithsonian Institution as one of a species. The retort was almost identically a rerun of the go-around a week earlier when Nixon had rushed out with his pathetic disclaimer of belief that Johnson was planning the halt for political purposes.

But this time, with a nationwide television audience, he went one step beyond. "I want to make it very clear that if I am elected President," he said by way of demonstrating his support of Johnson, "I will be willing to cooperate with the President in any way that he and the Secretary of State would deem helpful. If he, for example, and the Secretary of State would consider it helpful for me to go to Paris or go to Saigon in order to get the negotiations off dead center, I would be glad to do so." There had been, of course, no indication that Johnson or Dean Rusk had thought of that maneuver; yet lest anyone get the impression Nixon had anything in mind other than being helpful in suggesting it (such as a 1968 version of Eisenhower's effective 1952 pledge that "I shall go to Korea"), he added: "Let me make one thing clear. I don't suggest this as a grandstand stunt. I don't know that it would be helpful. But right now the key point, of course, is to get the South Vietnamese to that conference table. I believe they ought to go to the conference table. I think that semantical differences could be worked out, and if my influence could be helpful, I will be helpful."

The questions persisted, and Nixon continued to disavow his role in what Finch had said. ". . . The three Presidential candidates, I don't think, can be held responsible for what their campaign aides in the last forty-eight hours of the campaign are going to say about this. And I don't think Mr. Humphrey or I or anybody else—we may not agree with our aides—but there is no question they are going to answer questions to the press when they are put on this point." The answer completely sidestepped the fact that Finch had initiated the briefings with the reporters on the plane; it was not a case simply of responding to questions.

Later in the show, columnist Robert Novak asked Nixon whether it was true, as some aides on the plane had said, that Johnson in his phone call had implied or said that he had South Vietnam's approval for the bombing halt. Nixon said he had "assumed" that since Hanoi approval of Saigon's presence in Paris was "the major *quid pro quo*" for the bombing halt, that it had been approved by Saigon. Then Nixon referred to a New York *Times* story in which Xuan Thuy, the North Vietnamese representative in Paris, indicated that he too had assumed—in Nixon's words—"that all the ducks were in a row" (the same words Finch had used on the plane).

Nixon insisted that Johnson never would have agreed to the bombing halt if he had thought he did not have Saigon's support. ". . . The only *quid pro quo* we got from the bombing pause," he repeated, "at least publicly, was the right of South Vietnam to attend. Well now, if you played your trump card for the right of South Vietnam to attend and then did not know that South Vietnam was going to attend, you'd be giving away the card for nothing."

Lyndon Johnson by now had had enough of statements emanating from the Nixon camp that were disavowed by Nixon. He had heard about Finch's briefings to reporters as well as one other bit of intelligence that set off his legendary temper—and threatened to provide an incredibly bizarre final chapter to this stormiest of Presidential election years. A loyal—and individualistic—Nixon backer with connections in Southeast Asia, Mrs. Anna Chennault, the Chinese-born widow of the Flying Tigers General Claire Chennault, had been engaging in some free-lance diplomacy of her own and it had got back to the White House. In the name of the Nixon campaign, of which she was a woman's co-chairman along with Mamie Eisenhower and for which she boasted of having raised $250,000, Madame Chennault had been doing her best to throw a monkey wrench into the bombing halt talks. The White House information was that she had conveyed to her connections that Saigon would get a better deal by holding off and waiting for the Nixon administration. Not only that, but she was said to have played a role in an unusual spectacle of eleven South Vietnamese senators "endorsing" Nixon on the same day Thieu had announced rejection of the talks arrangement.

When Nixon aides found out about Madame Chennault's activities—or at least when they found out that the White House knew about them—they were aghast. Her monkey wrench, originally aimed at the Humphrey campaign, now threatened to clog the vital gears of the already clanking Nixon machine. They knew how a charge of trying to scuttle the peace talks for domestic political gain could ruin their candidate—just as they hoped that charge against Johnson would destroy Humphrey. Word that the White House was on to Mrs. Chennault's machinations came to the Nixon camp from Johnson himself, using his old friend Senate Republican Leader Everett Dirksen as an emissary. Dirksen quickly brought the word back to the President that Nixon was just as surprised and shocked about the revelation as he was.

The question now was what the Humphrey camp would do with this bombshell. And the answer—incredibly—was: nothing! After much soul-searching, and sifting of what admittedly was sketchy information, it was decided that the implications of the story simply were too hot to handle. They could completely scuttle the effort to get Saigon to the Paris peace table, which Humphrey now needed to make Johnson's total bombing halt credible. Also, some in the Humphrey camp actually argued, the revelation could make it impossible for Nixon, if elected, to govern.

The decision was either one of the noblest in American political history or one of the great tactical blunders. Possibly it was both. In any event, the Humphrey camp sat on the story, and the Nixon camp held its breath that it would not leak out. One Nixon insider theorized later that in the final reckoning, the idea that such a plot could have been concocted and carried out successfully may have been too far-fetched for the Humphrey camp to believe. "Thieu and Ky were Mrs. Chennault's friends, but to suggest she alone could change Saigon policy was ridiculous," he told me. "Theirs was a gut reaction. They resented the halt. They felt Johnson was using them. They were aware how important what they were doing was politically. These fellows aren't fools." One Nixon aide even suggested privately that Johnson had concocted the whole Chennault story just to confront Nixon with it!

Johnson in fact did call Nixon at his suite in the Century Plaza in Los Angeles Sunday afternoon, demanding to know what was going on. Nixon assured him that Mrs. Chennault had been acting on her own. Then Johnson is said to have asked Nixon who "this guy Fink" was who was making accusations in his behalf. Nixon assured him Finch too was speaking for himself.

Given Lyndon Johnson's own history of political dissembling, it seems incredible that he would have settled for Nixon's assurance on either point. Yet it is a fact that neither Johnson nor Humphrey aired the Chennault story on the final day before the balloting. Had either done so, and had the accusation of meddling in the peace talks taken hold, it could have swung to Humphrey this election that now was a cliff-hanger.

That, almost incredibly, is what the race had become. Humphrey now was working the key Northern states of New York, Pennsylvania and Ohio and gaining confidence with every step. With organized labor weaning away Wallace votes for him, he came roaring into Houston on Sunday afternoon. Johnson, shortly after having talked to Nixon on the phone, joined Humphrey for a rousing Texas-sized rally at the massive Astrodome, with Frank Sinatra leading an array of celebrities.

Among them, to the chagrin of the Nixon forces in Texas, was Democratic Governor John B. Connally. After having held Humphrey's feet to the fire at the Democratic convention, requiring him to stay in line behind the Johnson policy on Vietnam, Connally had studiously ignored the Minnesotan's campaign in the Lone Star State. He was busy with a "previous engagement" during an earlier Humphrey visit, and in fact had been helpful in more tangible ways to Nixon, privately lining up some politically influential Texans to work for the Republican candidate. It is not clear whether any outright promise was made to Connally by the Nixon camp, but he came to understand that as a former Secretary of the Navy and a Southern conservative, he had an excellent chance to be the Democrat in the Nixon Cabinet—as Secretary of Defense—if Nixon carried Texas. As the campaign came to a close, however, and Johnson himself was moved finally to help Humphrey, the President's look-alike Texas buddy apparently feared he might be left out in the cold in a state that went Democratic without him. Humphrey's final margin of victory, only 39,000 votes out of nearly 3,100,000 cast, suggests Connally could well have swung the state for Nixon had he not caved in at the end. Of the governor's last-minute leap off the Nixon train, a Nixon insider said later: "If the fellow had had a few more guts, he'd be Secretary of Defense today."

On another positive front for Humphrey, Gene McCarthy at last had given one of his predictably conditional endorsements to his Minnesota colleague, and that was expected to bring some more errant Democrats back to the fold. And then there were the polls. The final Gallup and Harris surveys were nothing short of amazing. Gallup on the last weekend had Nixon only two points ahead, 42 percent to 40 for Humphrey, in an election he said was "too close to call." Harris, polling a day later, actually had Humphrey ahead by three points, 43 percent to 40 for Nixon. From Houston, Humphrey also moved on to Los Angeles, and on Monday, while Nixon contented himself with an unscheduled visit to his southern California headquarters, Humphrey and his running mate, Senator Ed Muskie, rode in a triumphant motorcade through the same downtown streets where Robert Kennedy had received such an uproarious reception on the day after his defeat in Oregon. Crowds of Mexican-Americans and blacks who had turned out with such zeal for Kennedy repeated the performance for the beaming Humphrey, who now could look around and believe it finally, miraculously, all was coming his way. An authoritative poll in pivotal California showed him only one percentage point behind Nixon in a state he long ago had all but written off. After all the heartbreak and the heckling, the man they once had called "The Happy Warrior" was just that again.

As the Humphrey-Muskie motorcade was attracting all the publicity that last day, Nixon stood on a chair before about fifty party workers and told them new leadership was going to be needed to avoid "what could be a diplomatic disaster" in Paris. He called the situation "quite discouraging" and spoke of putting together "fragile hopes of peace that now seem to be hopelessly apart." Then Nixon went back to the Century Plaza for more reports on the impact of the bombing halt. Klein told reporters that spot phone calls to three hundred persons across the country on Saturday had turned up only two percent—six individuals—who felt the halt might change their vote. But the professional pollsters were finding it much otherwise. Both Mitchell and Nixon sought to discredit the Harris Survey, Mitchell calling it "a gratuitous concoction" that would not "con the voters," and Nixon saying he did not consider it "reliable." Nevertheless, the Nixon camp was very badly shaken.

"By Sunday night I thought we were finished," one of Nixon's speechwriters said later. "The bombing halt really had the women moving for Humphrey. I thought then we were down the tube. But when the South Vietnamese indicated they hadn't been plugged in, it started back. It knocked the hell out of the euphoria about a peace breakthrough. But 'the boss' stayed remarkably cool through all of it. He checked the polls and watched TV. He was as calm as he could be. The old fatalism was operating then."

More than fatalism was applied, however, to try to stem the collapse. Several hours before Nixon went on his final two-stage telethon on election eve, his staff released a statement they said had been written by General Eisenhower from his room at Walter Reed Army Hospital in Washington. (Officials at the hospital said it had come from an aide at the general's Gettysburg home.) "Opinion polls this morning," Eisenhower's statement said, "suggest to me that the American people may have been swayed by President Johnson's recent order to stop our attacks on North Vietnam. If that interpretation is correct, I feel an urgent obligation to offer these observations. First, Richard Nixon deserves the plaudits of the American people for his extraordinarily responsible conduct of his campaign respecting Vietnam. His outspoken support of the President throughout the campaign in major measures on the war gave the President the freedom to take his action. Second, even though the President's action, taken just before the election, seemed likely to have political repercussions adverse to his own fortunes, Nixon resisted all pressures to challenge the action on political grounds. In the circumstances, this must have taken extreme self-restraint. . . .

"Third, the adversities that have developed in the President's program since the bombing halt was announced have suggested to many people that the President acted hastily, perhaps seeking to influence the election. But again Nixon withheld criticism. I suggest that his statesmanlike conduct warrants national commendation."

The Eisenhower endorsement, quite obviously, was valued highly. To make sure it had maximum impact, David Eisenhower read parts of his grandfather's message later during the telethon.

The final TV extravaganza was conducted in two one-hour segments, with the Nixon girls on the team answering phone calls. The telethon was too extremely important for the campaign, however, to be left to random phone calls. So the Nixon media boys devised a shrewd system for preserving the appearance of authenticity without the substance. Questions were written by the staff on subjects and in language that would be most helpful to the candidate. Then, when questions in the same general area were called in, the ersatz questions were substituted, using the names of the original callers. Nixon sat with his old straight man, Bud Wilkinson, just off to the side, posing the questions. Once again Bud served them up soft and fat. Another carefully screened studio audience was brought in, and newsmen were banished to another studio where tables and numerous TV monitors were set up. There, they could watch not only Nixon but Humphrey and Wallace in their simultaneous telethons. Humphrey's was much more informal, using scores of Hollywood and television stars to keep the show moving. Muskie was with Humphrey; Agnew meanwhile was safely tucked away in one of the safest Nixon states, far-off Virginia.

The Agnew problem obviously was weighing heavy in Nixon's mind. In both segments of the telethon, Wilkinson led off with questions permitting Nixon to respond favorably about his controversial running mate. If Nixon could do it all over, Wilkinson asked solicitously, would he pick Agnew again? "I most certainly would," Nixon said. "I'm not unaware of the fact that Agnew has been the subject of some pretty vicious attacks by the opposition, but he's a man of great courage. He doesn't wilt under fire. . . . If he had to hold the highest position in the country, he'd be cool under pressure."

Nixon's pointed references to Agnew, and Agnew's absence from the studio, underlined how Humphrey, with repeated focus on Agnew, had been making points in the last weeks. In the homestretch, Humphrey constantly had contrasted his choice of Muskie with Nixon's choice of Agnew. The Democrats now ran a TV ad mentioning Agnew, followed by uproarious canned laughter, and another showing his face accompanied by the sound of a beating heart. Humphrey would tell his audiences: "My co-pilot, Ed Muskie, is ready to take over any time." It got so bad in the last week that James Doyle, then of the Boston *Globe,* composed a make-believe lead on his day's story that said: "Vice President Hubert H. Humphrey pledged today that if elected, he will resign immediately and let Senator Edmund S. Muskie become President."

Now, on election eve, Nixon told his vast TV audience that "to show you how really low they got, Humphrey three weeks ago said that we have to remember that there is one chance in three that the next man we elect won't live out his term in office." Then Nixon added: "If anything should happen to me, Agnew will be a strong, compassionate, good, firm man." Nobody knew better than Richard Nixon what it was to be a drag on a national ticket, a running mate under fire.

The two hours on television were an ordeal for Nixon, but he was equal to it. Knowing he had friends working on the questions and, of course, good old Bud Wilkinson, he rarely became rattled. There was one moment in the second segment, to emphasize a point, when Nixon startled his aides by talking

446

about getting down "to the nut-cutting." "As they say," he added, after the words had spilled out. Later he was able to laugh with the staff about the slip.

The telethon provided Nixon with one final opportunity to hammer home to the voters that the bombing halt decision had backfired. Johnson's order had appeared to offer real hope for a breakthrough, he said, "but then the negotiations came apart at the seams." He had heard "a very disturbing report," he also said, that in the days after the decision to halt all bombing, "the North Vietnamese are moving thousands of tons of supplies down the Ho Chi Minh Trail, and our bombers are not able to stop them." Humphrey's men, monitoring the Nixon show, informed their candidate about what Nixon had said. Humphrey responded directly in what was the closest the two major candidates were to come to a debate in all of 1968. "There is no indication of increased infiltration, Mr. Nixon," Humphrey said in his own telethon. He had checked with Washington and had been so informed, he said. "And let me say that it does not help the negotiations to falsely accuse anyone at this particular time."

And so it went, with each candidate trying to score last-minute points, yet trying more importantly to project his best image, his most relaxed and confident and Presidential image, to the huge television audiences. When it was all over, and Nixon's studio audience had given him a rousing ovation, the red eye of television that had brought him into America's living rooms all year was turned off for the last time. The candidate, dropping his hands from the overhead victory salute with which he had said good-bye to his television audience, stepped back, executed a brief Jackie Gleason shuffle and gagged, "And away we go." He strode quickly out of the studio and into his car, where he sat alone and unsmiling in the back seat, chin in his hand and staring straight ahead, a reading light overhead revealing his obvious tension. After six years in political exile, the day of reckoning, and possibly of atonement, had come.

Yet there was in this most media-oriented of all campaigns one remaining ploy, and one that cut through all the false optimism to reveal the near-desperation that now had gripped some in the Nixon camp. Humphrey's finishing spurt in the polls, and his more informal, breezier telethon compared to Nixon's one-man set piece, had them worried. At about two o'clock in the morning at the Century Plaza, David Eisenhower was rousted out of bed. They had him cut a radio tape quoting his famous and revered grandfather to the effect that Nixon was right on Vietnam, and if elected would end the war. The tape was quickly processed and fired off to radio stations in about forty states for saturation coverage on election day. At the very end, the cool and efficient Nixon machine was sputtering, improvising, just like any other political organization trying to squeeze out that last vote. The final public opinion polls said Richard Nixon would need every last one he could get, and for all the ridiculing and downgrading of the national pulse-takers along the way, they soon would be proved right.

18

Resurrection

RICHARD Nixon spent election day in a way no other candidate for the American Presidency ever had—flying across the country as the great electorate of 73,000,000 decided his fate 35,000 feet below. By the time he rose in his Century Plaza suite in Los Angeles on the clear, bright morning of November 5, voters in the East already had been at the polls for several hours. He phoned his brother Ed, John Mitchell, Murray Chotiner, Maury Stans and a number of other political associates in New York. He thanked them for their efforts and told those who expressed fears about the impact of the bombing halt that they all would know for sure pretty soon. He also called Mrs. Eisenhower, at the general's side at Walter Reed in Washington, and then with his family drove out to Los Angeles International Airport for the final cross-country flight on the *Tricia*.

Although the election day activities of the man still favored to be the next President were of considerable interest to the American people, only a single reporter was permitted aboard the plane. Nixon sat in his sheltered front compartment, summoning aides to him as the chartered jet flew across the nation then engaged in its single most important act of self-government. Bob Ellsworth, using the air-to-ground phone, took reports on voter turnouts in key states and relayed them to the

449

candidate. Nixon was said to be in good spirits, reminiscing about the campaign and kidding himself about the "nut-cutting" remark of the night before. He surprised Mrs. Nixon with a new pin and earrings and chatted with Tricia, Julie and David, who in a three-dollar pool on the plane gave his future father-in-law 47.3 percent of the vote, 36 states and 334 electoral votes.

Nixon then held brief sessions with speechwriters Pat Buchanan, Ray Price, Bill Safire and Jim Keogh, with his media team and with his political aides, Ellsworth, Finch and Charlie McWhorter. After lunch with Bebe Rebozo he strolled once through the main cabin, thanking his staff and trying to convey optimism to his restrained and sober subordinates. "The hay's in the barn," Herb Klein later quoted him as saying. Anthony Day, then of the Philadelphia *Bulletin,* sat expectantly in the rear but was ignored by the candidate. Repeated requests by Day for an interview were pigeonholed. It was, actually, a fitting way to mark the end of a campaign that had dedicated itself to isolating the candidate and neutralizing the press. It was an isolation and a neutralization that was to be maintained rigidly until the following morning, when Nixon appeared publicly for the first time to comment on the election's outcome.

The *Tricia* landed at Newark Airport at 6:15 P.M. Eastern Time, the flight across three time zones having shortened this longest day for a Presidential candidate. A black limousine was pulled up directly to the ramp, and Nixon, wearing a light raincoat, waved briefly and climbed in. He was trying to look casual but not quite making it. The car sped over the New Jersey Turnpike to the Lincoln Tunnel and into Manhattan to the Waldorf-Astoria, his election night headquarters. There, in a thirty-fifth-floor suite, he settled in for the long night. Only a handful of associates had ready access to him—Mitchell, Haldeman, Finch, Ehrlichman, Chapin, a few others. In other rooms on this and other floors, the Nixon organization prepared for its last campaign chore—the gathering and assessment of returns. Mitchell, Flanigan, Ellsworth, Finch each had a room on the Tower floor from which he could make calls around the country. Ellsworth as the political director set up an operations command post and kept shuttling state-by-state reports to Nixon. Chotiner checked the fourteen states that had been assigned to him, including five of the Big Seven—California, Illinois, Ohio, Michigan and Pennsylvania. From time to time Chapin would come into his room and say, "The boss wants to see you," and for Chotiner it would be just like old times. The image of the new Nixon organization, however, did not allow for much publicity about his presence at the center of power.

Elsewhere in the Waldorf, special television-viewing rooms were reserved for important contributors. In a style becoming the Nixon efficiency, the guests were herded in according to the amount they had contributed. Drinks were dispensed and aides were assigned to make the rounds, keeping the fat cats informed and feeling important. And in the grand ballroom thirty-two floors below Nixon's suite, the faithful and the press watched TV and waited. Lionel Hampton and his band played and Republican workers tried to muster up election-night gaiety, but the closeness of the polls—and the memories of 1960 and 1948—dampened the attempt.

In a large press conference room behind the ballroom, Ziegler and Klein appeared periodically to dispense noninformation. How did Nixon look? Ziegler: "Confident and relaxed." What was the atmosphere up there? Ziegler: "An atmosphere of confidence." What did Nixon do on arrival? Klein: "Like most people, he relaxed." The possibility of newsmen being admitted to the inner sanctum, even for a peek, was, of course, nil.

The first television returns, with their elaborate electronic projections, were meaningless. Nixon, knowing this full well, did not bother to tune in. In fact, remembering the anxiety that television had brought him on election nights in 1960 and 1962, he forbade anyone in his suite to turn on a set. Pat and the girls sat with Bebe, trying to cull trends from the aides who moved in and out with their own readings. Nixon relied on the Ellsworth operation, on Mitchell, Chotiner and Finch, and on his own calculations. For a time, as the votes were tallied across the nation and lieutenants brought him the latest state breakdowns and indications, the candidate soaked in a warm tub, combating the tensions and the fatigue that had overcome him with disastrous results on a similar night in Los Angeles six years earlier.

The first dangerous sign came in Connecticut, which went early and easily for Humphrey, 49.5 percent to 44.4 percent for Nixon and 6.1 for Wallace. Only eight electoral votes were at stake, but then, fairly early, it became clear that three of the Big Seven—New York (43), Pennsylvania (29) and Michigan (21) —were down the drain too. The New York loss was expected, but there had been some hope for the other two. It was the Wallace slippage going back home to the Democratic Party. Pennsylvania particularly had been tough to swallow, after that final-week swing. And on top of that, Humphrey was holding close in the national popular vote.

On the optimistic side for Nixon, North Carolina (13) was salvaged, Thurmond delivered South Carolina (12), and the outlook was good in border states Kentucky (9) and Tennessee (11). There was Wallace slippage there too, but this time Nixon was the beneficiary. The strategy was working; the only question would be how well Humphrey had come back in the North. Just as the Nixon strategists had expected, Ohio would be a key battleground, and also New Jersey and Illinois.

It was clear already, however, that the projection of "the geniuses in New York"—meaning Mitchell—that Nixon would win by three to five million was a pipe dream. The much-abused public polls, after a year in which their image had been severely strained, had turned out to be right; exactly eight years after he had participated in the greatest Presidential cliff-hanger of modern times, Richard Nixon was right back in the election-night pressure cooker again.

According to those who shared it with him, Nixon survived the night and its tensions with calm and control. Any early concession from Humphrey, who was at the Leamington Hotel in Minneapolis, and a victory statement of his own were banished from Nixon's mind by the realities of the big-state returns and the close popular vote. On past midnight the uncertainty lasted, with Klein occasionally being dispatched to the press below, just as he had been on those earlier nights of waiting, to mouth the usual words of optimism. The words were not all a pose this time, because it was becoming clear that only Nixon of the three candidates could hope for an electoral majority. One state after another in the "heartland," the border states, the Southwest and the Rockies was delivering for him. But the threat, as long feared, was Humphrey and Wallace together denying that clear majority to him, and sending the election into the unfriendly cloakrooms of the House of Representatives.

Finally, shortly before 3:00 A.M. on Wednesday, Nixon summoned Mitchell, Finch, Haldeman and Chotiner for a professional appraisal. They confirmed his own view that the Wallace slippage to Humphrey had not measured up in other key Northern states to what it was in Pennsylvania and Michigan; both New Jersey and Ohio, by the reckoning of his aides and the candidate himself, had moved into the Nixon column. Nixon was confident now that he had it. There then occurred an unusual suggestion from Nixon—one that will be particularly interesting to those aware of the man's penchant for canceling out black moments in his life by reliving them under happier circumstances. He wanted someone to go downstairs and claim victory—at the same hour when he himself had conceded the 1960 election to John Kennedy.* But when Haldeman objected that the outcome was not yet clear to the television audience, and that premature announcement of his victory would make Nixon look too eager to grasp the Presidency, he backed off. Still, one could see in his mind's eye that yellow legal pad listing all Richard Nixon's most bitter moments, and a checkmark next to yet another of them.

Thus, while much of the nation slept, Richard Nixon had declared himself, in the privacy of his own circle, the next President of the United States. Some of the Californians who had seen their hopes dashed twice before continued to sweat it out, and it was not until dawn that their fears finally were allayed. Before then, though, Nixon ordered Chapin to tell those on the staff still awake to come in for an informal victory celebration. As one by one they arrived, saying "Congratulations, Mr. President," there was at last a break in the tension, some joking and some drinking of champagne.

By dawn the only undecided states were Illinois and Cali-

---

* Cf. Theodore H. White, *The Making of the President 1968* (Atheneum, 1969).

fornia, and the strategists knew Illinois was okay; several Republican stronghold counties had been holding back reporting their totals to state election officials in anticipation of hanky-panky from Mayor Daley in Cook County. Now the word was passed to "let 'em go," and Illinois, and soon California too, were locked up.* The dimensions of the victory were far short of the clear mandate to govern that Nixon had asked from the voters in the last days: 31,770,000 votes or 43.4 percent of the total to 31,270,000 or 42.7 percent for Humphrey and 9,906,000 or 13.5 percent for Wallace, with the rest scattered among minor candidates. That 43 percent was just about what Nixon had started with back in September. He had sought to kill the clock and had done so—but just barely. He would be a plurality President, but President nonetheless. And the men who had pushed him, staggering, across the finish line—Mitchell foremost among them—now would take on the reputation of political masterminds, obscuring the fact that they had come within a hair of perpetrating the biggest political flop since Dewey—and maybe bigger even than that, considering the disarray of the foe.

Humphrey, holding out all night for Wallace to deny Nixon electoral votes in the border and Southern states, instead found himself undone by Wallace in New Jersey, Ohio and Illinois. At the same time, the Wallace ticket denied Nixon only the four redneck predictables—Mississippi, Louisiana, Alabama and Georgia—plus Arkansas. Wallace, watching the results at home in Montgomery with his seven-year-old daughter Lee, tried to take solace from the TV projections that his popular vote might reach ten million. He called the prospect "fantastic," and it was at that. Humphrey, meanwhile, had gone to bed expecting to lose, and he awoke sure of it. In midmorning he finally telephoned Nixon with his congratulations and advised the winner he was on his way to make a television concession.

---

* Determined he would not be "robbed" of the election in Illinois and elsewhere as Republicans had charged in 1960, Nixon had employed a former FBI agent, Lou Nichols, to organize a special poll-watching operation. In 1960, Republican strongholds were permitted to vote early, and once their vote was in, Daley knew how many votes his Democratic organization had to produce. This time, in key places under Republican control, Nixon supporters played a waiting game, just to be sure.

454

Now at last the time had come for Nixon, after eight years of frustration and a year of active if unprecedentedly controlled pursuit of the prize, to appear before the American people as their President-elect. As in 1960, they too had lived through a long night of great stress and uncertainty, and they needed reassurance. The 302 electoral votes Nixon had received, to 191 for Humphrey and 45 for Wallace, were 32 more than needed to keep the election out of the House, but those statistics could not obscure the tenuous nature of his victory. A word of humility, of reconciliation, was in order. Before going downstairs, Nixon recalled in conversations with his speechwriters, or so we are told, a single campaign sign that struck exactly the right note. Nixon descended with his family to the cheering ballroom crowd, where he expressed his thanks to his workers, the voters, to Humphrey for his call and to daughter Julie for a gift that reached into the hearts of many Americans—and the disbelief of others: a Presidential seal in crewelwork. Then the President-elect said:

". . . One final thought that I would like to leave with regard to the character of the new administration. I saw many signs in this campaign. Some of them were not friendly and some were very friendly. But the one that touched me the most was one that I saw in Deshler, Ohio, at the end of a long day of whistle-stopping—a little town, I suppose five times the population was there in the dusk—but a teen-ager held up a sign, 'Bring Us Together.' And that will be the great objective of this administration at the outset, to bring the American people together. This will be an open administration, open to new ideas, open to men and women of both parties, open to the critics as well as those who support us. We want to bridge the generation gap. We want to bridge the gap between the races. We want to bring America together. . . ."

It was an ironic reference to make when one recalled what Richard Nixon had said to that teenager and the others crowding around his railroad car on that night just two weeks earlier. "In the forty-five minutes it takes to ride from Lima to Deshler," he had told them, "this is what has happened in America: There has been one murder, two rapes, forty-five major crimes of violence, countless robberies and auto thefts . . . " But then

455

he was a candidate; white backlash votes that had been siphoned off by George Wallace were heading back toward their traditional Democratic roots in a pivotal state, and he was moving boldly to capture them for himself. Now he was the President-elect, and regardless of the irony, the message "Bring Us Together" was what the nation desperately needed to hear from him.*

In the ten weeks that followed, as Richard Nixon moved to create his new administration with the same deliberation and the same personal insulation from public and press that had marked the campaign, he sought to sustain the mood of that message of reconciliation. Immediately after giving his victory talk at the Waldorf, he boarded a plane for Key Biscayne (where he had gone in 1960 after losing). On the following night the Nixons dined with their key staff members and friends at the Jamaica Inn (just as he had done in 1960 after losing). And while there, he telephoned Humphrey, inviting him to stop off in Florida on his way to a Caribbean vacation the next day for a talk and show of national unity. (Aides recalled that in 1960, Nixon had been dining at the same Jamaica Inn when Kennedy called him and invited him to a similar meeting. Then Nixon attended as a loser; this time he met Humphrey as a winner. The next day, greeting Humphrey at a military field at Opa-Locka not far from Miami, Nixon stepped to the microphones, Humphrey at his side, and said: "I recall in 1960 after losing a very close election, President-elect Kennedy called on me when I was in Florida, and *history repeats itself, so I know exactly how you feel.*")

Now, with all the bitterest personal memories and associations of defeat canceled out, the President-elect turned to the task of transition. The assembling of his new administration was

---

* Shortly after Nixon's conciliatory victory speech, as hotel employees cleared debris from the ballroom, John Ehrlichman gathered perhaps twenty of his advance men in the center of the floor and congratulated them on "the most consummate job in the history of American politics." The mood was one of elation and, after all the months of cautious public relations, one of relief. "Why don't we all get a member of the press and beat them up?" offered Roy Good-earle. "I'm tired of being nice to them." One in the group who failed to see the humor of the remark was Joe Albright, chief of the Washington bureau of *Newsday,* who dutifully scribbled the quote in his notebook.

in a sense a continuation of the techniques and the thinking that had dominated the campaign of 1968. Whereas his style of the fifties and early sixties in the heat of partisanship had stimulated dissension, the very deliberateness and efficiency of 1968 now worked like a soothing salve on a nation frayed at its nerve ends by the events and the passions of its most spectacular election year in history. There was no talk now of Nixon going to Paris or Saigon; instead, the President-elect went into seclusion and made it known he was giving all his attention and energies to preparation for the most difficult job an American politician ever can be asked to perform. As he conducted the business of organizing the nation's new management in a calm and orderly manner, he intentionally suggested the hope of a new era of normalcy. To many, he made normalcy seem not only possible but the most desirable of conditions, even in a world wracked with abnormal troubles and challenges. He took more than a month to select his Cabinet, then introduced its members en masse on television, in a setting of utmost dignity—and under utmost control; the media boys had not been sent packing, just because the election had been won.

At noon on January 20, 1969, standing on the steps of the United States Capitol, Richard Nixon at long last took the Presidential oath of office, in clear and firm tones. Then, addressing himself to the task of national reconciliation, he sought to elicit from the American people two of the chief elements of his own political resurrection—self-analysis and self-control. Standing behind him as he spoke was the man he had succeeded, Lyndon B. Johnson; the man he had defeated, Hubert H. Humphrey; and the man who would serve as his Vice President, Spiro T. Agnew. The speech was simple in construction and in meaning, yet positive and full of hope.

"We are caught in war, wanting peace," he said evenly. "We are torn by division, wanting unity. We see around us empty lives, wanting fulfillment. We see tasks that need doing, waiting for hands to do them. To a crisis of the spirit, we need an answer of the spirit.

"To find that answer, we need only look within ourselves. When we listen to 'the better angels of our nature,' we find that

457

they celebrate the simple things, and the basic things—such as goodness, decency, love, kindness.

"Greatness comes in simple trappings. The simple things are the ones most needed today if we are to surmount what divides us, and cement what unites us.

"To lower our voices would be a simple thing.

"In these difficult years, America has suffered from a fever of words: from inflated rhetoric that promises more than it can possibly deliver; from angry rhetoric that fans discontent into hatreds; from bombastic rhetoric that postures instead of persuading.

"We cannot learn from one another until we stop shouting at one another—until we speak quietly enough so that our words can be heard as well as our voices."

The words and the familiar voice were heard by thousands of Americans crowded into the Capitol Plaza, and by other millions in their living rooms, where the new President had come to them so often and so reassuringly in the tumultuous year just ended. They were heard by Lyndon Johnson, who had not been accustomed to lowering his voice in the past, and by Ted Agnew, who would find it increasingly difficult in the future. They were heard by the good Americans, the forgotten Americans of the heartland who had elected this new President, and by the shouters and the dissenters who largely had ignored him as irrelevant; they were heard by Hubert Humphrey, who forlornly had been the major victim of the voices of war protest that would not be stilled.

Richard Nixon concluded his inaugural plea for a tempered national dialogue and strode with his wife and associates into the Capitol Building. There he lunched and then left for the traditional parade and, finally, occupancy of the White House that he had cherished and pursued with such single-mindedness for so long. In 1968, a year of political tempest seldom equaled in America, he had ridden out the worst, self-assured and always under control in the very eye of the storm. Now he was setting out onto a more fateful political sea, with the war abroad and the racial unrest at home still raging around him. The man who in so many earlier years had been regarded as a noisy, partisan catalyst of controversy now at last found himself at the wheel of the ship of state, quietly urging his people by their own conduct to calm the swirling waters. For his own part, self-analysis and self-control had performed a political miracle; he seemed now to be convinced that if these disciplines could save his own political life, applied on a national scale they could resurrect a nation.

Nixon's personal comeback was, without question, one of the most unexpected in American political history. Undeniably, there was in his success a heavy dose of luck, as developments not of his making opened the return route: John Kennedy's assassination; Barry Goldwater's debacle and the Republican Party's consequent desperation; Lyndon Johnson's credibility gap; the stalemated war abroad and the demonstrations, riots and racial polarization at home; George Romney's ineffectiveness as a campaigner and Nelson Rockefeller's indecisiveness; Johnson's astonishing decision to retire; Robert Kennedy's assassination and Hubert Humphrey's inability to be his own man; finally, Saigon's recalcitrance in accepting Johnson's eleventh-hour negotiations breakthrough.

Yet at every turn, Nixon moved deftly to convert circumstance into opportunity. In 1962, he moved himself resolutely out of the shadow of defeat and of the past. In 1963 he made a new beginning, and in 1964, after a lapse into political fantasy with his gropings toward the Republican nomination, he grasped the realistic perspective and acted on it. Having reconfirmed in the Goldwater disaster his credentials as the most loyal Republican, in 1965 he seized the center of his party and effectively isolated Rockefeller as a "spoilsport" and divider. In 1966, he cemented that center position and his own role as the man who brought the party back. In 1967, he exercised remarkable restraint and self-confidence in leaving the field to Romney, correctly anticipating Romney's performance and using it to reduce his own loser image. And in 1968, after destroying that image in uncontested primaries, he successfully occupied the middle ground first between Rockefeller and Reagan, then between Humphrey and Wallace. Nixon's performance, by any yardstick, was a remarkable exercise in political strategy and discipline.

Still, for all the astuteness, there was little inspirational about

459

the comeback along the way. Perhaps it was too dependent on the misfortunes of others in political life. John Kennedy, Barry Goldwater, Lyndon Johnson, Nelson Rockefeller, George Romney, Robert Kennedy, Hubert Humphrey all suffered at the hands of fate or folly in the course of Nixon's return. But it was more than that; there was such a cautionary caste to the whole effort—in the man's own demeanor and later in his political organization—as to obscure the drama in it. Caution became protectiveness and defensiveness, and at times suspiciousness. There developed a kind of fortress mentality that was to extend into the Nixon administration itself; within the first year, it would blossom into a collective persecution complex about "them"—the protesters, the Eastern press, "the shouters and the demonstrators," and in Agnew's incredible phrase, the "effete corps of impudent snobs."

The Nixon personal comeback and the Nixon campaign of 1968 were, after all, exercises in letting sleeping dogs lie. First, Richard Nixon's political excesses and failures of the past had to be shunted out of public remembrance. Once that much had been accomplished, it was mostly a matter of sustaining and drawing on the general discontent already existing in the country. The challenge, essentially, was to preach and promise change while running in place. This Nixon managed to do very well, though the strategy required that the level of public discontent remain high and that its focus remain on the party in power. Johnson's last-minute breakthrough on the peace talks severely jolted that focus and overnight nearly made of the hang-on Nixon strategy another Dewey collapse. After the election, pollster Louis Harris told me his studies indicated it was only Saigon's refusal on the Saturday before the election to send representatives to Paris that stopped a massive swing back to Humphrey and prevented his election. "Humphrey was ahead on Sunday," Harris said, "but Nixon made a comeback on Monday and Tuesday. Had the election been held two days later, Nixon would have won by an even bigger margin. Saigon's balking brought Johnson's credibility back into the picture. But had the election been ten days later, when Saigon had been brought into line, Nixon would have lost."

It was appropriate, therefore, that in the end it was not so much what Nixon had said or done, but once again a development not of his making, that provided him with his margin of victory. Yet the nature of his cautious, insulated campaign brought him to the Presidency as an unknown quantity in important areas. On the major issue facing the nation during the campaign, the war in Vietnam, he had elected to pass. In that regard he had built his narrow constituency largely on faith. Perhaps the best summation of the Nixon campaign was the candidate's peculiarly stilted, oversimplified lecture at every public rally: "When you're on the wrong road, you get off the wrong road and get onto a new road." Where that new road would go exactly, he never said—particularly where it would go concerning Vietnam. As a result, the people were not conditioned by the campaign about what to expect from the President they had elected. Many of those who voted for him were conditioned only to a climate—a climate of "trust me." Now, it turned out, Nixon was asking the electorate to give him as President what he shrewdly had taken as candidate—freedom from pressure, insulation from dissent, the peace and quiet of normalcy, though the times were not normal.

In return for lowered voices, he promised to bring the nation together. But for this promise too the citizenry had not been prepared by his campaign. The Nixon drive for the Presidency had been almost totally bereft of any reaching out to conflicting segments of the American society. It was, instead, a sophisticated effort to capitalize on the growing polarization among the nation's people, its races and its regions. The candidate spoke in the main to what in 1968 came to be called "Middle America"— white, comfortable, don't-let-them-take-it-away America. His two-track, media-oriented, carefully controlled campaign made the most of that approach. He deftly patterned his television effort to focus on Middle Americans—and to feature them in his "citizen panels." The requisite one black participant was included, but as a prop. He went out, when he did go out, to see "the good people" of white Middle America, ignoring the blacks; not once did he really campaign in a genuine black ghetto. As the nation trembled with division over the war, he wrapped himself in noble silence and even made a virtue of his reticence. Actually, America had two wars going on in 1968, one

461

abroad and one at home, and Richard Nixon declined to get very close to either one.

His posture was, no doubt, "smart politics." As long as his political challenge was merely to hold his constituency of the discontented it was not necessary or prudent for Nixon to go out on a limb on sensitive issues and situations. But a President who has been elected by a plurality must seek to enlarge his constituency, not merely to assure his reelection but to govern effectively in his first term. Now Nixon appeared to be striving toward that enlargement, with his appeal to temperate discussion and reconciliation. But again the electorate had not been readied for the effort by his campaign. In one of the few attempts Nixon the candidate had made to broaden his constituency, in Ohio late in the campaign when he sought to corral the Wallace slippage, his message had not been one of reconciliation, but of polarization. "The forgotten Americans" phrase of the campaign in itself was an invitation to polarization; beneath it ran an implication of their persecution by all those others who were speaking out—on the campuses, in the ghettos and on the streets. Within nine months of the new administration, "the forgotten Americans" were to become "the great silent majority"; they were to be encouraged by Nixon's newly assigned surrogate, Vice President Agnew, not to lower their voices but to raise them, and not to help bring Americans together but to drive them more clearly apart through what Agnew himself would call "positive polarization."

Perhaps the reason Nixon could make the kind of inaugural speech he delivered lies in the manner in which he traveled his long road to the White House. In the most antiseptic, controlled campaign in American history, he was a candidate in a glass booth. His smooth operation contrived for him appearances of enthusiastic support, and his own words attracted mostly those who already agreed with him. It was difficult for a candidate who had been so effectively sealed off from genuine dialogue with the public, and from debate with his opponents, to grasp the depth of the public passions of 1968 and the resoluteness of those who disagreed with him. Only one who had failed to properly gauge the intensity of the nation's dissent could ask, with any expectation of success, that its volume be modulated. The dissent could be isolated, yes, and put into perspective as a minority voice, but it could not be lullabyed to sleep—a lesson still not learned in his 1970 Cambodia decision.

In planning and implementing a campaign, of course, no serious candidate has as his primary objective self-education about the electorate. His first objective is to win. This was Nixon's goal and he reached it. Yet many candidates for public office learn a great deal about the electorate in the effort to win, simply by their intensive and intimate exposure to the people and to the unpredictable that Nixon strove so single-mindedly to avoid. The experience often brings life and emotion to a campaign, and to the candidate himself.

Such a result serves the best interests of both candidate and voter; John Kennedy in 1960, a rich man who never really had seen or understood the plight of the poor in explicit, individual terms, campaigned in West Virginia's coal-mine country and never was the same again. One afternoon during that state's Presidential primary campaign, Kennedy walked into a dust-black shack in one of his custom-made pinstripe blue suits, to shake hands and solicit votes from the miners. There he laid incredulous eyes on workers who like him were in their early forties but were bent and brittle like old men. Kennedy went down the mine shaft with them, came back up, then sat on coaldust-coated rail tracks in his suit that cost more than a miner earned in a week, asking questions about how they made ends meet. That searing experience and others in West Virginia lived with John Kennedy thereafter, coloring his candidacy and later his Presidency.

Richard Nixon, son of a grocer rather than son of a millionaire, perhaps did not need that particular lesson. But two of the critical lessons to be learned in 1968 were the broad-based and resolute nature of the war protest and the intensity of the black revolt. Nixon deliberately insulated himself from both these phenomena; had he not done so, he might have culled from the experience the knowledge that it would take much more than a plea for lower voices to still them. In less than a year, as it turned out, the new President did learn that lesson; he was compelled finally to ask "the great silent majority" to raise its voice to drown out the clamor.

One of the striking things about Richard Nixon all along his determined road back was that he seemed so often to be traveling it by helicopter—hovering above, studying the route, but never absorbing anything emotionally from the pilgrimage. In public, he seemed often to be a spectator in his own drama, or at best the guest of honor at a series of testimonials. Spontaneity was avoided like a Viet Cong land mine. And in his constant courting of the Presidential image, there never was the harried, loose-necktie image of the personally involved, seeking campaigner that often adds a humanizing element to his quest, and warms the voter to the candidate.

But Richard Nixon in 1960 had tried it the usual, the conventional way, and had lost. He had pushed himself from early morning until late at night, he had submitted himself to the crowds and to the press, and together they had brought him to exhaustion, to disorganization and ultimately to defeat. In 1960, and in 1962, he too had exposed himself to the educational process of traditional campaigning, and while he may not have been touched as emotionally as some others by the experiences, he did learn from them. What he learned was not to do it that way again.

There are feeling political candidates—men like Hubert Humphrey and George Romney—and there are thinking candidates like Richard Nixon. He learned from his political experiences not compassion for people but comprehension of a process that as traditionally practiced was ill-suited to him. And so he and his advisers conceived a new approach that blocked out those elements that had undone him in the past and accentuated those elements that could be used to his own best advantage. His innovations came at precisely a time when the technology for shaping public opinion had far outrun its use by most other politicians. Nixon enlisted this latest technology, and the media experts who knew how to employ it, and he adapted himself and every major aspect of his campaign to its requirements—while taking care always to preserve the façade of the traditional approach.

And in the end, he did the one thing he had become so good at: he survived. Through all the year's turbulent events, he had sought not enlightenment, not discourse, not public adulation, but survival. Over the previous six years, he had been like a soldier in combat whose only goal is not to be a daring hero, but to be alive when the battle is over. Richard Nixon kept his head down all the way, and when the smoke had cleared, he had made it; by the slimmest of margins, it is true, and without great public enthusiasm, but he had made it. In November, 1968, the system—and events—had offered up three men, none of whom fired the nation's imagination or its spirit. But that did not really matter because the system required that one of the three be chosen. Humphrey and Wallace were sorely wounded and could not bring the attack to Nixon, nor could the out-flanked press draw him out; having taken the most astute reading of the system, and having buttressed himself against its hazards, he persevered and—survived.

To state Richard Nixon's achievement in this way is not to denigrate the political significance of his controlled candidacy of 1968. That candidacy wrought a revolution in Presidential campaigning; innovations of the Nixon campaign, particularly the heavy reliance on the new opinion-shaping technology, will be adapted by future candidates who have the money and the shrewdness to do so. It is a disturbing prospect for anyone who sees the old, freewheeling campaigning as a vital crucible in which public men are tested in the public eye. As in 1968, the voter of the future may be ill-prepared to cope with the sophis-ticated salesmanship of the media-oriented politician and his new breed of political hucksters. And if the voter is deprived of seeing the candidate perform under pressure—either in person or in television appearances and debates not staged by the candidate's men—the loser in the end may be the country. Only once in every four years do the American people have a direct opportunity to endorse or change the national leader and the great public policies that shape their lives. Their ability to choose wisely depends critically on what they can learn during the campaign about the candidates and the ideas, the principles and the passions that move them.

Considering the physical risks and burdens imposed on to-day's Presidential candidates as they travel through a nation in turmoil, it may well be in the national interest to use more, rather than less, campaigning on television. But it must be television over which the candidate does not have control, and there must be sufficient traditional stumping—not simply the *appearance* of it—to permit the interplay between voter and candidate that can transmit to the candidate not only how various segments of the nation feel, but how deeply.

Yet for all that, it may be that the blueprint of Richard Nixon's success will not automatically chart the way for future candidates, simply because the essential ingredient was not the technology but the man who made use of it amid a series of spectacular events that helped clear the way for him. It may well be that the kind of incredibly insulated campaign that made Nixon the thirty-seventh President of the United States could not be carried off by someone else. Only a man of established national stature and reputation could have shunned discourse in an election year and remained in contention, and only a man of iron self-discipline could have hewed to the isolation imposed upon him by the strategy that succeeded so narrowly.

Nixon's self-control was forged in the fires of his bitter defeats of 1960 and 1962 and tempered in the next six uncertain years. He learned to master himself, and when his second chance at the Presidency finally came, he was ready. Others who study the way in which he fashioned his unprecedented comeback may marvel at the efficiency and discipline of his campaign machine, and at the cunning and ingenuity of his strategy. But in the end they will not comprehend how it happened unless they look at the man as the consummate political creature, and at the struggle he waged with the Richard Nixon who had been a loser—and won.

Index

Index

469

473

Index